# **500** GREATEST-EVER
## VEGETARIAN RECIPES

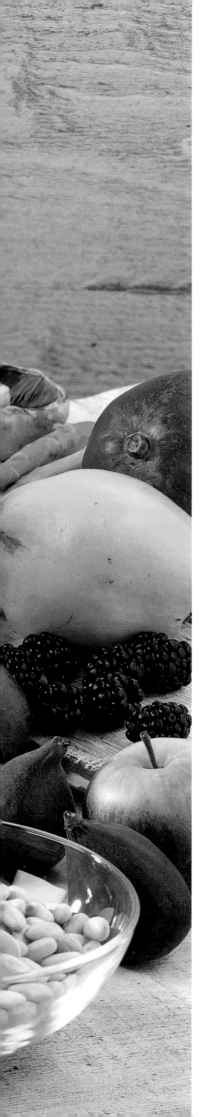

# 500 GREATEST-EVER
# VEGETARIAN RECIPES

A COOK'S GUIDE TO THE SENSATIONAL WORLD OF VEGETARIAN COOKING

**EDITOR** valerie ferguson

Published by World Publications Group, Inc.
140 Laurel Street, East Bridgewater, MA 02333
www.wrldpub.net

Produced by Anness Publishing Ltd, Hermes House, 88–89 Blackfriars Road, London SE1 8HA;
tel. 020 7401 2077; fax 020 7633 9499www.annesspublishing.com

If you like the images in this book and would like to investigate using them for publishing, promotions or advertising,
please visit our website www.practicalpictures.com for more information.

Publisher: Joanna Lorenz
Managing Editor: Helen Sudell
Editor: Valerie Ferguson
Designer: Carole Perks
Editorial Reader: Richard McGinlay
Production Controller: Wendy Lawson

ETHICAL TRADING POLICY
Because of our ongoing ecological investment programme, you, as our customer, can have the pleasure and reassurance of
knowing that a tree is being cultivated on your behalf to naturally replace the materials used to make the book you are holding.
For further information about this scheme, go to www.annesspublishing.com/trees

Recipes contributed by: Catherine Atkinson, Alex Barker, Michelle Berriedale-Johnson, Angela Boggiano, Kathy Brown,
Carla Capalbo, Kit Chan, Jacqueline Clark, Carole Clements, Trish Davies, Roz Denny, Patrizia Diemling, Matthew Drennan,
Sarah Edmonds, Rafi Fernandez, Christine France, Silvano Franco, Shirley Gill, Nicola Graimes, Rosamund Grant,
Carole Handslip, Rebekah Hassan, Deh-Ta Hsuing, Shehzad Husain, Christine Ingram, Judy Jackson, Manisha Kanani,
Sheila Kimberley, Sara Lewis, Patricia Lousada, Lesley Mackley, Sue Maggs, Kathy Man, Sally Mansfield, Norma Miller, Sallie Morris,
Annie Nichols, Maggie Pannell, Katherine Richmond, Jennie Shapter, Anne Sheasby, Liz Trigg, Hilaire Walden,
Laura Washburn, Steven Wheeler, Elizabeth Wolf-Cohen, Jeni Wright.
Photography: William Adams-Lingwood, Karl Adamson, Edward Allwright, Steve Baxter, Nicki Dowey, James Duncan,
John Freeman, Ian Garlick, Michelle Garrett, John Heseltine, Amanda Heywood, Ferguson Hill, Janine Hosegood,
David Jordan, Dave King, Don Last, Patrick McLeavey, Michael Michaels, Steve Moss, Thomas Odulate, Simon Smith,
Sam Stowell, Polly Wreford.

ISBN-10: 1-57215-492-6
ISBN-13: 978-1-57215-492-6

Previously published as *Vegetarian*

NOTES

Standard spoon and cup measures are level.

Large eggs are used unless otherwise stated.

Electric oven temperatures in this book are for conventional ovens.
When using a fan oven, the temperature will probably need to be
reduced by about 20–40°F. Since ovens vary, you should check with
your manufacturer's instruction book for guidance.

# Contents

# Introduction

Some of the most exciting and innovative food available today is vegetarian. Glorious colors and enticing flavors epitomize this type of cooking, and when you consider the superb soups, appetizers, snacks, salads and main courses that make up green cuisine, it seems inconceivable that vegetarian food could ever have been considered dull or unappetizing.

When it comes to vegetarian cooking, the pleasure starts long before the cook reaches the kitchen. What could be more sensual than stooping to pick fresh herbs, bruising them between the fingers and releasing those wonderful scents? Or meandering through a market, filling a basket with dark purple eggplant, fat red tomatoes, glossy peppers, tiny radishes or bulbs of fennel with their feathery fronds? Shopping for spices is another delight, as is discovering a new type of oil or vinegar, or a supplier of superb fresh pasta.

Vegetarian food has come a long way from the dreary days when it had a reputation for being brown and bland. It may once have been marginalized, but today it is very definitely mainstream. Visit any good restaurant, especially at lunchtime, and many of the most delectable items on the menu will be meatless. Broiled slices of eggplant or zucchini, layered with goat cheese and served with a rich tomato sauce, pasta with pesto and pine nuts, puff pastry shells filled with baby vegetables, asparagus risotto—such delicious dishes aren't on menus because they are vegetarian but because they are what people really love to eat.

The good news is that you don't have to go to a restaurant to taste treats like these. There are more than five hundred wonderful vegetarian dishes in this collection, each one as appealing to the eye as the palate. Many of the dishes will naturally promote good health, but

that's a bonus, not a basic requirement. You'll find the frivolous and indulgent as well as the sane and sensible, so if you start a meal with cocktails, you can pick a simple main course, such as the Harvest Vegetable & Lentil Casserole or the Spinach & Hazelnut Lasagne from the Low-fat Vegetarian chapter. A balanced diet is not difficult to achieve. Try to eat plenty of fruits and vegetables, legumes, nuts, seeds, rice, bread, pasta and potatoes, with some dairy foods or nondairy alternatives. Keep fats, desserts and high-calorie/low-nutrient foods to the minimum. (There are no recipes for desserts in this book, so that's a start!)

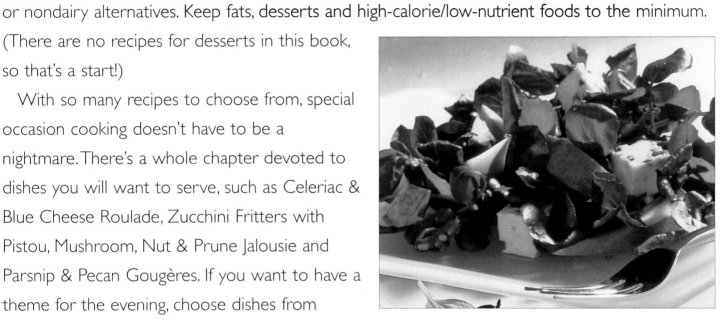

With so many recipes to choose from, special occasion cooking doesn't have to be a nightmare. There's a whole chapter devoted to dishes you will want to serve, such as Celeriac & Blue Cheese Roulade, Zucchini Fritters with Pistou, Mushroom, Nut & Prune Jalousie and Parsnip & Pecan Gougères. If you want to have a theme for the evening, choose dishes from China, India, Greece or Morocco, or seek some inspiration in the Hot & Spicy chapter.

It is likely that as many nonvegetarians as vegetarians will enjoy this book. Some of the former will adapt the recipes to include shrimp, perhaps, or strips of chicken, and some may use chicken stock instead of the vegetable stock featured. This is fine, but it is important to stress that if you are a carnivore cooking for a vegetarian, it is essential to follow the recipes scrupulously, avoiding not only the obvious things, such as meat, poultry and fish, but also any products that may contain derivatives of these foods, such as fish sauce or Worcestershire sauce (of which there are vegetarian versions). Guidance on ingredients is given in the pages that follow.

A number of the recipes feature cheese. We haven't stipulated vegetarian cheeses, assuming that committed vegetarians will choose varieties they feel comfortable using, while vegans will opt for recipes that exclude dairy products entirely. Although specific cheeses are listed, it is almost always possible to substitute alternatives, just as long as you match like with like. A vegetarian Cheddar won't give you the same results as Parmesan, for example, but the results will be perfectly acceptable.

# Vegetarian Ingredients

The cardinal rule when shopping for vegetarian ingredients is to choose the freshest possible produce, buying little and often. For dried goods, find a supplier with a healthy turnover, so stock doesn't have time to get stale. Keep a constant lookout for new and exciting products. Vegetarian food is a growth market, and the range of available foods is constantly increasing. Once the domain of the health food store, vegetarian ingredients are now stocked in every supermarket, and the demand for organic produce, and products made from organic ingredients, is huge.

## Vegetables & Fruits

Buy the bulk of your produce from local growers, if possible, balancing home-grown vegetables and fruits with exotic imports. Some supermarkets support local growers, including organic ones, so look out for labels that state the provenance of the produce. Several organic farms offer box plans, where you opt to buy a box of vegetables and/or fruits every week. What goes into the box depends on what is being harvested at the time, and because everything is picked to order, it is beautifully fresh. This is a great way of buying greens such as spinach or Swiss chard. Farmer's markets are excellent sources of fruits and vegetables. If you live in the country, look for roadside stalls. Gardeners often grow vegetables not generally available at stores, such as the more unusual types of squash, and sell them at very reasonable prices. Pick-your-own vegetable farms aren't as common as those offering pick-your-own fruit, but corn is sometimes sold that way. Don't forget essential aromatics such as fresh garlic and ginger root.

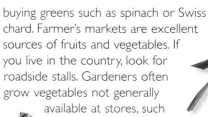

*tomatoes*

*winter squash*

*Swiss chard*

*garlic*

*apples*

*eggplant*

## Herbs & Spices

The most satisfying way to obtain herbs is from your own garden. You don't need acres of space, as even a window-box or a few pots on the patio will yield a generous harvest. Obvious candidates are mint and parsley, preferably the flat-leaf variety, but you should also aim to grow thyme, basil, sage and oregano or marjoram. If you possibly can, add cilantro, chives, chervil, tarragon, rosemary and bay, all of which feature in this book. Alternatively, buy herbs at the supermarket, but use them as soon as possible after purchase. Dried herbs lose their potency quite quickly, so buy small amounts at a time, keep them in a cool, dry place (out of direct sunlight) and replace them as soon as they start to get stale.

For the best flavor, buy whole spices and seeds, and grind them as needed in a spice mill or coffee grinder kept for the purpose. Dry-frying spices before grinding intensifies their flavor. Essential spices include cardamom pods, cumin and coriander seeds, cinnamon sticks, nutmeg, dried chiles and chili powder, cayenne, paprika, Chinese five-spice powder, garam masala, saffron, turmeric and curry powder.

*flat-leaf parsley*

*basil*

*cinnamon*

*chives and bay leaves*

*coriander seeds and leaves*

*Clockwise from top: celery seeds, chili powder, chile flakes and cayenne*

## Grains, Pasta & Pulses

The dried versions of these easy-to-use ingredients are staples. Rice is invaluable to the vegetarian cook, both as a base for vegetable stews and sautés and for stuffed vegetables. In addition to regular white and brown long-grain rice, try basmati, which has a wonderful fragrance and flavor. Rinse it well before use and, if there is time, soak it in the water used for the final rinse. For risotto you will need a short grain rice such as arborio, carnaroli or Vialone Nano. Bulghur wheat has already been partially prepared, so needs only a brief soaking before use. It is the basis for tabbouleh, and also tastes good in pilafs and casseroles. Another great grain that needs very little preparation is couscous, which is made from coarse semolina.

Dried pasta comes in an astonishing array of shapes. Some of the more unusual types are introduced in recipes in this book, but you can always substitute whatever you have in the pantry. Dried egg noodles are essential for many Asian dishes.

Fresh pasta is becoming widely available. Find a reliable source and buy it as needed, or make your own, using our basic recipe. Pulses, such as dried beans, split peas and lentils, keep well and play a vital role in vegetarian cooking. Most pulses need to be soaked overnight, so remember to take the time into account when you are planning your menu.

*rice*

*dried pasta*

*lentils*

*dried beans*

## From the Refrigerator & Freezer

Dairy products provide lacto-vegetarians (those who eat dairy products) with valuable protein, calcium and vitamins $B_{12}$, A and D, but can be high in fat. Like eggs, they should be eaten in moderation. Look for vegetarian versions of your favorite cheeses (produced with vegetable rennet). Yogurt, crème fraîche and fromage frais are also very useful, as is tofu (bean curd), a protein-rich food made from soybeans. Various forms are available, from soft silken tofu to a firm type that can be cubed and sautéed. Tempeh is similar to tofu, but has a nuttier taste.

Keep phyllo pastry, shortcrust and puff pastry in the freezer, but allow plenty of time for slow thawing. Nuts will also store well in the freezer.

*Parmesan cheese*

*tofu*

*sour cream and crème fraîche*

## From the Pantry

If your pantry is well stocked, spur-of-the-moment meals will never be a problem. In addition to pasta, pulses and grains, dry goods should include different types of flour, yeast, polenta and oats, and you'll also want a small supply of nuts. Don't buy these in bulk, as nuts become rancid if stored for too long. Dried mushrooms are useful, as are sun-dried tomatoes and peppers, but you may prefer to buy the ones that come packed in oil in jars. Also, look for pesto (both green and red), tahini, peanut butter, capers and olives. Useful sauces include passata (puréed tomatoes), creamed horseradish, soy sauce in various strengths, black bean sauce and the vegetarian versions of oyster sauce and Worcestershire sauce. You'll need various vinegars, including balsamic and rice vinegar, and oils, especially olive oil, sunflower oil, sesame oil, peanut oil and walnut oil. For low-fat cooking, a light oil spray is useful.

Cans take up quite a lot of space, but it is well worth keeping a stock of favorites, such as canned tomatoes, kidney beans, borlotti beans, flageolets and chickpeas, plus corn kernels, artichoke hearts and bamboo shoots. Canned coconut milk comes in handy for vegetable curries and some soups.

*mixed nuts*

*canned beans*

*wine vinegar*

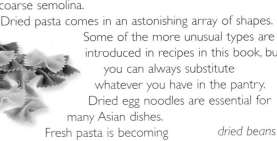

# Techniques

Even the simplest tasks in the kitchen can take longer than necessary if you don't know a few useful techniques and short cuts. Below are some step-by-step instructions for preparing a variety of ingredients that will save time and help to improve the presentation of the final dishes. No special equipment is required for most of them, just a sharp knife.

### Chopping Onions

**1** Cut a peeled onion in half lengthwise and place one half, cut-side down, on a board. Slice it vertically several times.

**2** Make two horizontal cuts in from the stalk end towards the root, but not through it. Holding the onion by the root end, cut it crosswise to form even diced pieces.

### Cutting Vegetable Matchsticks

**1** Peel firm vegetables and cut in 2-inch lengths. Cut these into ⅛-inch slices.

**2** Stack the slices and cut them neatly lengthwise into matchstick strips.

### Peeling & Chopping Tomatoes

**1** Cut a cross in the blossom end of each tomato. Put them in a heatproof bowl and pour in boiling water.

**2** Leave for 30 seconds, until the skins wrinkle and start to peel back from the crosses. Drain, peel off the skin and chop the flesh neatly.

### Chopping Herbs

**1** Remove any thick stems and discard. Pile the herbs on a board and chop them finely, first in one direction, then the other, using a sharp knife or a mezzaluna (half-moon herb chopper), which you use in a see-saw motion.

### Blanching Vegetables

**1** Bring a pan of water to a boil. Using a wire basket, if possible, lower the vegetables into the water and bring it back to a boil.

**2** Cook for 1–2 minutes, then drain the vegetables and cool them quickly under cold running water or by dipping them in a bowl of ice water. Drain well.

### Roasting & Peeling Bell Peppers

**1** Leave the peppers whole or cut them in half and scrape out the cores and seeds. Place them on a broiler pan under medium heat, turning them occasionally, until the skins are evenly blistered and charred but not too burnt, as this will make the flesh taste bitter.

**2** Seal the peppers in a plastic bag or place them in a bowl and cover them with several sheets of paper towels. When the steam has softened them, peel off the skins. Remove the bitter seeds if necessary, working over a bowl to catch any juices. The juices can be used in a salad dressing.

### Crushing Garlic

**1** Break off a clove of garlic and smash it firmly with the flat side of the blade of a cook's knife. Pick off all the papery skin.

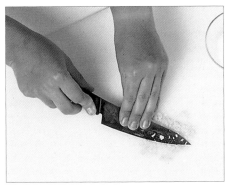

**2** Chop the clove roughly, sprinkle on a little table salt, then use the flat side of the knife blade to work the salt into the garlic until it is reduced to a fine paste.

### Preparing Chiles

**1** Wearing rubber gloves if possible, halve the chile lengthwise. Leave the seeds inside or scrape them out and discard them.

**2** Slice or chop the chile finely. Wash the knife, board and your hands (if not gloved) in hot soapy water, as chiles contain a substance that burns sensitive skin. Never rub your eyes or touch your lips after handling chiles.

### Preparing Fresh Ginger Root

**1** Using a vegetable peeler or a small knife, peel the skin off a piece of fresh ginger root. Cut the ginger in thin slices.

**2** Place each slice on a board. Cut it into thin strips and use, or turn the strips around and chop them finely. Ginger can also be grated, in which case it doesn't have to be peeled.

### Preparing Lemon Grass

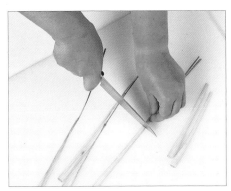

**1** Discard any tough outer layers from the lemongrass stem, then cut off the end and trim the top, leaving a piece 4 inches long.

**2** Split this in half lengthwise, then chop very finely. If the bulb is particularly fresh, it can be thinly sliced. Whole stems can be used for flavoring and removed before serving.

### Crushing Spices

**1** Dry-fry whole spices in a frying pan, then put them in a mortar and grind them with a pestle to make a smooth powder.

**2** Alternatively, grind them in a spice mill or a coffee grinder kept specifically for the purpose. Use a pastry brush to remove all the ground spice from the inside of the grinder.

### Preparing Pulses

**1** Rinse well, pick out any small stones, then put the pulses in a bowl with plenty of cold water. Soak for 4–8 hours.

**2** Drain the pulses, rinse them under cold water and drain them again. Put them in a pan. Add plenty of cold water but no salt. Bring to a boil, boil hard for 10 minutes, then simmer until tender. Drain and season.

*Lentils do not need to be soaked, although soaking will shorten the cooking time. Red lentils become very soft when cooked and are ideal for purées. Green or brown lentils are firmer and retain more texture. The finest flavored are Puy lentils.*

# Basic Recipes

The recipes in this book are largely complete in themselves, but there are a few basics that crop up again and again, such as vegetable stock, tomato sauce, flavored oils and doughs for pizzas and pastas. You can, of course, substitute bought ingredients, such as sauces, ready-made pasta and pizza crusts, but make your own when you have time.

### Pizza Dough
**Makes 1 10–12-inch round pizza crust**

1½ cups bread flour
¼ teaspoon salt
1 teaspoon active dry yeast
½–⅔ cup lukewarm water

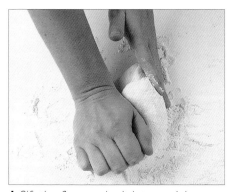

**1** Sift the flour and salt into a mixing bowl and stir in the yeast. Add the water and mix into a soft dough. Knead on a lightly floured surface for 10 minutes, until smooth and elastic. Return to the clean bowl, cover with lightly oiled plastic wrap and set in a warm place for about 1 hour, or until the dough has doubled.

**2** Punch down the dough, knead it for 2 minutes, then roll it out to a 10–12-inch round. Place on a greased baking sheet and turn up the edges. Top and bake as suggested in your recipes.

**Cook's Tip**
*Mix and knead the dough in a food processor, if you prefer, but transfer it to a bowl for rising.*

### Pasta Dough
**Serves 6**

2¾ cups Italian Tipo 00 flour or bread flour
1 teaspoon salt
3 eggs, beaten

**1** Put the flour and salt in a food processor fitted with the metal blade. Pour in one egg, cover and pulse to mix on maximum speed, add the remaining eggs through the feeder tube and mix briefly to form a dough.

**2** Knead the dough on a clean surface for 5 minutes if you are shaping it in a pasta machine, 10 minutes if shaping by hand. The dough should be very smooth and elastic. Wrap it in plastic wrap and let it rest for 15–20 minutes before rolling it and cutting it into shapes.

#### Making Pasta Dough by Hand

**1** Mound the flour on a work surface, make a well in the center and add the eggs and salt. Mix with a fork, gradually incorporating the surrounding flour until a rough dough forms. Knead as in the main recipe.

### Tomato Sauce
**Makes about 1½ cups**

1 tablespoon olive oil
1 onion, finely chopped
1 garlic clove, crushed
14-ounce can chopped tomatoes
1 tablespoon tomato paste
1 tablespoon chopped fresh mixed herbs
   (parsley, thyme, oregano, basil)
pinch of sugar
salt and ground black pepper

**1** Heat the oil in a pan and fry the onion and garlic gently until softened. Stir in the tomatoes, tomato paste, herbs and sugar, with salt and pepper to taste.

**2** Simmer, uncovered, for 15–20 minutes, stirring occasionally, until the mixture has reduced and is thick. Use at once or cool, cover and store in the refrigerator.

**Cook's Tip**
*Use this tomato sauce on pizzas or pasta. It is excellent in lasagne, and also tastes good with vegetables. Spoon it on cooked cauliflower, top with grated cheese and broil until bubbly.*

## Vegetable Stock
**Makes about 4 pints**
*2 large onions, roughly chopped*
*2 leeks, sliced*
*3 garlic cloves, crushed*
*3 carrots, roughly chopped*
*4 celery stalks, sliced*
*a large strip of pared lemon zest*
*12 fresh parsley stems*
*a few fresh thyme leaves*
*2 bay leaves*
*4 pints water*

**I** Put the onions, leeks, crushed garlic cloves, carrots and celery slices in a large saucepan. Add the strip of pared lemon zest, with the parsley, thyme and bay leaves. Pour in the water and bring to a boil. Skim off the foam that rises to the surface.

**2** Lower the heat and simmer, uncovered, for 30 minutes. Strain the stock, season it to taste and let it cool. Cover and keep in the refrigerator for up to 5 days, or freeze for up to 1 month.

*To save freezer space, boil vegetable stock down to concentrate it to about half the original quantity and then freeze in ice cube trays. When melting the frozen stock, add an equal amount of water.*

## French Dressing
**Makes about ¹/₂ cup**
*6 tablespoons olive oil or a mixture of olive and sunflower oils*
*I tablespoon white wine vinegar*
*I teaspoon French mustard*
*pinch of sugar*
*salt and ground black pepper*

**I** Place the oil and vinegar in a screw-top jar. Add the mustard and sugar.

**2** Close the lid tightly and shake well. Season to taste.

## Mayonnaise
**Makes about 1¹/₂ cups**
*2 egg yolks*
*I tablespoon Dijon mustard*
*2 tablespoons lemon juice or white wine vinegar*
*1¹/₄ cups oil (vegetable, corn or light olive)*
*salt and ground black pepper*

**I** Put the egg yolks, mustard, half the lemon juice or vinegar and a pinch of salt in a blender or food processor and process for 10 seconds to mix. With the motor running, add the oil through the funnel in the lid, drop by drop at first and then in a steady stream, processing constantly until the mayonnaise is thick and creamy. Taste and sharpen with the remaining juice or vinegar, if desired, and season to taste.

## Chili Oil
**Makes about ²/₃ cup**
*²/₃ cup olive oil*
*2 teaspoons tomato paste*
*I tablespoon dried red chile flakes*

**I** Heat the oil in a pan. When it is very hot, but not smoking, stir in the tomato paste and chile flakes. Let cool.

**2** Pour into a small jar or bottle. Cover well and store in the refrigerator for up to 2 months (the longer you keep it the hotter it gets).

## Garlic Oil
**Makes about ¹/₂ cup**
*3–4 garlic cloves*
*¹/₂ cup olive oil*

**I** Peel the garlic cloves and put them into a small jar or bottle. Pour in the oil, cover securely and store in the refrigerator for up to 1 month.

# Chilled Tomato & Sweet Bell Pepper Soup

Roasted red bell peppers give this chilled soup a sweet and slightly smoky flavor that is delicious with sun-ripened tomatoes.

**Serves 4**
2 red bell peppers, halved
  and seeded
3 tablespoons olive oil
1 onion, finely chopped
2 garlic cloves,
  crushed

1½ pounds ripe well-
  flavored tomatoes
⅔ cup red wine
2½ cups vegetable stock
salt and ground black pepper
snipped fresh chives,
  to garnish

**For the croutons**
2 slices day-old white bread,
  crusts removed
4 tablespoons olive oil

**1** Place the pepper halves, skin-side up, on a broiler pan and broil until the skins have charred. Transfer to a bowl and cover with crumpled paper towels. Let cool slightly.

**2** Heat the oil in a large pan. Add the onion and garlic and cook until soft. Meanwhile, remove the skin from the peppers and roughly chop them. Cut the tomatoes into chunks.

**3** Add the peppers and tomatoes to the pan, then cover and cook gently for 10 minutes. Pour in the wine and cook for 5 more minutes, then add the stock. Season well and continue to simmer for 20 minutes.

**4** To make the croutons, cut the bread into cubes. Heat the oil in a small frying pan, add the bread cubes and fry until golden. Drain on paper towels. When cold, store in an airtight container.

**5** Process the soup in a blender or food processor until smooth. Pour into a clean glass or ceramic bowl and let cool thoroughly before chilling in the refrigerator for at least 3 hours. Serve the soup in chilled bowls, topped with the croutons and garnished with snipped chives.

# Gazpacho

Tomatoes, cucumber and bell peppers form the basis of this classic chilled soup.

**Serves 4**
2 slices day-old white bread
2½ cups chilled water
2¼ pounds tomatoes
1 cucumber
1 red bell pepper, halved, seeded
  and chopped
1 fresh green chile, seeded
  and chopped
2 garlic cloves, chopped
2 tablespoons extra virgin olive oil

juice of 1 lime and 1 lemon
a few drops of Tabasco sauce
salt and ground black pepper
a handful of fresh basil leaves,
  to garnish
ice cubes and Avocado Salsa
  (optional), to serve

**For the garlic croutons**
2 slices day-old white bread,
  crusts removed
1 garlic clove, halved
1 tablespoon olive oil

**1** Soak the bread in ⅔ cup of the chilled water for 5 minutes. Meanwhile, place the tomatoes in a bowl and pour in boiling water to cover. Leave for 30 seconds, then drain, peel, seed and chop the flesh.

**2** Peel the cucumber thinly, then cut it in half lengthwise and scoop out the seeds with a teaspoon. Discard the seeds and chop the flesh.

**3** Place the soaked bread, tomatoes, cucumber, red pepper, chile, garlic, olive oil, lime juice, lemon juice and Tabasco sauce in a food processor or blender, with the remaining chilled water. Process until thoroughly combined but still chunky. Pour the soup into a bowl, season to taste with salt and pepper and chill in the refrigerator for 2–3 hours.

**4** Make the croutons. Rub the surface of the bread slices with the cut garlic clove. Cube the bread and toss with the olive oil until evenly coated. Heat a large nonstick frying pan and fry the croutons over medium heat until crisp and golden. Drain on paper towels.

**5** Ladle the soup into bowls and add two ice cubes to each portion. Garnish with the basil. Top with the avocado salsa, if using, and pass the croutons separately.

# Avocado Salsa

Serve a spoonful of this tasty salsa on top of each portion of Gazpacho, or enjoy it on its own, with chips or French bread.

**Serves 4**
1 ripe avocado
1 teaspoon lemon juice
1-inch piece cucumber, diced
½ fresh red chile, finely chopped

**1** Cut the avocado in half, remove the pit, then peel. Dice the flesh and put it in a bowl. Toss immediately with the lemon juice to prevent it from browning.

**2** Mix the avocado with the diced cucumber and finely chopped chile. Serve as soon as possible.

# Chilled Almond Soup

Unless you want to spend time pounding the ingredients for this refreshing Spanish soup by hand, a food processor is an essential kitchen tool.

**Serves 6**
4 slices day-old fresh white bread, crusts removed
3 cups chilled water
1 cup blanched almonds

2 garlic cloves, sliced
5 tablespoons olive oil
5 teaspoons sherry vinegar
salt and ground black pepper
toasted sliced almonds and skinned seedless grapes, to garnish

**1** Break the bread into a bowl and pour in ⅔ cup of the chilled water. Leave for 5 minutes.

**2** Put the almonds and garlic in a blender or food processor and process until very finely ground. Add the soaked white bread and process until smooth.

**3** With the motor running, gradually add the oil through the lid or feeder tube until the mixture forms a smooth paste. Add the sherry vinegar and remaining chilled water and process until smooth and thoroughly combined.

**4** Scrape the mixture into a bowl and season with salt and pepper, adding a little more water if the soup is very thick. Chill in the refrigerator for at least 3 hours.

**5** Ladle the soup into chilled bowls and sprinkle on the toasted almonds and skinned grapes.

**Cook's Tip**
*To blanch almonds, put the kernels in a bowl, pour in boiling water and leave for about 5 minutes. Drain, then rub off the skins with the palms of your hands.*

# Cold Cucumber & Yogurt Soup with Walnuts

Walnuts make a great addition to this refreshing cold soup.

1⅔ cups plain yogurt
½ cup chilled still mineral water
1–2 teaspoons lemon juice

**Serves 5–6**
1 cucumber
4 garlic cloves, peeled
½ teaspoon salt
¾ cup walnut pieces
1½ ounces day-old white bread, torn into pieces
2 tablespoons walnut oil

*For the garnish*
scant ½ cup walnuts, coarsely chopped
5 teaspoons olive oil
fresh dill sprigs

**1** Cut the cucumber in half lengthwise. Peel one half. Dice both halves, so that you have a mixture of peeled and unpeeled pieces of cucumber. Set aside.

**2** Crush the garlic and salt together in a mortar with a pestle. Add the walnuts and crush them into the mixture, then work in the bread. When the mixture is smooth, gradually add the walnut oil, using the pestle to ensure that the mixture is thoroughly combined.

**3** Scrape the mixture into a large bowl. Beat in the yogurt and diced cucumber, then beat in the mineral water and lemon juice to taste. Chill the soup if time permits.

**4** Pour the soup into chilled soup bowls. Sprinkle the coarsely chopped walnuts on top, then drizzle a little olive oil on the nuts. Complete the garnish with the fresh dill.

**Cook's Tip**
*If you prefer your soup smooth, process it in a food processor or blender into a purée before serving.*

# Chilled Leek & Potato Soup

This creamy-smooth soup is served with a tangy yogurt topping that beautifully complements its subtle but distinctive flavor.

**Serves 4**

2 tablespoons butter
1 tablespoon vegetable oil
1 small onion, chopped
3 leeks, sliced
2 medium floury potatoes, diced
about 2½ cups vegetable stock
about 1¼ cups milk
3 tablespoons light cream
salt and ground black pepper
4 tablespoons plain yogurt and
   fried chopped leeks, to serve

**1** Heat the butter and oil in a large, heavy pan and add the onion, leeks and potatoes. Cover and cook over low heat, stirring occasionally, for 15 minutes, until the vegetables have softened and the onion is golden.

**2** Stir in the stock and milk. Bring to a boil, lower the heat, cover and simmer for 10 minutes.

**3** Let cool slightly, then process the mixture, in batches if necessary, in a blender or a food processor into a purée. Pour the soup into a bowl, stir in the cream and season generously with salt and pepper.

**4** Set the soup aside to cool, then cover and chill in the refrigerator for 3–4 hours. You may need to add a little extra milk or cold vegetable stock to thin the soup before serving, as it will thicken slightly as it cools.

**5** Ladle the soup into chilled soup bowls and top each portion with a spoonful of yogurt and a sprinkling of fried leeks.

**Cook's Tip**
*You will need one or two thin young leeks for the garnish. Clean them, then slice them into rounds. Fry them in a mixture of butter and olive oil until they are crisp-tender.*

# Chilled Coconut Soup

Refreshing, cooling and not too filling, this soup makes an excellent summer appetizer, but it could also be served after a spicy curry, to refresh the palate.

**Serves 6**

5 cups milk
2⅔ cups unsweetened, dry, shredded coconut
1⅔ cups coconut milk
1⅔ cups vegetable stock
scant 1 cup heavy cream
½ teaspoon salt
½ teaspoon ground white pepper
1 teaspoon sugar
small bunch of cilantro

**1** Bring the milk to a boil in a large saucepan. Stir in the coconut, lower the heat and simmer, stirring occasionally, for 30 minutes. Spoon the mixture into a food processor and process until smooth. This may take a while—up to 5 minutes—so pause frequently and scrape down the sides of the bowl.

**2** Rinse the pan to remove any traces of coconut, pour in the processed mixture and add the coconut milk. Stir in the stock, cream, salt, pepper and sugar. Bring to a boil, stirring occasionally, then lower the heat and cook for 10 minutes.

**3** Reserve a few cilantro leaves for the garnish, then chop the rest finely and stir them into the soup. Pour the soup into a large bowl, let it cool, then cover and chill in the refrigerator.

**4** Just before serving, taste the soup and adjust the seasoning, as chilling will have altered the taste. Serve in chilled bowls, garnished with the reserved cilantro leaves.

**Cook's Tips**
*• Avoid using sweetened coconut, which would spoil the flavor of this soup.*
*• Use a tasty vegetable stock, boiling it down if necessary to concentrate the flavor.*

# French Onion Soup

This classic French soup is popular all over the world. It is always served with a slightly chewy topping of melted Gruyère cheese.

**Serves 4**

1/4 cup butter
2 onions, about 9 ounces total weight, sliced
2 teaspoons all-purpose flour
4 cups vegetable stock
4 tablespoons dry white wine or 2 tablespoons dry sherry
4 slices crusty white bread
1 1/4 cups grated Gruyère or Emmenthal cheese
salt and ground black pepper

**1** Melt the butter in a large, heavy saucepan. Add the sliced onions and cook over medium-low heat, stirring occasionally, for about 12 minutes or until lightly browned. Stir in the flour and continue to cook, stirring constantly, until the flour turns a sandy color.

**2** Pour in the stock and wine or sherry, then bring to a boil, stirring constantly. Season to taste with salt and pepper, cover and simmer for 15 minutes.

**3** Spread out the slices of bread in a broiler pan and toast them lightly. Divide the grated cheese among them. Return to the oven and heat until the cheese is bubbling. Place the cheese toasts in four warmed, heatproof bowls.

**4** Using a slotted spoon, scoop out the onions from the soup and divide them equally among the heated bowls. Pour in the soup and serve immediately.

> **Cook's Tips**
> • To give the soup a good color, make sure the onions are lightly browned before you add the stock.
> • Grated aged Cheddar cheese can be substituted for Gruyère or Emmenthal, but neither the flavor nor the texture will be strictly authentic.

# Cream of Zucchini Soup

The joys of this soup are its delicate color, creamy texture and subtle taste.

**Serves 4–6**

2 tablespoons olive oil
1 tablespoon butter
1 medium onion, roughly chopped
2 pounds zucchini, trimmed and sliced
1 teaspoon dried oregano
about 2 1/2 cups vegetable stock
4 ounces dolcelatte cheese, rind removed, diced
1 1/4 cups light cream
salt and ground black pepper
fresh oregano and extra dolcelatte, to garnish

**1** Heat the oil and butter in a large saucepan until foaming. Add the onion and cook gently, stirring frequently, for about 5 minutes, until softened but not brown.

**2** Add the sliced zucchini and dried oregano and season with salt and pepper to taste. Cook over medium heat, stirring frequently, for 10 minutes.

**3** Pour in the stock and bring to a boil, stirring constantly. Lower the heat and partially cover the pan. Simmer gently, stirring occasionally, for about 30 minutes. Stir in the diced dolcelatte until melted.

**4** Pour the mixture into a blender or food processor. Process until smooth, then press through a sieve into a clean pan.

**5** Add two-thirds of the cream. Stir over low heat until hot, but not boiling. Check the consistency and add more stock if the soup is too thick. Taste for seasoning, then pour into heated bowls. Swirl in the remaining cream. Garnish with fresh oregano and extra cheese and serve immediately.

> **Cook's Tip**
> There are vegetarian versions of a wide variety of cheeses. Look for them at large supermarkets or health food stores.

# Pear & Watercress Soup

Pears and Stilton are classic companions, although they are seldom served in soup. Try this sophisticated version—it is delicious!

**Serves 6**
1 bunch watercress
4 medium pears, peeled
  and sliced
3¾ cups vegetable stock

½ cup heavy cream
juice of 1 lime
salt and ground black pepper

***For the Stilton croutons***
2 tablespoons butter
1 tablespoon olive oil
3 slices day-old white bread,
  crusts removed, cubed
4 ounces Stilton cheese

**1** Reserve about one-third of the watercress leaves. Place the rest of the watercress leaves and the stems in a large pan and add the pears and stock. Bring to a boil, then lower the heat and simmer for 15–20 minutes.

**2** Let the mixture cool slightly, then pour it into a food processor. Add most of the reserved watercress leaves, reserving some for garnishing, and blend until smooth.

**3** Scrape the mixture into the clean pan and stir in the cream and lime juice. Season to taste with salt and pepper.

**4** Make the croutons. Melt the butter and oil and fry the bread cubes until golden brown. Drain on paper towels, then spread out in a shallow heatproof dish. Crumble the Stilton on top and heat under a hot broiler until bubbling.

**5** Meanwhile, reheat the soup gently, stirring constantly. Pour it into heated bowls. Divide the croutons and remaining watercress among the bowls and serve immediately.

**Cook's Tip**
*Watercress does not keep well, so use it within a day of purchase. Otherwise, the leaves will wilt and turn yellow.*

# Asparagus Soup

Homemade asparagus soup has a delicate flavor, quite unlike that from a can. Use young asparagus, which is tender and easy to blend.

**Serves 4**
1 pound young asparagus
3 tablespoons butter
6 shallots, sliced

2 tablespoons all-purpose flour
2½ cups vegetable stock
1 tablespoon lemon juice
1 cup milk
½ cup light cream
salt and ground black pepper
2 teaspoons chopped fresh
  chervil, to garnish

**1** Trim the stalks of the asparagus if necessary. Cut 1½ inches off the tops of half the asparagus and set aside for a garnish. Slice the remaining asparagus.

**2** Melt 2 tablespoons of the butter in a large, heavy saucepan. Add the sliced shallots and fry over low heat, stirring occasionally, for 2–3 minutes, until softened and translucent but not brown.

**3** Add the sliced asparagus and fry over low heat for about 1 minute. Stir in the flour and cook, stirring constantly, for 1 minute. Stir in the stock and lemon juice and season to taste with salt and pepper. Bring to a boil, then lower the heat and simmer, partially covered, for 15–20 minutes, until the asparagus is very tender.

**4** Cool the soup slightly, then process the mixture with the milk in a blender or food processor until smooth. Press the purée through a sieve into a clean pan.

**5** Melt the remaining butter in a frying pan over low heat. Add the reserved asparagus tips and fry gently for 3–4 minutes, until softened.

**6** Heat the soup gently for 3–4 minutes. Stir in the cream and the fried asparagus tips. Ladle into heated bowls, sprinkle with the chopped fresh chervil and serve immediately.

# Garlic & Cilantro Soup

This simple soup should be made with the best ingredients—plump garlic, cilantro, high-quality crusty country bread and extra virgin olive oil.

**Serves 6**

1 cup cilantro, leaves and stems chopped separately
6 cups vegetable stock
5–6 plump garlic cloves, peeled
6 eggs
3 slices day-old white bread, crusts removed and torn into bite-size pieces
6 tablespoons extra virgin olive oil, plus extra to serve
salt and ground black pepper

**1** Place the cilantro stems in a saucepan. Add the stock and bring to a boil over medium heat. Lower the heat and simmer for 10 minutes. Cool slightly, then process the mixture in a blender or food processor. Press through a sieve into the clean pan. Heat gently.

**2** Crush the garlic with 1 teaspoon salt, then stir in ½ cup of the hot cilantro stock. Return the mixture to the pan.

**3** Bring the soup to a boil and season to taste with salt and pepper. Leave over low heat. Poach the eggs.

**4** Divide the pieces of bread among six soup plates or bowls and drizzle the olive oil over it. Stir the chopped cilantro leaves into the soup, then ladle it onto the bread. Stir each portion once, then add a poached egg to each bowl. Serve immediately, passing more olive oil at the table so that it can be drizzled on the soup to taste.

# Tomato & Fresh Basil Soup

This is the perfect choice for late summer, when fresh tomatoes are at their most flavorful and sweet.

**Serves 4–6**

1 tablespoon olive oil
2 tablespoons butter
1 medium onion, finely chopped
2 pounds ripe Italian plum tomatoes, roughly chopped
1 garlic clove, roughly chopped
about 3 cups vegetable stock
½ cup dry white wine
2 tablespoons sun-dried tomato paste
2 tablespoons shredded fresh basil, plus a few whole leaves, to garnish
⅔ cup heavy cream
salt and ground black pepper

**1** Heat the oil and butter in a large, heavy saucepan. Add the chopped onion and cook over low heat, stirring occasionally, for about 5 minutes, until softened and translucent but not browned.

**2** Stir in the chopped tomatoes and garlic, then add the stock, white wine and sun-dried tomato paste, with salt and pepper to taste. Bring to a boil, then lower the heat, half-cover the pan and simmer gently for 20 minutes, stirring occasionally.

**3** Process the soup with the shredded basil in a blender or food processor, then press through a sieve into a clean pan.

**4** Stir in the heavy cream and heat through, stirring. Do not let the soup approach the boiling point. Check the consistency and flavor. Add more stock and seasoning if necessary. Pour into heated bowls and garnish with whole basil leaves. Serve immediately.

## Variation
*The soup can also be served chilled. Pour it into a container after sieving, cool, then chill in the refrigerator for at least 4 hours. Serve in chilled bowls.*

## Cook's Tip
*The olive oil is traditionally used to moisten the bread and flavor the soup, but you can use less than the recommended amount if you prefer.*

# Borscht

Beets are the main ingredient of this classic Russian soup, which is also very popular throughout Eastern Europe.

**Serves 4–6**
3 tablespoons butter
2 onions, sliced
2 pounds raw beet, peeled and
   cut into thick batons
2 carrots, cut into thick batons
2 celery stalks, cut into
   thick batons
2 garlic cloves, crushed
4 tomatoes, peeled, seeded
   and chopped
bouquet garni
4 whole peppercorns
5 cups vegetable stock
²/₃ cup beet kvas (see Cook's Tip)
   or the liquid from pickled beets
salt and ground black pepper
sour cream and snipped fresh
   chives, to garnish

**1** Melt the butter in a large pan and cook the onions over low heat for 5 minutes, stirring occasionally.

**2** Add the beet, carrots and celery and cook for 5 more minutes, stirring occasionally.

**3** Stir in the garlic and chopped tomatoes and continue to cook, stirring, for 2 more minutes.

**4** Add the bouquet garni, peppercorns and stock. Bring to a boil, lower the heat, cover and simmer for 1¼ hours, until all the vegetables are tender. Discard the bouquet garni. Stir in the beet kvas and season to taste. Bring to a boil. Ladle into bowls and serve with sour cream sprinkled with chives.

**Cook's Tip**
*Beet kvas, fermented beet juice, adds an intense color and a slight tartness. If unavailable, peel and grate 1 beet, add ²/₃ cup vegetable stock and 2 teaspoons lemon juice. Bring to a boil, cover and remove from heat. Leave for 30 minutes. Strain before using.*

# Wild Mushroom Soup

Dried porcini mushrooms have an intense flavor, so a small amount is sufficient to give this soup a truly superb taste.

**Serves 4**
2 cups dried porcini mushrooms
1 cup warm water
2 tablespoons olive oil
1 tablespoon butter
2 leeks, thinly sliced
2 shallots, roughly chopped
1 garlic clove, roughly chopped
3 cups fresh wild mushrooms
about 5 cups vegetable stock
½ teaspoon dried thyme
²/₃ cup heavy cream
salt and ground black pepper
fresh thyme sprigs, to garnish

**1** Soak the dried porcini in the warm water for 20–30 minutes. Lift out of the liquid and squeeze out as much of the liquid as possible. Strain all the liquid and reserve. Chop the mushrooms.

**2** Heat the oil and butter in a large pan and cook the leeks, shallots and garlic gently for about 5 minutes, stirring frequently.

**3** Slice the fresh mushrooms and add them to the pan. Stir over medium heat until they begin to soften, then pour in the stock and bring to a boil. Add the porcini, soaking liquid and dried thyme and season to taste. Lower the heat, half-cover the pan and simmer gently for 30 minutes, stirring occasionally.

**4** Process three-quarters of the soup in a blender or food processor until smooth. Return it to the pan, stir in the cream and heat through. Add more stock if the soup is too thick. Taste for seasoning. Serve hot, garnished with the thyme sprigs.

**Cook's Tip**
*Look for packages of fresh mixed wild mushrooms in the supermarket. Use them on the day of purchase, if possible, as they don't keep well.*

# Pea, Leek & Broccoli Soup

A delicious and nutritious soup, ideal for a family supper to warm those chilly winter evenings.

**Serves 4–6**

1 onion, chopped
2 cups sliced leeks
8 ounces unpeeled
  potatoes, diced
4 cups vegetable stock
1 bay leaf
2 cups broccoli florets
1 1/2 cups frozen peas
2–3 tablespoons chopped
  fresh parsley
salt and ground black pepper
fresh parsley leaves, to garnish

**1** Put the onion, leeks, potatoes, stock and bay leaf in a large, heavy saucepan and mix together well. Cover and bring to a boil over medium heat. Lower the heat and simmer, stirring frequently, for 10 minutes.

**2** Add the broccoli and peas, cover and return to a boil. Lower the heat and simmer, stirring occasionally, for another 10 minutes.

**3** Set aside to cool slightly. Remove and discard the bay leaf. Process the soup in a blender or food processor, in batches if necessary, until you have a smooth purée.

**4** Add the parsley, season to taste with salt and pepper and process again briefly. Return to the saucepan and reheat gently until piping hot. Ladle into heated soup bowls and garnish with parsley leaves. Serve immediately.

---

**Variations**
• If you prefer, cut the vegetables finely and leave the cooked soup chunky rather than puréeing it.
• If you prefer, peel the potatoes before cooking, but the soup will contain less fiber and fewer nutrients.
• Substitute frozen or drained, canned corn kernels for the frozen peas.

---

# Spiced Indian Cauliflower Soup

Light and tasty, this creamy, mildly spicy soup makes a wonderfully warming first course. It would also make a delicious light lunch with some Indian bread.

**Serves 4–6**

1 large potato, diced
1 small cauliflower, chopped
1 onion, chopped
1 tablespoon sunflower oil
3 tablespoons water
1 garlic clove, crushed
1 tablespoon grated fresh
  ginger root
2 teaspoons ground turmeric
1 teaspoon cumin seeds
1 teaspoon black mustard seeds
2 teaspoons ground coriander
4 cups vegetable stock
1 1/4 cups plain yogurt
salt and ground black pepper
cilantro or parsley sprigs,
  to garnish

**1** Put the potato, cauliflower and onion into a large, heavy saucepan with the oil and water. Cook over medium heat until hot and bubbling, then cover and lower the heat. Continue cooking the mixture for about 10 minutes.

**2** Add the garlic, ginger, turmeric, cumin seeds, mustard seeds and ground coriander. Stir well and cook for 2 more minutes, stirring occasionally.

**3** Pour in the stock and season to taste with salt and pepper. Bring to a boil, then lower the heat, cover and simmer for about 20 minutes.

**4** Stir in the yogurt and adjust the seasoning, if necessary. Ladle the soup into heated bowls, garnish with cilantro or parsley sprigs and serve immediately.

---

**Variation**
This soup is equally delicious chilled. After simmering, let it cool, then stir in the yogurt. Chill in the refrigerator for 4–6 hours before serving in chilled bowls.

# Roasted Vegetable Soup

Roasting the vegetables gives this winter soup a wonderful depth of flavor.

**Serves 6**
4 tablespoons olive oil
1 small butternut squash, peeled, seeded and cubed
2 carrots, cut into thick rounds
1 large parsnip, cubed
1 small rutabaga, cubed
2 leeks, thickly sliced
1 onion, quartered
3 bay leaves
4 fresh thyme sprigs, plus extra to garnish
3 fresh rosemary sprigs
5 cups vegetable stock
salt and ground black pepper
sour cream, to serve

**1** Preheat the oven to 400°F. Put the olive oil into a large bowl. Add the vegetables and toss until well coated.

**2** Spread out the vegetables in a single layer on one large or two small baking sheets. Tuck the bay leaves and thyme and rosemary sprigs among the vegetables.

**3** Roast the vegetables for about 50 minutes, until tender, turning them occasionally to make sure that they brown evenly. Remove from the oven, discard the herbs and transfer the vegetables to a large saucepan.

**4** Pour the stock into the pan and bring to a boil. Lower the heat, season to taste with salt and pepper, then simmer for 10 minutes. Transfer the soup to a food processor or blender and process for a few minutes until thick and smooth.

**5** Return the soup to the pan and heat through. Season well. Serve in heated bowls, adding a swirl of sour cream to each portion. Garnish with the extra thyme sprigs.

> **Cook's Tip**
> A hand-held blender makes short work of puréeing the soup and saves some dishwashing time.

# Spicy Peanut Soup

When you serve a lot of soups, it is good to have some more unusual recipes in your repertoire. This one comes from Africa, and it tastes delicious.

**Serves 6**
2 tablespoons vegetable oil
1 large onion, finely chopped
2 garlic cloves, crushed
1 teaspoon mild chili powder
2 red bell peppers, seeded and finely chopped
8 ounces carrots, finely chopped
8 ounces potatoes, finely chopped
3 celery stalks, sliced
4 cups vegetable stock
6 tablespoons crunchy peanut butter
2/3 cup corn kernels
salt and ground black pepper
roughly chopped unsalted roasted peanuts, to garnish

**1** Heat the oil in a large, heavy pan. Add the onion and garlic and cook, stirring occasionally, for about 3 minutes, until softened and translucent. Stir in the chili powder and cook for 1 more minute.

**2** Add the peppers, carrots, potatoes and celery. Stir well, then cook for 4 more minutes, stirring occasionally.

**3** Add the stock, peanut butter and corn and stir well until thoroughly combined.

**4** Season to taste with salt and pepper. Bring to a boil, lower the heat, cover and simmer for about 20 minutes or until the vegetables are tender. Adjust the seasoning, if necessary. Ladle the soup into heated bowls, sprinkle with the chopped peanuts and serve immediately.

> **Cook's Tip**
> Different brands of chili powder vary in strength, so it is best to use it with caution to begin with. Some varieties also include added ingredients, which may not go with your recipe.

# Butternut Squash Soup

The rich golden color, creamy texture and mild curry flavor combine to make this soup a winter winner with the whole family.

**Serves 6**

1 butternut squash
1 cooking apple
2 tablespoons butter
1 onion, finely chopped
1–2 teaspoons curry powder
3¾ cups vegetable stock
1 teaspoon chopped fresh sage
⅔ cup apple juice
salt and ground black pepper
curry powder and finely shredded
  lime zest, to garnish
Curried Horseradish Cream
  (optional), to serve

**1** Peel the squash, cut it in half and remove the seeds. Chop the flesh. Peel, core and chop the apple.

**2** Heat the butter in a large, heavy saucepan. Add the onion and cook, stirring occasionally, for 5 minutes, until soft and translucent. Stir in the curry powder. Cook, stirring constantly, for 2 minutes.

**3** Pour in the stock, then add the squash, apple and sage. Bring to a boil, lower the heat, cover and simmer for 20 minutes, until the squash and apple are tender.

**4** Process the soup in a blender or food processor into a smooth purée. Return to the clean pan and add the apple juice. Season with salt and pepper to taste. Reheat gently, without letting the soup boil.

**5** Serve the soup in heated bowls, topping each portion with a dusting of curry powder. Garnish with a few lime shreds. Add a spoonful of Curried Horseradish Cream, if desired.

> **Cook's Tip**
> *Butternut squash looks like an oversize, elongated yellow pear. It is descriptively named, as the deep golden-yellow flesh has a buttery consistency and a nutty taste. However, other varieties of winter squash could also be used in this soup.*

# Curried Horseradish Cream

This is particularly good as a topping for the Butternut Squash Soup but can be used with other vegetable soups as well. It is also excellent as a dipping sauce for crudités—use double or triple the amount.

**Serves 6 as a topping**

4 tablespoons heavy cream
2 teaspoons creamed horseradish
½ teaspoon curry powder

**1** Whip the cream in a bowl until stiff, then stir in the creamed horseradish and curry powder.
**2** Cover and chill in the refrigerator for up to 3 days.

# Spiced Lentil Soup

A subtle blend of spices takes this warming soup to new heights. Serve it with warm crusty bread for a satisfying lunch.

**Serves 6**

2 onions, finely chopped
2 garlic cloves, crushed
4 tomatoes, roughly chopped
½ teaspoon ground turmeric
1 teaspoon ground cumin
6 cardamom pods
½ cinnamon stick
1 cup red lentils
3¾ cups water
1 4-ounce can coconut milk
1 tablespoon fresh lime juice
salt and ground black pepper
cumin seeds, to garnish

**1** Put the onions, garlic, tomatoes, turmeric, cumin, cardamoms, cinnamon and lentils into a saucepan. Pour in the water. Bring to a boil, lower the heat, cover and simmer gently for about 20 minutes or until the lentils are soft.

**2** Remove the cardamoms and cinnamon stick. Process the mixture in a blender or food processor into a smooth purée. Press the soup through a sieve, then return it to the clean pan.

**3** Reserve a little of the coconut milk for the garnish and add the remainder to the pan, together with the lime juice. Stir well. Season to taste with salt and pepper. Reheat the soup gently without boiling. Ladle into heated bowls, swirl in the reserved coconut milk, garnish with the cumin seeds and serve.

> **Cook's Tips**
> • *For maximum flavor, use sun-ripened vine tomatoes, rather than those ripened under glass. Alternatively, stir in a little tomato paste or use canned tomatoes.*
> • *When whole cardamom pods are used for flavoring—usually in soups and casseroles—they are removed before serving or processing into a purée. The small black seeds—usually used for flavoring desserts—may be eaten.*
> • *The cooking time for lentils may vary, depending on how long they have been stored.*

# Hot-&-Sour Soup

This spicy, warming soup is the perfect introduction to a simple Chinese meal. Cloud Ears are a type of Chinese fungi.

**Serves 4**
1/4 ounce dried cloud ears
8 fresh shiitake mushrooms
3 ounces tofu (bean curd)
1/2 cup sliced, drained, canned bamboo shoots
4 cups vegetable stock
1 tablespoon sugar
3 tablespoons rice vinegar
1 tablespoon light soy sauce
1/4 teaspoon chili oil
1/2 teaspoon salt
large pinch of ground white pepper
1 tablespoon cornstarch
1 tablespoon cold water
1 egg white
1 teaspoon sesame oil
2 scallions, sliced into fine rings

**1** Soak the cloud ears in hot water to cover for 30 minutes or until soft. Drain, trim off and discard the hard bottom from each and chop the cloud ears roughly.

**2** Remove and discard the stems from the shiitake mushrooms. Cut the caps into thin strips. Cut the tofu into 1/2-inch cubes and shred the bamboo shoots finely.

**3** Place the stock, shiitake mushrooms, tofu, bamboo shoots and cloud ears in a large, heavy saucepan. Bring the stock to a boil, lower the heat and simmer for about 5 minutes.

**4** Stir in the sugar, vinegar, soy sauce, chili oil, salt and pepper. Mix the cornstarch into a paste with the water. Add the mixture to the soup and stir constantly until it thickens slightly.

**5** Lightly beat the egg white, then pour it slowly into the soup in a steady stream, stirring constantly. Cook, stirring constantly, until the egg white changes color.

**6** Add the sesame oil just before serving. Ladle into heated bowls and top each portion with scallion rings.

# North African Spiced Soup

Warm spices, such as cinnamon and ginger, give this thick vegetable and chickpea soup an unforgettable flavor.

**Serves 6**
1 large onion, chopped
5 cups vegetable stock
1 teaspoon ground cinnamon
1 teaspoon ground turmeric
1 tablespoon grated fresh ginger root
pinch of cayenne pepper
2 carrots, diced
2 celery stalks, diced
14-ounce can chopped tomatoes
1 pound floury potatoes, diced
5 saffron threads
14-ounce can chickpeas, drained
2 tablespoons chopped cilantro
1 tablespoon lemon juice
salt and ground black pepper
fried lemon wedges, to serve

**1** Place the onion in a large pan with 1 1/4 cups of the vegetable stock. Bring to a boil, lower the heat and simmer gently for about 10 minutes.

**2** Meanwhile, spoon the cinnamon, turmeric, ginger and cayenne pepper into a bowl. Stir in 2 tablespoons of the remaining stock to form a paste. Stir the spice paste into the onion mixture, together with the carrots and celery. Pour in the rest of the stock.

**3** Bring the mixture to a boil, lower the heat, then cover and simmer gently for 5 minutes.

**4** Stir in the tomatoes and potatoes. Cover and simmer gently for 20 minutes. Add the saffron, chickpeas, cilantro and lemon juice. Season to taste with salt and pepper. When piping hot, serve in heated bowls with fried lemon wedges.

**Cook's Tip**
*Although it is very expensive, do not stint on the saffron, as it adds a unique flavor to the spice combination.*

# Jerusalem Artichoke Soup

Thanks to their mild, nutty flavor, Jerusalem artichokes make a remarkably good, creamy soup.

**Serves 4**
2 tablespoons olive oil
1 large onion, chopped
1 garlic clove, chopped
1 celery stalk, chopped
1½ pounds Jerusalem artichokes, peeled or scrubbed and chopped
5 cups vegetable stock
1¼ cups milk
salt and ground black pepper
Gruyère Toasts, to serve (optional)

**1** Heat the oil in a large saucepan and cook the onion, garlic and celery over medium heat, stirring occasionally, for about 5 minutes or until softened. Add the Jerusalem artichokes and cook for 5 more minutes.

**2** Add the stock and season with salt and pepper to taste. Bring to a boil, lower the heat and simmer, stirring occasionally, for 20–25 minutes, until the artichokes are tender.

**3** Transfer the soup to a food processor or blender and process until smooth. Return the soup to the pan, stir in the milk and heat through gently for 2 minutes. Ladle the soup into bowls and top with Gruyère Toasts, if using, and ground black pepper.

# Gruyère Toasts

These are very good when floated on Jerusalem Artichoke Soup, but can also be served as snacks.

**Makes 8**
8 slices French bread
1 cup grated Gruyère cheese

**1** Spread out the slices of French bread in a broiler pan and toast them lightly on one side under a hot broiler.
**2** Turn over the slices of bread and sprinkle the untoasted side of each with the grated Gruyère. Broil until the cheese melts and is golden.

# Spinach & Rice Soup

Use baby spinach leaves to prepare this light and fresh-tasting soup.

**Serves 4**
1½ pounds fresh young spinach, washed
3 tablespoons extra virgin olive oil
1 small onion, finely chopped
2 garlic cloves, finely chopped
1 small fresh red chile, seeded and finely chopped
1 cup risotto rice
5 cups vegetable stock
salt and ground black pepper
4 tablespoons grated Pecorino cheese, to serve

**1** Place the spinach in a large pan with just the water that clings to its leaves after washing. Add a large pinch of salt. Heat gently until the spinach has just wilted, then remove from heat and drain, reserving any liquid.

**2** Either chop the spinach finely using a large knife or place it in a food processor and process into a fairly coarse purée.

**3** Heat the oil in a large, heavy saucepan. Add the onion, garlic and chile and cook over low heat, stirring occasionally, for 4–5 minutes, until softened.

**4** Add the rice and stir until all the grains are well coated, then pour in the stock and reserved spinach liquid. Bring to a boil over medium heat, then lower the heat and simmer for about 10 minutes.

**5** Add the spinach and season with salt and pepper to taste. Cook for 5–7 more minutes, until the rice is tender. Check the seasoning and serve in warmed soup plates with the grated Pecorino cheese.

**Cook's Tip**
*Use arborio or carnaroli rice for the rice soup, or try one of the less familiar risotto rices, such as Vialone Nano.*

# Ribollita

Ribollita is an Italian soup, like minestrone, but with beans instead of pasta. It is traditionally served ladled over bread and a rich green vegetable.

**Serves 6–8**
3 tablespoons olive oil
2 onions, chopped
2 carrots, sliced
4 garlic cloves, crushed
2 celery stalks, thinly sliced
1 fennel bulb, trimmed
   and chopped
2 large zucchini, thinly sliced

14-ounce can chopped tomatoes
2 tablespoons homemade or
   ready-made pesto
3³/₄ cups vegetable stock
14-ounce can haricot or borlotti
   beans, drained
salt and ground black pepper

**To finish**
1 tablespoon extra virgin olive oil,
   plus extra for drizzling
1 pound fresh young spinach
6–8 slices white bread
freshly ground black pepper

**1** Heat the oil in a large saucepan. Add the onions, carrots, garlic, celery and fennel and fry gently for 10 minutes. Add the zucchini and fry for 2 more minutes.

**2** Stir in the chopped tomatoes, pesto, stock and beans and bring to a boil. Lower the heat, cover and simmer gently for 25–30 minutes, until the vegetables are completely tender. Season with salt and pepper to taste.

**3** To serve, heat the oil in a heavy frying pan and fry the spinach for 2 minutes or until wilted. Put a slice of bread in each heated soup bowl, spoon the spinach on top, then ladle the soup onto the spinach. Pass extra olive oil at the table, so that guests can drizzle it on the soup. Freshly ground black pepper can be sprinkled on top.

**Variation**
*Use other dark greens, such as chard or cabbage, instead of the spinach; shred and cook until tender.*

# Corn & Potato Chowder

This creamy yet chunky soup is rich with the sweet taste of corn. Serve it topped with grated Cheddar cheese.

**Serves 4**
2 tablespoons sunflower oil
2 tablespoons butter
1 onion, chopped
1 garlic clove, crushed
1 medium baking potato, chopped

2 celery stalks, sliced
1 small green bell pepper, halved,
   seeded and sliced
2¹/₂ cups vegetable stock or water
1¹/₄ cups milk
7-ounce can flageolet beans
11-ounce can corn kernels
good pinch of dried sage
salt and ground black pepper
grated Cheddar cheese, to serve
fresh sage leaves, to garnish

**1** Heat the oil and butter in a large heavy pan. Add the onion, garlic, potato, celery and green pepper and cook over low heat, stirring occasionally, for about 10 minutes, until the onion is softened and golden.

**2** Pour in the stock or water, season with salt and pepper to taste and bring to a boil. Lower the heat, cover and simmer gently for about 15 minutes, until the vegetables are tender.

**3** Add the milk, beans and corn—including the can liquids. Stir in the sage. Simmer, uncovered, for 5 minutes. Serve, sprinkled with the grated cheese, garnished with sage leaves.

**Cook's Tip**
*Although the word "chowder" is most closely associated with a soup made from clams, this recipe contains the two traditional ingredients—vegetables and milk—so it is quite authentic.*

**Variation**
*If you are unable to locate canned flageolet beans, use frozen peas instead.*

# Borlotti Bean & Pasta Soup

A complete meal in a bowl, this is based on a classic Italian soup. Traditionally, the person who finds the bay leaf is honored with a kiss from the cook.

**Serves 4**

5 tablespoons olive oil
1 onion, chopped
1 celery stalk, chopped
2 carrots, chopped
1 bay leaf
5 cups vegetable stock
14-ounce can chopped tomatoes
1½ cups dried pasta shapes
14-ounce can borlotti
  beans, drained
9 ounces fresh young spinach
salt and ground black pepper
⅔ cup freshly grated Parmesan
  cheese, to serve

**1** Heat the olive oil in a large, heavy saucepan and add the chopped onion, celery and carrots. Cook over medium heat, stirring occasionally, for 5 minutes or until the vegetables soften and the onion is translucent.

**2** Add the bay leaf, stock and tomatoes and bring to a boil. Lower the heat and simmer for about 10 minutes, until the vegetables are just tender.

**3** Bring the soup back to a boil, add the pasta and beans and simmer for 8 minutes, until the pasta is *al dente*. Stir the soup frequently to prevent the pasta from sticking to the bottom of the pan.

**4** Season to taste with salt and pepper, add the spinach and cook for 2 more minutes. Serve in heated bowls, sprinkled with the grated Parmesan.

**Variations**
• Add a glass of white wine with the stock, if desired.
• Substitute two shallots for the onion and ½ small fennel bulb for the celery.

# Garlic, Chickpea & Spinach Soup

Tahini, sesame seed paste, is the secret ingredient that gives this thick, creamy soup such a superb taste.

**Serves 4**

2 tablespoons olive oil
4 garlic cloves, crushed
1 onion, roughly chopped
2 teaspoons ground cumin
2 teaspoons ground
  coriander
5 cups vegetable stock
12 ounces potatoes,
  finely chopped
15-ounce can chickpeas, drained
1 tablespoon cornstarch
⅔ cup heavy cream
2 tablespoons light tahini (sesame
  seed paste)
7 ounces fresh young
  spinach, shredded
salt and ground black pepper
cayenne pepper, to serve

**1** Heat the olive oil in a large, heavy saucepan. Add the garlic and onion and cook over medium heat, stirring occasionally, for 5 minutes or until the onion has softened and is golden brown.

**2** Stir in the cumin and coriander and cook for 1 more minute, then pour in the stock. Add the potatoes. Bring to a boil, lower the heat and simmer for 10 minutes.

**3** Add the drained chickpeas and simmer for another 5 minutes or until the potatoes are just tender.

**4** Mix the cornstarch, cream and tahini in a bowl. Stir in plenty of seasoning. Stir the mixture into the soup and add the spinach. Bring to a boil, stirring constantly, then simmer for 2 minutes. Ladle the soup into heated bowls, sprinkle with a little cayenne pepper and serve immediately.

**Variation**
*Ful medames would make a delicious alternative to chickpeas, but you would probably have to use dried beans. Soak them overnight and then simmer for 3–4 hours before using.*

# Pear & Parmesan Salad with Poppy Seed Dressing

This is a good salad when pears are at their seasonal best. Drizzle on poppy-seed dressing and top them with shavings of Parmesan cheese.

**Serves 4**

4 just-ripe dessert pears
2-ounce piece of
    Parmesan cheese
watercress, to garnish
water crackers or rye bread, to
    serve (optional)

**For the dressing**

2 tablespoons cider vinegar
1/2 teaspoon light brown sugar
good pinch of dried thyme
2 tablespoons extra virgin olive oil
1 tablespoon sunflower oil
1 tablespoon poppy seeds
salt and ground black pepper

**1** Peel the pears if desired, although they look more attractive with the skin on. Cut them in quarters and remove the cores.

**2** Cut each pear quarter in half lengthwise and arrange them on four small serving plates.

**3** Make the dressing. Mix the vinegar, sugar and thyme in a pitcher. Gradually whisk in the olive oil, then the sunflower oil. Season with salt and pepper, then add the poppy seeds.

**4** Trickle the dressing on the pears. Shave Parmesan on top and garnish with watercress. Serve with water crackers or thinly sliced rye bread, if desired.

**Variation**
Blue cheeses and pears also have a natural affinity. Stilton, dolcelatte, Gorgonzola or Danish blue (Danablu) can be used instead of the shavings of Parmesan. Allow about 7 ounces and cut into wedges or cubes.

# Dressed Salad of Fresh Cèpes

Mushrooms are great in salad, especially if you are able to obtain fresh cèpes or bay boletus. Any wild or cultivated mushrooms can be used; remove the stems from shiitake mushrooms.

**Serves 4**

4 cups fresh cèpes or bay boletus,
    thinly sliced
6 ounces ready-to-serve mixed
    salad greens
1/2 cup broken walnut
    pieces, toasted

2-ounce piece of
    Parmesan cheese
salt and ground black pepper

**For the dressing**

2 egg yolks
1/2 teaspoon French mustard
5 tablespoons peanut oil
3 tablespoons walnut oil
2 tablespoons lemon juice
2 tablespoons chopped
    fresh parsley
pinch of sugar

**1** Make the dressing. Place the egg yolks in a screw-top jar with the mustard, peanut oil, walnut oil, lemon juice, parsley and sugar. Close the jar tightly and shake well.

**2** Place the mushrooms in a large salad bowl and pour on the dressing. Toss to coat, then set aside for 10–15 minutes to allow the flavors to mingle.

**3** Add the salad greens to the mushrooms and toss lightly. Season with plenty of salt and pepper.

**4** Divide the salad among four large plates. Sprinkle on toasted walnuts and shavings of Parmesan cheese.

**Cook's Tip**
The dressing for this salad uses raw egg yolks. Be sure to use only the freshest eggs from a reputable supplier. Expectant mothers, young children and the elderly are advised to avoid raw egg yolks. If this presents a problem, the dressing can be made without the egg yolks.

# Broiled Goat Cheese Salad

The fresh tangy flavor of goat cheese contrasts beautifully with the mild greens in this satisfying and attractive salad.

**Serves 4**
2 firm round whole goat cheeses, about 2¹/₂–4 ounces each
4 slices French bread
extra virgin olive oil, for drizzling
6 ounces ready-to-serve mixed salad greens
snipped fresh chives, to garnish

***For the vinaigrette dressing***
¹/₂ garlic clove
1 teaspoon Dijon mustard
1 teaspoon white wine vinegar
1 teaspoon dry white wine
3 tablespoons extra virgin olive oil
salt and ground black pepper

**1** To make the dressing, rub a large salad bowl with the cut side of the garlic clove. Combine the mustard, vinegar and wine in the bowl. Add salt and pepper to taste, then whisk in the oil, 1 tablespoon at a time, to form a thick vinaigrette.

**2** Using a sharp knife, cut the goat cheeses in half across their width to make four "cakes."

**3** Arrange the bread slices in a broiler pan and toast them on one side under a hot broiler. Turn them over and place a piece of cheese, cut-side up, on each slice. Drizzle with olive oil and broil until the cheese is lightly browned.

**4** Add the leaves to the salad bowl and toss to coat them with the dressing. Divide the salad among four plates, top each with a goat cheese crouton and garnish with chives. Serve immediately.

> **Cook's Tip**
> *The best-known goat cheeses are French, known generically as chèvre, and are also sold under specific names, such as Crottin de Chavignol. There are other excellent goat's milk cheeses, such as the English Cerney, Capricorn Goat and Vulscombe, and the American Caprile Banon and Chèvre de Provence.*

# Asparagus in Egg & Lemon Sauce

As as appetizer or light lunch, fresh asparagus is a special treat, especially when topped with a tangy, fresh-tasting sauce.

**Serves 4**
1¹/₂ pounds asparagus
1 tablespoon cornstarch
2 teaspoons sugar
2 egg yolks
juice of 1¹/₂ lemons
salt

**1** Trim the asparagus stalks, discarding the tough ends, then tie them in a bundle. Cook in a tall pan of boiling salted water over medium heat for 7–10 minutes.

**2** Drain well, reserving a scant 1 cup of the cooking liquid. Untie the asparagus stems and arrange them in a shallow serving dish.

**3** Put the cornstarch in a small pan. Stir in enough of the reserved cooking liquid to form a smooth paste, then stir in the remaining cooking liquid. Bring to a boil, stirring constantly, and cook over low heat until the sauce thickens slightly. Stir in the sugar, then remove the pan from heat. Set the sauce aside to cool slightly.

**4** Beat the egg yolks with the lemon juice. Gradually stir the mixture into the cooled sauce. Cook over very low heat, stirring constantly, until the sauce is fairly thick. Immediately remove the pan from heat. Continue stirring for 1 minute.

**5** Taste the sauce and add salt or sugar if needed. Let it cool slightly, then pour a little on the asparagus. Cover and chill for at least 2 hours before serving with the rest of the sauce.

> **Variation**
> *This sauce goes very well with all sorts of young vegetables. Try it with baby leeks, cooked whole or chopped, or serve it with other baby vegetables, such as carrots and zucchini.*

# Baby Onions & Mushrooms à la Grecque

There are many variations of this classic dish. The mushrooms may be omitted, but they add immeasurably to the flavor.

**Serves 4**
2 carrots
12 ounces baby onions
4 tablespoons olive oil
½ cup dry white wine
1 teaspoon coriander seeds, lightly crushed
2 bay leaves

pinch of cayenne pepper
1 garlic clove, crushed
4 cups button mushrooms
3 tomatoes, peeled, seeded and quartered
salt and ground black pepper
3 tablespoons chopped fresh parsley, to garnish
crusty bread, to serve

**1** Peel the carrots and cut them into small dice. Peel the baby onions and trim the tops and roots.

**2** Heat 3 tablespoons of the olive oil in a deep frying pan. Add the carrots and onions and cook, stirring occasionally, for about 20 minutes, until the vegetables have browned lightly.

**3** Add the white wine, coriander seeds, bay leaves, cayenne, garlic, button mushrooms and tomatoes, with salt and pepper to taste. Cook, uncovered, for 20–30 minutes, until the vegetables are soft and the sauce has thickened.

**4** Transfer to a serving dish and let cool. Cover and chill until needed. Before serving, pour on the remaining olive oil and sprinkle with the parsley. Serve with crusty bread.

> **Cook's Tip**
> Don't trim too much from either the top or root end of the onions: if you do, the centers will pop out during cooking.

# Marinated Vegetable Antipasto

If you ever want to prove just how delectable vegetables can be, serve this sensational selection of Italian-style appetizers.

**Serves 4**
**For the bell peppers**
3 red bell peppers, halved and seeded
3 yellow bell peppers, halved and seeded
4 garlic cloves, sliced
a handful of fresh basil leaves, plus extra to garnish
extra virgin olive oil
salt

**For the mushrooms**
6 cups open cap mushrooms
4 tablespoons extra virgin olive oil

1 large garlic clove, crushed
1 tablespoon chopped fresh rosemary
1 cup dry white wine
salt and ground black pepper
fresh rosemary sprigs, to garnish

**For the olives**
½ cup extra virgin olive oil
1 dried red chile
grated zest of 1 lemon
1¼ cups Italian black olives
2 tablespoons chopped fresh flat-leaf parsley
1 lemon wedge, to serve

**1** Place the pepper halves, skin-side up, on a broiler pan and cook until the skins have charred. Transfer to a bowl and cover with crumpled paper towels. Let cool slightly.

**2** When the pepper halves are cool enough to handle, peel off their skins, then cut the flesh into strips. Place the strips in a bowl and add the sliced garlic and basil leaves. Sprinkle on salt to taste, cover with olive oil and set aside to marinate for 3–4 hours, tossing occasionally. Chill in the refrigerator.

**3** Slice the mushrooms thickly and place them in a large heatproof bowl. Heat the oil in a small pan and add the garlic and rosemary. Pour in the wine. Bring the mixture to a boil, then lower the heat and simmer for 3 minutes. Season with salt and pepper to taste.

**4** Pour the mixture onto the mushrooms. Mix thoroughly and set aside until cool, stirring occasionally. Cover and let marinate overnight in the refrigerator.

**5** Prepare the olives. Place the oil in a small pan and crumble in the chile. Add the lemon zest. Heat gently for about 3 minutes. Add the olives and heat for 1 more minute. Put into a bowl and let cool. Set aside to marinate overnight.

**6** Let the marinated mushrooms come to room temperature before serving. Garnish them with rosemary sprigs. Garnish the chilled peppers with basil leaves. Sprinkle parsley on the olives and serve with the lemon wedge.

> **Cook's Tip**
> The pepper antipasto can be stored in a screw-top jar in the refrigerator for up to 2 weeks.

# Vegetable Terrine with Brandy

A feast for the eye and the palate—that's this luscious layer of brandy-flavored custard and a colorful combination of vegetables.

**Serves 4**
oil, for greasing
1 red bell pepper, quartered
    and seeded
1 green bell pepper, quartered
    and seeded
3/4 cup fresh or frozen peas
6 fresh green asparagus stalks
2 carrots, cut into batons
2/3 cup milk
2/3 cup heavy cream
6 eggs, beaten
1 tablespoon brandy
3/4 cup low-fat cream cheese
1 tablespoon chopped
    fresh parsley
salt and ground black pepper
salad greens, cucumber slices and
    halved tomatoes, to serve

**1** Preheat the oven to 350°F. Grease and line the bottom of a 2-pound loaf pan. Place the pepper quarters, skin-side up, on a broiler pan and cook until the skins have charred. Transfer to a bowl and cover with crumpled paper towels. Let cool.

**2** Cook the peas, asparagus and carrots in separate pans of lightly salted boiling water until tender. Drain and dry on paper towels. Peel off the skins from the pepper quarters.

**3** In a bowl, combine the milk, cream, eggs, brandy, cream cheese and parsley. Mix well and season with plenty of salt and pepper.

**4** Arrange some of the vegetables in the bottom of the loaf pan, trimming to fit if necessary. Spoon some of the cheese mixture onto the vegetables. Continue layering the vegetables and the cheese mixture, ending with a layer of peppers. Cover the pan with aluminum foil and stand it in a roasting pan. Pour in boiling water to come halfway up the sides of the loaf pan.

**5** Bake for 45 minutes or until the custard is just firm. Leave the terrine in the pan until cold, then remove it from the roasting pan. Invert it onto a plate. Lift off the lining paper and slice the terrine. Serve with the salad greens, cucumber and tomatoes.

# Eggplant & Spinach Terrines

These individual terrines make an elegant first course.

**Serves 4**
1 eggplant
2 tablespoons extra virgin olive oil
2 zucchini, thinly sliced
leaves from 1 small fresh
    thyme sprig
4 firm tomatoes, peeled
    and seeded
4 fresh basil leaves, finely sliced
10 ounces fresh baby
    spinach leaves
1 garlic clove, crushed
1 tablespoon butter
pinch of freshly grated nutmeg
salt and ground black pepper
1/2 roasted red bell pepper,
    skinned and chopped, plus a
    little balsamic vinegar, to serve

**1** Preheat the oven to 375°F. Seal four 2 1/2-inch diameter metal cake rings at one end with plastic wrap.

**2** Slice the eggplant into four rounds of equal size. Heat half the oil in a frying pan and fry the eggplant slices on both sides until brown. Place them on a baking sheet and cook in the oven for 10 minutes. Transfer to a plate lined with paper towels.

**3** Heat half the remaining oil in the same pan and fry the zucchini for 2 minutes, then drain on the paper towels. Season with salt and pepper and sprinkle with thyme leaves.

**4** Place the tomatoes, basil and remaining oil in a heavy frying pan and cook for 5–8 minutes. Cook the spinach, garlic and butter in a saucepan, allowing all the water to evaporate. Drain well, add the nutmeg, then season with salt and pepper.

**5** Line the bottom and 1/2 inch of the sides of the cake rings with the spinach leaves, leaving no gaps. Place zucchini slices around the edges of each ring, overlapping them slightly. Divide the tomato mixture equally among the rings, pressing it down well. Place the eggplant on top, trimming the edges to fit.

**6** Seal the top with plastic wrap and pierce the bottom to allow any liquid to escape. Chill overnight. Remove from the rings and serve with roasted pepper and drizzled with balsamic vinegar.

# Red Bell Pepper Polenta with Pipian

This recipe is inspired by the fusion of Italian and Mexican influences. A polenta loaf, layered with brightly colored vegetables, is served with a spicy salsa.

**Serves 4**
oil, for greasing
3 young zucchini, trimmed
5 cups vegetable stock
2 cups fine polenta
  or cornmeal
7-ounce can red bell peppers,
  drained and sliced
4 ounces salad greens

**For the pipian**
generous 1 cup roasted
  sunflower seeds
1 slice white bread, crust removed
scant 1 cup vegetable stock
1 garlic clove, crushed
$\frac{1}{2}$ fresh red chile, seeded
  and chopped
2 tablespoons chopped cilantro
1 teaspoon sugar
1 tablespoon freshly squeezed
  lime juice
pinch of salt

**1** Lightly oil a 9-inch loaf pan and line with a single sheet of waxed paper. Cook the zucchini in a pan of lightly salted simmering water for 2–3 minutes. Refresh under cold running water and drain. When they are cool, cut into strips.

**2** Heat the stock in a heavy saucepan until it is simmering. Add the polenta in a steady stream, stirring constantly, and continue to stir over the heat for 2–3 minutes, until thickened.

**3** Partly fill the lined pan with the polenta mixture. Layer the sliced zucchini and peppers over the polenta. Fill the pan with the remaining polenta and let set for 10–15 minutes.

**4** Meanwhile, make the pipian. Process the sunflower seeds in a food processor into a thick paste. Add the remaining ingredients and process again until well combined. Spoon into a bowl.

**5** Turn the warm polenta loaf onto a board, remove the paper and cut into thick slices with a large wet knife. Serve with the salad greens and the pipian salsa.

# Sweet Potato Roulade

Sweet potato works particularly well as the base for this roulade. Slice thinly for an impressive appetizer.

**Serves 8**
oil, for greasing
1 cup low-fat cream cheese
5 tablespoons plain yogurt
6–8 scallions, thinly sliced
2 tablespoons chopped Brazil
  nuts, roasted

1 pound sweet potatoes, peeled
  and cubed
12 allspice berries, crushed
4 eggs, separated
$\frac{1}{2}$ cup finely grated Edam cheese
salt and ground black pepper
1 tablespoon sesame seeds
ready-to-serve mixed salad greens,
  to serve

**1** Preheat the oven to 400°F. Grease and line a 13 × 10-inch jelly roll pan with nonstick baking parchment. In a small bowl, mix the cream cheese, yogurt, scallions and Brazil nuts. Set this filling aside.

**2** Boil or steam the sweet potatoes until tender. Drain well. Place in a food processor with the allspice and process until smooth. Spoon into a bowl and stir in the egg yolks and grated cheese. Season to taste with salt and pepper.

**3** Whisk the egg whites until stiff, but not dry. Fold one-third of the egg whites into the sweet potatoes to lighten the mixture before gently folding in the rest.

**4** Pour into the prepared pan, tilting it to get the mixture into the corners. Smooth gently with a knife and bake for 10–15 minutes.

**5** Meanwhile, lay a large sheet of waxed paper on a clean dish towel and sprinkle on the sesame seeds.

**6** When the roulade is cooked, turn it onto the paper, remove the lining paper, trim the edges and roll it up. Let cool. When cool, carefully unroll, spread with the filling and roll up again. Cut into slices and serve with salad greens.

# Stuffed Grape Leaves

Whether you serve these as part of a meze or as a solo starter, they are certain to prove popular.

**Makes about 40**
40 fresh grape leaves
4 tablespoons olive oil
lemon wedges and a crisp salad,
   to serve

**For the stuffing**
¾ cup long-grain rice, rinsed
2 bunches scallions,
   finely chopped
½ cup pine nuts
3 tablespoons seedless raisins
2 tablespoons chopped fresh
   mint leaves
4 tablespoons chopped
   fresh parsley
¾ teaspoon ground black pepper
salt

**1** Using a knife or a pair of scissors, snip out the thick, coarse stems from the grape leaves. Blanch the leaves in a large pan of boiling salted water until they just begin to change color. Drain, refresh in cold water, then drain again.

**2** To make the stuffing, mix all the ingredients in a bowl and season to taste with salt. Open out the grape leaves, ribbed side facing up. Place a heaping teaspoonful of the stuffing on each.

**3** Fold over the two outer edges to secure the stuffing, then roll up each grape leaf from the stem end to form a neat roll.

**4** Arrange the stuffed grape leaves neatly in a steamer and sprinkle on the olive oil. Steam over boiling water for 50–60 minutes or until the rice is completely cooked. Serve cold, but not chilled, with lemon wedges and a salad.

**Cook's Tip**
If you can't obtain fresh grape leaves, use two packages of grape leaves preserved in brine. Rinse and drain them well, then pat dry with paper towels before filling.

# Vermicelli with Lemon

Fresh and tangy, this makes an excellent first course for a dinner party. It has the additional advantage of being extremely quick and easy to prepare.

**Serves 4**
12 ounces dried vermicelli
juice of 2 large lemons
¼ cup butter
scant 1 cup heavy cream
1 tablespoon finely grated
   lemon zest
1⅓ cups freshly grated
   Parmesan cheese
salt and ground black pepper

**1** Cook the vermicelli in a large pan of lightly salted boiling water until *al dente*.

**2** Meanwhile, pour the lemon juice into a medium saucepan. Add the butter and cream, then stir in the lemon zest. Season with salt and pepper to taste.

**3** Bring to a boil, stirring frequently. Lower the heat and simmer, stirring occasionally, for about 5 minutes, until the cream has reduced slightly.

**4** Drain the pasta and return it to the pan. Add the grated Parmesan to the sauce, then taste for seasoning and adjust if necessary. Pour the sauce onto the pasta. Toss quickly over medium heat until the pasta is evenly coated with the sauce, then divide among four warmed bowls and serve immediately.

**Cook's Tips**
• Lemons vary in the amount of juice they yield. On average, a large fresh lemon will yield 4–6 tablespoons. The lemony flavor of this dish is quite pronounced—you can use less juice if you prefer.
• Try to find unwaxed lemons if you are going to grate the zest. (Waxed lemons have been treated to preserve the zest.) Otherwise, wash the lemons thoroughly first.

## Chilled Stuffed Zucchini

Full of flavor but low in calories and fat, this makes a superb summer appetizer.

**Serves 6**
6 zucchini, trimmed
1 Spanish onion, very
  finely chopped
1 garlic clove, crushed
4–6 tablespoons well-flavored
  French dressing
1 green bell pepper, seeded
  and diced
3 tomatoes, peeled, seeded
  and diced
1 tablespoon drained and
  chopped rinsed capers
1 teaspoon chopped fresh parsley
1 teaspoon snipped fresh basil
sea salt and ground black pepper
fresh parsley sprigs, to garnish

**1** Bring a large shallow pan of lightly salted water to a boil. Add the zucchini and simmer for 2–3 minutes, until they are lightly cooked. Drain well.

**2** Cut the zucchini in half lengthwise. Carefully scoop out the flesh, leaving the zucchini shells intact. Chop the flesh into small cubes. Place in a bowl and cover with half the chopped onion. Dot with the crushed garlic.

**3** Drizzle on 2 tablespoons of the dressing, cover and marinate for 2–3 hours. Wrap the zucchini shells tightly in plastic wrap, and chill them until they are needed.

**4** Stir the pepper, tomatoes and capers into the zucchini mixture, with the remaining onion and the herbs. Season to taste with sea salt and pepper. Pour on enough of the remaining dressing to moisten the mixture and toss well. Chill.

**5** Spoon the filling into the zucchini shells, arrange on a platter and serve garnished with parsley.

> **Cook's Tip**
> To make French dressing, whisk together 1 tablespoon wine vinegar, 1 teaspoon Dijon mustard and 5 tablespoons olive oil.

## Stuffed Mushrooms

This is a classic mushroom dish, strongly flavored with garlic. Use very fresh mushrooms.

**Serves 6**
12 large or 18 medium
  flat mushrooms
butter, for greasing
3 tablespoons olive oil
2 garlic cloves, very finely chopped
3 tablespoons finely chopped
  fresh parsley
3/4–1 cup fresh white
  bread crumbs
salt and ground black pepper
flat-leaf parsley sprig,
  to garnish

**1** Preheat the oven to 350°F. Cut off the mushroom stems and set them aside. Grease a shallow ovenproof dish with butter. Arrange the mushroom caps, gills-side up, in the dish.

**2** Heat 1 tablespoon of the olive oil in a frying pan and fry the garlic briefly. Chop the mushroom stems finely and mix them with the parsley and bread crumbs. Add the garlic and 1 tablespoon of the remaining oil and season with salt and pepper to taste. Mix thoroughly, then pile a little of the mixture on each mushroom cap.

**3** Drizzle the remaining oil on the mushrooms, then cover them with buttered waxed paper. Bake for 15–20 minutes, removing the paper for the last 5 minutes to brown the tops.

**4** Serve two or three mushrooms per portion, garnishing with flat-leaf parsley.

> **Cook's Tips**
> • The cooking time for the mushroom caps depends on their size and thickness. If they are fairly thin, cook for slightly less time. They should be tender, but not too soft when cooked. Test them with the point of a sharp knife.
> • If a stronger garlic flavor is preferred, do not cook the garlic before adding it to the bread crumb mixture.

# Hot Halloumi with Bell Peppers

Salty and full of flavor, Halloumi cheese takes on a wonderful texture when broiled or fried. A tumble of roasted sweet bell peppers makes an especially fine accompaniment.

**Serves 4**

6 bell peppers of mixed colors,
   halved and seeded
olive oil
2 tablespoons balsamic vinegar
small handful of raisins (optional)
11 ounces Halloumi cheese,
   thickly sliced
salt and ground black pepper
flat-leaf parsley, to garnish

**1** Place the pepper halves, skin-side up, on a broiler pan and broil until the skins have blistered and charred. Transfer to a bowl and cover with crumpled paper towels. Let cool slightly, then peel off the skins. Slice the flesh into a bowl. Save any juices and mix these with the peppers.

**2** Pour a little olive oil on the peppers. Add the vinegar and raisins, if using, and season with salt and pepper to taste. Toss lightly and let cool.

**3** When ready to serve, divide the pepper salad among four plates. In a large heavy frying pan heat olive oil to a depth of about ¼ inch. Fry the Halloumi slices over a medium-high heat for 2–3 minutes or until golden brown on both sides, turning them halfway through cooking.

**4** Drain the Halloumi thoroughly on paper towels and serve with the roasted peppers and a parsley garnish.

---

**Cook's Tips**
• *For a crisp coating on the Halloumi, toss the slices in all-purpose flour before frying them.*
• *Plain Halloumi can be broiled instead of fried. Preheat a broiler or ridged grill pan, add the cheese and cook until golden brown, turning once. It is good cooked on a grill, too.*

---

# Malfatti with Bell Pepper Sauce

Deliciously light spinach dumplings are wonderful when served with a smoky pepper and tomato sauce.

**Serves 5**

1¼ pounds fresh leaf spinach
1 onion, finely chopped
1 garlic clove, crushed
1 tablespoon extra virgin olive oil
1½ cups ricotta cheese
3 eggs, beaten
½ cup natural-colored dried
   bread crumbs
½ cup all-purpose flour

⅔ cup freshly grated
   Parmesan cheese
freshly grated nutmeg
2 tablespoons butter, melted
salt and ground black pepper

**For the sauce**
2 red bell peppers, quartered
   and seeded
2 tablespoons extra virgin olive oil
1 onion, chopped
14-ounce can chopped tomatoes
⅔ cup water

**1** Make the sauce. Broil the peppers, skin-side up, until the skins have charred. Place in a bowl, cover with crumpled paper towels and let cool. Peel off the skins and chop the flesh.

**2** Heat the oil in a saucepan and sauté the onion and peppers for 5 minutes. Add the tomatoes and water and season. Bring to a boil, lower the heat and simmer for 15 minutes. Process in a food processor or blender, then return to the clean pan.

**3** Trim any thick stems from the spinach, then blanch in a pan of boiling water for about 1 minute. Drain, refresh under cold water and drain again. Squeeze dry, then chop finely. Put the onion, garlic, oil, ricotta, eggs, bread crumbs and spinach in a bowl. Mix well, then stir in the flour and 1 teaspoon salt. Add half the Parmesan, then season to taste with pepper and nutmeg. Roll the mixture into 15 small logs and chill lightly.

**4** Bring a large saucepan of water to a boil. Cook the malfatti, in batches, for 5 minutes. Remove them with a spatula and toss them with the melted butter. To serve, reheat the sauce and divide it among five plates. Arrange three malfatti on each and sprinkle on the remaining Parmesan. Serve immediately.

# Vegetable Tempura

These deep-fried fritters are based on Kaki-age, a popular Japanese dish.

**Makes 8**

2 medium zucchini
½ medium eggplant
1 large carrot
½ small Spanish onion

vegetable oil, for deep-frying
salt and ground black pepper
sea salt flakes, lemon slices and
    Japanese soy sauce, to serve

**For the batter**
1 egg
½ cup ice water
1 cup all-purpose flour

**1** Using a potato peeler, pare strips of peel from the zucchini and eggplant to give a striped effect. Cut the zucchini, eggplant and carrot into strips 3–4 inches long and ⅛ inch wide and put them in a colander.

**2** Sprinkle the vegetable strips liberally with salt. Leave for about 30 minutes, then rinse thoroughly under cold running water. Drain well.

**3** Thinly slice the onion from top to bottom, discarding the plump pieces in the middle. Separate the layers so that there are lots of fine long strips. Mix all the vegetables and season to taste with salt and pepper.

**4** Make the batter immediately before frying: mix the egg and ice water in a bowl, then sift in the flour. Mix very briefly with a fork or chopsticks—the batter should remain lumpy. Add the vegetables to the batter and mix to combine.

**5** Half-fill a wok with oil and heat to 350°F or until a cube of day-old bread browns in 60 seconds. Scoop up one heaping tablespoon of the mixture at a time and carefully lower it into the oil to make a fritter. Deep-fry in batches for about 3 minutes, until golden brown and crisp.

**6** Drain the cooked fritters on paper towels, and serve immediately, offering each diner sea salt flakes, lemon slices and a tiny bowl of Japanese soy sauce for dipping.

# Scallion & Ricotta Fritters

These melt-in-your-mouth fritters make an unusual appetizer and are very tasty, especially if you serve them with a spicy avocado salsa.

**Serves 4–6**

generous 1 cup ricotta cheese
1 large egg, beaten
6 tablespoons self-rising flour
6 tablespoons milk
1 bunch scallions,
    thinly sliced
2 tablespoons chopped cilantro

sunflower oil, for frying
salt and ground black pepper

**To garnish**
cilantro sprigs
lime wedges

**To serve**
Avocado & Tomato
    Dipping Sauce
scant 1 cup crème fraîche

**1** Beat the ricotta in a bowl until smooth, then beat in the egg and flour, followed by the milk to make a smooth, thick batter. Beat in the scallions and cilantro. Season well with pepper and a little salt.

**2** Heat a little oil in a nonstick frying pan over medium heat. Add spoonfuls of the mixture, in batches, to make fritters about 3 inches across. Fry for 4–5 minutes on each side, until set and browned. The mixture makes 12 fritters.

**3** Drain the fritters on paper towels and serve immediately. Garnish with the cilantro sprigs and lime wedges, and serve with the dipping sauce and crème fraîche.

> **Cook's Tip**
> It is important that the ricotta is well beaten before the other ingredients are added to make the batter. Once the flour has been added, beat lightly, just to ensure that it is thoroughly combined. Over-beating develops the gluten in the flour, and the fritters will become dense.

# Avocado & Tomato Dipping Sauce

This tastes superb with the Scallion & Ricotta Fritters, but can also be served with fried potato skins, crudités, pretzels or breadsticks.

**Serves 4–6**

2 ripe, but not soft, avocados
1 small red onion, diced
grated zest and juice of 1 lime

½–1 fresh green or red chile,
    seeded and finely chopped
8 ounces tomatoes, peeled,
    seeded and diced
2–3 tablespoons chopped mixed
    fresh mint and cilantro
pinch of sugar
salt and ground black pepper

**1** Peel, pit and dice the avocados. Place in a bowl with the red onion, lime zest and juice. Add chile to taste, the tomatoes, mint and cilantro. Season, then stir in the sugar.

**2** Cover closely and set aside for 30 minutes before using.

# Indian Potato Pancakes

Although described as pancakes, these classic, crisp cakes are more like bhajis. They make an ideal appetizer for an Indian meal.

**Makes 10**
2 potatoes, about 11 ounces
  total weight
1½ teaspoons garam masala or
  curry powder
4 scallions, finely chopped
1 large egg white, lightly beaten
2 tablespoons vegetable oil
salt and ground black pepper
chutney and relishes, to serve

**1** Peel the potatoes, then grate them into a large bowl. Taking a handful at a time, squeeze out the excess liquid, then pat the potatoes dry with paper towels and put them in a separate medium bowl.

**2** Add the garam masala or curry powder, scallions and egg white to the potatoes. Stir to combine, then season to taste with salt and pepper.

**3** Heat the oil in a nonstick frying pan over medium heat. Taking care not to overcrowd the pan, drop tablespoonfuls of the batter onto the surface and flatten each to a pancake with the back of the spoon.

**4** Cook for a few minutes and then flip over each pancake. Cook for 3 more minutes.

**5** Drain on paper towels and keep hot while cooking more pancakes in the same way. Serve hot, with chutney and relishes.

---

**Cook's Tips**
• *Grate the potatoes at the last minute, as the flesh will turn brown if they are left standing.*
• *Garam masala is a mixture of spices that usually includes dried chiles, cinnamon, curry leaves, coriander, cumin, mustard and fenugreek seeds, and black peppercorns.*

---

# Baked Eggs en Cocotte with Wild Mushrooms & Chives

These simple but utterly delicious baked eggs, served with toast, make a splendid start to a light meal.

**Serves 6**
5 tablespoons butter
2 shallots, finely chopped
1 small garlic clove,
  finely chopped
3 cups wild mushrooms,
  finely chopped
1 tablespoon lemon juice
1 teaspoon chopped fresh tarragon
2 tablespoons crème fraîche
2 tablespoons snipped fresh chives
6 eggs
salt and ground black pepper
whole chives, to garnish
buttered whole-wheat toast, to serve

**1** Melt 4 tablespoons of the butter in a frying pan and cook the shallots and garlic until softened but not browned.

**2** Increase the heat and add the mushrooms, then cook briskly, stirring frequently, until the mushrooms lose their moisture and are just starting to brown slightly.

**3** Stir in the lemon juice and tarragon and continue to cook, stirring occasionally, until the mushrooms have absorbed the liquid. Stir in half the crème fraîche and half the snipped chives and season to taste with salt and pepper.

**4** Preheat the oven to 375°F. Distribute the mushroom mixture equally among six ramekins. Sprinkle the remaining snipped chives on the mushrooms.

**5** Break an egg into each dish, add a dab of crème fraîche and season to taste with pepper. Dot with the remaining butter. Bake for 10–15 minutes or until the whites of the eggs are set and the yolks cooked to your liking.

**6** Serve immediately, garnished with the fresh chives and accompanied by lots of hot, buttered whole-wheat toast.

# Baked Eggs with Heavy Cream

This rich dish is very easy and quick to make.

**Serves 4**
1 tablespoon unsalted
  butter, softened,
  for greasing
½ cup heavy cream
2 tablespoons snipped
  fresh chives
4 eggs
1 cup finely grated Gruyère
  cheese
salt and ground black pepper

**1** Preheat the oven to 350°F. Grease four individual gratin dishes. Mix the cream with the chives, and season to taste with salt and pepper.

**2** Break an egg into each dish and top with the cream mixture. Sprinkle the cheese around the edge of each dish. Bake for 15–20 minutes. When cooked, brown the tops briefly under a hot broiler, then serve.

# Twice Baked Gruyère & Potato Soufflés

These were popular a few years ago and should not be forgotten. Easily prepared in advance, they are perfect for entertaining.

**Serves 4**
butter, for greasing
8 ounces floury potatoes

2 eggs, separated
1 1/2 cups grated Gruyère cheese
1/2 cup self-rising flour
2 ounces fresh young spinach
    leaves, finely chopped
salt and ground black pepper
ready-to-serve salad greens,
    to serve

**1** Preheat the oven to 400°F. Grease four large ramekins. Cook the potatoes in lightly salted boiling water for 20 minutes, until very tender. Drain thoroughly and mash with the egg yolks.

**2** Stir in half the Gruyère cheese and all the flour. Season to taste with salt and pepper, then fold in the spinach.

**3** Whisk the egg whites until they form soft peaks. Stir a little of the egg white into the spinach mixture to loosen it slightly, then fold in the rest.

**4** Place the ramekins on a baking sheet. Divide the mixture among them. Bake for 20 minutes. Remove from the oven and let cool.

**5** Reheat the oven to 400°F. Carefully invert the soufflés on a baking sheet and sprinkle on the remaining Gruyère cheese. Bake for 5 minutes. Serve immediately with salad greens.

> **Variation**
> For a different flavoring, try replacing the Gruyère with a crumbled blue cheese, such as Stilton.

# Cheese & Pesto Turnovers

Dispense with a formal appetizer and serve these with drinks instead. They are also perfect for parties.

**Serves 8**
8-ounces package frozen
    chopped spinach
2 tablespoons pine nuts

4 tablespoons pesto sauce
1 cup grated Gruyère cheese
2/3 cup freshly grated
    Parmesan cheese
2 10-ounce packages frozen
    phyllo pastry, thawed
2 tablespoons olive oil
salt and ground black pepper

**1** Preheat the oven to 375°F. Prepare the filling. Put the frozen spinach into a pan. Heat it gently, breaking it up as it thaws. Increase the heat to cook any excess moisture. Transfer to a bowl and cool.

**2** Spread out the pine nuts in a frying pan and stir over very low heat until they are lightly toasted. Chop them and add them to the spinach, with the pesto. Stir in the Gruyère and Parmesan cheeses. Season to taste with salt and pepper.

**3** Keeping the rest of the phyllo pastry covered, cut one sheet into 2-inch wide strips. Brush each strip with oil. Put a teaspoon of filling on one end of a strip of pastry. Fold the end over in a triangle, enclosing the filling.

**4** Continue to fold the triangle over and over again until the end of the strip is reached. Repeat with the other strips, until all the filling has been used up.

**5** Place the turnovers on baking sheets, brush them with oil and bake for 20–25 minutes or until golden brown. Cool slightly on a wire rack. Serve warm.

> **Cook's Tip**
> Keep the phyllo moist and pliable by keeping it covered with plastic wrap and a damp dish towel. Remove one sheet at a time.

# Quail's Egg & Vermouth Tartlets

The hard-boiled eggs have an attractive marbled surface.

**Serves 4**
10 quail's eggs
2 tablespoons soy sauce
2 tablespoons mustard seeds
1 tablespoon green tea leaves
6 phyllo pastry sheets, thawed
  if frozen

1/4 cup butter, melted
1 small avocado
3 tablespoons dry white vermouth
2 tablespoons mayonnaise
2 teaspoons freshly squeezed
  lime juice
salt and ground black pepper
paprika, for dusting
mâche, to serve

**1** Put the quail's eggs into a saucepan. Pour in cold water to cover. Add the soy sauce, mustard seeds and tea leaves. Bring to a boil, then lower the heat and simmer for 3 minutes.

**2** Remove the pan from heat and lift out the eggs with a draining spoon. Gently tap them on a firm surface so that the shells crack all over. Put the eggs back into the liquid and set in a cool place for 8 hours or overnight.

**3** Preheat the oven to 375°F. Grease four 4-inch tartlet shells. Brush each sheet of phyllo pastry with a little melted butter and stack the six sheets on top of each other. Stamp out four rounds with a 6-inch cutter.

**4** Line the tartlet shells with the pastry and frill the edge of each. Put a crumpled piece of aluminum foil in each phyllo shell and bake for 12–15 minutes, until cooked and golden. Remove the foil and set the cases aside to cool.

**5** Cut the avocado in half, remove the pit and scoop the flesh into a blender or food processor. Add the vermouth, mayonnaise and lime juice, and season to taste with salt and pepper. Process until smooth.

**6** Shell and halve the eggs. Pipe or spoon the avocado mixture into the pastry shells and arrange the eggs on top. Dust them with a little paprika and serve immediately, with the mâche.

# Brandied Roquefort Tarts

Light puff pastry rounds are topped with the irresistible combination of brandy and Roquefort cheese.

**Makes 6**
5 ounces Roquefort cheese
2 tablespoons brandy
2 tablespoons olive oil
2 red onions (total weight about
  8 ounces), thinly sliced

8-ounce puff pastry, thawed
  if frozen
all-purpose flour, for dusting
beaten egg or milk, to glaze
6 walnut halves, chopped
2 tablespoons snipped
  fresh chives
salt and ground black pepper
chive knots, to garnish
salad greens, diced cucumber and
  thin tomato wedges, to serve

**1** Crumble the Roquefort into a small bowl, pour on the brandy and let marinate for 1 hour. Meanwhile, heat the oil in a frying pan and fry the onions gently for 20 minutes, stirring occasionally. Set the pan aside.

**2** Preheat the oven to 425°F. Grease a baking sheet. Roll out the pastry on a floured surface to a 1/4-inch thickness and stamp out six rounds with a 4-inch fluted cutter. Put them on the baking sheet and prick with a fork.

**3** Brush the edges of the pastry with a little beaten egg or milk. Add the walnuts and chives to the onion mixture and season with salt and pepper to taste. Divide the mixture among the pastry shapes, leaving the edges clear.

**4** Spoon the brandied cheese mixture on top of the pastries and bake for 12–15 minutes, until golden. Serve warm, garnished with chive knots, on a bed of salad greens, diced cucumber and thin tomato wedges.

**Cook's Tip**
*To make the chive knots, simply tie chives together in groups of three, with a central knot. Blanch the chives briefly if they are not very pliable.*

# Spiced Carrot Dip

This is a delicious low-fat dip with a sweet and spicy flavor. Serve with wheat crackers or tortilla chips.

**Serves 4**

1 onion
4 carrots
grated zest and juice of 2 oranges
1 tablespoon hot curry paste
⅔ cup low-fat plain yogurt
a handful of fresh basil leaves
1–2 tablespoons fresh lemon juice, to taste
Tabasco sauce, to taste
salt and ground black pepper

**1** Chop the onion finely. Peel and grate the carrots. Place three-quarters of the grated carrot in a small saucepan and add the onion, orange zest and juice and curry paste. Bring to a boil, lower the heat, cover and simmer for 10 minutes, until tender.

**2** Let cool slightly, then process the mixture in a blender or food processor until smooth. Scrape into a bowl and let cool completely.

**3** Stir in the yogurt, a little at a time. Tear the basil leaves into small pieces and stir them into the mixture.

**4** Season with lemon juice, Tabasco, salt and pepper to taste. Mix well. Serve at room temperature within a few hours of making. Garnish with the remaining grated carrot.

---

**Cook's Tip**
The original Tabasco sauce, dating from the mid-nineteenth century, is made from red bell peppers, vinegar and salt. A green bell pepper version is also available.

---

**Variation**
Sour cream can be used instead of plain yogurt to make a richer, creamy dip.

---

# Fat-free Saffron Dip

Serve this mild dip with fresh vegetable crudités—it is particularly good with crunchy vegetables, such as cauliflower florets, baby corn and celery.

**Serves 4**

1 tablespoon boiling water
small pinch of saffron threads
scant 1 cup fat-free fromage frais
10 fresh chives
10 fresh basil leaves
salt and ground black pepper

**1** Pour the boiling water into a small bowl and add the saffron threads. Let infuse for 3 minutes.

**2** Beat the fromage frais until smooth, then stir in the infused saffron liquid.

**3** Use a pair of scissors to snip the chives into the dip. Tear the basil leaves into small pieces and stir them in. Season with salt and pepper to taste and stir to combine. Serve immediately.

---

**Variation**
If preferred, you can omit the saffron and flavor the dip with a squeeze of lemon or lime juice instead.

---

# Pesto Dip

This tastes great with roasted vegetables and also goes well with baked potato skins and chips.

**Serves 4**

1 cup sour cream or low-fat fromage frais
1 tablespoon ready-made red or green pesto

**1** Spoon the sour cream or fromage frais into a bowl. Stir in the pesto, swirling it on the surface of the dip.
**2** Cover and chill until ready to serve.

# Lemon Oil Dip with Charred Artichokes

A tangy lemon and garlic dip makes the perfect accompaniment to roasted globe artichokes. It would also go well with grilled baby artichokes.

**Serves 4**
1 tablespoon lemon juice or white wine vinegar
2 globe artichokes, trimmed
12 garlic cloves, unpeeled
6 tablespoons olive oil
1 lemon
sea salt
flat-leaf parsley sprigs, to garnish

**1** Preheat the oven to 400°F. Add the lemon juice or vinegar to a bowl of cold water. Cut each artichoke lengthwise into wedges. Pull out and discard the hairy choke from the center of each wedge, then drop the wedges into the acidulated water to prevent discoloration.

**2** Drain the artichoke wedges and place them in a roasting pan with the garlic. Add half the olive oil and toss well to coat. Sprinkle with sea salt and roast for 40 minutes, stirring once or twice, until the artichokes are tender and a little charred.

**3** Meanwhile, make the dip. Using a small, sharp knife, thinly pare two strips of zest from the lemon. Lay the strips on a board and carefully scrape off any remaining pith. Place the zest in a small pan with water to cover. Bring to a boil, then simmer for 5 minutes. Drain the zest, refresh it in cold water, then chop it roughly and set it aside.

**4** Arrange the cooked artichokes on a serving plate and set them aside to cool for 5 minutes.

**5** Press the garlic cloves to extract the flesh and put it in a bowl. Mash it into a purée, then add the lemon zest. Squeeze the juice from the lemon and whisk it into the garlic mixture. Finally, whisk in the remaining oil. Season with sea salt and serve with the warm artichokes. Garnish with flat-leaf parsley.

# Aïoli with Fried Potatoes

Today, aïoli is usually made in a food processor, rather than pounded with a pestle in a mortar, and is more like garlic mayonnaise.

**Serves 4**
vegetable oil, for deep-frying
4 potatoes, each cut into eight wedges
coarse sea salt

**For the aïoli**
1 large egg yolk, at room temperature
1 teaspoon white wine vinegar
5 tablespoons olive oil
5 tablespoons sunflower oil
4 garlic cloves, crushed
parsley sprig, to garnish

**1** First, make the aïoli. Place the egg yolk and vinegar in a food processor. With the motor running, gradually add the olive oil, then the sunflower oil through the feeder tube, until the mixture has the consistency of a thick mayonnaise.

**2** Scrape the mixture into a serving bowl and stir in the crushed garlic. Season with salt to taste, then cover closely and chill in the refrigerator until needed.

**3** Heat the vegetable oil in a saucepan or deep-fryer to a temperature of 350°F or until a cube of day-old bread turns golden in about 60 seconds. Add the potato wedges and fry for about 7 minutes, until pale golden.

**4** Lift out the potato wedges with a draining spoon and drain them on paper towels. Increase the heat of the oil slightly, then return the potato wedges to the pan and fry them for a second time until crisp and golden brown. Remove with a slotted spoon and drain thoroughly on paper towels. Sprinkle with sea salt and serve hot with the aïoli, garnished with parsley.

**Cook's Tip**
*For an aïoli with a milder flavor, use three parts sunflower oil to one part olive oil.*

# Mellow Garlic Dip

Two whole heads of garlic may seem like a lot but, once cooked, their flavor becomes sweet and mellow.

4 tablespoons mayonnaise
5 tablespoons plain yogurt
1 teaspoon whole-grain mustard
salt and ground black pepper
crunchy breadsticks, to
    serve (optional)

**Serves 4**
2 whole heads of garlic
1 tablespoon olive oil

**1** Preheat the oven to 400°F. Separate the garlic cloves and place them in a small roasting pan. Pour the olive oil over them and turn them with a spoon to coat evenly. Roast for 20–30 minutes, until tender and softened. Set aside to cool for 5 minutes.

**2** Trim off the root end from each garlic clove, then peel. Place the garlic cloves on a cutting board and sprinkle with salt. Mash with a fork until puréed. Scrape the purée into a small bowl and stir in the mayonnaise, yogurt and mustard.

**3** Check and adjust the seasoning, then spoon the dip into a serving bowl. Cover closely and chill until ready to serve.

# Easy Garlic and Coconut Dip

This tastes fabulous with crudités or breadsticks.

2 tablespoons chili powder
²⁄₃ cup plain yogurt
salt
crudités, to serve

**Serves 4**
5 garlic cloves
2 cups dry, shredded grated
    coconut

**1** Pound the garlic with a pinch of salt. Gradually work in the coconut and chili powder to make a paste.
**2** Stir the paste into the yogurt and serve with crudités.

# Butternut Squash & Parmesan Dip

Butternut squash makes an unusual but very tasty dip, which is best served warm.

4 garlic cloves, unpeeled
2 tablespoons freshly grated
    Parmesan cheese
3–5 tablespoons heavy cream
salt and ground black pepper
Melba toast, cheese straws or
    crudités, to serve

**Serves 4**
1 butternut squash
1 tablespoon butter

**1** Preheat the oven to 400°F. Cut the butternut squash in half lengthwise, then scoop out and discard the seeds.

**2** Use a small, sharp knife to score the flesh deeply in a criss-cross pattern; cut as close to the skin as possible, but take care not to cut through it. Arrange both halves in a small roasting pan and dot them with the butter. Sprinkle with salt and pepper and roast for 20 minutes. Tuck the garlic cloves around the squash in the roasting pan. Bake for 20 more minutes, until the squash is tender and softened.

**3** Scoop the flesh out of the squash shells and place it in a blender or food processor. Slip the garlic cloves out of their skins and add the pulp to the squash. Process until smooth.

**4** With the motor running, add half the grated Parmesan cheese, then add the cream. Check the seasoning. Spoon the dip into a serving bowl, sprinkle on the reserved cheese and serve warm with Melba toast, cheese straws or crudités.

> **Cook's Tip**
> To make Melba toast, broil a slice of white bread on both sides until golden. Let cool slightly, then cut off and discard the crusts. Using a long, thin, very sharp knife, slice the bread in half horizontally to make two thinner slices. Toast the inner slices under the broiler until golden. Let cool, then store in an airtight container until needed.

# Tzatziki

Cool, creamy and refreshing, tzatziki is wonderfully easy to make and even easier to eat. Serve this classic Greek dip with pita bread, potato wedges or a selection of grilled vegetables.

**Serves 4**

*1 mini cucumber, trimmed*
*4 scallions*
*1 garlic clove*
*scant 1 cup plain yogurt*
*3 tablespoons chopped fresh mint*
*salt and ground black pepper*
*fresh mint sprig, to garnish*
*toasted mini pita breads, to serve*

**1** Cut the cucumber into ¼-inch dice. Trim the scallions and garlic, then chop both very finely.

**2** Beat the yogurt until smooth, if necessary, then gently stir in the cucumber, onions, garlic and mint.

**3** Scrape the mixture into a serving bowl and season with salt and plenty of ground black pepper to taste. Cover and chill in the refrigerator until needed. Garnish with a small mint sprig and serve with toasted mini pita breads.

**Cook's Tip**
*Choose Greek-style yogurt for this dip—it has a higher fat content than most yogurts, which gives it a deliciously rich, creamy texture.*

**Variation**
*A similar, but smoother dip can be made in the food processor. Peel one small cucumber and process with two garlic cloves and 3 cups mixed fresh herbs to a purée. Stir the purée into scant 1 cup sour cream and season to taste with salt and pepper.*

# Blue Cheese Dip

This dip can be mixed up in next to no time and is delicious served with ripe pears cut into wedges. If you add a little more yogurt to give a softer consistency, it makes a good salad dressing.

**Serves 4**

*5 ounces blue cheese, such as Stilton or Danish blue*
*⅔ cup low-fat cream cheese*
*5 tablespoons plain yogurt*
*salt and ground black pepper*

**1** Crumble the blue cheese into a bowl. Using a wooden spoon, beat the cheese to soften it.

**2** Add the cream cheese and beat well to blend the cheeses.

**3** Gradually beat in the yogurt, adding enough to give you the consistency you prefer.

**4** Season with lots of black pepper and a little salt. Cover and chill in the refrigerator until ready to serve.

# Sun-dried Tomato Swirl

Try this with celery stalks or carrot batons. It is also delicious as a topping on baked potatoes.

**Serves 4**
*2 tablespoons sun-dried tomato paste*

*1 cup plain yogurt*
*2 scallions, finely chopped*
*2 sun-dried tomatoes in oil, drained and finely chopped*
*dash of Tabasco sauce (optional)*
*salt and ground black pepper*

**1** Mix the sun-dried tomato paste with a little of the yogurt until smooth, then gradually stir in the remaining yogurt.
**2** Add the scallions and chopped sun-dried tomatoes, season to taste with salt and pepper and mix well. If desired, spike the swirl with a dash of Tabasco.

# Guacamole

One of the best-loved Mexican salsas, this blend of creamy avocado, tomatoes, garlic, chiles, cilantro and lime now appears on tables all over the world.

**Serves 6–8**
4 ripe avocados
juice of 1 lime
½ small onion
2 garlic cloves
small bunch of cilantro, chopped
3 fresh red chiles
4 medium tomatoes, peeled,
 seeded and roughly chopped
salt
tortilla chips, to serve

**1** Cut the avocados in half and remove the pits. Scoop the flesh out of the shells and place it in a food processor or blender. Process until almost smooth, then scrape into a bowl and stir in the lime juice. For a chunkier dip, mash the avocado flesh roughly with a fork.

**2** Chop the onion finely, then crush the garlic. Add both to the avocado and mix well. Stir in the cilantro.

**3** Remove the stems from the chiles, slit the pods and scrape out the seeds with a small sharp knife. Chop the chiles finely and add them to the avocado mixture, together with the chopped tomatoes. Mix well.

**4** Check the seasoning and add salt to taste. Cover closely with plastic wrap or a tight-fitting lid and chill for 1 hour before serving as a dip with tortilla chips.

**Cook's Tips**
• If it is well covered, guacamole will keep in the refrigerator for 2–3 days, but it will tend to turn grayish.
• Submerging an avocado pit in the guacamole is said to inhibit discoloration.
• Traditionally, avocados are cut with a silver-bladed knife— again to prevent discoloration.

# Eggplant & Bell Pepper Spread

With its rich color and robust texture, this mixture makes an excellent contrast to a creamy cheese dip. It goes especially well with black olives.

**Serves 6–8**
2 eggplant, total weight about
 1½ pounds, halved lengthwise
2 green bell peppers, seeded
 and quartered
3 tablespoons olive oil
2 firm ripe tomatoes, halved,
 seeded and finely chopped
3 tablespoons chopped fresh
 parsley or cilantro
2 garlic cloves, crushed
2 tablespoons red wine vinegar
lemon juice, to taste
salt and ground black pepper
fresh parsley or cilantro sprigs,
 to garnish
dark rye bread, lemon wedges
 and black olives, to serve

**1** Place the eggplant and pepper quarters, skin-side up, on a broiler pan and broil until the skins have blistered and charred. Turn over the vegetables and cook for 3 more minutes. Transfer to a bowl, cover with crumpled paper towels and let cool for about 10 minutes.

**2** Peel off the blackened skin. Place the eggplant and pepper flesh in a food processor and process into a purée.

**3** With the motor running, pour the olive oil in a continuous stream through the feeder tube and process until smooth and thoroughly combined.

**4** Scrape the mixture into a serving bowl and stir in the chopped tomatoes, parsley or cilantro, garlic, vinegar and lemon juice. Season to taste with salt and pepper, garnish with the parsley or cilantro sprigs and serve with dark rye bread and wedges of lemon.

**Cook's Tip**
This dip is delicious served with any rustic bread, such as olive bread or ciabatta.

# Baba Ganoush with Lebanese Flatbread

Baba Ganoush is a delectable eggplant dip from the Middle East.

**Serves 6**
2 small eggplant, halved
1 garlic clove, crushed
4 tablespoons tahini
1/4 cup ground almonds
juice of 1/2 lemon
1/2 teaspoon ground cumin
2 tablespoons fresh mint leaves

olive oil, for drizzling
salt and ground black pepper

**For the Lebanese flatbread**
4 pita breads
3 tablespoons toasted sesame seeds
3 tablespoons chopped fresh thyme leaves
3 tablespoons poppy seeds
2/3 cup olive oil

**1** Make the flatbread. Split the pita breads through the middle and carefully open them out. Mix the sesame seeds, thyme and poppy seeds in a mortar and crush them lightly with a pestle.

**2** Stir in the olive oil. Spread the mixture lightly on the cut-sides of the pita bread. Broil until golden brown and crisp. When cool, break into rough pieces and set aside.

**3** Place the eggplant, skin-side up, on a broiler pan and broil until the skins have blistered and charred. Transfer to a bowl, cover with crumpled paper towels and let cool for 10 minutes. Peel the eggplant, chop the flesh roughly and let it drain in a colander.

**4** Squeeze out as much liquid from the eggplant as possible. Place the flesh in a blender or food processor. Add the garlic, tahini, ground almonds, lemon juice and cumin and process into a smooth paste. Roughly chop half the mint and stir into the dip. Season to taste with salt and pepper.

**5** Spoon the dip into a serving bowl, sprinkle on the remaining mint and drizzle lightly with olive oil. Serve the dip with the Lebanese flatbread.

# Lemon & Coconut Dhal

A warm spicy dish, this is perfect with poppadums or can be served as a main-meal accompaniment.

**Serves 8**
2 tablespoons sunflower oil
2-inch piece of fresh ginger root, chopped
1 onion, chopped
2 garlic cloves, crushed
2 small fresh red chiles, seeded and chopped

1 teaspoon cumin seeds
2/3 cup red lentils
1 cup water
1 tablespoon hot curry paste
scant 1 cup coconut milk
juice of 1 lemon
handful of cilantro leaves
1/4 cup sliced almonds
salt and ground black pepper
warm poppadums, to serve
a few thin slices of red chile, to garnish

**1** Heat the sunflower oil in a large, shallow saucepan. Add the ginger, onion, garlic, red chiles and cumin seeds. Cook over medium heat, stirring occasionally, for about 5 minutes, until the onion is softened but not colored.

**2** Stir the lentils, water and curry paste into the pan and bring to a boil over medium heat. Lower the heat, cover and cook gently for 15–20 minutes, stirring occasionally, until the lentils are just tender but not yet broken.

**3** Stir in all but 2 tablespoons of the coconut cream. Bring to a boil and cook, uncovered, for another 15–20 minutes, until the mixture is thick and pulpy. Remove the pan from heat, then stir in the lemon juice and the whole cilantro leaves. Season with salt and pepper to taste.

**4** Heat a large, heavy frying pan. Add the almonds and dry-fry briefly over medium heat, stirring frequently, until golden brown. Stir about three-quarters of the toasted almonds into the dhal.

**5** Transfer the dhal to a serving bowl and swirl in the remaining coconut milk. Sprinkle on the remaining toasted almonds and chile slices. Serve warm, with poppadums.

# Cannellini Bean Dip

This soft bean dip or pâté is good spread on wheat crackers. Serve it with wedges of tomato and salad.

**Serves 4**
14-ounce can cannellini beans, rinsed and drained
grated zest and juice of 1 lemon
2 tablespoons olive oil
1 garlic clove, finely chopped
2 tablespoons chopped fresh parsley, plus extra to garnish
Tabasco sauce, to taste
cayenne pepper
salt and ground black pepper

**1** Put the beans in a shallow bowl and break them up roughly with a potato masher.

**2** Stir in the lemon zest and juice and olive oil, then the chopped garlic and parsley. Add Tabasco sauce, salt and black pepper to taste.

**3** Spoon the mixture into a small bowl, dust lightly with cayenne and sprinkle with parsley. Chill until ready to serve.

# Vegetarian Tapenade

This famous black olive paste usually contains anchovies, but the vegetarian version is just as delicious.

**Serves 4**
3 cups pitted black olives
5 pieces of sun-dried tomatoes in oil, drained
2 tablespoons drained capers
1–2 garlic cloves, roughly chopped
1 teaspoon chopped fresh thyme
1 tablespoon Dijon mustard
juice of 1/2 lemon
3 tablespoons olive oil

**1** Place all the ingredients in a food processor. Process into a smooth purée, then scrape into a serving dish. Cover and chill slightly before serving.

# Bean Dip

This creamy bean dip is best served warm with pita bread.

**Serves 4**
2 tablespoons vegetable oil
2 garlic cloves, crushed
1 onion, finely chopped
2 fresh green chiles, seeded and finely chopped
1–2 teaspoons hot chili powder
14-ounce can kidney beans
3/4 cup grated mature Cheddar cheese, plus extra to garnish
1 fresh red chile, seeded
salt and ground black pepper
green chiles, to garnish
triangles of pita bread, to serve

**1** Heat the oil in a deep, heavy frying pan. Add the garlic, onion, green chiles and chili powder and fry over low heat, stirring frequently, for about 5 minutes, until the onions are softened and transparent, but not browned.

**2** Drain the kidney beans, reserving the can juices. Set aside 2 tablespoons of the beans and put the remainder in a food processor. Process into a purée.

**3** Add the puréed beans to the onion mixture and moisten with 2–3 tablespoons of the reserved can juices. Heat gently, stirring to mix well.

**4** Stir in the reserved whole kidney beans and the grated Cheddar. Cook over low heat, stirring constantly, for 2–3 minutes, until the cheese has melted. Season with salt and pepper to taste.

**5** Cut the red chile into thin strips. Spoon the dip into four individual serving bowls and sprinkle the chile strips on top. Serve warm, garnished with green chiles, with the pita triangles.

**Cook's Tip**
*For a dip with a coarser texture, do not purée the beans; instead, mash them with a potato masher.*

# Lima Bean, Watercress & Herb Dip

A refreshing dip that is especially good served with crudités and breadsticks.

**Serves 4–6**
1 cup plain cottage cheese
14-ounce can lima beans, drained and rinsed
1 bunch scallions, chopped
2 ounces watercress, chopped
4 tablespoons mayonnaise
3 tablespoons chopped fresh mixed herbs
salt and ground black pepper
watercress sprigs, to garnish
crudités and breadsticks, to serve

**1** Put the cottage cheese, butter beans, scallions, watercress, mayonnaise and herbs in a blender or food processor and process into a rough purée.

**2** Spoon the mixture into a dish, season to taste with salt and pepper and cover tightly with plastic wrap. Chill in the refrigerator for several hours.

**3** Transfer to a serving dish (or individual dishes) and garnish with watercress sprigs. Serve with crudités and breadsticks.

# Curried Corn Dip

Serve this spicy dip with crudités, breadsticks or Melba toast.

**Serves 6–8**
2 tablespoons mayonnaise
2–3 teaspoons curry paste
1 cup cottage cheese
1 cup grated Cheddar cheese
1¼ cups sour cream
⅔ cup canned corn, drained
salt and ground black pepper

**1** Blend the mayonnaise, curry paste and cottage cheese together in a bowl. Stir in the grated Cheddar.
**2** Stir in the sour cream and corn and season with salt and pepper to taste. Transfer to a serving bowl and serve.

# Hummus with Crudités

Always a great family favorite, hummus can be made quickly at home with the help of a blender.

**Serves 2–3**
14-ounce can chickpeas
2 tablespoons tahini
2 tablespoons lemon juice
1 garlic clove, crushed
salt and ground black pepper
olive oil and paprika, to garnish

**To serve**
whole baby carrots and radishes
strips of green and red bell pepper, endive, celery and cucumber
bite-size chunks of bread, pita or grissini sticks

**1** Drain the chickpeas and put them in a blender or food processor. Add the tahini, lemon juice and garlic. Process into a smooth paste.

**2** Season the hummus with plenty of salt and pepper. Spoon it into a bowl and swirl the top with the back of a spoon. Trickle on a little olive oil and sprinkle with paprika.

**3** Arrange the baby carrots, radishes and the strips of salad vegetables around the rim of a large plate.

**4** Add chunks of bread, pieces of pita or grissini. Place the bowl of hummus in the center. Serve immediately.

---

**Variation**
*Hummus is delicious served with hot celeriac fritters. Peel and slice one medium celeriac into strips about ½ inch wide and 2 inches long. Drop them into a bowl of water mixed with a little lemon juice. Lightly beat one egg in a shallow dish. In another shallow dish, combine 1 cup ground almonds, 3 tablespoons grated Parmesan cheese and 3 tablespoons chopped fresh parsley. Heat vegetable oil for deep-frying to 350°F or until a cube of bread browns in about 60 seconds. Pat the celeriac dry and dip, first, in the egg and then in the almond mixture. Deep-fry, in batches, and serve.*

---

# Nutty Mushroom Pâté

Spread this delicious, medium-texture pâté on chunks of crusty French bread and eat with crisp leaves of lettuce and sweet cherry tomatoes.

**Serves 4–6**

1 tablespoon sunflower oil
1 onion, chopped
1 garlic clove, crushed
2 tablespoons water
1 tablespoon dry sherry
3 cups button mushrooms, chopped
¾ cup cashews or walnuts, chopped
⅔ cup low-fat cream cheese
1 tablespoon soy sauce
few dashes of vegetarian Worcestershire sauce
salt and ground black pepper
fresh parsley, chopped, and a little paprika, to garnish

**1** Heat the oil in a saucepan. Add the onion and garlic and fry over medium heat, stirring occasionally, for 3 minutes. Stir in the water, sherry and mushrooms. Cook, stirring constantly, for about 5 minutes. Season to taste with salt and pepper. Remove the pan from heat and let cool a little.

**2** Put the mixture into a food processor and add the cashews or walnuts, cheese, soy sauce and Worcestershire sauce. Process into a coarse purée—do not let the mixture become too smooth.

**3** Check and adjust the seasoning, if necessary, then scrape the pâté into a serving dish. Swirl the top and chill lightly in the refrigerator. Serve the pâté sprinkled with parsley and paprika.

### Cook's Tips
• Conventional Worcestershire sauce is off-limits for vegetarians, as it contains anchovies. Look out for the vegetarian version of this popular sauce. It is available at health-food stores.
• For extra flavor, add ½ ounce dried porcini mushrooms, soaked in hot water for 30 minutes. Substitute 2 tablespoons of the strained soaking water for the plain water.

# Roast Garlic & Goat Cheese Pâté

The flavor of mellow roasted garlic goes well with this classic goat's cheese, walnut and herb pâté.

**Serves 2–4**

4 large garlic bulbs
4 fresh rosemary sprigs
8 fresh thyme sprigs
4 tablespoons extra virgin olive oil
salt and ground black pepper

**For the pâté**
6 ounces soft goat cheese
1 teaspoon finely chopped fresh thyme
1 tablespoon chopped fresh parsley
½ cup shelled walnuts, chopped
1 tablespoon walnut oil (optional)

**To serve**
4–8 slices sourdough bread
shelled walnuts
sea salt

**1** Preheat the oven to 350°F. Strip the papery skin from the garlic bulbs. Place them in an ovenproof dish large enough to hold them snugly.

**2** Tuck in the rosemary and thyme, drizzle on the oil and season to taste with salt and pepper. Cover the dish closely with aluminum foil and bake for 50–60 minutes, basting once. Remove from the oven and let cool.

**3** Make the pâté. Cream the cheese with the thyme, parsley and chopped walnuts. Beat in 1 tablespoon of the cooking oil from the garlic. Season to taste with salt and pepper, then transfer the pâté to a serving bowl.

**4** Spread out the slices of sourdough bread in a broiler pan and brush them with the remaining cooking oil from the garlic. Broil until toasted.

**5** If using the walnut oil, drizzle it on the goat cheese pâté. Grind some black pepper on it. Place one or two bulbs of garlic on each plate and serve with the pâté and a couple of slices of toasted sourdough bread. Serve a few freshly shelled walnuts and a little sea salt with each portion.

# Fontina Pan Bagna

When the weather is hot, a crusty flute or baguette filled with juicy tomatoes, crisp red onion, green bell pepper, thinly sliced Fontina cheese and sliced black olives makes a refreshing and substantial snack.

**Serves 2–4**

1 small red onion, thinly sliced
1 fresh flute or baguette
*extra virgin olive oil*
*3 ripe plum tomatoes, thinly sliced*
*1 small green bell pepper, halved, seeded and thinly sliced*
*7 ounces Fontina cheese, thinly sliced*
*about 12 pitted black olives, sliced*
*a handful of flat-leaf parsley or basil leaves*
*salt and ground black pepper*
*fresh basil sprigs, to garnish*

**1** Soak the slices of red onion in plenty of cold water for at least 1 hour, then drain well in a colander, spread out on paper towels and pat dry.

**2** Slice the flute or baguette in half lengthwise and brush the cut-sides well with olive oil. Lay the tomato slices down one side and season well with salt and black pepper.

**3** Top with the green pepper slices, then add the onion slices. Arrange the cheese and olives on top. Sprinkle on the parsley or basil leaves and season with salt and pepper again.

**4** Press the halves together, then wrap the filled loaf tightly in plastic wrap to compress it. Chill for at least 1 hour. Unwrap and cut diagonally into thick slices. Garnish with basil sprigs and serve immediately.

> **Cook's Tips**
> • *This is a good choice for a picnic. Pack the loaf, uncut and still wrapped in plastic wrap, and cut into slices just before serving. Do not forget to take a sharp knife with you.*
> • *Other cheeses, such as Taleggio and Havarti, could be used instead of Fontina.*

# Four Cheese Ciabatta Pizzas

Few dishes are as simple—or as satisfying—as this pizza made by topping a halved loaf of ciabatta.

**Serves 2**

1 loaf of ciabatta
1 garlic clove, halved
2–3 tablespoons olive oil
about 6 tablespoons passata
1 small red onion, thinly sliced
2 tablespoons chopped pitted black olives
*about 2 ounces each of four cheeses, one aged (Parmesan or Cheddar), one blue-veined (Gorgonzola or Stilton), one mild (Fontina or Emmenthal) and a goat cheese, sliced, grated or crumbled*
*pine nuts or cumin seeds, to sprinkle*
*salt and ground black pepper*
*fresh basil sprigs, to garnish*

**1** Preheat the oven to 400°F. Split the ciabatta loaf in half. Rub the cut-sides with the cut-sides of the garlic clove, then brush on the olive oil.

**2** Spread the passata evenly on the ciabatta halves. Separate the onion slices into rings and arrange them on each cut loaf, with the chopped olives on top. Season generously with salt and pepper.

**3** Divide the sliced, grated or crumbled cheeses equally among the ciabatta halves and then sprinkle the pine nuts or cumin seeds on top.

**4** Bake for 10–12 minutes, until the cheese topping is bubbling and golden brown. Cut the ciabatta pizzas into slices and serve immediately, garnished with basil sprigs.

> **Cook's Tip**
> *Passata is a very useful ingredient to keep on hand. Strained, puréed tomato pulp with an intense flavor, it comes in jars, cans and cartons and is widely available. Sugocasa can be used instead.*

# Cannellini Bean & Rosemary Bruschetta

More brunch than breakfast, this dish is a sophisticated version of beans on toast.

**Serves 4**
2/3 cup dried cannellini beans
5 tomatoes
3 tablespoons olive oil, plus extra
 for drizzling
2 sun-dried tomatoes in oil,
 drained and finely chopped
1 garlic clove, crushed

2 tablespoons chopped
 fresh rosemary
salt and ground black pepper
a handful of fresh basil leaves,
 to garnish

**To serve**
8 slices Italian-style bread,
 such as ciabatta
1 large garlic clove, halved

**1** Place the beans in a large bowl and cover with water. Let soak overnight. Drain and rinse the beans, then place in a saucepan and cover with fresh water. Bring to a boil and boil rapidly for 10 minutes. Reduce the heat and simmer for 50–60 minutes or until tender. Drain and set aside.

**2** Meanwhile, place the tomatoes in a bowl, cover with boiling water and leave for 30 seconds. Remove with a draining spoon, then peel, seed and chop the flesh.

**3** Heat the oil in a frying pan, add the fresh and sun-dried tomatoes, garlic and rosemary. Cook over medium heat, stirring occasionally, for 2 minutes, until the tomatoes begin to break down and soften.

**4** Add the tomato mixture to the cannellini beans, season to taste with salt and pepper and mix well. Keep warm.

**5** When ready to serve, rub both sides of the bread slices with the cut-sides of the garlic clove, then toast lightly. Spoon the cannellini bean and tomato mixture on top of the toast. Sprinkle with fresh basil leaves and drizzle on a little extra olive oil before serving.

# Goat Cheese & Gin Crostini

A gin marinade accentuates the flavor of goat cheese, which melts beautifully over the scallions.

**Serves 4**
8 slices chèvre
1 tablespoon gin
2 tablespoons walnut oil
2 tablespoons olive oil
4 slices Italian or French bread
1 garlic clove, halved

2 scallions, sliced
6 walnut halves, roughly broken
1 tablespoon chopped
 fresh parsley
ground black pepper
cherry tomatoes and mixed salad
 greens, to garnish
Orange and Tomato Salsa,
 to serve

**1** Spread out the cheese slices in a single layer in a shallow bowl. Pour on the gin, walnut oil and olive oil, then cover and set in a cool place to marinate for 1 hour.

**2** Put the slices of bread on a broiler pan. Toast them under a broiler on one side, then turn them over and rub the untoasted surfaces with the cut pieces of garlic. Brush with a little of the marinade used for the goat cheese, then sprinkle on the sliced scallions. Top with the slices of marinated cheese.

**3** Pour on any remaining marinade, season with pepper and cook the crostini under a hot broiler until the cheese has melted and browned. Sprinkle on the walnuts and parsley. Garnish with the tomatoes and salad greens and serve with the salsa.

> **Cook's Tip**
> Chèvre is French goat's milk cheese. It is often cylindrical in shape, which makes it perfect for this dish. Use a natural-rind cheese with a firm but not hard texture. Do not let it get wet in storage, as this will spoil it.

# Orange & Tomato Salsa

Fruity, but not too sweet, this salsa is the perfect accompaniment for the crostini. It also tastes wonderful with Lancashire or Cheddar cheese and French bread as part of a simple lunch.

**Serves 4**
2 oranges
5 tomatoes, peeled, seeded
 and chopped
1 tablespoon shredded fresh basil
2 tablespoons olive oil
pinch of light brown sugar
fresh basil sprig, to garnish

**1** Cut a slice off the top and bottom of each orange. Place each orange in turn on a board and cut off the skin, taking care to remove all the bitter white pith. Working over a bowl to catch the juices, cut between the membranes to release the segments.

**2** Add the segments to the bowl, with the tomatoes, shredded basil, olive oil and brown sugar. Mix well. Serve at room temperature, garnished with the basil.

# Falafel

In North Africa, these spicy fritters are made using dried fava beans, but chickpeas are much easier to buy. They are great served as a snack with creamy yogurt or stuffed into warmed pita bread pockets.

**Serves 4**
⅔ cup dried chickpeas
1 large onion, roughly chopped
2 garlic cloves,
  roughly chopped
4 tablespoons roughly
  chopped parsley
1 teaspoon cumin seeds, crushed
1 teaspoon coriander
  seeds, crushed
½ teaspoon baking powder
vegetable oil, for deep-frying
salt and ground black pepper

**To serve**
pita bread
salad
plain yogurt

**1** Put the chickpeas in a bowl with plenty of cold water. Let soak overnight.

**2** Drain the chickpeas and put them in a large pan. Pour in enough water to cover them by at least 2 inches. Bring to a boil. Boil rapidly for 10 minutes, then lower the heat and simmer for 1–1½ hours, until soft.

**3** Drain the chickpeas and place them in a food processor. Add the onion, garlic, parsley, cumin seeds, coriander seeds and baking powder. Season with salt and pepper to taste. Process until the mixture forms a fine paste.

**4** As soon as the paste is cool enough to handle, shape it into walnut-size balls, flattening them slightly.

**5** Pour oil to a depth of 2 inches into a deep frying pan. Heat until a little of the falafel mixture added to the hot oil sizzles on the surface.

**6** Fry the falafel, in batches, until golden. Drain on paper towels and keep hot while frying the remainder. Serve warm in pita bread, with salad and yogurt.

# Zucchini, Carrots & Pecans in Pita Bread

Easy to eat and very tasty, this makes a good, healthy after-school snack or a nourishing light lunch.

**Serves 2**
2 carrots
¼ cup pecans
4 scallions, sliced
4 tablespoons plain yogurt
3 tablespoons olive oil
1 teaspoon lemon juice
1 tablespoon chopped fresh mint
2 zucchini
¼ cup all-purpose flour
2 pita breads
salt and ground black pepper
shredded lettuce, to serve

**1** Trim the carrots. Grate them coarsely into a bowl. Stir in the pecans and scallions and toss well.

**2** In a clean bowl, whisk the yogurt with ½ teaspoon of the olive oil, the lemon juice and the fresh mint. Stir the dressing into the carrot mixture and mix thoroughly. Cover and chill in the refrigerator until needed.

**3** Top and tail the zucchini. Cut them diagonally into fairly thin slices. Season the flour with a little salt and pepper. Spread it out on a plate and coat the zucchini slices. Shake off any excess flour.

**4** Heat the remaining oil in a large frying pan. Add the coated zucchini slices and cook for 3–4 minutes, turning once, until browned. Drain the zucchini on paper towels.

**5** Make a slit in each pita bread to form a pocket. Fill the pitas with the carrot mixture and the zucchini slices. Serve immediately on a bed of shredded lettuce.

**Cook's Tip**
*Warm the pita breads, if desired. Do not fill them too soon or the carrot mixture will make the bread soggy.*

# Creamy Cannellini Beans with Asparagus

In this tasty toast topper, cannellini beans in a creamy sauce contrast with tender asparagus spears.

**Serves 2**

2 teaspoons butter
1 small onion, finely chopped
1 small carrot, grated
1 teaspoon fresh thyme leaves
14-ounce can cannellini beans, drained
⅔ cup light cream
4 ounces young asparagus spears, trimmed
2 slices whole-grain bread
salt and ground black pepper

**1** Melt the butter in a pan. Add the onion and carrot and fry over medium heat, stirring occasionally, for 4 minutes, until soft. Add the thyme leaves.

**2** Put the cannellini beans into a sieve and rinse them under cold running water. Drain thoroughly, then add to the onion and carrot. Mix lightly.

**3** Pour in the cream and heat slowly to just below the boiling point, stirring occasionally. Remove the pan from heat and season with salt and pepper to taste.

**4** Place the asparagus spears in a saucepan. Pour in just enough boiling water to cover. Poach for 3–4 minutes, until the spears are just tender.

**5** Meanwhile, toast the bread under a hot broiler until both sides are golden. Place the toast on individual plates. Drain the asparagus and divide the spears between the slices of toast. Spoon the bean mixture onto each portion and serve.

---

**Variation**
Try making this with other canned beans, such as borlotti, haricot or flageolets.

---

# Parsley, Lemon & Garlic Mushrooms on Toast

Don't overwhelm the delicate flavor of wild mushrooms by adding too much garlic. Temper the taste with sherry, parsley and lemon juice.

**Serves 4**

2 tablespoons butter, plus extra for spreading
1 medium onion, chopped
1 garlic clove, crushed
4 cups assorted wild mushrooms, sliced
3 tablespoons dry sherry
5 tablespoons chopped fresh flat-leaf parsley
1 tablespoon lemon juice
salt and ground black pepper
4 slices of brown or white bread

**1** Melt the butter in a large nonstick frying pan. Add the onion and fry over low heat, stirring occasionally, for 5 minutes without letting it color.

**2** Add the garlic and mushrooms, cover and cook over medium heat for 3–5 minutes. Stir in the sherry, and cook, uncovered, until all the liquid has been absorbed.

**3** Stir in the parsley and lemon juice, and then season to taste with salt and pepper.

**4** Toast the bread, spread it with butter and place each piece on a serving plate. Spoon the mushroom mixture on the toast and serve immediately.

---

**Cook's Tips**
• Flat-leaf parsley, also known as French parsley, has a good flavor and keeps well in the refrigerator. To keep it fresh, stand the bunch in a jar of water and cover with a plastic bag.
• Use any mixture of wild mushrooms, such as field mushrooms, horse mushrooms and shaggy ink caps or, more economically, a mixture of wild and cultivated mushrooms.

---

# Mozzarella in Carozza with Fresh Tomato Salsa

These upmarket toasted sandwiches come from Italy. After being filled, they are dipped in beaten egg and fried like French toast.

**Serves 4**

7 ounces mozzarella cheese,
 thinly sliced
8 thin slices of bread,
 crusts removed
pinch of dried oregano
2 tablespoons freshly grated
 Parmesan cheese

3 eggs, beaten
olive oil, for frying
salt and ground black pepper
fresh herbs, to garnish

**For the salsa**
4 ripe plum tomatoes, peeled,
 seeded and finely chopped
1 tablespoon chopped
 fresh parsley
1 teaspoon balsamic vinegar
1 tablespoon extra virgin olive oil

**1** Arrange the mozzarella on four slices of the bread. Season with salt and pepper and sprinkle with a little dried oregano and the Parmesan. Top with the other bread slices and press them firmly together.

**2** Pour the beaten eggs into a large shallow dish and season with salt and pepper. Add the cheese sandwiches, two at a time, pressing them into the eggs with a spatula until they are well coated. Repeat with the remaining sandwiches, then let them stand for 10 minutes.

**3** Meanwhile, make the salsa. Put the chopped tomatoes in a bowl and add the parsley. Stir in the balsamic vinegar and the extra virgin olive oil. Season to taste with salt and pepper and set aside.

**4** Pour olive oil to a depth of ¼ inch into a large frying pan. When it is hot, add the sandwiches carefully in batches and cook for about 2 minutes on each side, until golden and crisp. Drain well on paper towels. Cut in half. Serve on individual plates, garnished with fresh herbs and accompanied by the salsa.

# Scrambled Eggs in Brioches

Lift the lids on baked brioches and discover a glorious mixture of creamy scrambled eggs and fried brown cap mushrooms.

**Serves 4**
½ cup butter
generous 1 cup brown cap
 mushrooms, finely sliced
4 individual brioches
8 eggs, lightly mixed
1 tablespoon snipped fresh chives,
 plus extra to garnish
salt and ground black pepper

**1** Preheat the oven to 350°F. Melt one-quarter of the butter in a frying pan. Fry the mushrooms for about 3 minutes or until soft, then set aside and keep warm.

**2** Slice the tops off the brioches, then scoop out the centers and save them for making bread crumbs. Put the brioches and lids on a baking sheet and bake for 5 minutes, until hot and slightly crisp.

**3** Meanwhile, beat the eggs lightly and season to taste. Heat the remaining butter in a heavy saucepan over low heat.

**4** Add the eggs. Using a wooden spoon, stir constantly until about three-quarters of the egg is semi-solid and creamy—this should take 2–3 minutes. Remove the pan from heat and stir in the snipped chives.

**5** Immediately spoon one-quarter of the fried mushrooms into the bottom of each brioche and top with the scrambled eggs, divided equally among them. Sprinkle with extra chives, balance the brioche lids on top and serve immediately.

---

**Cook's Tip**
*Timing and temperature are crucial for perfect scrambled eggs. When cooked for too long over too high heat, eggs become dry and crumbly; undercooked eggs are sloppy and unappealing.*

---

# Eggs Benedict with Quick Hollandaise

This classic brunch dish originated in New York, and is ideal for serving on a special occasion, such as a birthday treat or New Year's day.

**Serves 4**
4 large eggs, plus 2 egg yolks
1 teaspoon dry mustard
1 tablespoon white wine vinegar
    or lemon juice
¾ cup butter, plus extra
    for spreading
4 English muffins, split
2 tablespoons rinsed capers
salt and ground black pepper
a little chopped fresh parsley,
    to garnish

**1** Put the egg yolks in a blender or food processor. Add the mustard and a pinch of salt and pepper and process for a few seconds. Add the vinegar or lemon juice and process again.

**2** Heat the butter until it is on the point of bubbling, then, with the motor running, slowly pour it through the lid or feeder tube. When the mixture is thick and creamy, switch off the blender or food processor and set the sauce aside.

**3** Toast the split muffins under a broiler. Cut four of the halves in two and butter them lightly. Place the four uncut halves on warmed plates and leave unbuttered.

**4** Poach the eggs either in gently simmering water or in an egg poacher. Drain well and slip carefully onto the muffin halves. Spoon the hollandaise sauce onto the English muffins, then sprinkle with capers and parsley. Serve immediately with the buttered muffin quarters.

> **Variation**
> *Instead of the toasted English muffin, you could serve the poached eggs and sauce on a bed of lightly steamed or blanched spinach.*

# Mixed Bell Pepper Pipérade

Every cook needs recipes like this one. Tasty, nourishing and made in moments, Pipérade is based on everyday ingredients.

**Serves 4**
2 tablespoons olive oil
1 onion, chopped
1 red bell pepper
1 green bell pepper
4 tomatoes, peeled and chopped
1 garlic clove, crushed
4 large eggs, beaten with
    1 tablespoon water
4 large, thick slices of
    whole-wheat bread
butter, for spreading (optional)
ground black pepper
fresh herbs, to garnish

**1** Heat the oil in a large frying pan. Add the onion and sauté over low heat, stirring occasionally, for 5 minutes, until it has softened but not browned.

**2** Cut the peppers in half, remove the seeds and slice them thinly. Stir the pepper slices into the onion and cook gently for about 5 minutes.

**3** Stir in the tomatoes and garlic, season generously with black pepper, and cook for 5 more minutes.

**4** Pour the egg mixture onto the vegetables and cook for 2–3 minutes, stirring occasionally, until the pipérade has thickened to the consistency of lightly scrambled eggs.

**5** While the egg mixture is cooking, toast the bread. Butter it, if desired, and serve the toast and pipérade on individual plates, garnished with fresh herbs.

> **Cook's Tip**
> *Choose eggs that have been date-stamped to ensure that they are fresh. Do not stir the pipérade too much or the eggs may become unpleasantly rubbery.*

# Cheese Scrolls

Fascinating phyllo pastries with a feta and yogurt filling, Cheese Scrolls make very good snacks.

**Makes 14–16**

2 cups feta cheese, well drained and finely crumbled
6 tablespoons plain yogurt
2 eggs, beaten
14–16 sheets, 16 x 12-inch ready-made phyllo pastry, thawed if frozen
1 cup butter, melted
sea salt and chopped scallions, for the topping

**1** Preheat the oven to 400°F. In a large bowl mix the feta, yogurt and eggs, beating well until the mixture is smooth.

**2** Fit a piping bag with a ½-inch plain round nozzle. Spoon half the cheese mixture into the bag.

**3** Keeping the rest of the phyllo covered, lay one sheet on the work surface. Fold it in half to make a 12 x 8-inch rectangle, then brush with a little of the melted butter. Pipe a thick line of cheese mixture along one long edge, leaving a ¼-inch clear border.

**4** Roll up the pastry to form a sausage shape, tucking in each end to prevent the filling from escaping. Brush with more melted butter. Form the "sausage" into a tight "S" or scroll-shape. Make more scrolls in the same way, refilling the piping bag as necessary.

**5** Arrange the scrolls on a buttered baking sheet and sprinkle with a little sea salt and chopped scallion. Bake for about 20 minutes or until crisp and golden brown. Cool on a wire rack, before serving.

> **Cook's Tip**
> If you find it easier, you can shape the filled phyllo into crescents instead of scrolls.

# Cheese Aigrettes

These choux buns, flavored with aged Gruyère cheese and dusted with grated Parmesan, can be prepared ahead and deep-fried to serve.

**Makes about 30**

scant 1 cup all-purpose flour
½ teaspoon paprika
½ teaspoon salt
6 tablespoons cold butter, diced
scant 1 cup water
3 eggs, beaten
¾ cup coarsely grated aged Gruyère cheese
vegetable oil, for deep-frying
2-ounce piece of Parmesan cheese
ground black pepper
fresh flat-leaf parsley sprigs, to garnish

**1** Sift the flour, paprika and salt onto a sheet of waxed paper. Add a generous grinding of black pepper.

**2** Put the butter and water into a medium saucepan and heat gently. As soon as the butter has melted and the liquid starts to boil, add all the seasoned flour at once and beat vigorously with a wooden spoon until the dough comes away from the sides of the pan.

**3** Remove the pan from heat and set the paste aside to cool for about 5 minutes. Gradually beat in enough of the beaten eggs to make a stiff dropping consistency. Add the grated Gruyère and mix well.

**4** Heat the oil for deep-frying to 350°F or until a cube of day-old bread turns golden brown in 60 seconds. Take a teaspoonful of the choux paste and use a second spoon to slide it into the hot oil. Make more aigrettes in the same way, but don't overcrowd the pan. Fry for 3–4 minutes, until golden brown. Remove with a draining spoon and drain the aigrettes thoroughly on paper towels. Keep warm while cooking successive batches.

**5** To serve, pile the aigrettes on a warmed serving dish, grate Parmesan on top and garnish with fresh parsley sprigs.

# Artichoke Rice Cakes with Melting Manchego

Cold cooked rice is very easy to mold. Shape it into balls, fill the centers with diced cheese and deep-fry to make a delectable snack.

**Makes about 12 cakes**
1 globe artichoke
1/4 cup butter
1 small onion, finely chopped
1 garlic clove, finely chopped

2/3 cup risotto rice
scant 2 cups hot vegetable stock
1/4 cup freshly grated
    Parmesan cheese
5 ounces Manchego cheese,
    very finely diced
3–4 tablespoons fine cornmeal
olive oil, for frying
salt and ground black pepper
flat-leaf parsley, to garnish

**1** Remove the stem, leaves and choke to leave just the heart of the artichoke. Chop the heart finely. Melt the butter in a saucepan and gently fry the artichoke heart, onion and garlic for 5 minutes, until softened. Stir in the rice and cook for about 1 minute.

**2** Add the stock a little at a time, stirring constantly and waiting until each addition has been absorbed before adding more.

**3** After about 20 minutes the rice will be tender, but still firm at the center of the grain, and all the liquid will have been absorbed. Season well, then stir in the Parmesan. Transfer to a bowl. Let cool, then cover and chill for at least 2 hours.

**4** Spoon about 1 tablespoon of the rice mixture into the palm of one hand, flatten slightly, and place a few pieces of diced Manchego in the center. Shape the rice around the cheese to make a small ball. Flatten slightly then roll in the cornmeal, shaking off any excess. Repeat with the remaining mixture to make about 12 cakes.

**5** Fry in hot olive oil for 4–5 minutes, until the rice cakes are crisp and golden brown. Drain on paper towels and serve hot, garnished with flat-leaf parsley.

# Wild Mushroom Pancakes with Chive Butter

Pancakes are easy to make and taste wonderful with wild mushrooms. The unusual hedgehog has been used here, but any wild or cultivated mushrooms could be used instead.

**Makes 12 pancakes**
about 5 cups hedgehog fungus or
    other wild mushrooms
1/4 cup butter

1 1/2 cups self-rising flour
2 eggs
scant 1 cup milk
salt and ground white pepper

**For the chive butter**
scant 1 cup fresh finely
    snipped chives
1/2 cup butter, softened
1 teaspoon lemon juice

**1** First make the chive butter by mixing all the ingredients. Turn out onto a 10-inch square of waxed paper and form into a sausage. Roll up, twist both ends of the paper and chill for about 1 hour, until the chive butter is firm.

**2** Slice one-quarter of the mushrooms and set them aside. Chop the remaining mushrooms finely. Melt half the butter in a frying pan and fry the chopped mushrooms until they are soft and all the moisture has evaporated. Spread them on a tray and let cool. Cook the sliced mushrooms in a pat of butter.

**3** Sift the flour into a bowl and season with salt and pepper. Beat the eggs with the milk in a bowl. Add to the flour, stirring to make a thick batter. Add the chopped mushrooms.

**4** Heat the remaining butter in the clean frying pan. Arrange small heaps of sliced mushrooms on the bottom of the pan, using five mushroom slices each time, then pour a little batter onto each heap to make 2-inch pancakes.

**5** When bubbles appear on the surface, turn the pancakes over and cook for another 10–15 seconds. Serve warm with slices of the chive butter.

## Potato Pancakes

Crisp on the outside, with tender centers, these potato pancakes are delicious with sour cream and a refreshing salad or salsa.

1 teaspoon chopped
   fresh marjoram
1/4 cup butter
4 tablespoons vegetable oil
salt and ground black pepper

**Serves 6–8**
6 large waxy potatoes, peeled
2 eggs, beaten
1–2 garlic cloves, crushed
1 cup all-purpose flour

**To serve**
sour cream
chopped fresh parsley
tomato salad

**1** Coarsely grate the potatoes onto a clean dish towel, then gather up the sides and squeeze tightly to remove as much moisture as possible.

**2** Put the potatoes into a bowl and add the beaten eggs, garlic, flour and marjoram. Season to taste with salt and pepper and mix well.

**3** Heat half the butter and half the oil in a large frying pan, then add large spoonfuls of the potato mixture to form rounds. Using the back of a dampened spoon, carefully flatten the rounds into pancakes.

**4** Fry the pancakes until crisp and golden brown, then turn them over carefully and cook on the other side. Drain on paper towels and keep hot while cooking the rest of the pancakes, adding the remaining butter and oil to the frying pan as necessary.

**5** Serve the pancakes topped with sour cream, sprinkled with parsley, and accompanied by a fresh, juicy tomato salad.

> **Cook's Tip**
> *Choose firm-fleshed potatoes, such as Charlotte or Kipfler.*

## Eggs in Baked Potatoes

Nestled in creamy baked potatoes, cheese-topped eggs make a substantial, nourishing and inexpensive snack for all the family.

2 tablespoons hot light cream
   or milk
2 tablespoons snipped
   fresh chives
4 eggs
about 1/2 cup finely grated aged
   Cheddar cheese
salt and ground black pepper
celery stalks and chives, to garnish

**Serves 4**
4 large baking potatoes
3 tablespoons butter

**1** Preheat the oven to 400°F. Prick the potatoes with a fork and bake for 1–1¼ hours, until soft.

**2** Working quickly, cut a slice about a quarter to a third of the way down from the top of each potato, then scoop the flesh into a bowl with a teaspoon, taking care not to pierce the potato skins. Reserve the skins.

**3** Add the butter and cream or milk to the potato flesh, together with the chives. Season to taste with salt and pepper. Mash the ingredients together.

**4** Divide the potato mixture among the potato skins, and make a hollow in each with the back of a spoon.

**5** Break an egg into each hollow, season to taste with salt and pepper, then return to the oven for about 10 minutes, until the eggs are just set.

**6** Sprinkle the cheese on the eggs, then place under a broiler until golden. Serve immediately, garnished with celery and chives.

> **Cook's Tip**
> *Bake the potatoes in the microwave, if you prefer. For crisp skins, pop them into a preheated 400°F oven for about 10 minutes after microwave cooking.*

# Potato Casserole

This dish is made from layered potatoes, cheese and herbs. Cooking the ingredients together gives them a very rich flavor.

**Serves 4**
3 large potatoes
butter, for greasing
1 small onion, thinly sliced
   into rings

1¾ cups grated red Leicester or
   aged Cheddar cheese
fresh thyme sprigs
⅔ cup light cream
salt and ground black pepper
salad greens, to serve

**1** Preheat the oven to 400°F. Peel the potatoes and cook them in a large pan of lightly salted boiling water for 10 minutes, until they are just starting to soften. Remove from the water and pat dry.

**2** Slice the potatoes thinly, using the straight edge of a grater or a mandoline. Grease the bottom and sides of an 7-inch cake pan with butter and lay some of the potatoes on the bottom to cover it completely. Season to taste with salt and pepper.

**3** Sprinkle some of the onion rings on the potatoes and top with a little of the grated cheese. Sprinkle on some thyme leaves. Continue to layer the ingredients, finishing with a layer of cheese. Season to taste with salt and pepper. Press the potato layers right down. (The mixture may seem quite high at this point, but it will cook down.)

**4** Pour on the cream and bake for 35–45 minutes. Remove from the oven and cool. Invert onto a plate and cut into wedges. Serve with a few salad greens.

**Variation**
If you want to make this snack more substantial, top with grilled red bell peppers.

# Potato Skins with Cajun Dip

Divinely crisp and naughty, these potato skins taste great with this piquant dip.

**Serves 2**
2 large baking potatoes
vegetable oil, for deep-frying

**For the dip**
½ cup plain yogurt
1 garlic clove, crushed
1 teaspoon tomato paste
½ teaspoon green chili purée
   or ½ small fresh green
   chile, chopped
¼ teaspoon celery salt
pinch of cayenne
   pepper (optional)
salt and ground black pepper

**1** Preheat the oven to 350°F. Prick the potatoes and bake for 1–1¼ hours, until tender. Cut them in half and scoop out the flesh, leaving a thin layer on the skins. Keep the flesh for another meal.

**2** Meanwhile, make the dip. Put the yogurt, garlic, tomato paste, chili purée or fresh chile and celery salt in a bowl and mix thoroughly. Season to taste with cayenne, if using, salt and pepper. Cover with plastic wrap and chill in the refrigerator.

**3** Pour vegetable oil to a depth of about ½ inch into a large saucepan or deep-fat fryer. Heat to 350°F or until a cube of day-old bread turns golden brown in about 60 seconds. Cut each potato-skin half in half again, then fry them until crisp and golden on both sides.

**4** Drain the fried potato skins on paper towels, sprinkle with salt and black pepper and serve with a bowl of dip or with a dollop of dip in each skin.

**Cook's Tip**
If you prefer, you can microwave the potatoes to save time. On the maximum setting, this will take about 10 minutes.

# Thai Tempeh Cakes with Sweet Dipping Sauce

Made from soybeans, tempeh is similar to tofu (bean curd), but has a nuttier taste. Here, it is combined with spices and formed into small patties.

**Makes 8 cakes**

1 lemongrass stalk, outer leaves removed, roughly chopped
2 garlic cloves, chopped
2 scallions, finely chopped
2 shallots, roughly chopped
2 fresh chiles, seeded and roughly chopped
1-inch piece of fresh ginger root, finely chopped
4 tablespoons chopped cilantro, plus extra to garnish

2¼ cups tempeh, thawed if frozen, sliced
1 tablespoon freshly squeezed lime juice
1 teaspoon sugar
3 tablespoons all-purpose flour
1 large egg, lightly beaten
vegetable oil, for frying
salt and ground black pepper

**For the dipping sauce**

3 tablespoons mirin
3 tablespoons white wine vinegar
2 scallions, finely sliced
1 tablespoon sugar
2 fresh red chiles, chopped
2 tablespoons chopped cilantro

**1** To make the dipping sauce, mix the mirin, vinegar, scallions, sugar, chiles, cilantro and a large pinch of salt in a small bowl and set aside.

**2** Place the lemongrass, garlic, scallions, shallots, chiles, ginger and cilantro in a food processor or blender and process into a coarse paste.

**3** Add the tempeh, lime juice and sugar, then process until thoroughly combined. Add the flour and egg and season with plenty of salt and pepper. Process again until the mixture forms a coarse, sticky paste.

**4** Using a tablespoon, scoop up a generous amount of the tempeh mixture. Dampen your hands, then shape the mixture into a round, slightly flattened cake. Make seven more tempeh cakes in the same way.

**5** Heat enough oil to cover the bottom of a large frying pan. Fry the tempeh cakes, in batches, for 5–6 minutes, turning once, until golden. Drain on paper towels and keep warm while cooking the remainder. Serve warm with the dipping sauce, garnished with the reserved cilantro.

**Cook's Tip**
*Use red or green chiles, choosing a variety with the degree of fieriness you require. In general, dark green chiles tend to be hotter than pale green ones, which, in turn, are hotter than red chiles. (As the chiles ripen, they become red and relatively sweeter.) Also, the small, pointed chiles tend to be fiercer than the larger, rounder ones. However, there are always exceptions, and even different pods from the same plant can vary in their level of spiciness. Err on the side of caution, if in doubt.*

# Zucchini Fritters with Chili Jam

Much like a thick chutney, chili jam is hot, sweet and sticky. It adds a piquancy to these light zucchini fritters but is also delicious with pies or a chunk of cheese.

**Makes 12 fritters**

1 pound zucchini
⅔ cup freshly grated Parmesan cheese
2 eggs, beaten
4 tablespoons unbleached all-purpose flour

vegetable oil, for frying
salt and ground black pepper

**For the chili jam**

5 tablespoons olive oil
4 large onions, diced
4 garlic cloves, chopped
1–2 fresh Thai chiles, seeded and sliced
3 tablespoons dark brown sugar
a few thin slices of fresh red chile, to garnish

**1** First, make the chili jam. Heat the oil in a frying pan, add the onions and garlic, then lower the heat and cook the mixture, stirring frequently, for 20 minutes, until the onions are very soft.

**2** Let the onion mixture cool, then put it into a food processor or blender. Add the Thai red chiles and brown sugar and process until smooth, then return the mixture to the saucepan. Cook over low heat, stirring frequently, for about 10 minutes or until the liquid evaporates and the mixture has the consistency of jam. Cool slightly.

**3** To make the fritters, grate the zucchini roughly onto a clean dish towel, then gather up the sides and squeeze tightly to remove any excess moisture. Put the zucchini into a bowl and stir in the grated Parmesan, eggs and flour and season to taste with salt and pepper.

**4** Heat enough vegetable oil to cover the bottom of a large frying pan. Add 2 tablespoons of the mixture for each fritter and cook three fritters at a time. Cook for 2–3 minutes on each side until golden, then keep warm while you cook the remaining fritters. Drain on paper towels and serve hot with a spoonful of the chili jam, garnished with a slice of chile.

# Mexican Tortilla Parcels

Seeded green chiles add just
a flicker of fire to the spicy
filling in these parcels.

**Serves 4**

4 tablespoons sunflower oil
1 large onion, thinly sliced
1 garlic clove, crushed
2 teaspoons cumin seeds
2 fresh green chiles, seeded
    and chopped
1½ pounds tomatoes, peeled
    and chopped
2 tablespoons tomato paste
1 vegetable stock cube
7-ounce can corn kernels, drained
1 tablespoon chopped cilantro
1 cup grated Cheddar cheese
12 wheat flour tortillas
cilantro leaves, shredded lettuce
    and sour cream, to serve
1 fresh red chile, sliced, to garnish

**1** Heat half the oil in a frying pan and fry the onion with the garlic and cumin seeds for 5 minutes, until the onion softens. Add the chiles and tomatoes, then stir in the tomato paste.

**2** Crumble in the stock cube, stir well and cook gently for 5 minutes, until the chile is soft but the tomatoes have not broken down completely. Stir in the corn and cilantro and heat gently to warm through. Keep hot.

**3** Sprinkle grated cheese in the middle of each tortilla. Spoon some tomato mixture on the cheese. Fold over one edge of the tortilla, then the sides and finally the remaining edge to enclose the filling completely.

**4** Heat the remaining oil in a frying pan and fry the filled tortillas for 1–2 minutes on each side, until crisp. Garnish with chiles and serve with cilantro, lettuce and sour cream.

> **Cook's Tip**
> Mexican wheat flour tortillas are available at most supermarkets. Keep them in the cupboard as instant wraps for a variety of vegetable and cheese mixtures.

# Spiced Sweet Potato Turnovers

A subtle hint of sweetness
underscores the spicy flavor
of these turnovers.

**Serves 4**

1 tablespoon olive oil
1 small egg
⅔ cup plain yogurt
½ cup butter, melted
¼ teaspoon baking soda
2½ cups all-purpose flour
2 teaspoons paprika
beaten egg, to glaze
salt and ground black pepper

fresh mint sprigs, to garnish

**For the filling**

1 sweet potato, about 8 ounces
2 tablespoons vegetable oil
2 shallots, finely chopped
2 teaspoons coriander
    seeds, crushed
1 teaspoon ground cumin
1 teaspoon garam masala
1 cup frozen petit pois, thawed
1 tablespoon chopped fresh mint

**1** To make the filling, cook the sweet potato in boiling salted water for 15–20 minutes, until tender. Drain and let cool, then peel the potato and cut into ½-inch cubes.

**2** Heat the vegetable oil in a frying pan and cook the shallots until softened. Add the potato and fry until it browns at the edges. Sprinkle on the spices and fry, stirring, for a few seconds. Remove the pan from heat and add the peas and mint and season with salt and pepper to taste. Let cool.

**3** Preheat the oven to 400°F. Grease a baking sheet. To make the pastry, whisk together the olive oil and egg, stir in the yogurt, then add the melted butter. Sift the baking soda, flour, paprika and 1 teaspoon salt into a bowl, then stir into the yogurt mixture to form a soft dough.

**4** Turn out the dough, and knead gently. Roll it out, then stamp out 4-inch rounds. Spoon 2 teaspoons of the filling onto one side of each round, fold over and seal the edges. Re-roll the trimmings and stamp out more rounds until the filling is used.

**5** Arrange the turnovers on the baking sheet and brush with beaten egg. Bake for 20 minutes, until crisp. Garnish and serve.

# Samosas

These are far too good to be served only as cocktail party nibbles. Enjoy them as snacks or lunches, too.

**Makes about 20**

1 package 10-inch square spring roll wrappers, thawed if frozen
2 tablespoons all-purpose flour, mixed into a paste with water
vegetable oil, for deep-frying
cilantro leaves, to garnish

**For the filling**
2 tablespoons ghee
1 small onion, finely chopped
$\frac{1}{2}$-inch piece of fresh ginger root, chopped
1 garlic clove, crushed
$\frac{1}{2}$ teaspoon chili powder
1 large potato, about 8 ounces, cooked until just tender, then finely diced
$\frac{1}{2}$ cup cauliflower florets, lightly cooked, chopped
$\frac{1}{2}$ cup frozen peas, thawed
1–2 teaspoons garam masala
1 tablespoon chopped cilantro (leaves and stems)
squeeze of lemon juice
salt

**1** To make the filling, heat the ghee in a large wok or frying pan and fry the onion, ginger and garlic for 5 minutes, until the onion has softened but not browned. Stir in the chili powder and cook for 1 minute, then add the potato, cauliflower and peas. Mix well. Sprinkle with garam masala and set aside to cool. Stir in the chopped cilantro, lemon juice and salt.

**2** Cut the spring roll wrappers into three strips. Brush the edges with a little of the flour paste. Place a small spoonful of filling about ¾ inch from the edge of one strip. Fold one corner over it to make a triangle and continue this folding until the entire strip has been used and a triangular pastry has been formed. Seal any open edges with more flour and water paste.

**3** Heat the oil for deep-frying to 350°F or until a cube of day-old bread turns golden brown in 60 seconds. Fry the samosas, a few at a time, until golden and crisp.

**4** Drain well on paper towels. Serve hot, garnished with cilantro leaves.

# Spinach Empanadillas

These little Spanish pastry turnovers are filled with ingredients that have a strong Moorish influence— pine nuts and raisins.

**Makes 20**

3 tablespoons raisins
1$\frac{1}{2}$ tablespoons olive oil
1 pound fresh young spinach, chopped
2 garlic cloves, finely chopped
$\frac{1}{3}$ cup pine nuts, chopped
12 ounces puff pastry, thawed if frozen
butter, for greasing
1 egg, beaten, to glaze
salt and ground black pepper

**1** Put the raisins in bowl and pour in enough warm water to cover. Set aside to soak for 10 minutes. Drain thoroughly, then chop roughly.

**2** Heat the oil in a large sauté pan or wok. Add the spinach, stir, then cover and cook over low heat for about 2 minutes.

**3** Take the lid off the pan, turn up the heat and let any liquid evaporate. Add the garlic and season with plenty of salt and pepper. Cook, stirring constantly, for 1 more minute. Remove the pan from heat, stir in the raisins and pine nuts and set aside to cool.

**4** Preheat the oven to 350°F. Roll out the pastry thinly. Using a 3-inch cookie cutter, cut out 20 rounds, re-rolling the dough if necessary.

**5** Place about 2 teaspoons of the filling in the middle of a round, then brush the edges with a little water. Bring up the sides of the pastry and seal well to make a turnover. Press the edges together with the back of a fork. Make more turnovers in the same way.

**6** Place the turnovers on a lightly greased baking sheet, brush with the beaten egg and bake for about 15 minutes, until golden. Serve warm.

# Herb Omelet

It takes only moments to make a simple, herb-flavored omelet. Serve it with a salad and a chunk of crusty bread, and it becomes a nutritious light meal.

**Serves 1**
2 eggs
1 tablespoon chopped fresh
  herbs, such as parsley or chives
1 teaspoon butter
salt and ground black pepper
fresh parsley, to garnish

**1** Lightly beat the eggs in a bowl, add the fresh herbs and season to taste with salt and pepper.

**2** Melt the butter in a heavy omelet pan or nonstick frying pan and swirl it around to coat the bottom evenly.

**3** Keeping the heat fairly high, pour in the egg mixture. Let it start to set for 1–2 minutes, then lower the heat. Using a spoon or spatula, lift the edges of the omelet and push them gently toward the center, so that the raw egg runs in to fill the gap then starts to set as well.

**4** Cook for about 2 minutes, without stirring, until the omelet is lightly set. Quickly fold it over and slide onto a plate. Serve immediately, garnished with parsley.

### Cook's Tips
• It is important to serve omelets as soon as they are cooked, so this is one occasion when it would be unrealistic to expect everyone to be served simultaneously. Seat your guests and serve each omelet as soon as it is cooked.
• Omelets have an undeserved reputation for being difficult to make. There are two secrets to success. A good-quality, heavy omelet or frying pan ensures an even distribution of heat throughout. It is essential to ensure that the butter has melted completely and to swirl it around so the entire pan is evenly coated before adding the beaten egg mixture.

# Classic Cheese Omelet

Perhaps the ultimate fast food—a couple of eggs, some well-flavored cheese, a pat of butter and a good pan and you soon have a satisfying meal.

**Serves 1**
2 large eggs
1 tablespoon chopped fresh herbs,
  such as chives, parsley or dill
1 teaspoon butter
1/2 cup grated full-flavored cheese,
  such as Gruyère, Gouda
  or Cheddar
salt and ground black pepper
fresh flat-leaf parsley, to garnish
tomato wedges, to serve

**1** Lightly beat the eggs in a bowl and quickly mix in the herbs. Season to taste with salt and pepper.

**2** Melt the butter in an 8-inch heavy omelet pan or nonstick frying pan, swirling it around to coat the bottom evenly.

**3** Keeping the heat fairly high, pour in the egg mixture. Let it set for 1–2 minutes, then lower the heat. Using a spoon or spatula, lift the edges of the omelet and push them gently toward the center, so that the raw egg runs in to fill the gap then starts to set as well.

**4** When the egg at the sides is firm, but the center remains soft, sprinkle on the cheese. Leave undisturbed to cook for about 30 seconds.

**5** Fold over the edge of the omelet nearest the handle, then roll the omelet over onto a warmed plate. Serve immediately with a garnish of fresh flat-leaf parsley and tomato wedges.

### Variation
You can add other ingredients to the cheese. Crunchy, garlicky croutons are good, as are sautéed sliced mushrooms or chopped tomatoes.

# Soufflé Omelet with Mushrooms

A soufflé omelet makes an ideal meal for one, especially with this delicious filling. Use a combination of different mushrooms, such as oyster and chestnut, if desired.

**Serves 1**

2 eggs, separated
1 tablespoon water
1 tablespoon butter
fresh flat-leaf parsley or cilantro
    leaves, to garnish

**For the mushroom sauce**

1 tablespoon butter
generous 1 cup button
    mushrooms, thinly sliced
1 tablespoon all-purpose flour
$1/3$–$1/2$ cup milk
1 teaspoon chopped fresh
    parsley (optional)
salt and ground black pepper

**1** Start by making the mushroom sauce. Melt the butter in a pan over low heat. Add the sliced mushrooms and fry gently, stirring occasionally, for 4–5 minutes, until tender.

**2** Stir in the flour and cook, stirring constantly, for 1 minute, then gradually add the milk, stirring constantly until the sauce boils and thickens. Add the parsley, if using, and season to taste with salt and pepper. Keep the sauce hot while you are making the omelet.

**3** Beat the egg yolks with the water and season with a little salt and pepper. Whisk the egg whites until stiff, then gently fold them into the egg yolks, using a metal spoon. Preheat the broiler.

**4** Melt the butter in a large, heavy frying pan that can safely be used under the boiler. (Cover a wooden handle with aluminum foil to protect it.) Pour in the egg mixture. Cook over low heat for 2–4 minutes, then place the frying pan under the broiler and cook for 3–4 more minutes, until the top of the omelet is golden brown.

**5** Slide the omelet onto a warmed serving plate, pour the mushroom sauce on top and fold the omelet in half. Garnish with parsley or cilantro leaves and serve.

# Cilantro Omelet Parcels with Asian Vegetables

Stir-fried vegetables in black bean sauce make a remarkably good omelet filling, which is quick and easy to prepare.

**Serves 4**

$4^{1}/_{2}$ ounces broccoli, cut into
    small florets
2 tablespoons peanut oil
$1/2$-inch piece of fresh ginger root,
    finely grated

1 large garlic clove, crushed
2 fresh red chiles, seeded and
    finely sliced
4 scallions, sliced diagonally
3 cups shredded bok choy
2 cups cilantro leaves, plus extra
    to garnish
2 cups bean sprouts
3 tablespoons black bean sauce
4 eggs
salt and ground black pepper

**1** Bring a large pan of lightly salted water to a boil, add the broccoli and blanch for 2 minutes. Drain, refresh under cold running water, then drain again.

**2** Heat half the oil in a wok and stir-fry the ginger, garlic and half the chiles for 1 minute. Add the scallions, broccoli and bok choy, and stir-fry for 2 more minutes.

**3** Chop three-quarters of the cilantro leaves and add to the wok with the bean sprouts. Stir-fry for 1 minute, then add the black bean sauce and toss over the heat for 1 more minute. Remove the pan from heat and keep the vegetables hot.

**4** Lightly beat the eggs and season well. Heat a little of the remaining oil in a small frying pan and add one-quarter of the beaten egg. Swirl the egg to cover the bottom of the pan, then sprinkle on one-quarter of the whole cilantro leaves. Cook the omelet until set, then turn it out onto a plate. Make three more omelets, adding more oil as needed.

**5** Divide the stir-fry among the omelets and roll them up. Cut each one in half crosswise and arrange the pieces on a plate. Garnish with cilantro leaves and the remaining chiles.

# Potato & Onion Tortilla

One of the signature dishes of Spain, this delicious thick potato and onion omelet is eaten anytime of the day, hot or cold.

**Serves 4**
1¼ cups olive oil
6 large potatoes, sliced
2 Spanish onions, sliced
6 large eggs
salt and ground black pepper
cherry tomatoes, halved, to serve

**1** Heat the oil in a large nonstick frying pan. Stir in the potato and onion slices and a little salt. Cover and cook gently for 20 minutes, until soft.

**2** Beat the eggs. Transfer the onion and potato slices to the eggs with a draining spoon. Season to taste. Pour off some of the oil from the frying pan, leaving about 4 tablespoons.

**3** When the oil is very hot, pour in the egg mixture. Cook for 2–3 minutes. Cover the pan with a plate, then, holding them together, invert the tortilla onto the plate. Slide it back into the pan and cook for 5 more minutes. Serve with the tomatoes.

# Pasta Frittata

This is a great way to use up cold leftover pasta.

**Serves 4**
8 ounces cold cooked pasta, with any sauce

⅔ cup freshly grated Parmesan cheese
5 eggs, lightly beaten
5 tablespoons butter
salt and ground black pepper

**1** Stir the pasta and Parmesan into the eggs. Season to taste.
**2** Heat half the butter in a large pan. Pour in the egg mixture and cook for 4–5 minutes, gently shaking the pan.
**3** Place a plate over the pan, then, holding them together, invert the frittata onto the plate. Melt the remaining butter in the pan, slide the frittata back in and cook for 3–4 more minutes.

# Bell Pepper & Zucchini Frittata

Eggs, cheese and vegetables form the basis of this excellent supper dish. Served cold, in wedges, it makes tasty picnic fare too.

**Serves 4**
3 tablespoons olive oil
1 red onion, thinly sliced
1 large red bell pepper, seeded and thinly sliced

1 large yellow bell pepper, seeded and thinly sliced
2 garlic cloves, crushed
1 medium zucchini, thinly sliced
6 eggs
1¼ cups grated Italian cheese, such as Fontina, Provolone or Taleggio
salt and ground black pepper
dressed mixed salad greens, to serve

**1** Heat 2 tablespoons of the olive oil in a large heavy frying pan that can safely be used under the broiler. (Cover a wooden handle with aluminum foil to protect it.) Add the onion and red and yellow pepper slices and fry over low heat, stirring occasionally, for about 10 minutes, until softened.

**2** Add the remaining oil to the pan. When it is hot, add the garlic and the zucchini slices. Fry over low heat, stirring constantly, for 5 minutes.

**3** Beat the eggs with salt and pepper to taste. Stir in the grated cheese. Pour the mixture over the vegetables, stirring lightly to mix. Cook over low heat until the mixture is just set.

**4** Meanwhile, preheat the boiler. When it is hot, slide the pan underneath and brown the top of the frittata lightly. Let the frittata stand in the pan for about 5 minutes before cutting into wedges. Serve hot or cold, with the salad.

**Cook's Tips**
• *When adding the egg mixture to the vegetables, make sure that it covers the bottom of the pan evenly.*
• *Make sure that you use the freshest possible free-range eggs for maximum flavor.*

# Irish Colcannon

Curly kale is a vegetable that is often neglected, but if you mix it with mashed potatoes, eggs and cheese you will find that you have a dish fit for a king.

**Serves 4**
2¼ pounds potatoes, quartered
8 ounces curly kale or crisp green
   cabbage, shredded
2 scallions, chopped
butter, to taste
grated nutmeg
4 large eggs
¾ cup grated aged
   Cheddar cheese
salt and ground black pepper

**1** Cook the potatoes in a pan of lightly salted boiling water for about 30 minutes, until tender, then drain and mash well. Preheat the oven to 375°F.

**2** Steam the kale or cabbage over boiling water until crisp-tender. Drain well. Add the greens to the potato with the onions, butter and nutmeg. Mix well and season to taste with salt and pepper.

**3** Spoon the mixture into a shallow ovenproof dish and make four hollows in the mixture. Crack an egg into each hollow and season well with salt and pepper.

**4** Bake for about 12 minutes or until the eggs are just set, then sprinkle on the cheese and serve.

# Patrick's Potatoes

This is one of many tasty variations on traditional Irish Colcannon.

**Serves 6**
1½ pounds potatoes, quartered
½ cup butter, plus extra
   for mashing
4 ounces onion, finely chopped

4 ounces celery stalks,
   finely chopped
8 ounces green cabbage,
   finely shredded
6 juniper berries, lightly crushed
4 tablespoons water
6 eggs
pinch of cayenne pepper
salt and ground black pepper

**1** Cook the potatoes in a pan of lightly salted boiling water for about 30 minutes, until tender. Drain and mash well with butter to taste. Preheat the oven to 375°F.

**2** Melt ½ cup butter in a frying pan. Add the onion and celery and fry over low heat, stirring occasionally, for about 5 minutes, until softened but not colored.

**3** Meanwhile, put the cabbage, juniper berries and water in a saucepan and cook over low heat for 5 minutes, until tender. Drain well then add to the mashed potatoes.

**4** Combine the potato mixture with the onion and celery and season to taste with salt and pepper. Spoon into an ovenproof dish and make six hollows in the mixture. Break an egg into each hollow and season with cayenne, salt and black pepper.

**5** Bake for about 12 minutes or until the eggs are just set. Serve immediately.

# Vegetable Stir-fry with Eggs

A perfect family supper dish, this is very easy to prepare. Serve with plenty of fresh crusty bread.

**Serves 4**
2 tablespoons olive oil
1 onion, roughly chopped
2 garlic cloves, crushed
8 ounces zucchini, cut in
   long strips
1 red bell pepper, seeded and
   thinly sliced
1 yellow bell pepper, seeded and
   thinly sliced
2 teaspoons paprika
14-ounce can chopped tomatoes
1 tablespoon sun-dried tomato
   paste or tomato paste
4 eggs
1 cup grated Cheddar cheese
salt and ground black pepper
crusty bread, to serve

**1** Heat the oil in a deep, heavy frying pan that can safely be used under the broiler. (Cover a wooden handle with aluminum foil to protect it.) Add the onion and garlic and cook over low heat, stirring occasionally, for about 4 minutes or until just beginning to soften.

**2** Add the zucchini and red and yellow peppers to the onion. Cook over medium heat, stirring occasionally, for 3–4 minutes, until beginning to soften.

**3** Stir in the paprika, tomatoes and sun-dried tomato paste or tomato paste. Season with salt and pepper to taste. Bring to a boil, lower the heat and simmer gently for 15 minutes, until the vegetables are just tender.

**4** Reduce the heat to a low setting. Make four wells in the tomato mixture, break an egg into each and season to taste with salt and pepper. Cook until the egg whites begin to set. Preheat the broiler.

**5** Sprinkle the cheese on the stir-fry, then slide the pan under the hot broiler. Cook for about 5 minutes, until the cheese is melted golden and the eggs are lightly set. Serve immediately with plenty of crusty bread.

# Spring Vegetable Stir-fry

A dazzling and colorful medley of fresh and sweet young vegetables.

**Serves 4**

1 tablespoon peanut oil
1 garlic clove, sliced
1-inch piece of fresh ginger root, finely chopped
4 ounces baby carrots
4 ounces small patty pan squash
4 ounces baby corn
4 ounces green beans, trimmed

4 ounces sugar snap peas, trimmed
4 ounces young asparagus, cut into 3-inch pieces
8 scallions, trimmed and cut into 2-inch pieces
4 ounces cherry tomatoes

**For the dressing**
juice of 2 limes
1 tablespoon honey
1 tablespoon soy sauce
1 teaspoon sesame oil

**1** Heat the peanut oil in a wok and stir-fry the garlic and ginger over high heat for 30 seconds.

**2** Reduce the heat slightly and add the baby carrots, patty pan squash, corn and beans and stir-fry for 3–4 more minutes.

**3** Add the sugar snap peas, asparagus, scallions and cherry tomatoes. Toss for another 1–2 minutes.

**4** Mix the dressing ingredients in a pitcher and pour them over the stir-fried vegetables. Stir well, cover and cook for 2–3 more minutes, until the vegetables are crisp-tender. Serve immediately.

> **Variation**
> You can use any seasonal vegetables, provided they are tender enough to cook quickly. Cauliflower or broccoli florets, snow peas, bell pepper strips and sliced zucchini would all be suitable. Make sure they are cut into similar sized pieces so that they cook simultaneously. Add thinly sliced red onion and celery when frying the garlic, if desired.

# Lentil Stir-fry

Mushrooms, artichokes, sugar snap peas and lentils make a satisfying stir-fry for a mid-week supper.

**Serves 2–3**

4 ounces sugar snap peas
2 tablespoons butter
1 small onion, chopped
1½ cups cup or brown cap mushrooms, sliced

14-ounce can artichoke hearts, drained and halved
14-ounce can cooked green lentils, drained
4 tablespoons light cream
¼ cup sliced almonds, toasted
salt and ground black pepper
French bread, to serve

**1** Bring a pan of lightly salted water to a boil and cook the sugar snap peas for 4 minutes or until just tender. Drain, refresh under cold running water, then drain again. Pat the peas dry with paper towels and set them aside.

**2** Melt the butter in a large, heavy frying pan. Add the chopped onion and cook over medium heat, stirring occasionally for 2–3 minutes.

**3** Stir in the sliced mushrooms, then cook, stirring occasionally, for 2–3 minutes, until just tender. Add the artichoke hearts, sugar snap peas and lentils to the pan. Stir-fry over medium heat for 2 minutes.

**4** Stir in the cream and almonds and cook for 1 minute. Season to taste. Serve immediately, with chunks of French bread.

> **Cook's Tip**
> Canned lentils are convenient, but it doesn't take long to cook dried lentils. Unlike most pulses, they don't need soaking. To add flavor, simmer them in vegetable stock or water to which you have added a little yeast extract. Do not add salt, as this tends to make the lentils tough. They will take 20–30 minutes, depending on type and the degree of freshness.

# Quorn with Ginger, Chile & Leeks

If you've never eaten Quorn, this would be a good recipe to try. Serve it over noodles or rice.

**Serves 4**

3 tablespoons soy sauce
2 tablespoons dry sherry
  or vermouth
2 cups Quorn cubes
2 teaspoons honey
²⁄₃ cup vegetable stock
2 teaspoons cornstarch
3 tablespoons sunflower oil
3 leeks, thinly sliced
1 fresh red chile, seeded
  and sliced
1-inch piece of fresh ginger
  root, shredded
salt and ground black pepper

**1** Mix the soy sauce and sherry or vermouth in a bowl. Add the Quorn cubes, toss until well coated and let marinate for about 30 minutes.

**2** Using a draining spoon, lift out the Quorn cubes from the marinade and set them aside. Stir the honey, stock and cornstarch into the remaining marinade to make a paste.

**3** Heat the oil in a wok. When it is hot, stir-fry the Quorn cubes until they are crisp on the outside. Remove the Quorn and set aside.

**4** Reheat the oil and stir-fry the leeks, chile and ginger for about 2 minutes, until they are just soft. Season lightly.

**5** Add the Quorn cubes to the vegetables in the wok and mix well. Stir the marinade mixture, pour it into the wok and stir until it forms a thick, glossy coating for the Quorn and vegetables. Serve immediately.

> **Cook's Tip**
> Quorn is a versatile mycoprotein food, which easily absorbs different flavors and retains a good firm texture. It is available at most supermarkets.

# Spiced Tofu Stir-fry

Like Quorn, firm tofu (bean curd) is a boon to the vegetarian cook, as it readily absorbs the flavors of the other ingredients. In this recipe it is coated with warm spices before being stir-fried with a medley of mixed vegetables.

**Serves 4**

2 teaspoons ground cumin
1 tablespoon paprika
1 teaspoon ground ginger
good pinch of cayenne pepper
1 tablespoon sugar
10 ounces tofu (bean curd), cubed
2 tablespoons vegetable oil
2 garlic cloves, crushed
1 bunch scallions, sliced
1 red bell pepper, seeded
  and sliced
1 yellow bell pepper, seeded
  and sliced
generous 3 cups brown cap
  mushrooms, halved or
  quartered, if necessary
1 large zucchini, sliced
1 cup fine green beans, halved
²⁄₃ cup pine nuts
1 tablespoon freshly squeezed
  lime juice
1 tablespoon honey
salt and ground black pepper

**1** Mix the cumin, paprika, ginger, cayenne and sugar in a bowl and add plenty of salt and pepper. Coat the tofu cubes in the spice mixture.

**2** Heat 1 tablespoon of the oil in a wok or large, heavy frying pan and cook the tofu cubes over high heat for 3–4 minutes, turning occasionally and taking care not to break them up too much. Remove the tofu cubes with a draining spoon. Wipe out the pan with paper towels and return it to the heat.

**3** Heat the remaining oil in the wok and stir-fry the garlic and scallions for 3 minutes. Add the red and yellow peppers, mushrooms, zucchini and beans and toss over medium heat for about 6 minutes or until beginning to soften and turn golden. Season well with salt and pepper.

**4** Return the tofu cubes to the wok with the pine nuts, lime juice and honey. Heat through, stirring occasionally, then serve immediately.

# Stir-fried Chickpeas

Most of the ingredients in this nourishing supper dish come straight from the pantry, so it is a useful standby for unexpected guests.

**Serves 2–4**
2 tablespoons sunflower seeds
14-ounce can chickpeas, drained and rinsed
1 teaspoon chili powder
1 teaspoon paprika
2 tablespoons vegetable oil
1 garlic clove, crushed
7-ounce can chopped tomatoes
8 ounces fresh spinach, coarse stems removed
2 teaspoons chili oil
salt and ground black pepper

**1** Heat the wok and then add the sunflower seeds. Dry-fry, stirring frequently, until the seeds are golden and toasted, then put them into a bowl.

**2** Toss the chickpeas in the chili powder and paprika. Heat the oil in the wok and stir-fry the garlic for 30 seconds. Add the chickpeas and stir-fry for 1 minute.

**3** Stir in the tomatoes and stir-fry for 4 minutes. Add the spinach, season well with salt and pepper and toss over the heat for 1 minute.

**4** Spoon the stir-fry into a serving dish and drizzle with chili oil. Sprinkle on the sunflower seeds and serve immediately.

**Cook's Tips**
• If you have time, use dried chickpeas, but be prepared to soak them overnight. They are notorious for the time they take to cook, so it is worth making a big batch and either freezing the surplus or using it to make hummus.
• Ready-chopped canned tomatoes are usually slightly less watery than canned whole tomatoes but are more expensive.
• Paprika, while never as hot as chili powder, is available in two forms—mild (or sweet) and hot.

# Black Bean & Vegetable Stir-fry

The secret of a quick stir-fry is to have everything ready before you begin to cook. This colorful vegetable mixture is coated in a classic Chinese sauce.

**Serves 4**
8 scallions
3 cups button mushrooms
1 red bell pepper
1 green bell pepper
2 large carrots
4 tablespoons sesame oil
2 garlic cloves, crushed
4 tablespoons black bean sauce
6 tablespoons warm water
4 cups bean sprouts
salt and ground black pepper

**1** Thinly slice the scallions and button mushrooms. Cut both the peppers in half, remove the seeds and slice the flesh into thin strips.

**2** Cut the carrots in half widthwise, then cut each half into thin strips lengthwise. Stack the slices and cut through them to make very fine strips.

**3** Heat the oil in a large wok until it is very hot. Add the scallions and garlic and stir-fry for 30 seconds.

**4** Add the mushrooms, peppers and carrots and stir-fry over high heat for 5–6 minutes, until the vegetables are just beginning to soften.

**5** Mix the black bean sauce with the water. Add to the wok and cook, stirring occasionally, for 3–4 minutes. Stir in the bean sprouts and stir-fry for 1 more minute, until all the vegetables are coated in the sauce. Season to taste with salt and pepper. Serve immediately.

**Cook's Tip**
For best results the oil in the wok must be very hot before adding the vegetables.

# Spaghetti with Garlic & Oil

This classic Italian dish has only a few ingredients, which must be of the very best quality. Chile is always included to give the dish some bite.

**Serves 4**
14 ounces fresh or
   dried spaghetti
6 tablespoons extra virgin olive oil
2–4 garlic cloves, chopped
1 dried red chile
1 small handful of fresh flat-leaf
   parsley, roughly chopped
salt

**1** Bring a large pan of generously salted water to a boil and cook the spaghetti until it is *al dente*. Dried spaghetti will take 10–12 minutes; fresh spaghetti will be ready in 2–3 minutes.

**2** While the pasta is cooking, heat the oil in a small frying pan over very low heat. Add the crushed garlic and whole dried chile and stir over low heat until the garlic is just beginning to brown. Remove the chile and save as a garnish.

**3** Drain the pasta and put it into a warmed serving bowl. Pour on the oil and garlic mixture, add the parsley and toss until the pasta glistens. Serve immediately, garnished with the chile.

---

**Cook's Tips**
• Don't use salt in the oil and garlic mixture, because it will not dissolve sufficiently. This is why plenty of salt is recommended for cooking the pasta.
• For an authentic Italian flavor, use peperoncino, fiery, dried, red chiles from Abruzzi. They are so hot that they are known locally as diavoletto—little devils. They are available at some Italian delicatessens.

---

**Variation** If desired, serve the pasta with 4 tablespoons freshly grated Parmesan or Pecorino cheese.

---

# Eliche with Pesto

Ready-made pesto is a useful standby, but nothing beats the flavor of the freshly made mixture.

**Serves 4**
1½ cups fresh basil leaves, plus
   extra, to garnish
2–4 garlic cloves, chopped
4 tablespoons pine nuts
½ cup extra virgin olive oil
1⅓ cups freshly grated Parmesan
   cheese, plus shaved Parmesan
   to serve
⅓ cup freshly grated
   Pecorino cheese
3½ cups dried eliche or other
   pasta shapes
salt and ground black pepper

**1** Put the basil leaves, garlic and pine nuts in a food processor. Add 4 tablespoons of the olive oil. Process until the ingredients are finely chopped, then stop the machine, remove the lid and scrape down the sides of the bowl.

**2** Switch the machine on again and slowly add the remaining oil in a thin, steady stream through the feeder tube. You may need to stop the machine and scrape down the sides of the bowl once or twice to make sure everything is evenly mixed.

**3** Scrape the mixture into a large bowl and beat in the cheeses with a wooden spoon. Taste and season if necessary.

**4** Bring a large pan of lightly salted water to a boil and cook the pasta for about 12 minutes, until it is *al dente*. Drain it thoroughly, then add it to the bowl of pesto and toss well. Serve immediately, garnished with the fresh basil leaves. Pass shaved Parmesan separately.

---

**Cook's Tip**
*The pesto can be made up to 2–3 days in advance. To store pesto, transfer it to a bowl and pour a thin film of olive oil on the surface. Cover the bowl tightly with plastic wrap and keep it in the refrigerator.*

---

# Spaghetti with Fresh Tomato Sauce

This famous Neapolitan sauce is very simple, so nothing detracts from the rich, sweet flavor of the tomatoes themselves.

**Serves 4**
1½ pounds ripe Italian plum tomatoes
4 tablespoons olive oil
1 onion, finely chopped
12 ounces fresh or dried spaghetti
a small handful of fresh basil leaves, shredded
salt and ground black pepper
coarsely shaved Parmesan cheese, to serve

**1** Cut a cross in the blossom end of each tomato and put them in a heatproof bowl. Pour in boiling water to cover and leave for about 30 seconds or until the skins wrinkle and start to peel back from the crosses. Drain, peel off the skin and roughly chop the flesh.

**2** Heat the oil in a large saucepan and cook the onion over low heat, for 5 minutes, until softened and lightly colored. Stir in the tomatoes and season with salt and pepper to taste. Cover the pan and cook over low heat for 30–40 minutes, stirring occasionally.

**3** Bring a large pan of lightly salted water to a boil and cook the spaghetti until it is *al dente*. Dried pasta will take about 12 minutes and fresh spaghetti about 3–4 minutes.

**4** Remove the sauce from heat and taste for seasoning. Drain the pasta, put it into a warmed bowl, pour on the sauce and toss well. Sprinkle the fresh basil over the top and serve immediately, with shaved Parmesan passed separately.

**Cook's Tip**
*In summer, when sun-ripened tomatoes are plentiful, make this sauce in bulk and freeze it for later use. Let it cool, then freeze in usable quantities in rigid containers. Thaw before reheating.*

# Penne Rigate with Green Vegetable Sauce

Strictly speaking, this isn't a sauced dish, but a medley of vegetables and pasta tossed in butter and oil.

**Serves 4**
2 tablespoons butter
3 tablespoons extra virgin olive oil
1 small leek, thinly sliced
2 carrots, diced
½ teaspoon sugar
1 zucchini, diced
3 ounces green beans, cut in short lengths
1 cup frozen peas
4 cups dried penne rigate or other pasta shapes
a handful of fresh flat-leaf parsley, chopped
2 ripe Italian plum tomatoes, peeled and diced
salt and ground black pepper

**1** Melt the butter in the oil in a pan. When the mixture sizzles, add the leek and carrots. Sprinkle on the sugar and fry, stirring frequently, for about 5 minutes.

**2** Stir in the zucchini, beans and peas, and season with salt and pepper. Cover and cook over low heat for about 10 minutes, until the vegetables are tender, stirring occasionally.

**3** Meanwhile, bring a large pan of lightly salted water to a boil and cook the pasta until it is *al dente*.

**4** Drain the pasta and return it to the pan. Stir the parsley and plum tomatoes into the sauce and adjust the seasoning to taste. Pour the sauce on the pasta, toss to mix, then serve.

**Variation**
*For a quick and easy dish, make the vegetable mixture without the tomatoes. Toss it with the pasta and spoon into an ovenproof dish. Slice three tomatoes and arrange the slices on the vegetable mixture. Top with a thick layer of grated cheese, then broil until the cheese melts to form a delicious topping.*

# Pasta with Slow-cooked Cabbage, Parmesan & Pine Nuts

This is an unusual but quite delicious, way of serving pasta. Use cavolo nero, Italy's delicious black cabbage, if you can locate it.

**Serves 4**

2 tablespoons butter
1 tablespoon extra virgin olive oil
1¼ pounds Spanish onions, halved and thinly sliced
1–2 teaspoons balsamic vinegar
14 ounces cavolo nero, collard greens or kale, shredded
4 cups dried pasta, such as penne or fusilli
1 cup freshly grated Parmesan cheese
⅔ cup pine nuts, toasted
salt and ground black pepper

**1** Heat the butter and olive oil in a large saucepan. Add the onions, stirring to coat them in the butter mixture. Cover and cook over very low heat, stirring occasionally, for about 20 minutes, until the onions are very soft.

**2** Remove the lid and continue to cook the onions until they have turned golden yellow. Add the balsamic vinegar and season well with salt and pepper, then cook for another 1–2 minutes. Set aside.

**3** Bring a large pan of lightly salted water to a boil and blanch the greens for about 3 minutes. Remove the greens from the pan using a slotted spoon and drain them thoroughly. Add them to the onions, stir thoroughly to mix and cook over the lowest possible heat.

**4** Bring the water in the pan back to a boil, add the pasta and cook for about 12 minutes, until *al dente*. Drain and return it to the pan. Add the onion mixture and toss over medium heat until warmed through.

**5** Season well with salt and pepper and stir in half the grated Parmesan. Spoon onto warmed plates. Sprinkle the pine nuts and more Parmesan on top and serve immediately.

# Rustic Buckwheat Pasta Casserole

A spicy combination of nutty-flavored buckwheat pasta, vegetables and Fontina cheese, this makes a wonderful family supper.

**Serves 6**

3 tablespoons olive oil, plus extra for greasing
2 potatoes, peeled and cubed
2 cups dried buckwheat pasta shapes
2½ cups shredded Savoy cabbage
1 onion, chopped
2 leeks, sliced
2 garlic cloves, chopped
2½ cups brown cap mushrooms, sliced
1 teaspoon caraway seeds
1 teaspoon cumin seeds
⅔ cup vegetable stock
5 ounces Fontina cheese, diced
¼ cup walnuts, roughly chopped
salt and ground black pepper

**1** Preheat the oven to 400°F. Grease a deep ovenproof dish with oil. Cook the cubed potatoes in a pan of lightly salted water for 8–10 minutes, until tender, then drain and set aside.

**2** Meanwhile, bring a large pan of lightly salted water to a boil. Add the pasta and cook until it is just tender. Add the cabbage in the last minute of cooking time. Drain, then rinse under cold running water.

**3** Heat the olive oil in a large heavy saucepan and fry the onion and leeks over medium heat, stirring occasionally, for 5 minutes, until softened.

**4** Add the garlic and mushrooms and cook, stirring occasionally, for 3 more minutes, until tender. Stir in the caraway seeds and cumin seeds and cook, stirring constantly, for 1 minute.

**5** Stir in the cooked potatoes, pasta and cabbage. Season well with salt and pepper. Spoon the mixture into the prepared dish. Pour the stock on the mixture, then sprinkle with the cheese and walnuts. Bake for 15 minutes or until the cheese is melted and bubbling.

# Five-spice Vegetable Noodles

Vary this stir-fry by substituting mushrooms, bamboo shoots, bean sprouts, snow peas or water chestnuts for some or all of the vegetables.

**Serves 2–3**
8 ounces dried egg noodles
2 tablespoons sesame oil
2 carrots
1 celery stalk

1 small fennel bulb
2 zucchini, halved lengthwise
    and sliced
1 fresh red chile
1-inch piece of fresh ginger
    root, grated
1 garlic clove, crushed
1½ teaspoons Chinese five-
    spice powder
½ teaspoon ground cinnamon
4 scallions, sliced
4 tablespoons warm water

**1** Bring a large pan of salted water to a boil. Add the noodles and cook for 2–3 minutes, until they are just tender. Drain the noodles, return them to the pan and toss them with a little of the oil. Set aside.

**2** Cut the carrots and celery into matchstick strips. Cut the fennel bulb in half and cut out the hard core. Cut into slices, then cut the slices into matchstick strips.

**3** Heat the remaining oil in a wok until very hot. Add the carrots, celery, fennel and zucchini and stir-fry over medium heat for 7–8 minutes.

**4** Cut half the chile into rings, discarding any seeds, and set aside. Chop the rest of the chile and add it to the wok.

**5** Add the ginger and garlic and stir-fry for 2 minutes, then add the Chinese five-spice powder and cinnamon. Stir-fry for 1 minute, then toss in the scallions and stir-fry for another minute.

**6** Pour in the warm water and cook for 1 minute. Stir in the noodles and toss over the heat until they have warmed through. Transfer to a warmed serving dish and serve sprinkled with the reserved sliced red chile.

# Fried Noodles with Bean sprouts & Asparagus

Soft fried noodles contrast beautifully with crisp bean sprouts and asparagus.

**Serves 2**
4 ounces dried egg noodles
3 tablespoons vegetable oil
1 small onion, chopped
1-inch piece of fresh ginger
    root, grated

2 garlic cloves, crushed
6 ounces young asparagus
    spears, trimmed
2 cups bean sprouts
4 scallions, sliced
3 tablespoons soy sauce
salt and ground black pepper

**1** Bring a pan of lightly salted water to a boil. Add the noodles and cook for 2–3 minutes, until just tender. Drain and toss with 1 tablespoon of the oil.

**2** Heat the remaining oil in a wok until very hot. Add the onion, ginger and garlic and stir-fry for 2–3 minutes. Add the asparagus and stir-fry for 2–3 more minutes.

**3** Add the noodles and bean sprouts and toss over high heat for 2 minutes.

**4** Stir in the scallions and soy sauce. Season to taste with salt and pepper. Stir-fry for 1 minute, then serve.

**Cook's Tip**
*When seasoning the stir-fry, add salt sparingly, as the soy sauce will impart quite a salty flavor.*

**Variation**
*If preferred, substitute the same quantity of snow peas for the asparagus spears.*

# Pizza Margherita

This classic pizza is simple to prepare. The sweet flavor of sun-ripe tomatoes works wonderfully with the basil and mozzarella.

**Serves 2–3**

1 pizza crust, about
  10–12 inches in diameter
2 tablespoons olive oil
1½ cups tomato sauce
5 ounces mozzarella cheese
2 ripe tomatoes, thinly sliced
6–8 fresh basil leaves
2 tablespoons freshly grated
  Parmesan cheese
ground black pepper

**1** Preheat the oven to 425°F. Support the pizza crust on a baking sheet. Brush it with 1 tablespoon of the olive oil, then spread the tomato sauce evenly over the surface, leaving a ½-inch rim all around.

**2** Cut the mozzarella into thin slices, and arrange the slices on top of the pizza crust, alternating them with overlapping slices of tomato.

**3** Tear the basil leaves into large pieces and sprinkle them on the pizza. Sprinkle on the Parmesan. Drizzle on the remaining oil and season with black pepper. Bake the pizza for 15–20 minutes, until crisp and golden. Serve immediately.

> **Cook's Tips**
> • Depending on the amount of time—and energy—you have, you can use a ready-made pizza crust, make one from a packaged mix or prepare your own dough.
> • Make your own tomato sauce if possible, but use a good bottled sauce if you are in a hurry.

# Pizza with Onions & Olives

The sweetness of slow-cooked onions is the perfect foil for the salty bitterness of the olives.

**Serves 2–3**

4 tablespoons olive oil
4 medium onions, finely sliced
1 pizza crust, about
  10–12 inches in diameter
12 ounces mozzarella cheese, cut
  into small dice
32 pitted black olives, halved
3 tablespoons chopped
  fresh parsley
salt and ground black pepper

**1** Preheat the oven to 425°F. Heat half the olive oil in a large frying pan. Add the onions and fry over low heat, stirring occasionally, for about 15 minutes, until they are soft, translucent and beginning to brown.

**2** Support the pizza crust on a baking sheet. Spread the onions evenly on the surface, leaving the rim clear. Sprinkle on with the diced mozzarella.

**3** Dot with the olives. Sprinkle on parsley and the remaining olive oil. Season to taste. Bake the pizza for 15–20 minutes, until crisp and golden. Serve immediately.

# Fresh Herb Pizza

Sometimes it is the simplest ideas that prove to be the most successful. This pizza is the perfect excuse to raid your herb garden.

**Serves 2–3**

about 3 cups mixed fresh herbs,
  such as parsley, basil
  and oregano
3 garlic cloves, crushed
½ cup heavy cream
1 pizza crust, 10–12 inches
  in diameter
1 tablespoon garlic oil (see
  Cook's Tip)
1⅓ cups grated Pecorino cheese
salt and ground black pepper

**1** Preheat the oven to 425°F. Chop the herbs by hand or in a food processor, then put them into a bowl. Stir in the garlic and cream. Season with plenty of salt and pepper.

**2** Support the pizza crust on a baking sheet. Brush it with the garlic oil, then spread the herb mixture evenly on the surface, leaving a ½-inch rim all around.

**3** Sprinkle on the Pecorino. Bake the pizza for 15–20 minutes. until the crust is crisp and golden but the topping is still moist. Cut into thin wedges and serve immediately.

> **Cook's Tip**
> Making garlic oil couldn't be simpler. It has lots of applications, from tossing with pasta to drizzling on tomatoes before grilling, and is an excellent basis for a salad dressing. Peel four garlic cloves, put them in a small jar or bottle and pour on about ½ cup olive oil. Cover and keep in the refrigerator for up to 1 month.

> **Variation**
> You can substitute baby spinach for half the fresh herbs.

# Fiorentina Pizza

An egg adds the finishing touch to this spinach pizza; it's best when the yolk is still slightly soft.

**Serves 2–3**

3 tablespoons olive oil
1 small red onion, thinly sliced
6 ounces fresh spinach,
    stems removed
1 pizza crust, about
    10–12 inches in diameter
1½ cups tomato sauce
freshly grated nutmeg
5 ounces mozzarella cheese
1 egg
¼ cup grated Gruyère cheese

**1** Heat 1 tablespoon of the olive oil. Add the onion and fry over low heat, stirring occasionally, for 5 minutes, until soft. Add the spinach and fry until wilted. Drain any excess liquid.

**2** Preheat the oven to 425°F. Support the pizza crust on a baking sheet, then brush it with half the remaining olive oil. Spread the tomato sauce evenly on the crust, using the back of a spoon, leaving a ½-inch rim all around. Then cover the top of the pizza with the spinach mixture. Sprinkle on a little freshly grated nutmeg.

**3** Slice the mozzarella thinly and arrange it on the spinach. Drizzle on the remaining oil. Bake for 10 minutes, then remove from the oven.

**4** Make a small well in the center of the pizza topping and carefully break the egg into the hole. Sprinkle on the grated Gruyère. Return the pizza to the oven for 5–10 minutes, until crisp and golden. Serve immediately.

### Variation
If you make your own dough, you can easily transform this into a calzone. Add the egg to the spinach mixture, spread it on half the pizza dough, then add the cheeses. Fold the pizza dough over, seal the edges and bake for 20 minutes.

# Butternut Squash & Sage Pizza

The combination of the sweet butternut squash, pungent sage and sharp goat cheese works wonderfully on this pizza.

**Serves 2–3**

1 tablespoon butter
2 tablespoons olive oil
1 shallot, finely chopped
1 small butternut squash, peeled,
    seeded and cubed
8 fresh sage leaves
1 pizza crust, about
    10–12 inches in diameter
1½ cups tomato sauce
3 ounces mozzarella
    cheese, sliced
3 ounces firm goat cheese
salt and ground black pepper

**1** Preheat the oven to 400°F. Melt the butter in the oil in a roasting pan. Add the shallot, squash and half the sage leaves. Toss well to coat all over in oil. Roast the vegetables for 15–20 minutes, until tender.

**2** Increase the oven temperature to 425°F. Support the pizza crust on a baking sheet. Spread the tomato sauce evenly on the surface with the back of a spoon, leaving a ½-inch rim all around.

**3** Spoon the squash and shallot mixture evenly on the pizza, arrange the slices of mozzarella on top and crumble the goat cheese on the surface.

**4** Sprinkle the remaining sage leaves on the pizza and season with plenty of salt and pepper. Bake for 15–20 minutes, until the cheese has melted and the crust is golden. Serve immediately.

### Cook's Tip
If you don't have time to make a yeast-based pizza dough, use scone batter. Mix 2 cups self-rising flour with a pinch of salt, then rub in ¼ cup diced butter. Pour in about ⅔ cup milk and mix into a soft dough. Pat out to a 10-inch round, top as suggested above and bake for about 20 minutes.

# New Potato, Rosemary & Garlic Pizza

New potatoes, smoked mozzarella, rosemary and garlic make the flavor of this pizza unique.

**Serves 2–3**
12 ounces new potatoes
3 tablespoons olive oil
2 garlic cloves, crushed
1 pizza crust, 10–12 inches
  in diameter

1 red onion, very thinly sliced
1¼ cups grated smoked
  mozzarella cheese
2 teaspoons chopped
  fresh rosemary
salt and ground black pepper
2 tablespoons freshly grated
  Parmesan cheese, to garnish

**1** Preheat the oven to 425°F. Bring a large pan of lightly salted water to a boil and cook the potatoes for 5 minutes. Drain well. When cool, peel the potatoes and slice them thinly.

**2** Heat 2 tablespoons of the oil in a frying pan. Add the sliced potatoes and garlic and fry over medium heat, stirring occasionally, for 5–8 minutes, until tender.

**3** Brush the pizza crust with the remaining oil. Sprinkle on the onion, then arrange the potatoes on top.

**4** Sprinkle on the mozzarella and rosemary. Grind on plenty of black pepper. Bake for 15–20 minutes, until the crust is crisp and golden. Sprinkle on the grated Parmesan and serve.

**Cook's Tips**
• It's easy to overestimate how many new potatoes you need to cook for a family meal. Next time you find yourself with leftovers, use them to make this tasty pizza.
• Smoked mozzarella, also known as mozzarella affumicata, is available at supermarkets and delicatessens.

# Quattro Formaggi Pizzas

As the Italian title suggests, these tasty little pizzas are topped with four different types of cheese and have a very rich flavor.

**Serves 4**
1 batch Basic Pizza Dough
all-purpose flour, for dusting
1 tablespoon olive oil

1 small red onion, very
  thinly sliced
2 ounces dolcelatte cheese
2 ounces mozzarella cheese
2 ounces Gruyère cheese
2 tablespoons freshly grated
  Parmesan cheese
1 tablespoon chopped
  fresh thyme
ground black pepper

**1** Preheat the oven to 425°F. Divide the dough into four pieces and roll out each one on a lightly floured surface into a 5-inch circle.

**2** Place well apart on two greased baking sheets, then push up the dough edges to make a thin rim.

**3** Heat the olive oil in a small frying pan. Add the red onion slices and fry over low heat, stirring occasionally for 4–5 minutes, until softened. Divide them among the pizza crusts, then brush on any oil remaining in the pan.

**4** Cut the dolcelatte and mozzarella into cubes and sprinkle on the pizza crusts. Grate the Gruyère cheese into a bowl. Add the Parmesan and thyme and mix thoroughly. Sprinkle the mixture on the crusts.

**5** Grind on plenty of black pepper. Bake for 15–20 minutes, until the crust of each pizza is crisp and golden and the cheese is bubbling. Serve immediately.

**Variations**
There's no need to stick slavishly to the suggested cheeses. Any variety that melts readily can be used, but a mixture of soft and hard cheeses gives the best result.

# Polenta Pan-pizza

This yeast-free pizza is cooked in a frying pan rather than in the oven.

**Serves 2**

2 tablespoons olive oil
1 large red onion, sliced
3 garlic cloves, crushed
1 ½ cups brown cap
   mushrooms, sliced
1 teaspoon dried oregano
4 ounces mozzarella
   cheese, sliced
tomato wedges and fresh basil
   leaves, to garnish

*For the pizza crust*
½ cup all-purpose flour, sifted
½ teaspoon salt
scant 1 cup fine polenta
1 teaspoon baking powder
1 egg, beaten
⅔ cup milk
⅓ cup freshly grated
   Parmesan cheese
½ teaspoon dried chile flakes
1 tablespoon olive oil
baby plum tomatoes, halved and
   basil, to serve

**1** Heat half the oil in a heavy frying pan, and fry the onion for 10 minutes, stirring occasionally. Remove the onion from the pan and set aside. Heat the remaining oil in the pan and fry the garlic for 1 minute. Add the mushrooms and oregano and cook for 5 minutes.

**2** To make the pizza crust, mix the flour, salt, polenta and baking powder in a bowl. Make a well in the center and add the egg. Gradually add the milk, mixing well to make a thick, smooth batter. Stir in the Parmesan and chile flakes.

**3** Heat the oil in a 10-inch heavy frying pan that can safely be used under the broiler. (Cover a wooden handle with aluminum foil to protect it.) Spoon in the batter in an even layer. Cook for 3 minutes or until set. Remove the pan from heat and run a knife around the edge of the pizza crust. Place a plate over the pan and, holding them together, invert the pizza onto the plate. Slide it back into the pan. Cook for 2 minutes, until golden.

**4** Preheat the broiler to high. Spoon the onion on the crust, then top with the mushroom mixture and the mozzarella, then broil for about 6 minutes. Serve in wedges with tomatoes and basil.

# Potato Gnocchi

These tasty Italian dumplings are made with mashed potatoes and flour.

**Serves 4–6**

2¼ pounds waxy potatoes
2¼–2¾ cups all-purpose flour,
   plus more if necessary
1 egg

pinch of freshly grated nutmeg
2 tablespoons butter
salt
fresh basil leaves shaved
   Parmesan cheese and freshly
   ground black pepper,
   to garnish

**1** Bring a large saucepan of lightly salted water to a boil. Add the potatoes and cook for 25–30 minutes, until tender but not falling apart. Drain and peel while the potatoes are still hot.

**2** Spread a layer of flour on a work surface. Pass the hot potatoes through a food mill, dropping them directly onto the flour. Sprinkle with about half the remaining flour and mix in very lightly. Break the egg into the mixture. Finally, add the nutmeg to the dough and knead lightly, adding more flour if needed in order to make a dough that is light to the touch and no longer moist.

**3** Divide the dough into four pieces. On a lightly floured surface, form each into a roll about ¾ inch in diameter. Cut the rolls crosswise into pieces about ¾ inch long.

**4** Press and roll the gnocchi lightly along the tines of a fork toward the points, making ridges on one side, and a depression from your thumb on the other.

**5** Bring a large pan of salted water to a fast boil, then drop in about half the prepared gnocchi. As soon as they rise to the surface, after 3–4 minutes, lift them out with a draining spoon, drain well, and place in a warmed serving bowl. Dot with butter. Cover to keep warm while cooking the remainder.

**6** As soon as all the gnocchi are cooked, toss them with the butter, garnish with basil, Parmesan and black pepper and serve.

# Saffron Risotto

This classic risotto makes a delicious first course or light supper dish.

**Serves 4**
about 5 cups vegetable stock
good pinch of saffron threads
6 tablespoons butter
1 onion, finely chopped
1 ½ cups risotto rice
1 cup freshly grated
    Parmesan cheese
salt and ground black pepper
freshly ground black pepper,
    to garnish

**1** Bring the stock to a boil in a large pan, then lower the heat so that it barely simmers. Ladle a little stock into a small bowl. Add the saffron threads and let infuse.

**2** Melt 4 tablespoons of the butter in a large saucepan and cook the onion over low heat for 3 minutes, stirring frequently, until softened.

**3** Add the rice. Stir until coated, then add a few ladlefuls of the stock, with the saffron liquid and salt and pepper to taste. Stir over low heat until the stock has been absorbed.

**4** Add the remaining stock in the same way, allowing the rice to absorb all the liquid before adding more, and stirring constantly. After 20–25 minutes, the rice should be *al dente* and the risotto golden yellow, moist and creamy.

**5** Gently stir in about two-thirds of the grated Parmesan and the remaining butter. Cover the pan and let risotto stand for 2–3 minutes. Spoon it into a warmed serving bowl and serve immediately, with the remaining grated Parmesan sprinkled on top and some freshly ground black pepper.

> **Cook's Tip**
> Risotto rice, such as arborio, has rounder grains than long-grain rice and is able to absorb large amounts of liquid, giving the dish its characteristic creamy texture.

# Risotto with Summer Vegetables

This is one of the prettiest risottos, especially if you can get summer squash.

**Serves 4**
1 ¼ cups shelled fresh peas
1 cup green beans, cut into
    short lengths
2 tablespoons olive oil
6 tablespoons butter
2 small summer squash, cut into
    matchstick strips
1 onion, finely chopped
1 ½ cups risotto rice
½ cup Italian dry white vermouth
about 4 cups simmering
    vegetable stock
1 cup freshly grated
    Parmesan cheese
a small handful of fresh basil
    leaves, finely shredded, plus a
    few whole leaves, to garnish
salt and ground black pepper

**1** Bring a large pan of lightly salted water to a boil and blanch the peas and beans for 2–3 minutes, until just tender. Drain, refresh under cold running water, drain again and set aside.

**2** Heat the oil and 2 tablespoons of the butter in a medium saucepan. Add the squash and cook over low heat for 2–3 minutes. Remove with a draining spoon and set aside.

**3** Add the onion to the pan and cook, stirring occasionally, for about 3 minutes, until softened.

**4** Stir in the rice until coated, then add the vermouth. When most of it has been absorbed, add a few ladlefuls of the stock and season with salt and pepper to taste. Stir over low heat until the stock has been absorbed.

**5** Continue adding the stock, a little at a time, stirring constantly for about 20 minutes, until all the stock has been added and the risotto is moist and creamy.

**6** Gently stir in the vegetables, the remaining butter and about half the grated Parmesan. Heat through, then stir in the shredded basil. Serve immediately, garnished with a few whole basil leaves. Pass the remaining grated Parmesan separately.

# Leek, Mushroom & Lemon Risotto

Leeks and lemon go together beautifully in this light risotto, while mushrooms add texture and extra flavor.

**Serves 4**

2 tablespoons olive oil
3 garlic cloves, crushed
8 ounces trimmed leeks, sliced
2–3 cups brown cap
   mushrooms, sliced
6 tablespoons butter
1 large onion, roughly chopped
1¾ cups risotto rice
5 cups simmering vegetable stock
grated zest of 1 lemon
3 tablespoons lemon juice
²/₃ cup freshly grated
   Parmesan cheese
4 tablespoons mixed chopped
   fresh chives and
   flat-leaf parsley
salt and ground black pepper

**1** Heat the olive oil in a large pan and cook the garlic for 1 minute. Add the leeks and mushrooms and season to taste with salt and pepper. Cook over low heat, stirring occasionally, for about 10 minutes or until the leeks have softened and browned. Spoon the mixture into a bowl and set aside.

**2** Melt 2 tablespoons of the butter in the pan and cook the onion, stirring occasionally, for 5 minutes, until it has softened and is golden. Stir in the rice until coated, then add a ladleful of hot stock. Cook gently, stirring frequently, until all the liquid has been absorbed.

**3** Continue to add the remaining stock, a little at a time, and stirring constantly. After about 25–30 minutes, the rice will have absorbed all the stock, and the risotto will be moist and creamy.

**4** Add the leeks and mushrooms, with the remaining butter. Stir in the lemon zest and juice, then the grated Parmesan and the herbs. Adjust the seasoning, spoon into a bowl and serve.

**Cook's Tip**
*Always wash leeks very thoroughly, as soil and grit may be trapped within the leaves.*

# Nutty Rice with Mushrooms

This delicious and substantial supper dish can be eaten either hot, or cold with salads.

**Serves 4–6**

1¾ cups long-grain rice
3 tablespoons sunflower oil
1 small onion, roughly chopped
3 cups field mushrooms, sliced
½ cup hazelnuts,
   roughly chopped
½ cup pecans, roughly chopped
½ cup almonds, roughly chopped
4 tablespoons chopped
   fresh parsley
salt and ground black pepper
fresh flat-leaf parsley sprigs,
   to garnish

**1** Bring a large pan of water to a boil. Add the rice and cook for about 10 minutes or until just tender. Drain, refresh under cold water and drain again. Let dry.

**2** Heat half the oil in a wok. Add the rice and stir-fry over medium heat for 2–3 minutes. Remove and set aside.

**3** Add the remaining oil to the wok. Add the onion and stir-fry for 2 minutes, until softened, then mix in the sliced mushrooms and stir-fry for 2 more minutes.

**4** Add all the nuts and stir-fry for 1 minute. Return the rice to the wok and toss over the heat for 3 minutes. Season with salt and pepper to taste. Stir in the chopped parsley and serve with a garnish of flat-leaf parsley sprigs.

**Cook's Tips**
• *When cooking in a wok, always preheat it. When it is hot, add the oil and swirl it around to coat the sides. Then let the oil heat up before adding any ingredients.*
• *It is possible to stir-fry in a frying pan, if you don't have a wok. However, the heat will be less evenly distributed, and it is harder to toss the ingredients without making a mess.*

# Rice with Green Beans & Mushrooms

Crunchy green beans and mushrooms are the star ingredients in this vegetarian dish.

**Serves 2**
¾ cup basmati rice
3 eggs
1½ cups green beans, trimmed
¼ cup butter
1 onion, finely chopped
3 cups brown cap
  mushrooms, quartered
2 tablespoons light cream
1 tablespoon chopped
  fresh parsley
salt and ground black pepper

**1** Rinse the rice several times in cold water. Drain thoroughly. Bring a large saucepan of lightly salted water to a boil, add the rice and cook for 10–12 minutes, until tender. Drain thoroughly and set aside.

**2** Half fill a second pan with water, add the eggs and bring to a boil over medium heat. Lower the heat and simmer gently for 8 minutes. Drain the eggs, cool them under cold water, then remove the shells.

**3** Bring another pan of water to a boil and cook the beans for 5 minutes. Drain, refresh under cold running water, then drain again.

**4** Melt the butter in a large, heavy frying pan. Add the onion and mushrooms and fry over medium heat, stirring occasionally, for 2–3 minutes.

**5** Stir in the beans and rice and cook for 2 minutes. Cut the hard-boiled eggs into wedges and add them to the pan.

**6** Stir in the cream and parsley, taking care not to break up the eggs. Season to taste with salt and pepper. Reheat the dish, but do not let it boil. Transfer to a warmed serving dish and serve immediately.

# Golden Vegetable Paella

Hearty enough for the hungriest guests, this takes very little time to prepare and cook.

**Serves 4**
pinch of saffron threads
3 cups hot vegetable stock
6 tablespoons olive oil
2 large onions, sliced
3 garlic cloves, chopped
1½ cups long-grain rice
⅓ cup wild rice
6 ounces pumpkin, chopped
1 large carrot, cut into
  matchstick strips
1 yellow bell pepper, seeded
  and sliced
4 tomatoes, peeled and chopped
1½ cups oyster
  mushrooms, quartered
salt and ground black pepper
strips of red, yellow and green bell
  pepper, to garnish

**1** Place the saffron in a small bowl with 4 tablespoons of the hot stock. Let stand for 5 minutes.

**2** Meanwhile, heat the oil in a paella pan or large, heavy frying pan. Add the onions and garlic and fry over low heat, stirring occasionally, for 3 minutes, until just beginning to soften.

**3** Add the long-grain rice and wild rice to the pan and toss for 2–3 minutes, until coated in oil. Add the stock to the pan, together with the pumpkin and the saffron threads and liquid. Stir the mixture as it comes to a boil, then reduce the heat to the lowest setting.

**4** Cover and cook very gently for 15 minutes, without lifting the lid. Add the carrot strips, yellow pepper and chopped tomatoes and season to taste with salt and pepper. Replace the lid and cook very gently for another 5 minutes or until the rice is almost tender.

**5** Add the oyster mushrooms, check the seasoning and cook, uncovered, for just enough time to soften the mushrooms without letting the paella stick to the pan. Garnish with the peppers and serve.

# Middle-Eastern Rice with Lentils

Part of the appeal of this spicy main meal dish lies in its sheer simplicity as well as the speed with which it can be cooked.

**Serves 4**
2 tablespoons sunflower oil
1 large onion, sliced
4–5 cardamom pods
½ teaspoon coriander
  seeds, crushed
½ teaspoon cumin
  seeds, crushed

small piece of fresh ginger root,
  finely chopped
1 cinnamon stick
1 garlic clove, crushed
¾ cup brown rice
about 3¾ cups vegetable stock
½ teaspoon ground turmeric
½ cup split red lentils
¼ cup sliced almonds, toasted
⅓ cup raisins
plain yogurt, to serve

**1** Heat the sunflower oil in a large saucepan. Add the onion and fry over medium heat, stirring occasionally, for 5 minutes, until softened.

**2** Crush the cardamom pods, extract the seeds and add them to the pan, together with the coriander seeds, cumin seeds, ginger, cinnamon stick and garlic. Stir over medium heat for 2–3 minutes.

**3** Add the rice, stirring to coat the grains in the spice mixture, then pour in the stock. Stir in the turmeric. Bring to a boil and then lower the heat, cover the pan with a tight-fitting lid and simmer for 15 minutes.

**4** Add the lentils to the pan, replace the lid and cook for 20 more minutes or until the rice and lentils are tender and all the stock has been absorbed. If the mixture seems to be drying out, stir in a little more stock.

**5** When all the stock has been absorbed, put the rice mixture into a heated serving dish. Remove and discard the cinnamon stick. Sprinkle the toasted almonds and raisins on top. Serve with the yogurt.

# Quick Basmati & Nut Pilaf

Light and fragrant basmati rice cooks perfectly using this simple pilaf method.

**Serves 4–6**
generous 1 cup basmati rice
1–2 tablespoons sunflower oil
1 onion, chopped
1 garlic clove, crushed
1 large carrot, coarsely grated
1 teaspoon cumin seeds

2 teaspoons ground coriander
2 teaspoons black mustard seeds
4 cardamom pods
scant 2 cups vegetable stock
1 bay leaf
¾ cup unsalted nuts
salt and ground black pepper
chopped fresh parsley or cilantro
  to garnish

**1** Rinse the rice in several changes of cold water. If there is enough time, let it soak for 30 minutes in the water used for the final rinse.

**2** Heat the oil in a large shallow pan and fry the onion, garlic and carrot for 2–3 minutes. Stir in the rice and spices and cook for 1–2 minutes, so that the grains are coated in oil.

**3** Pour in the stock, add the bay leaf and season to taste with salt and pepper. Bring to a boil, then lower the heat, cover and simmer very gently for about 10 minutes.

**4** Remove from heat without lifting the lid—this helps the rice to firm up and cook more. Leave for about 5 minutes, then check the rice. If it is cooked, there will be small steam holes in the center. Discard the bay leaf and cardamom pods.

**5** Stir in the nuts and check the seasoning. Spoon the mixture into a serving dish and sprinkle the chopped parsley or cilantro on the surface. Serve immediately.

> **Cook's Tip**
> *Use whatever nuts are your favorites, such as almonds, cashews or pistachios—even unsalted peanuts are good.*

# Vegetable Couscous with Saffron & Harissa

A North African favorite, this spicy dish makes an excellent midweek supper.

**Serves 4**

3 tablespoons olive oil
1 onion, chopped
2 garlic cloves, crushed
1 teaspoon ground cumin
1 teaspoon paprika
14-ounce can chopped tomatoes
1¼ cups vegetable stock
1 cinnamon stick
generous pinch of saffron threads
4 baby eggplant, quartered

8 baby zucchini, trimmed and
    quartered lengthways
8 baby carrots
1⅓ cups couscous
14-ounce can chickpeas, drained
    and rinsed
¾ cup prunes
3 tablespoons chopped
    fresh parsley
3 tablespoons chopped cilantro
2–3 teaspoons harissa
salt

**1** Heat the olive oil in a large saucepan and cook the onion and garlic gently for 5 minutes, until soft. Add the cumin and paprika and cook, stirring, for 1 minute. Stir in the tomatoes, stock, cinnamon stick, saffron, eggplant, zucchini and carrots. Season with salt. Bring to a boil, lower the heat, cover and cook for 20 minutes.

**2** Select a colander that will fit over the pan of vegetables. Line it with a double thickness of muslin. Soak the couscous according to the instructions on the package.

**3** Add the chickpeas and prunes to the vegetables and cook for 5 minutes. Fork the couscous to break up any lumps and spread it in the colander. Place it on top of the vegetables, cover, and cook for 5 minutes, until the couscous is hot.

**4** Put the couscous into a warmed dish. Using a draining spoon, add the vegetables. Spoon on a little of the cooking liquid, add the parsley and cilantro and toss gently to combine. Stir the harissa into the remaining sauce and serve separately.

# Spiced Couscous with Halloumi

Zucchini ribbons add color and flavor to this delicious dish.

**Serves 4**

1⅔ cups couscous
generous 2 cups boiling water
1 bay leaf
1 cinnamon stick
2 tablespoons olive oil, plus extra
    for brushing
1 large red onion, chopped
2 garlic cloves, chopped
1 teaspoon mild chili powder

1 teaspoon ground cumin
1 teaspoon ground coriander
5 cardamom pods, bruised
¼ cup whole blanched
    almonds, toasted
1 peach, pitted and diced
2 tablespoons butter
3 zucchini, sliced lengthwise
    into ribbons
8 ounces Halloumi cheese, sliced
salt and ground black pepper
chopped fresh flat-leaf parsley,
    to garnish

**1** Place the couscous in a bowl and pour in the boiling water. Add the bay leaf and cinnamon stick and season with salt. Leave the couscous for 10 minutes.

**2** Meanwhile, heat the oil in a large heavy pan and sauté the onion and garlic until the onion has softened, stirring occasionally. Stir in the chili powder, cumin, coriander and cardamom pods and cook for another 3 minutes.

**3** Fork the couscous to break up any lumps, then add it to the pan, with the almonds, diced peach and butter. Heat through for 2 minutes.

**4** Brush a griddle with olive oil and heat until very hot. Turn down the heat to medium, then place the zucchini on the griddle and cook for 5 minutes, until tender and slightly charred. Turn them over, add the Halloumi and continue cooking for 5 more minutes, turning the Halloumi halfway through.

**5** Remove the cinnamon stick, bay leaf and cardamom pods from the couscous mixture, then pile it on a plate and season to taste with salt and pepper. Top with the Halloumi and zucchini. Sprinkle the parsley on top and serve.

# Goat Cheese Kasha

Kasha is a Russian staple of cooked grains. Buckwheat is conventionally used but has a strong flavor. Here it is moderated with couscous.

**Serves 4**
1 cup couscous
3 tablespoons buckwheat
¼ cup dried cèpes
3 eggs, lightly beaten
4 tablespoons chopped
   fresh parsley

2 teaspoons chopped fresh thyme
4 tablespoons olive oil
3 tablespoons walnut oil
6 ounces crumbly white
   goat cheese
½ cup broken walnuts, toasted
salt and ground black pepper
fresh parsley sprigs,
   to garnish
rye bread and a mixed salad,
   to serve

**1** Place the couscous, buckwheat and cèpes in a bowl, cover with boiling water and let soak for 15 minutes. Drain off any excess liquid.

**2** Place the mixture in a large nonstick frying pan and stir in the eggs. Season with plenty of salt and pepper. Cook over medium heat, stirring with a wooden spoon, until the mixture looks like grainy scrambled eggs. Do not let it get too dry.

**3** Stir in the parsley, thyme, olive oil and walnut oil. Crumble in the goat cheese and stir in the walnuts.

**4** Transfer to a large serving dish, garnish with fresh parsley sprigs, and serve hot with rye bread and a mixed salad.

### Cook's Tip
*Cèpe is the French name for the* Boletus edulis *mushroom. As the dried mushrooms are widely used in Italian cuisine, packages may also be labeled porcini (little pigs), the Italian name. Dried bay boletus mushrooms* (Boletus badius) *are also available, but the flavor is inferior to that of cèpes.*

# Eggplant Pilaf

This hearty dish is made with bulghur and eggplant, flavored with fresh mint. It is a perfect choice for a mid-week supper, as it can be prepared within 15 minutes.

**Serves 2**
2 medium eggplant
4–6 tablespoons sunflower oil
1 small onion, finely chopped
1 cup bulghur wheat

scant 2 cups vegetable stock
2 tablespoons pine nuts, toasted
1 tablespoon chopped fresh mint
salt and ground black pepper

**For the garnish**
lime wedges
lemon wedges
torn mint leaves

**1** Trim the ends from the eggplant, then slice them lengthwise. Cut each slice into neat sticks and then into ½-inch dice.

**2** Heat 4 tablespoons of the oil in a large, heavy frying pan. Add the onion and fry over medium heat for 1 minute. Add the diced eggplant. Increase the heat to high and cook, stirring frequently, for about 4 minutes, until just tender. Add the remaining oil if needed.

**3** Stir in the bulghur, mixing well, then pour in the vegetable stock. Bring to a boil, then lower the heat and simmer for 10 minutes or until all the liquid has evaporated. Season to taste with salt and pepper.

**4** Stir in the pine nuts and mint, then spoon the pilaf onto individual plates. Garnish each portion with lime and lemon wedges. Sprinkle with torn mint leaves for extra color and serve immediately.

### Variation
*Use zucchini instead of eggplant, or, for something completely different, substitute pumpkin or acorn squash.*

# Braised Barley & Vegetables

One of the oldest cultivated cereals, barley has a nutty color and slightly chewy texture. It makes a warming and filling dish when combined with a selection of root vegetables.

**Serves 4**
2 tablespoons sunflower oil
1 large onion, chopped
2 celery stalks, sliced
2 carrots, halved lengthwise
   and sliced
1 cup pearl barley
1 large piece of rutabaga, about
   8 ounces, cubed
1 large potato, about
   8 ounces, cubed
2 cups vegetable stock
salt and ground black pepper
celery leaves, to garnish

**1** Heat the oil in a large pan. Add the onion and fry over low heat, stirring occasionally, for 5 minutes, until softened. Add the sliced celery and carrots and cook for 3–4 minutes or until the onion is starting to brown.

**2** Add the barley, then stir in the rutabaga and potato. Pour in the stock and season to taste with salt and pepper. Bring to a boil, then lower the heat and cover the pan.

**3** Simmer, stirring occasionally, for 40 minutes or until most of the stock has been absorbed and the barley is tender.

**4** Spoon onto warmed serving plates, garnish with the celery leaves and serve.

**Variations**
• This tastes good with feta cheese, especially if you use the cubes that are conveniently packed in oil. Toss them in to the mixture just before serving and drizzle on a little of the oil from the jar, if desired.
• You can substitute or add other vegetables, such as celeriac or parsnips. For a more summery version of the dish, use fennel, zucchini and fava beans.

# Beet Casserole

Maybe beets aren't the obvious choice for a casserole, but this sweet-and-sour dish is delicious.

**Serves 4**
1/4 cup butter
1 onion, chopped
2 garlic cloves, crushed
1 1/2 pounds raw beets, peeled
   and diced
2 large carrots, diced
1 1/2 cups button mushrooms
1 1/4 cups vegetable stock
grated zest and juice of 1/2 lemon
2 bay leaves
1 tablespoon chopped fresh mint
salt and ground black pepper

**For the hot dressing**
2/3 cup sour cream
1/2 teaspoon paprika, plus extra
   to garnish

**1** Melt the butter in a nonaluminum pan. Add the onion and garlic and fry over low heat for 5 minutes. Add the beets, carrots and mushrooms and fry for 5 more minutes. Pour in the stock, then add the lemon zest and bay leaves. Season with salt and pepper. Bring to a boil, lower the heat, cover and simmer for 1 hour or until the vegetables are soft.

**2** Turn off the heat and stir in the lemon juice and mint. Cover the pan and let it stand for 5 minutes.

**3** Meanwhile, make the dressing. Gently heat the sour cream and paprika in a small pan, stirring constantly, until bubbling.

**4** Transfer the beet mixture to a serving bowl, spoon on the dressing and sprinkle with a little more paprika. Serve.

**Cook's Tips**
• Wear rubber or plastic gloves to avoid staining your hands when preparing beets.
• Cooking beets in an aluminum pan may cause discoloration of pan and food.

# Vegetable Casserole with Cheese Triangles

A sort of savory cobbler, this casserole is topped with scone batter. The combination is irresistible.

**Serves 6**
2 tablespoons oil
2 garlic cloves, crushed
1 onion, roughly chopped
1 teaspoon mild chili powder
1 pound potatoes, peeled and
   roughly chopped
1 pound celeriac, peeled and
   roughly chopped
12 ounces carrots,
   roughly chopped
12 ounces trimmed leeks,
   roughly chopped
3 cups brown cap
   mushrooms, halved

4 teaspoons all-purpose flour
2¹/₂ cups vegetable stock
14-ounce can chopped tomatoes
1 tablespoon tomato paste
2 tablespoons chopped
   fresh thyme
14-ounce can kidney beans,
   drained and rinsed
salt and ground black pepper

**For the topping**
2 cups self-rising flour
¹/₂ cup butter
1 cup grated Cheddar cheese
2 tablespoons snipped
   fresh chives
about 5 tablespoons milk

**1** Preheat the oven to 350°F. Heat the oil in a large flameproof casserole. Add the garlic and onion and fry over low heat, stirring occasionally, for 5 minutes. Stir in the chili powder and cook for 1 more minute.

**2** Add the potatoes, celeriac, carrots, leeks and mushrooms. Cook for 3–4 minutes. Stir in the flour and cook, stirring constantly, for 1 more minute.

**3** Stir in the stock, then the tomatoes, tomato paste and thyme and season well with salt and pepper. Bring to a boil, stirring. Cover and bake for 30 minutes.

**4** Meanwhile, make the topping. Sift the flour into a bowl and rub in the butter with your fingertips, then stir in half the grated cheese, together with the chives and plenty of seasoning. Add just enough milk to bind the dry ingredients and mix quickly to form a soft dough.

**5** Pat out the dough to a round, about 1 inch thick. Cut it into 12 triangles. Brush with a little milk.

**6** Remove the casserole from the oven and stir in the beans. Overlap the triangles on top, and sprinkle with the remaining cheese. Return to the oven, uncovered, for 20–25 minutes or until the scone topping is golden brown and cooked through. Serve immediately.

**Cook's Tip**
*Use any of your favorite vegetables, as long as the overall weight remains the same. Firm vegetables may need a little more cooking.*

# Vegetarian Cassoulet

Every town in southwest France has its own version of this popular classic. Serve this hearty vegetable version with warm French bread.

**Serves 4–6**
1³/₄ cups dried haricot beans,
   soaked overnight in water
   to cover
1 bay leaf
7 cups cold water
2 onions
3 cloves
1 teaspoon olive oil
2 garlic cloves, crushed

2 leeks, thickly sliced
12 baby carrots
1¹/₂ cups button mushrooms
14-ounce can chopped tomatoes
1 tablespoon tomato paste
1 teaspoon paprika
1 tablespoon chopped
   fresh thyme
2 tablespoons chopped
   fresh parsley
2 cups fresh white bread crumbs
salt and ground black pepper

**1** Drain the beans. Rinse them under cold running water, then put them in a large pan. Add the bay leaf, then pour in the water. Bring to a boil and cook rapidly for 10 minutes.

**2** Peel one of the onions and spike it with cloves. Add it to the beans and lower the heat. Cover and simmer gently for 1 hour, until the beans are almost tender. Drain, reserving the stock but discarding the bay leaf and onion.

**3** Preheat the oven to 325°F. Chop the remaining onion. Heat the oil in a large flameproof casserole. Add the chopped onion and garlic and fry over low heat, stirring occasionally, for 5 minutes or until softened. Add the leeks, carrots, mushrooms, chopped tomatoes, tomato paste, paprika and thyme to the casserole. Stir in 1⅔ cups of the reserved stock.

**4** Bring to a boil, cover and simmer gently for 10 minutes. Stir in the cooked beans and parsley. Season to taste, sprinkle with the fresh bread crumbs and bake, uncovered, for 35 minutes or until the topping is golden brown and crisp.

# Baked Cheese Polenta with Tomato Sauce

Polenta, or cornmeal, is a staple food in Italy. It is cooked like porridge and can be eaten soft. This version uses squares of set polenta, baked in a rich tomato sauce.

**Serves 4**

4 cups water
1 teaspoon salt
2 cups quick-cook polenta
1 teaspoon paprika
½ teaspoon ground nutmeg
2 tablespoons olive oil, plus extra
    for greasing
1 large onion, finely chopped
2 garlic cloves, crushed
2 14-ounce cans
    chopped tomatoes
1 tablespoon tomato paste
1 teaspoon sugar
3 ounces Gruyère cheese, grated
salt and ground black pepper

**1** Preheat the oven to 400°F. Line a 11 × 7-inch baking pan with plastic wrap. Pour the water into a large heavy pan and add the salt.

**2** Bring the water to a boil. Pour in the polenta in a steady stream and cook, stirring constantly, for 5 minutes. Beat in the paprika and nutmeg, then pour the mixture into the prepared pan. Level the surface. Let cool.

**3** Heat the oil in a pan. Add the onion and garlic and fry over low heat, stirring occasionally, for 5 minutes, until soft. Stir in the tomatoes, tomato paste and sugar and season with salt and pepper to taste. Simmer for 20 minutes.

**4** Turn out the polenta onto a chopping board and cut it into 2-inch squares. Place half the polenta squares in a greased ovenproof dish. Spoon on half the tomato sauce and sprinkle with half the grated cheese. Repeat the layers of polenta, sauce and cheese.

**5** Bake the polenta for about 25 minutes, until the top is golden and bubbling. Serve immediately.

# Polenta with Mushroom Sauce

This is a fine example of just how absolutely delicious soft polenta can be. Topped with a robust mushroom and tomato sauce, it tastes quite sublime.

**Serves 4**

5 cups vegetable stock
3 cups fine polenta
    or cornmeal
⅔ cup freshly grated
    Parmesan cheese
salt and ground black pepper

**For the sauce**

¼ cup dried porcini mushrooms
⅔ cup hot water
1 tablespoon olive oil
¼ cup butter
1 onion, finely chopped
1 carrot, finely chopped
1 celery stalk, finely chopped
2 garlic cloves, crushed
6 cups mixed chestnut and
    large flat mushrooms,
    roughly chopped
½ cup red wine
14-ounce can chopped tomatoes
1 teaspoon tomato paste
1 tablespoon chopped
    fresh thyme

**1** Make the sauce. Soak the dried mushrooms in the hot water for 20 minutes. Drain, reserving the liquid, and chop roughly.

**2** Heat the oil and butter in a saucepan and fry the onion, carrot, celery and garlic gently for 5 minutes, until beginning to soften. Raise the heat and add the fresh and dried mushrooms. Cook for 10 minutes. Pour in the wine and cook rapidly for 2–3 minutes, then add the tomatoes and strained, reserved soaking liquid. Stir in the tomato paste and thyme and season. Lower the heat and simmer for 20 minutes.

**3** Meanwhile, heat the stock in a large heavy saucepan. Add a pinch of salt. As soon as it simmers, add the polenta in a fine stream, whisking until the mixture is smooth. Cook for 30 minutes, stirring constantly, until the polenta comes away from the pan. Stir in half the Parmesan and some pepper.

**4** Divide among four heated bowls and top each with sauce. Sprinkle with the remaining Parmesan.

# Onions Stuffed with Goat Cheese & Sun-dried Tomatoes

Roasted onions and creamy goat cheese truly are a winning combination.

**Serves 4**
4 large onions
oil, for greasing
5 ounces goat cheese, crumbled
1 cup fresh bread crumbs
8 sun-dried tomatoes in olive oil, drained and chopped

1–2 garlic cloves, finely chopped
½ teaspoon chopped fresh thyme
2 tablespoons chopped fresh parsley, plus extra to garnish
1 small egg, beaten
3 tablespoons pine nuts, toasted
2 tablespoons olive oil (from the tomatoes)
salt and ground black pepper

**1** Bring a large pan of lightly salted water to a boil. Add the whole onions in their skins and boil for 10 minutes. Drain and cool, then cut each onion in half horizontally and peel.

**2** Using a teaspoon to scoop out the flesh, remove the center of each onion, leaving a thick shell. Reserve the flesh and place the shells in an oiled ovenproof dish. Preheat the oven to 375°F.

**3** Chop the scooped-out onion flesh and place it in a bowl. Add the goat cheese, bread crumbs, sun-dried tomatoes, garlic, thyme, parsley and egg. Mix well, then season to taste with salt and pepper. Add the toasted pine nuts.

**4** Divide the stuffing among the onions and cover with aluminum foil. Bake for about 25 minutes. Uncover, drizzle with the oil and cook for 30–40 more minutes, until bubbling and well cooked. Baste occasionally during cooking.

**Variation**
• Omit the goat cheese and add 4 ounces finely chopped mushrooms and 1 grated carrot.

# Bell Peppers with Egg & Lentils

A bread crumb or rice filling is commonly used for bell peppers. Lentils make a delicious change and the eggs add extra protein.

**Serves 4**
scant ½ cup Puy lentils
½ teaspoon ground turmeric
½ teaspoon ground coriander
½ teaspoon paprika

scant 2 cups vegetable stock
2 large bell peppers, halved lengthwise and seeded
a little vegetable oil
1 tablespoon chopped fresh mint
4 eggs
salt and ground black pepper
cilantro sprigs, to garnish

**1** Put the lentils in a pan with the spices and stock. Bring to a boil, stirring occasionally, then lower the heat and simmer for 30–40 minutes. If necessary, add some water during cooking.

**2** Preheat the oven to 375°F. Brush the peppers lightly with oil and place them close together, cut-sides facing up, in a roasting pan. Stir the mint into the lentils, then fill the peppers with the mixture.

**3** Beat one egg in a small bowl and carefully pour it over the lentil mixture in one of the peppers. Using a small spoon, gently stir it into the lentils and season with salt and pepper to taste. Repeat with the remaining eggs and peppers. Bake for 10 minutes, garnish with cilantro and serve.

**Variations**
• Add a little extra flavor to the lentil mixture by mixing in chopped onion and tomatoes sautéed in olive oil before filling the peppers.
• Use beef tomatoes instead of peppers. Cut a lid off the tomatoes and scoop out the flesh with a teaspoon. Fill with the lentils and egg and bake.
• For an extra touch of spice, add one or two finely chopped fresh green chiles to the lentils.

# Baked Stuffed Squash

A creamy, sweet and nutty filling makes the perfect topping for tender squash.

**Serves 4**
2 butternut or acorn squash, about 1¼ pounds each
1 tablespoon olive oil
1 cup drained canned corn kernels
½ cup unsweetened chestnut purée
5 tablespoons low-fat yogurt
2 ounces fresh goat cheese
salt and ground black pepper
snipped chives, to garnish
mixed salad greens, to serve

**1** Preheat the oven to 350°F. Cut the squash in half lengthwise, scoop out the seeds and place the halves, skin-side down, on a baking sheet.

**2** Brush the squash flesh lightly with the olive oil, then bake for about 30 minutes.

**3** Meanwhile, mix the corn, chestnut purée and yogurt in a bowl. Season to taste with salt and pepper.

**4** Remove the squash from the oven and divide the chestnut mixture between them, spooning it into the hollows.

**5** Top each half with one-quarter of the goat cheese and return to the oven for 10–15 minutes. Garnish with snipped chives and serve immediately with salad greens.

> **Variations**
> • Use mozzarella or other mild, soft cheeses instead of the goat cheese. The cheese can be omitted entirely for a lower-fat alternative.
> • Add 1–2 tablespoons finely chopped nuts, such as almonds or pistachios to the filling.
> • This filling also goes well with zucchini. Cut four to six large zucchini in half lengthwise and bake for about 20 minutes.

# Stuffed Mushrooms with Pine Nut Tarator

Portabello mushrooms have a rich flavor and a meaty texture. They go well with this fragrant and tasty herb and lemon stuffing.

**Serves 4–6**
3 tablespoons olive oil, plus extra for brushing
1 onion, finely chopped
2 garlic cloves, crushed
2 tablespoons chopped fresh thyme or 1 teaspoon dried thyme
8 portabello mushrooms, stems removed and finely chopped
14-ounce can adzuki beans, drained and rinsed
1 cup fresh whole-wheat bread crumbs
juice of 1 lemon
6½ ounces goat cheese, crumbled
salt and ground black pepper

**For the pine nut tarator**
⅔ cup pine nuts, toasted
1 cup cubed white bread
2 garlic cloves, chopped
scant 1 cup milk
3 tablespoons olive oil

**1** Preheat the oven to 400°F. Heat the oil in a large, heavy frying pan. Add the onion and garlic and fry over low heat, stirring occasionally, for 5 minutes, until softened. Add the thyme and the mushroom stems and cook for 3 more minutes, stirring occasionally, until tender.

**2** Stir the adzuki beans into the mixture with the bread crumbs and lemon juice, season well with salt and pepper, then cook for 2 minutes, until heated through.

**3** Remove the pan from heat and, using a fork or potato masher, mash the mixture until about two-thirds of the beans are broken up, leaving the remaining beans whole.

**4** Brush an ovenproof dish and the tops and sides of the mushroom caps with oil. Place them, gills facing up, in the dish and top each one with a spoonful of the bean mixture. Cover with aluminum foil and bake for 20 minutes.

**5** Remove the foil. Top each mushroom with goat cheese and bake for 15 more minutes or until the cheese has melted and the mushrooms are tender.

**6** Meanwhile, make the pine nut tarator. Put the pine nuts, bread and garlic in a food processor and process briefly. Add the milk and olive oil and process until creamy. Serve the tarator with the mushrooms.

> **Cook's Tip**
> Use dried beans if you prefer. Soak 1 cup beans overnight in cold water, then drain and rinse well. Place in a pan with water to cover and boil rapidly for 10 minutes. Reduce the heat, cook for 30 minutes, until tender, then drain. Alternatively, cover the dried beans with boiling water and let soak for about 3 hours before draining and cooking.

# Eggplant Parmigiana

A classic Italian dish, in which blissfully tender sliced eggplant are layered with melting creamy mozzarella, fresh Parmesan and a good homemade tomato sauce.

**Serves 4–6**
3 medium eggplant, thinly sliced
olive oil, for brushing
11 ounces mozzarella
  cheese, sliced
1 1/3 cups freshly grated
  Parmesan cheese

2–3 tablespoons natural-colored
  dried bread crumbs
salt and ground black pepper
fresh basil sprigs, to garnish

**For the sauce**
2 tablespoons olive oil
1 onion, finely chopped
2 garlic cloves, crushed
14-ounce can chopped tomatoes
1 teaspoon sugar
about 6 fresh basil leaves

**1** Layer the eggplant slices in a colander, sprinkling each layer with a little salt. Drain over a sink for about 20 minutes, then rinse thoroughly under cold running water and pat dry with paper towels.

**2** Preheat the oven to 400°F. Lay the eggplant slices on nonstick baking sheets, brush the tops with olive oil and bake for 10–15 minutes, until softened.

**3** Meanwhile, make the sauce. Heat the oil in a pan. Add the onion and garlic and fry over low heat, stirring occasionally, for 5 minutes. Add the canned tomatoes and sugar and season with salt and pepper to taste. Bring to a boil, then lower the heat and simmer for about 10 minutes, until reduced and thickened. Tear the basil leaves into small pieces and stir them into the sauce.

**4** Layer the eggplant in a greased shallow ovenproof dish with the sliced mozzarella, the tomato sauce and the grated Parmesan, ending with a layer of Parmesan mixed with the bread crumbs. Bake for 20–25 minutes, until golden brown and bubbling. Let stand for 5 minutes before cutting. Serve garnished with basil.

# Savoy Cabbage Stuffed with Mushroom Barley

Savoy cabbage is delicious with this hearty stuffing of barley and wild mushrooms.

**Serves 4**
1/4 cup butter
2 medium onions,
  chopped
1 celery stalk, sliced

3 cups assorted wild and
  cultivated mushrooms
3/4 cup pearl barley
1 fresh thyme sprig
3 cups water
2 tablespoons cashew butter
1/2 vegetable stock cube
1 head Savoy cabbage
salt and ground black pepper

**1** Melt the butter in a large pan and fry the onions and celery over low heat, stirring occasionally, for 5 minutes, until soft. Add the mushrooms and cook until they release their juices, then add the barley, thyme, water and the nut butter. Bring to a boil, lower the heat, cover and simmer for 30 minutes. Crumble in the piece of stock cube, cover again and simmer for 20 more minutes. Season to taste with salt and pepper.

**2** Separate the cabbage leaves and cut out the thick stem. Blanch the leaves in a pan of lightly salted boiling water for 3–4 minutes. Drain, refresh under cold running water and then drain well again.

**3** Lay an 18-inch square of muslin over a steaming basket. Reconstruct the cabbage by lining the muslin with large cabbage leaves. Spread a layer of mushroom barley over the leaves.

**4** Cover with a second layer of leaves and filling. Continue until the center is full. Draw together the opposite corners of the muslin and tie firmly.

**5** Set the steaming basket in a saucepan containing 1 inch of simmering water. Cover and steam for 30 minutes.

**6** To serve, place on a warmed serving plate, untie the muslin and carefully pull it from underneath the cabbage.

# Potato Rösti & Tofu Stacks

Although this dish has several components, it is not difficult to make. Serve it with mixed salad greens.

**Serves 4**

5 ounces firm tofu (bean curd), cut into 1/2-inch cubes
4 large potatoes, total weight about 2 pounds, peeled
sunflower oil, for frying
2 tablespoons sesame seeds, toasted
salt and ground black pepper

**For the marinade**

2 tablespoons tamari or dark soy sauce
1 tablespoon honey
2 garlic cloves, crushed
1 1/2-inch piece of fresh ginger root, grated
1 teaspoon toasted sesame oil

**For the sauce**

1 tablespoon olive oil
8 tomatoes, halved, seeded and chopped

**1** Mix all the marinade ingredients in a shallow dish. Add the tofu, spoon on the marinade and marinate for 1 hour.

**2** Cook the potatoes in a large pan of boiling water for 10–15 minutes, until almost tender. Let cool, then grate coarsely. Season well. Preheat the oven to 400°F.

**3** Lift out the tofu from the marinade. Spread it out on a baking sheet and bake for 20 minutes, turning occasionally, until the cubes are golden and crisp.

**4** Form the potato mixture into four cakes. Heat a frying pan with just enough oil to cover the bottom. Place the cakes in the pan and flatten them to rounds about 1/2 inch thick. Cook for 6 minutes, until golden and crisp underneath. Carefully turn them over and cook the undersides for 6 minutes, until golden.

**5** Meanwhile, make the sauce. Heat the oil in a pan, add the reserved marinade and the tomatoes and simmer, stirring occasionally, for 10 minutes. Press through a sieve, then reheat.

**6** To serve, place a rösti on each plate. Pile the tofu on top, spoon on the sauce and sprinkle with the sesame seeds.

# Tomato Bread & Butter Pudding

This is a great family dish and is ideal when you don't have time to cook because it can be prepared in advance.

**Serves 4**

1/4 cup butter, softened
1 tablespoon red pesto sauce
1 garlic and herb focaccia

5 ounces mozzarella cheese, thinly sliced
2 large ripe tomatoes, sliced
1 1/4 cups milk
3 large eggs
1 teaspoon fresh chopped oregano, plus extra leaves to garnish
2/3 cup grated Pecorino cheese
salt and ground black pepper

**1** Preheat the oven to 350°F. Mix the butter and pesto sauce in a small bowl. Slice the herb bread and spread one side of each slice with the pesto mixture.

**2** In an oval ovenproof dish, layer the slices of herb bread with the mozzarella and tomatoes, overlapping each new layer with the next.

**3** Beat the milk, eggs and oregano in a pitcher, season well with salt and pepper and pour on the bread. Let stand for at least 5 minutes.

**4** Sprinkle on the grated cheese and bake for 40 minutes or until golden brown and just set. Sprinkle with whole oregano leaves, and serve immediately.

**Cook's Tip**
*The longer this stands before baking, the better it will be. Try to leave it for at least half an hour before baking, if you have time.*

**Variation**
*Other cheeses that would go well with this dish include Fontina, Beaufort, Bel Paese and Taleggio.*

# Vegetable Crumble

This dish is popular with children, and even those who claim to dislike Brussels sprouts will dig into it eagerly.

**Serves 8**

1 pound potatoes, peeled and halved
2 tablespoons butter
8 ounces leeks, sliced
1 pound carrots, chopped
2 garlic cloves, crushed
3 cups mushrooms, thinly sliced
1 pound Brussels sprouts, sliced

salt and ground black pepper

**For the cheese crumble**

1/2 cup all-purpose flour
1/4 cup butter
1 cup fresh white bread crumbs
1/2 cup grated Cheddar cheese
2 tablespoons chopped fresh parsley
1 teaspoon English mustard powder

**1** Add the potatoes to a pan of lightly salted water. Bring to a boil and cook for about 15 minutes, until just tender.

**2** Meanwhile, melt the butter in a large pan. Add the leeks and carrots and cook over low heat, stirring occasionally, for 2–3 minutes. Add the garlic and mushrooms and cook, stirring occasionally, for 3 more minutes.

**3** Add the Brussels sprouts to the pan. Season to taste with pepper. Transfer the vegetable mixture to a 10-cup ovenproof dish.

**4** Preheat the oven to 400°F. Drain the potatoes and cut them into 1/2-inch-thick slices. Arrange them in an even layer on top of the other vegetables.

**5** To make the topping, sift the flour into a bowl and rub in the butter with your fingertips. Alternatively, process in a food processor until combined. Add the bread crumbs and mix in the grated Cheddar, parsley and mustard powder. Spoon the mixture evenly on the vegetables and bake for 20–30 minutes. Serve hot.

# Gorgonzola, Cauliflower & Walnut Gratin

A bubbly blue cheese sauce sprinkled with chopped nuts makes a great topping for cauliflower.

**Serves 4**

1 large cauliflower, broken into florets
2 tablespoons butter
1 medium onion, finely chopped

3 tablespoons all-purpose flour
scant 2 cups milk
5 ounces Gorgonzola, cut into pieces
1/2 teaspoon celery salt
pinch of cayenne pepper
3/4 cup chopped walnuts
salt
fresh parsley, to garnish

**1** Bring a large saucepan of lightly salted water to a boil and cook the cauliflower for 6 minutes. Drain and place in a flameproof gratin dish.

**2** Heat the butter in a heavy pan. Add the onion and fry over low heat, stirring occasionally, for 4–5 minutes, until softened but not colored.

**3** Stir in the flour and cook, stirring constantly, for 1 minute, then gradually add the milk, stirring until the sauce boils and thickens. Stir in the cheese, celery salt and cayenne.

**4** Preheat the broiler to medium hot. Spoon the sauce on the cauliflower, sprinkle on the chopped walnuts and broil until golden. Garnish with the parsley and serve.

**Variations**
• For a delicious alternative, replace the cauliflower with 2 1/2 pounds fresh broccoli or use a combination.
• For a milder flavor, use dolcelatte or Buxton blue cheese instead of Gorgonzola.
• For an even richer sauce, substitute 1 cup light cream for the same amount of milk.

# Pan Haggerty

A wonderfully old-fashioned dish, this has endured because it is easy to make and always tastes delicious.

**Serves 2**
2 tablespoons olive oil
2 tablespoons butter
1 pound potatoes, thinly sliced
1 large onion, halved and sliced
2 garlic cloves, crushed
1 cup grated aged
    Cheddar cheese
3 tablespoons snipped fresh
    chives, plus extra to garnish
salt and ground black pepper

**1** Heat the oil and butter in a large heavy frying pan that can safely be used under the broiler. (Cover a wooden handle with aluminum foil to protect it.) Remove the pan from heat and cover the bottom with a layer of potatoes, followed by layers of onion, garlic, cheese, chives and seasoning.

**2** Continue layering, ending with cheese. Cover with aluminum foil and cook over low heat for about 30 minutes or until the potatoes and onion are tender. Remove the foil.

**3** Preheat the broiler and slide the frying pan under it. Cook until the topping has browned. Garnish with chives and serve.

# Bubble & Squeak

Another classic British dish, this is very easy to make. It is a traditional way of using up leftover vegetables but is also worth cooking with fresh ingredients.

**Serves 4**
6 cups mashed potatoes
2 cups cooked cabbage
4 tablespoons sunflower oil
salt and ground black pepper

**1** Mix the potatoes and cabbage and season to taste.
**2** Heat the oil in a frying pan. Add the potato mixture and press down to make a cake. Fry over low heat until golden underneath. Invert onto a plate and return to the pan. Cook for about 10 minutes, until golden.

# Root Vegetable Gratin with Indian Spices

Subtly spiced with curry powder, turmeric, coriander and mild chili powder, this rich gratin is substantial enough to serve on its own for lunch or supper.

**Serves 4**
2 large potatoes, total weight
    about 1 pound
2 sweet potatoes, total weight
    about 10 ounces
6 ounces celeriac
1 tablespoon butter
1 teaspoon curry powder
1 teaspoon ground turmeric
1/2 teaspoon ground coriander
1 teaspoon mild chili powder
3 shallots, chopped
2/3 cup light cream
2/3 cup low-fat milk
salt and ground black pepper
chopped fresh flat-leaf parsley,
    to garnish

**1** Using a sharp knife or the slicing attachment of a food processor, slice the potatoes, sweet potatoes and celeriac thinly. Immediately place the vegetables in a bowl of cold water to prevent them from discoloring.

**2** Preheat the oven to 350°F. Heat half the butter in a heavy pan, and add the curry powder, turmeric and coriander and half the chili powder. Cook for 2 minutes, then let cool slightly.

**3** Drain the vegetables, then pat them dry with paper towels. Place them in a bowl, add the spice mixture and the shallots and mix well.

**4** Arrange the vegetables in a gratin dish, seasoning each layer. Mix the cream and milk in a pitcher. Pour the mixture on the vegetables, then sprinkle the remaining chili powder on top.

**5** Cover with waxed paper and bake for 45 minutes. Remove the waxed paper, dot with the remaining butter and bake for 50 more minutes, until the top is golden. Serve garnished with chopped fresh parsley.

# Mushroom Tart

A mixture of fresh wild mushrooms is best for this simple tart, but if the only mushrooms you can find are cultivated, it is still well worth making.

**Serves 4**

12 ounces shortcrust pastry, thawed if frozen
¼ cup butter
3 medium onions, halved and sliced
4 cups mushrooms, such as field mushrooms, cèpes and oyster mushrooms, sliced
leaves from 1 fresh thyme sprig, chopped
pinch of freshly grated nutmeg
3 tablespoons milk
4 tablespoons light cream
1 egg, plus 2 egg yolks
salt and ground black pepper

**1** Roll out the pastry on a lightly floured surface and line a 9-inch loose-bottomed tart pan. Place the flan case in the refrigerator to rest for about 1 hour.

**2** Preheat the oven to 375°F. Prick the pastry shell a few times with a fork, then line with aluminum foil and fill with baking beans. Bake blind for 25 minutes. Lift out the paper and baking beans and let the crust cool without removing it from the pan.

**3** Melt the butter in a heavy frying pan, add the sliced onions, cover and cook over very low heat, stirring occasionally, for about 20 minutes, until very soft and beginning to caramelize. Add the sliced mushrooms and thyme leaves, and continue cooking, stirring occasionally, for another 10 minutes. Season to taste with salt, freshly ground black pepper and nutmeg.

**4** Mix the milk and cream in a bowl and beat in the egg and egg yolks. Spoon the mushroom mixture into the crust and level the surface. Pour in the milk and egg mixture. Bake for 15–20 minutes, until the center is just firm to the touch. Cool slightly, then gently ease the tart out of the pan and place it on a plate for serving.

# Cheese & Onion Quiche

Perfect for picnics, parties and family suppers, this classic quiche celebrates a timeless combination.

**Serves 6–8**

1¾ cups all-purpose flour
½ teaspoon salt
scant ½ cup butter
about 4 tablespoons ice water

**For the filling**

2 tablespoons butter
1 large onion, thinly sliced
3 eggs
1¼ cups light cream
¼ teaspoon freshly grated nutmeg
scant 1 cup grated hard cheese, such as aged Cheddar, Gruyère or Manchego
salt and ground black pepper

**1** To make the pastry, sift the flour and salt into a bowl. Rub in the butter with your fingertips, then add enough ice water to make a firm dough. Knead lightly, wrap in plastic wrap and chill in the refrigerator for 20 minutes.

**2** Roll out the dough and line a 9-inch loose-bottomed tart pan. Prick the pastry shell a few times. Line the shell with aluminum foil and baking beans and chill again for about 15 minutes.

**3** Preheat the oven to 400°F. Place a baking sheet in the oven. Stand the tart pan on the baking sheet and bake blind for 15 minutes. Remove the beans and foil and return the pastry shell to the oven for 5 more minutes. Reduce the oven temperature to 350°F.

**4** To make the filling, melt the butter in a heavy frying pan. Add the onion and fry over low heat, stirring occasionally, for 5 minutes, until softened. In a bowl, beat together the eggs and cream. Add the nutmeg and season with salt and pepper.

**5** Spoon the onion mixture into the cooked pastry shell and sprinkle on the grated cheese. Pour in the egg and cream mixture. Bake the quiche for 35–40 minutes or until the filling has just set. Cool, then gently ease the quiche out of the pan and place it on a plate for serving.

# Cheese & Leek Sausages with Spicy Tomato Sauce

These are based on Glamorgan sausages, which are traditionally made using white or whole-wheat bread crumbs alone. However, adding mashed potatoes lightens the sausages and makes them much easier to handle.

**Serves 4**

2 tablespoons butter
6 ounces leeks, finely chopped
6 tablespoons cold
   mashed potatoes
2 cups fresh white bread crumbs
1¼ cups grated Caerphilly cheese
2 tablespoons chopped
   fresh parsley
1 teaspoon chopped fresh sage
2 large eggs, beaten

cayenne pepper
1 cup dry white bread crumbs
oil, for shallow frying
salt and ground black pepper

**For the sauce**

2 tablespoons olive oil
2 garlic cloves, thinly sliced
1 fresh red chile, seeded and
   finely chopped
1 small onion, finely chopped
1¼ pounds tomatoes, peeled,
   seeded and chopped
2–3 fresh thyme sprigs
2 teaspoons balsamic vinegar
pinch of light brown sugar
1–2 tablespoons chopped
   fresh marjoram

**1** Melt the butter in a frying pan. Add the leeks and fry over low heat, stirring occasionally, for 4–5 minutes, until softened but not browned.

**2** Mix the leeks with the mashed potatoes, fresh bread crumbs, grated cheese, parsley and sage. Add about two-thirds of the beaten eggs to bind the mixture. Season well with salt and pepper and add a good pinch of cayenne.

**3** Shape the mixture into 12 sausages. Put the remaining egg in a shallow dish and the dry bread crumbs in another shallow dish. Dip the sausages first in egg, then in the dry bread crumbs, shaking off any excess. Place the coated sausages on a plate, cover and chill in the refrigerator.

**4** To make the sauce, heat the olive oil over low heat. Add the garlic, chile and onion and fry, stirring occasionally, for 3–4 minutes. Add the tomatoes, thyme and vinegar. Season to taste with salt, pepper and sugar.

**5** Cook the sauce for 40–50 minutes, until much reduced. Remove the thyme and process the sauce in a blender into a purée. Return to the clean pan and add the marjoram. Reheat gently, then adjust the seasoning, adding more sugar, if necessary.

**6** Fry the sausages in shallow oil until golden brown on all sides. Drain on paper towels and serve with the sauce.

> **Variation**
> These sausages are also delicious served with aïoli, guacamole or chili jam.

# Mixed Vegetables with Artichokes

Baking a vegetable medley is a wonderfully easy way of producing a quick, simple, wholesome mid-week meal.

**Serves 4**

2 tablespoons olive oil
1½ pounds frozen fava beans
4 turnips, peeled and sliced
4 leeks, sliced

1 red bell pepper, seeded
   and sliced
7 ounces fresh spinach leaves
2 14-ounce cans artichoke
   hearts, drained
4 tablespoons pumpkin seeds
soy sauce
salt and ground black pepper

**1** Preheat the oven to 350°F. Pour the olive oil into a casserole and set aside.

**2** Cook the fava beans in a saucepan of lightly salted boiling water for about 10 minutes.

**3** Drain the fava beans and place them in the casserole. Add the turnips, leeks, red pepper slices, spinach and canned artichoke hearts.

**4** Cover the casserole and place it in the oven. Bake for 30–40 minutes or until the turnips are soft.

**5** Stir in the pumpkin seeds and a little soy sauce to taste. Season with ground black pepper and serve.

> **Cook's Tip**
> Serve this with pasta, rice, new potatoes or bread.

> **Variation**
> For a delicious change, top the cooked vegetables with a mixture of whole-wheat bread crumbs and grated Cheddar cheese. Broil until the cheese melts and the topping is golden.

# Vegetable Stew with Roasted Tomato & Garlic Sauce

This lightly-spiced, richly flavored stew makes a perfect match for couscous.

**Serves 6**

3 tablespoons olive oil
9 ounces shallots
1 large onion, chopped
2 garlic cloves, chopped
1 teaspoon cumin seeds
1 teaspoon ground
 coriander seeds
1 teaspoon paprika
2-inch piece cinnamon stick
2 fresh bay leaves
scant 2 cups vegetable stock
good pinch of saffron threads
1 pound carrots, thickly sliced
2 green bell peppers, seeded and
 thickly sliced

½ cup dried apricots, halved
 if large
1–1½ teaspoons ground toasted
 cumin seeds
1 pound squash, peeled, seeded
 and cut into chunks
salt and ground black pepper
3 tablespoons cilantro leaves,
 to garnish

**For the sauce**

2¼ pounds tomatoes, halved
about 1 teaspoon sugar
3 tablespoons olive oil
1–2 fresh red chiles, seeded
 and chopped
2–3 garlic cloves, chopped
1 teaspoon fresh thyme leaves

**1** Preheat the oven to 350°F. First make the sauce. Place the tomatoes, cut-sides facing up, in an ovenproof dish. Season with salt and pepper to taste, sprinkle the sugar on top, then drizzle on the olive oil. Roast for 30 minutes.

**2** Sprinkle the chiles, garlic and thyme on the tomatoes. Stir, then roast for another 30–45 minutes, until the tomatoes have collapsed but are still a little juicy. Cool, then process in a food processor or blender to make a thick sauce. Sieve to remove the seeds.

**3** Heat 2 tablespoons of the oil in a large, deep, frying pan. Add the shallots and cook over low heat, stirring frequently, until browned all over. Remove them from the pan and set aside.

**4** Add the chopped onion to the pan and cook over low heat, stirring occasionally, for 5–7 minutes, until softened. Stir in the garlic and cumin seeds and cook for 3–4 more minutes.

**5** Add the ground coriander seeds, paprika, cinnamon stick and bay leaves. Cook, stirring constantly, for 2 minutes, then mix in the stock, saffron, carrots and peppers. Season well with salt and pepper, cover and simmer gently for 10 minutes.

**6** Stir in the apricots, 1 teaspoon of the ground toasted cumin, the browned shallots and the squash. Stir in the tomato sauce. Cover and cook for another 5 minutes.

**7** Uncover the pan and continue to cook, stirring occasionally, for 10–15 minutes, until the vegetables are all fully cooked. Adjust the seasoning, adding more cumin and a pinch of sugar to taste. Remove and discard the cinnamon stick and bay leaves. Serve with the cilantro leaves.

# Roasted Vegetables with Salsa Verde

Fresh herbs are at the heart of the Italian salsa verde (green sauce). It tastes wonderful with the vegetable mixture. Serve it with rice or a mixture of rice and vermicelli.

**Serves 4**

3 zucchini, sliced lengthwise
1 large fennel bulb, cut
 into wedges
1 pound butternut squash, cut
 into ¾-inch chunks
12 shallots
2 red bell peppers, seeded and
 thickly sliced

4 plum tomatoes, halved
 and seeded
3 tablespoons olive oil
2 garlic cloves, crushed
1 teaspoon balsamic vinegar
salt and ground black pepper

**For the salsa verde**

3 tablespoons chopped fresh mint
6 tablespoons chopped fresh flat-
 leaf parsley
1 tablespoon Dijon mustard
juice of ½ lemon
2 tablespoons olive oil

**1** Preheat the oven to 425°F. Make the salsa verde. Place all the ingredients, except the olive oil, in a food processor or blender. Blend into a coarse paste, then add the oil, a little at a time, until the mixture forms a smooth purée. Season to taste with salt and pepper.

**2** In a large bowl, toss the zucchini, fennel, squash, shallots, peppers and tomatoes in the olive oil, garlic and balsamic vinegar. Leave for 10 minutes to allow the flavors to mingle.

**3** Place all the vegetables—other than the squash and tomatoes—in a roasting pan. Brush with half the oil and vinegar mixture and season with plenty of salt and pepper.

**4** Roast for 25 minutes. Remove the roasting pan from the oven, turn over the vegetables and brush with the rest of the oil and vinegar mixture. Add the squash and tomatoes and cook for 20–25 more minutes, until all the vegetables are tender and lightly charred around the edges. Spoon the roasted vegetables onto a serving platter and serve with the salsa verde.

# Bean Feast with Mexican Salsa

Canned beans really come into their own when you need to make a nutritious meal fast.

**Serves 4**

14-ounce can red kidney beans
14-ounce can flageolet beans
14-ounce can borlotti beans
1 tablespoon olive oil
1 small onion, finely chopped
3 garlic cloves, finely chopped
1 fresh red chile, seeded and
  finely chopped
1 red bell pepper, seeded and
  coarsely chopped
2 bay leaves
2 teaspoons chopped
  fresh oregano
2 teaspoons ground cumin
1 teaspoon ground coriander
½ teaspoon ground cloves
1 tablespoon dark
  brown sugar
1¼ cups vegetable stock
salt and ground black pepper
cilantro sprigs, to garnish

**For the salsa**

1 ripe but firm avocado
3 tablespoons freshly squeezed
  lime juice
1 small red onion, chopped
1 small fresh hot green chile,
  finely sliced
3 ripe plum tomatoes, peeled,
  seeded and chopped
3 tablespoons chopped cilantro

**1** Drain all the beans in a colander and rinse thoroughly. Heat the oil in a heavy saucepan. Add the onion and fry over low heat, stirring occasionally, for 3 minutes, until soft and transparent. Add the garlic, chile, red pepper, bay leaves, oregano, cumin, coriander and cloves.

**2** Stir well and cook for another 3 minutes, then add the sugar, beans and stock and cook for 8 minutes. Season with salt and pepper, and leave over low heat while you make the salsa.

**3** Cut the avocado in half, remove the pit, then peel it and dice the flesh. Toss it with the lime juice, then add all the remaining salsa ingredients and season with plenty of black pepper. Mix well.

**4** Spoon the beans into four serving bowls. Garnish with sprigs of cilantro and serve with the salsa.

# Tuscan Baked Beans

Cannellini beans are delicious with garlic and sage in this tasty dish, which can be served hot or at room temperature.

**Serves 6–8**

3½ cups dried cannellini beans
4 tablespoons olive oil
2 garlic cloves, crushed
3 fresh sage leaves
1 leek, thinly sliced
14-ounce can chopped tomatoes
salt and ground black pepper

**1** Carefully pick over the beans, place them in a large bowl and cover with water. Soak for at least 6 hours or overnight.

**2** Preheat the oven to 350°F. Heat the oil in a small saucepan. Add the garlic cloves and sage leaves and sauté over low heat, stirring occasionally, for 3–4 minutes. Remove the pan from heat.

**3** Drain the cannellini beans and put them in a saucepan with cold water to cover. Bring to a boil and boil vigorously for 10 minutes. Drain again.

**4** Put the beans into a casserole and add the leek and tomatoes. Stir in the garlic and sage, with the oil in which they were cooked. Add enough cold water to cover the beans by 1 inch. Mix well. Cover the casserole and bake for 1¾ hours.

**5** Remove the casserole from the oven, stir the bean mixture, and season to taste with salt and pepper. Return the casserole to the oven, uncovered, and cook for 15 more minutes, until the beans are tender. Remove from the oven and let stand for 7–8 minutes before serving.

**Cook's Tip**
*Cannellini beans are also known as Italian haricot beans.*

# Chickpea Stew

This hearty chickpea and vegetable stew makes a filling meal.

**Serves 4**
2 tablespoons olive oil
1 small onion, chopped
8 ounces carrots, halved and thinly sliced
1/2 teaspoon ground cumin
1 teaspoon ground coriander
2 tablespoons all-purpose flour

8 ounces zucchini, halved lengthwise and sliced
7-ounce can corn kernels, drained
14-ounce can chickpeas, drained and rinsed
2 tablespoons tomato paste
scant 1 cup hot vegetable stock
salt and ground black pepper
garlic-flavored mashed potatoes, to serve

**1** Heat the oil in a frying pan. Add the onion and carrots. Toss to coat the vegetables in the oil, then cook over medium heat, stirring occasionally, for 4 minutes.

**2** Stir in the ground cumin, coriander and flour. Cook, stirring constantly, for 1 minute.

**3** Add the zucchini slices to the pan with the corn, chickpeas, tomato paste and vegetable stock. Stir well. Cook for 10 minutes, stirring frequently.

**4** Taste the stew and season with salt and pepper. Serve immediately, with garlic-flavored mashed potatoes (see Cook's Tip), if you like.

**Cook's Tip**
For speedy garlic-flavored mashed potatoes, simply mash 1 1/2 pounds potatoes with garlic butter and stir in chopped fresh parsley and a little crème fraîche. Alternatively, add 10–12 peeled garlic cloves to the potatoes during cooking and then mash with the potatoes, adding butter, herbs and crème fraîche to taste. This may seem like an alarming quantity of garlic, but the flavor is actually quite subtle.

# Shepherdess Pie

A no-meat version of the timeless classic, this dish does not contain any dairy products, so it is also suitable for vegans.

**Serves 6–8**
2 1/4 pounds potatoes
3 tablespoons extra virgin olive oil
3 tablespoons sunflower oil
1 large onion, chopped
1 green bell pepper, chopped
2 carrots, coarsely grated

2 garlic cloves
1 1/4 cups mushrooms, roughly chopped
2 14-ounce cans adzuki beans, drained
2 1/2 cups vegetable stock
1 teaspoon yeast extract
2 bay leaves
1 teaspoon dried mixed herbs
dried bread crumbs or chopped nuts, for the topping
salt and ground black pepper

**1** Bring a large pan of water to a boil. Add the unpeeled potatoes and cook for about 30 minutes, until tender. Drain, reserving a little of the cooking water.

**2** As soon as the potatoes are cool enough to handle, remove the skins. Put the skinned potatoes in a bowl and mash them with the olive oil, adding enough of the reserved cooking water to make a smooth purée. Season well with salt and pepper.

**3** Heat the sunflower oil in a large, heavy frying pan. Add the chopped onion, green pepper, carrots and garlic and fry over low heat, stirring occasionally, for about 5 minutes, until softened.

**4** Stir in the mushrooms and beans. Cook for 2 more minutes, then stir in the stock, yeast extract, bay leaves and mixed herbs. Simmer for 15 minutes.

**5** Preheat the broiler. Remove and discard the bay leaves from the vegetable and bean mixture, then put into a gratin dish. Spoon on the mashed potatoes in dollops and sprinkle the bread crumbs or chopped nuts on top. Broil for 5 minutes, until the topping is golden brown. Serve immediately, right from the dish.

# Veggie Burgers

Unlike some commercially-produced veggie burgers, which are tasteless, these are full of flavor.

**Serves 4**

1 1/4 cups mushrooms, finely chopped
1 small onion, chopped
1 small zucchini, chopped
1 carrot, chopped
1/4 cup unsalted peanuts or cashews
2 cups fresh bread crumbs
2 tablespoons chopped fresh parsley
1 teaspoon yeast extract
fine oats or flour, for shaping
a little vegetable oil, for frying
salt and ground black pepper
salad, to serve

**1** Cook the mushrooms in a nonstick pan without oil, stirring them constantly, for 8–10 minutes to cook off all the moisture.

**2** Process the onion, zucchini, carrot and nuts in a food processor until the mixture starts to bind together. Scrape it into a bowl.

**3** Stir in the mushrooms, bread crumbs, parsley and yeast extract to taste. Season to taste. Coat your hands and a board with the oats or flour, then shape the mixture into four burgers. Chill in the refrigerator for 30 minutes.

**4** Heat a little oil in a nonstick frying pan and cook the burgers for 8–10 minutes, turning once, until they are cooked and golden brown. Serve hot with a crisp salad.

> **Cook's Tip**
> *These burgers can be cooked on a grill, but do not place them directly on the rack, as they are quite delicate and likely to break up. Use an aluminum foil pan and brush with a little vegetable oil on both sides.*

# Marinated Tofu Kebabs

Perfect partners for both the vegetarian burgers featured here, these kebabs are very easy to make.

**Serves 4**

2 tablespoons soy sauce
1 teaspoon peanut oil
1 teaspoon sesame oil
1 garlic clove, crushed
1 tablespoon grated fresh ginger root
1 tablespoon honey
2 cups firm tofu (bean curd), cut into 1/2-inch cubes
2 small zucchini, thickly sliced
8 baby onions
8 mushrooms

**1** Mix the soy sauce, peanut oil, sesame oil, garlic, ginger and honey in a shallow dish. Add the tofu cubes and marinate for 1–2 hours.

**2** Drain the tofu cubes, reserving the marinade, and thread onto four long metal skewers, alternating with the vegetables. Brush with the reserved marinade and broil or grill until golden, turning occasionally.

# Red Bean & Mushroom Burgers

Whether you cook these tasty burgers under the broiler or on the grill, they are sure to prove popular with everyone.

**Serves 4**

1 tablespoon olive oil, plus extra for brushing
1 small onion, finely chopped
1 garlic clove, crushed
1 teaspoon ground cumin
1 teaspoon ground coriander
1/2 teaspoon ground turmeric
1 1/2 cups finely chopped mushrooms
14-ounce can red kidney beans, drained and rinsed
2 tablespoons chopped cilantro
whole-wheat flour, for forming the burgers
salt and ground black pepper

**To serve**

warm pita bread
plain yogurt
green salad
tomatoes

**1** Heat the olive oil in a deep, heavy frying pan. Add the onion and garlic and fry over medium heat, stirring occasionally, for about 4 minutes, until softened. Add the cumin, ground coriander and turmeric and cook for 1 more minute, stirring constantly.

**2** Add the mushrooms and cook, stirring, until softened and dry. Remove the pan from heat.

**3** Put the beans into a bowl and then mash them with a fork. Stir them into the mushroom mixture, then add the cilantro, mixing thoroughly. Season well with salt and pepper.

**4** Using floured hands, form the mixture into four flat burger shapes. If the mixture is too sticky to handle, mix in a little flour. Preheat the broiler.

**5** Brush the burgers with oil and broil them for 8–10 minutes, turning once, until golden brown. Alternatively, cook on the grill, using a wire rack to turn them easily.

**6** Serve immediately with warm pita bread, yogurt, a crisp green salad and tomatoes.

## Pasta with Spicy Eggplant Sauce

There's no better way to satisfy hearty appetites than with a big bowl of pasta in a rich and robust sauce.

**Serves 4–6**
2 tablespoons olive oil
1 small fresh red chile
2 garlic cloves
2 handfuls fresh flat-leaf parsley, roughly chopped
1 pound eggplant, roughly chopped

1 handful of fresh basil leaves
scant 1 cup water
1 vegetable stock cube
8 ripe Italian plum tomatoes, peeled and finely chopped
4 tablespoons red wine
1 teaspoon sugar
1 envelope saffron powder
½ teaspoon ground paprika
3 cups dried pasta shapes
salt and ground black pepper
chopped fresh herb, to garnish

**1** Heat the oil in a large pan and add the chile, garlic cloves and half the chopped parsley. Smash the garlic cloves with a wooden spoon to release their juices, then cover the pan and cook over low heat, stirring occasionally, for about 10 minutes.

**2** Remove and discard the chile. Add the eggplant to the pan with the rest of the parsley and all the basil. Pour in half the water. Crumble in the stock cube and stir until it has dissolved, then cover and cook, stirring frequently, for about 10 minutes.

**3** Add the tomatoes, wine, sugar, saffron and paprika, season with salt and pepper, then pour in the remaining water. Stir well, replace the lid and cook, stirring occasionally, for 30–40 minutes.

**4** When the sauce is almost ready, bring a pan of lightly salted water to a boil. Cook the pasta for about 12 minutes, until it is *al dente*. Drain, put into a bowl and toss with the eggplant sauce. Garnish with fresh herbs, and serve.

> **Variation**
> This sauce can be layered with sheets of pasta and béchamel or cheese sauce to make a delicious vegetarian lasagne.

## Pasta with Sugocasa & Chile

This is a quick version of a popular Italian dish, *pasta arrabbiata*. The name literally translates as "furious pasta," a reference to the heat generated by the chile.

**Serves 4**
2 cups bottled sugocasa (see Cook's Tip)
2 garlic cloves, crushed
⅔ cup dry white wine

1 tablespoon sun-dried tomato paste
1 fresh red chile
11 ounces dried penne or other pasta shapes
4 tablespoons finely chopped fresh flat-leaf parsley
salt and ground black pepper
freshly grated Pecorino cheese, to serve

**1** Put the sugocasa, garlic, wine, sun-dried tomato paste and chile in a saucepan and bring to a boil. Lower the heat, cover and simmer for about 15 minutes, until thick.

**2** Meanwhile, bring a large pan of lightly salted water to a boil. Add the pasta shapes and cook for 10–12 minutes, until they are *al dente*.

**3** Using tongs, remove the chile from the sauce. Taste for seasoning. If you prefer a hotter taste, chop some or all of the chile and return it to the sauce.

**4** Drain the pasta and put it into a large bowl. Stir half the parsley into the sauce, then pour the sauce on the pasta and toss to mix. Serve immediately, sprinkled with grated Pecorino and the remaining parsley.

> **Cook's Tip**
> Sugocasa is sold in bottles and is sometimes labeled "crushed Italian tomatoes." It is finer than canned chopped tomatoes and coarser than passata, and so is ideal for pasta sauces, soups and stews.

# Mushroom & Chile Carbonara

Classic spaghetti carbonara hits the spot when chiles and mushrooms enter the equation.

**Serves 4**

$\frac{1}{2}$ ounce dried porcini mushrooms
$1\frac{1}{4}$ cups hot water
8 ounces spaghetti
2 tablespoons butter
1 tablespoon olive oil
1 garlic clove, crushed
3 cups button or chestnut mushrooms, sliced
1 teaspoon dried chile flakes
2 eggs
$1\frac{1}{4}$ cups light cream
salt and ground black pepper
freshly Parmesan cheese shavings and chopped parsley, to serve

**1** Put the dried mushrooms in a bowl, cover with the hot water and soak for 20–30 minutes. Drain, reserving the soaking liquid.

**2** Bring a large pan of lightly salted water to a boil and cook the spaghetti for 10–12 minutes, until it is *al dente*. Drain, rinse under cold water and drain again.

**3** Melt the butter in the oil in a separate pan. Add the garlic and cook gently for 30 seconds, then add the mushrooms, including the soaked dried mushrooms. Stir in the dried chile flakes and cook for about 2 minutes. Strain the liquid used for soaking the mushrooms and add it to the pan. Bring to a boil and cook over high heat until the sauce has reduced slightly.

**4** Beat the eggs with the cream and plenty of salt and pepper. Add the cooked spaghetti to the mushroom mixture and toss in the eggs and cream. Reheat, without boiling, and serve hot, sprinkled with the Parmesan and chopped parsley.

> **Variation**
> *If chile flakes are too hot and spicy for your taste, try the delicious alternative of peeled and chopped tomatoes with torn, fresh basil leaves.*

# Spinach, Tomato & Chile Pizza

The fiery flavor of hot chiles is soothed slightly by the spinach in the colorful topping on this pizza.

**Serves 2–3**

6 sun-dried tomatoes in oil, drained, plus 3 tablespoons oil from the jar
1 onion, chopped
2 garlic cloves, chopped
1–2 fresh red chiles, seeded and finely chopped
14-ounce can chopped tomatoes
1 tablespoon tomato paste
6 ounces fresh spinach
1 pizza crust, 10–12 inches in diameter
$\frac{3}{4}$ cup grated smoked Bavarian cheese
$1\frac{1}{2}$ cups grated aged Cheddar cheese
salt and ground black pepper

**1** Pour 2 tablespoons of the oil from the jar of sun-dried tomatoes into a large, heavy pan. Heat gently, then add the onion, garlic and chiles and fry over low heat, stirring occasionally, for about 5 minutes, until softened.

**2** Roughly chop the sun-dried tomatoes. Add them to the pan, together with the chopped tomatoes and tomato paste. Season with plenty of salt and pepper. Simmer uncovered, over low heat, stirring occasionally, for 15 minutes.

**3** Remove the stems from the spinach and wash the leaves in plenty of cold water. Drain well and pat dry with paper towels. Chop the spinach roughly.

**4** Stir the spinach into the sauce. Cook, stirring constantly, for 5–10 more minutes, until the spinach has just wilted and no excess moisture remains. Remove the pan from heat and set aside to cool.

**5** Preheat the oven to 425°F. Brush the pizza crust with the remaining tomato oil, then spoon the spinach mixture evenly over the surface, leaving a $\frac{1}{2}$-inch border all around. Sprinkle on the grated cheeses and bake the pizza for 15–20 minutes, until crisp and golden. Serve immediately.

# Indian Mee Goreng

This is a truly international dish combining Indian, Chinese and Western ingredients. It is a delicious treat for lunch or supper.

**Serves 4–6**

1 pound fresh yellow egg noodles
4–6 tablespoons vegetable oil
5 ounces firm tofu
  (bean curd), cubed
2 eggs
2 tablespoons water
1 onion, sliced
1 garlic clove, crushed
1 tablespoon light soy sauce
2–3 tablespoons ketchup
1 tablespoon chili sauce
1 large cooked potato, diced
4 scallions, shredded
1–2 fresh green chiles and
  1 red chile, seeded and
  finely sliced
salt and ground black pepper

**1** Bring a large pan of water to a boil, add the fresh egg noodles and cook for just 2 minutes. Drain the noodles and immediately rinse them under cold water. Drain well again and then set aside.

**2** Heat 2 tablespoons of the oil in a large frying pan. Fry the tofu until brown, then lift it out with a draining spoon and set it aside.

**3** Beat the eggs with the water and a little seasoning. Make an omelet by adding it to the oil in the frying pan and cooking it, without stirring, until it sets. Flip over, cook the other side, then slide it out of the pan, roll up and slice thinly.

**4** Heat the remaining oil in a wok and fry the onion and garlic for 2–3 minutes. Add the drained noodles, soy sauce, ketchup and chili sauce. Toss well over medium heat for 2 minutes, then add the diced potato.

**5** Reserve a few scallions for garnishing, then stir the rest into the noodles. Add the chiles and the tofu and toss lightly until heated through.

**6** Stir in the omelet. Pile on a hot platter, garnish with the remaining scallions and serve immediately.

# Crispy Noodles with Mixed Vegetables

Deep-frying noodles gives them a crunchy texture. They taste great in this colorful stir-fry.

**Serves 3–4**

4 ounces dried vermicelli rice
  noodles or cellophane noodles
peanut oil, for deep-frying
4 ounces yard-long beans or
  green beans, cut into
  short lengths
1-inch piece of fresh ginger root,
  cut into shreds
1 fresh red chile, sliced
1½ cups fresh shiitake or button
  mushrooms, thickly sliced
2 large carrots, cut into thin strips
2 zucchini, cut into thin strips
a few Chinese cabbage leaves,
  coarsely shredded
1½ cups bean sprouts
4 scallions, shredded
2 tablespoons light soy sauce
2 tablespoons Chinese rice wine
1 teaspoon sugar
2 tablespoons roughly torn
  cilantro leaves

**1** Break the noodles into 3-inch lengths. Half-fill a wok with oil and heat it to 350°F. Deep-fry the raw noodles, in batches, for 1–2 minutes until puffed and crispy. Drain on paper towels. Carefully pour off all but 2 tablespoons of the oil.

**2** Reheat the oil in the wok. When hot, add the beans and stir-fry for 2–3 minutes. Add the ginger, chile, mushrooms, carrots and zucchini and stir-fry for 1–2 minutes.

**3** Add the Chinese cabbage, bean sprouts and scallions. Toss over the heat for 1 minute, then add the soy sauce, rice wine and sugar. Cook, stirring, for about 30 seconds.

**4** Add the noodles and cilantro and toss to mix, without crushing the noodles. Serve immediately, piled on a plate.

**Cook's Tip**
*If a milder flavor is preferred, remove the seeds from the chile.*

# Chiles Rellenos

Slice open one of these delicious deep-fried chiles or peppers and you'll be rewarded with a melted cheese filling.

**Serves 4**
8 large fresh green chiles or small green bell peppers
1–2 tablespoons vegetable oil, plus extra for frying
4 cups grated Cheddar cheese
4 eggs, separated
²/₃ cup all-purpose flour

cilantro sprigs, to garnish

**For the sauce**
1 tablespoon vegetable oil
1 small onion, finely chopped
¼ teaspoon salt
1–2 teaspoons dried chile flakes
½ teaspoon ground cumin
1 cup vegetable stock
2 14-ounce cans chopped tomatoes

**1** First, make the sauce. Heat the oil in a heavy frying pan. Add the onion and fry over low heat, stirring occasionally, for 5 minutes, until just soft. Stir in the salt, chile flakes, cumin, stock and tomatoes. Cover and simmer gently for 5 minutes, stirring occasionally.

**2** Remove the pan from heat and cool slightly. Put the mixture into a food processor or blender and process until smooth. Strain into a clean pan. Bring to a boil, then lower the heat to a bare simmer.

**3** Preheat the broiler. Brush the chiles or peppers lightly all over with vegetable oil. Spread them out in a single layer on a baking sheet. Broil as close to the heat as possible until charred all over. Place them in a bowl, cover with paper towels and set aside for 5–10 minutes.

**4** When the chiles or peppers are cool enough to handle, rub off the skins. Carefully slit the chiles or peppers and scoop out the seeds.

**5** Form the cheese into eight cylinders and place them inside the chiles or peppers. Secure the slits with wooden toothpicks. Set aside.

**6** Beat the egg whites until just stiff. Add the egg yolks, one at a time, beating on low speed just to incorporate them. Beat in 1 tablespoon of the flour.

**7** Pour vegetable oil into a large frying pan to a depth of 1 inch and heat. Coat the chiles or peppers lightly in flour. Dip them into the egg batter, then place in the hot oil. Fry for about 2 minutes, until brown on one side. Turn carefully and brown the other side. Drain, garnish with cilantro sprigs and serve immediately with the sauce.

> **Variation**
> If using peppers instead of fresh chiles, mix the grated cheese with about 2 teaspoons hot chili powder for a more authentic, Tex-Mex taste.

# Jalapeño & Onion Quiche

Not too fiery, but with a distinctive Tex-Mex flavor, this is good served hot or at room temperature.

**Serves 6**
1 tablespoon butter
2 onions, sliced
4 scallions, chopped
½ teaspoon ground cumin
1–2 tablespoons chopped canned jalapeño chiles
4 eggs

1¼ cups milk
½ teaspoon salt
¾ cup grated Cheddar cheese

**For the pastry**
1½ cups all-purpose flour
¼ teaspoon salt
¼ teaspoon cayenne pepper
6 tablespoons cold butter
6 tablespoons cold margarine
2–4 tablespoons ice water
fresh parsley sprig, to garnish

**1** First, make the pastry. Sift the flour, salt and cayenne into a bowl. Rub in the butter and margarine until the mixture resembles bread crumbs, then add enough ice water to bind the mixture. Wrap in plastic wrap and chill for at least 30 minutes.

**2** Preheat the oven to 375°F. Roll out the pastry and line a 9-inch loose-bottomed tart pan. Prick the pan with the pastry shell, then line with nonstick baking parchment and fill with baking beans.

**3** Bake for 15 minutes, then remove from the oven and carefully lift out the paper and baking beans. Return the pastry shell to the oven and bake for 5–8 more minutes, until golden. Leave the oven on.

**4** Melt the butter in a pan and cook the sliced onions until softened. Add the scallions and cook for 1 more minute. Stir in the cumin and jalapeños and set aside.

**5** In a bowl, whisk the eggs with the milk and salt.

**6** Spoon the onion mixture into the pastry shell. Sprinkle with the cheese, then pour in the egg mixture. Bake for about 40 minutes, until the filling is golden and set. Garnish with parsley.

# Chile Cheese Tortilla with Salsa

Good warm or cold, this is like a quiche without the pastry shell. Cheese and chiles are a great match for each other.

**Serves 4**
3 tablespoons olive oil
I small onion, thinly sliced
2–3 fresh green jalapeño chiles, sliced
7 ounces cold cooked potato, thinly sliced
generous I cup grated Cheddar cheese

6 eggs, beaten
salt and ground black pepper
fresh herbs, to garnish

**For the salsa**
1 1/4 pounds tomatoes, peeled, seeded and finely chopped
I fresh mild green chile, seeded and finely chopped
2 garlic cloves, crushed
3 tablespoons chopped cilantro
juice of I lime
1/2 teaspoon salt

I First, make the salsa. Put the tomatoes in a bowl and add the chile, garlic, cilantro, lime juice and salt. Mix well and set aside.

2 Heat half the oil in a large omelet pan and gently fry the onion and jalapeños, stirring occasionally, for 5 minutes, until softened. Add the potato and cook for 5 more minutes, until lightly browned, being careful to keep the slices whole.

3 Using a draining spoon, transfer the vegetables to a warm plate. Wipe the pan with paper towels, then pour in the remaining oil. Heat well, return the vegetable mixture to the pan and season to taste. Sprinkle the cheese on top.

4 Pour in the eggs, making sure that they seep under the vegetables. Cook over low heat until set. Serve in wedges, garnished with fresh herbs, with the salsa on the side.

**Cook's Tip**
*If you use a frying pan with a flameproof handle, you can brown the top of the tortilla under a hot broiler.*

# Rice & Beans with Avocado Salsa

Mexican-style rice and beans make a tasty supper dish.

**Serves 4**
4 tomatoes, halved and seeded
2 garlic cloves, chopped
I onion, sliced
3 tablespoons olive oil
generous I cup long-grain brown rice, rinsed
2 1/2 cups vegetable stock
1/2 cup canned kidney beans, rinsed and drained
2 carrots, diced

3 ounces green beans
salt and ground black pepper
4 wheat tortillas and sour cream, to serve

**For the salsa**
I avocado
juice of I lime
I small red onion, diced
I small fresh red chile, seeded and chopped
I tablespoon chopped cilantro

I Preheat the broiler. Spread out the tomatoes, garlic and onion in a broiler pan. Pour in I tablespoon of the olive oil and toss to coat. Broil for 10 minutes, turning once. Set aside to cool.

2 Heat the remaining oil in a saucepan, add the rice and cook for 2 minutes, stirring constantly, until light golden.

3 Process the cooked tomato mixture in a food processor or blender, then scrape into the rice and cook for 2 more minutes, stirring frequently. Pour in the stock, cover and cook gently for 20 minutes, stirring occasionally.

4 Reserve 2 tablespoons of the kidney beans for the salsa. Add the rest to the rice mixture with the carrots and green beans. Cook for 10 minutes, until the vegetables are tender. Season well. Remove the pan from heat and let stand, covered, for 15 minutes.

5 Make the salsa. Halve and pit the avocado. Peel and dice the flesh, then toss it in the lime juice. Add the onion, chile, cilantro and reserved kidney beans, then season with salt. To serve, spoon the hot rice and beans onto warm tortillas. Pass the salsa and sour cream.

# Vegetable Fajitas

A colorful medley of mushrooms and peppers in a spicy sauce, wrapped in tortillas and served with creamy guacamole.

**Serves 2**

1 onion, sliced
1 red bell pepper, seeded and sliced
1 green bell pepper, seeded and sliced
1 yellow bell pepper, seeded and sliced
1 garlic clove, crushed
3 cups mushrooms, sliced
6 tablespoons vegetable oil
2 tablespoons medium chili powder
6 warm wheat flour tortillas
salt and ground black pepper
cilantro sprigs and lime wedges, to garnish

**For the guacamole**

1 ripe avocado
1 shallot, roughly chopped
1 fresh green chile, seeded and roughly chopped
juice of 1 lime

**1** Combine the onion and red, green and yellow peppers in a large bowl. Add the garlic and mushrooms and mix lightly. Mix the oil and chili powder in a cup, pour onto the vegetable mixture and stir well. Set aside.

**2** To make the guacamole, cut the avocado in half lengthwise and remove the pit. Scoop the flesh into a food processor or blender and add the chopped shallot, green chile and lime juice. Process for about 1 minute, until smooth. Scrape the guacamole into a small bowl, cover closely with plastic wrap and chill in the refrigerator as needed.

**3** Heat a large, heavy frying pan or wok until very hot. Add the marinated vegetables and stir-fry over high heat for 5–6 minutes, until the mushrooms and peppers are just tender. Season well with salt and pepper.

**4** Spoon a little of the filling onto each warm tortilla and roll up. Place three fajitas on each of two individual serving plates, garnishing them with the cilantro and lime wedges. Pass the guacamole separately.

# Black Bean Burritos

Some of the world's most delectable vegetarian dishes come from Mexico. Burritos make a delicious supper.

**Serves 4**

1 cup dried black beans, soaked overnight
1 bay leaf
2 tablespoons coarse salt
oil, for greasing
1 small red onion, finely chopped
2 cups grated Cheddar cheese
1–3 tablespoons chopped pickled jalapeño chiles
1 tablespoon chopped cilantro
3¾ cups ready-made tomato salsa
8 wheat flour tortillas
diced avocado and salad, to serve

**1** Drain the beans and put them in a large pan. Add fresh cold water to cover and the bay leaf. Bring to a boil, then lower the heat, and simmer, covered, for 30 minutes. Add the salt and continue to simmer for about 30 minutes, until tender. Drain and put into a bowl. Discard the bay leaf and let cool.

**2** Preheat the oven to 350°F. Grease a rectangular ovenproof dish. Add the onion, half the cheese, the jalapeños and cilantro to the beans, with 1 cup of the salsa. Stir and taste for seasoning.

**3** Place one tortilla on a board. Spread a spoonful of the filling down the middle, then roll up. Place the burrito in the prepared dish, seam side down. Repeat with the remaining tortillas.

**4** Sprinkle the remaining cheese on the burritos, in a line down the middle. Bake for about 15 minutes, until the cheese melts. Serve the burritos immediately, with diced avocado, salad and the remaining salsa.

> **Variation**
> • Use passata if you don't have any ready-made salsa. Add some chopped onion and diced peppers to the portion used as a serving sauce.

# Spiced Coconut Mushrooms

These delicious mushrooms can be served with almost any vegetarian meal, and are also good as a toast topping.

**Serves 3–4**
2 tablespoons peanut oil
2 garlic cloves, finely chopped
2 fresh red chiles, seeded and
   sliced into rings

3 shallots, finely chopped
1 1/2 cups brown cap mushrooms,
   thickly sliced
2/3 cup coconut milk
2 tablespoons chopped cilantro
salt and ground black pepper

**I** Heat the oil in a wok, add the garlic and chiles, then stir-fry for a few seconds. Add the shallots and stir-fry for 2–3 minutes, until softened. Add the mushrooms and cook for 3 minutes.

**2** Pour in the coconut milk and bring to a boil. Boil rapidly until the liquid is reduced by half and coats the mushrooms. Season to taste with salt and pepper. Sprinkle on the chopped cilantro and toss gently to mix. Serve immediately.

# Pickled Mushrooms

Add a little olive oil to the liquid when serving these spicy mushrooms.

**Makes I jar**
1 cup white wine vinegar
2/3 cup water
1 teaspoon salt

1 fresh red chile
2 teaspoons coriander seeds
2 teaspoons black peppercorns
1 1/2 cups firm button mushrooms

**I** Pour the vinegar and water into a stainless steel pan. Bring to the simmering point, add the remaining ingredients and cook for 10 minutes.
**2** Pour into a hot sterilized jar. Seal, label and let cool. Store in the refrigerator for at least 10 days before opening.

# Sprouting Beans & Bok Choy

Health-food stores are a good source of the more unusual sprouting beans, or you can sprout your own.

**Serves 4**
3 tablespoons peanut oil
3 scallions, sliced
2 garlic cloves, cut in slivers
1-inch piece of fresh ginger root,
   cut in slivers
1 carrot, cut in thin sticks
2 1/2 cups sprouting beans
7 ounces bok choy,
   shredded
1/2 cup unsalted cashews or
   halved almonds

**For the sauce**
3 tablespoons light soy sauce
2 tablespoons dry sherry
1 tablespoon sesame oil
1 tablespoon chili sauce
2/3 cup cold water
1 teaspoon cornstarch
1 teaspoon honey
ground black pepper

**I** Heat the oil in a large wok and stir-fry the onions, garlic, ginger and carrot for 2 minutes. Add the sprouting beans and stir-fry for 2 more minutes, stirring and tossing them together.

**2** Add the bok choy and cashews or almonds. Toss over the heat for 2–3 minutes, until the cabbage leaves are just wilting.

**3** Quickly mix all the sauce ingredients in a pitcher and pour them into the wok, stirring constantly until the sauce is hot and coats the vegetables. Season and serve immediately.

**Cook's Tip**
*To sprout your own beans, put dried mung beans, soybeans, lentils, adzuki beans or chickpeas in a large glass jar, filling it no more than one-sixth full. Pour in cold water and cover with muslin, kept in place by a rubber band. Pour out the water, so that the beans are just damp, and put the jar in a cool, dark place. Rinse daily. You should have edible sprouts in 5–6 days.*

# Spiced Vegetables with Coconut

This spicy and substantial dish could be served as an appetizer for four people, or as a vegetarian main course for two.

**Serves 2–4**
2 tablespoons grapeseed oil
1-inch piece of fresh ginger root, grated
1 garlic clove, crushed
1 fresh red chile, seeded and chopped

2 large carrots, diagonally sliced
6 celery stalks, diagonally sliced
1 fennel bulb, roughly chopped
3 scallions, sliced
14-fluid ounce can coconut milk
1 tablespoon chopped cilantro
salt and ground black pepper
cilantro sprigs, to garnish

**1** Swirl the grapeseed oil into a preheated wok and heat. Lower the heat and add the grated ginger and garlic. Stir-fry over medium heat for 1–2 minutes, until the garlic is pale golden in color.

**2** Add the chile, carrots, celery, fennel and scallions. Stir-fry for 2 minutes.

**3** Stir in the coconut milk with a large spoon and bring to a boil. Cook, stirring constantly, until the coconut milk reduces slightly and the vegetables are crisp-tender.

**4** Toss in the chopped cilantro, season to taste with salt and pepper and serve immediately, garnished with the sprigs of cilantro.

> **Cook's Tips**
> • Serve this with rice or chunks of farmhouse-style bread for mopping up the sauce.
> • Slicing the vegetables diagonally ensures the maximum surface area so that they cook quickly and evenly. When stir-frying, try to make the ingredients about the same size.

# Spicy Potatoes & Cauliflower

Serve this easy dish with a cucumber and yogurt raita.

**Serves 2**
about 8 ounces potatoes
5 tablespoons peanut oil
1 teaspoon ground cumin
1 teaspoon ground coriander
1/4 teaspoon ground turmeric
1/4 teaspoon cayenne pepper

1 fresh green chile, seeded and finely chopped
1 medium cauliflower, broken into small florets
4 tablespoons water
1 teaspoon cumin seeds
2 garlic cloves, cut into shreds
1–2 tablespoons chopped cilantro
salt

**1** Bring a pan of lightly salted water to a boil and cook the potatoes in their skins for 20 minutes, until just tender. Drain and let cool, then peel and cut into 1-inch cubes.

**2** Heat 3 tablespoons of the oil in a wok. Add the ground spices and chile. Let them sizzle for a few seconds, then add the cauliflower and water. Stir-fry for 6–8 minutes over medium heat. Add the potatoes, tossing them until coated. Stir-fry for 2–3 minutes. Season with salt and remove from heat.

**3** Heat the remaining oil in a frying pan. Add the cumin seeds and garlic and cook until golden. Pour the mixture onto the vegetables. Sprinkle with the chopped cilantro and serve.

# Cucumber & Yogurt Raita

Refreshing and cooling, this tastes wonderful with any spicy vegetable dish.

**Serves 2–4**
1 cucumber, finely diced
1 cup plain yogurt
4 teaspoons chopped fresh mint
salt and ground black pepper

**1** Place the cucumber in a colander and sprinkle with salt. Leave for 2 hours, then rinse well, drain and pat dry.
**2** Mix the yogurt and mint, stir in the cucumber and season.

# Middle-Eastern Vegetable Stew

Serve this spicy dish of mixed vegetables as a side dish for six or as a main course for four. Children may prefer less chile.

**Serves 4–6**
3 tablespoons vegetable stock
1 green bell pepper, seeded
   and sliced
2 medium zucchini, sliced
2 medium carrots, sliced
2 celery stalks, sliced
2 medium potatoes, diced
14-ounce can chopped tomatoes
1 teaspoon hot chili powder
2 tablespoons chopped fresh mint
1 tablespoon ground cumin
14-ounce can chickpeas, drained
   and rinsed
salt and ground black pepper
fresh mint sprigs, to garnish

**1** Pour the vegetable stock into a large flameproof casserole and bring to a boil, then add the sliced pepper, zucchini, carrots and celery. Stir over high heat for 2–3 minutes, until the vegetables are just beginning to soften.

**2** Add the diced potatoes, tomatoes, chili powder, chopped mint and cumin. Stir in the chickpeas and bring the mixture back to a boil.

**3** Lower the heat, cover the casserole and simmer for about 30 minutes or until all the vegetables are tender. Season to taste with salt and pepper and serve immediately, garnished with mint sprigs.

**Cook's Tip**
*Cooking the vegetables in a small amount of stock rather than oil works extremely well, and makes this dish ideal for anyone on a low-fat diet.*

**Variation**
*You can use kidney beans or haricot beans instead of chickpeas, if desired.*

# Deep-fried Zucchini with Chili Sauce

Crunchy coated zucchini is great served with a fiery tomato sauce.

**Serves 2**
1 tablespoon olive oil
1 onion, finely chopped
1 fresh red chile, seeded and
   finely diced
2 teaspoons hot chili powder
14-ounce can chopped tomatoes
1 vegetable stock cube
4 tablespoons hot water
⅔ cup milk
½ cup all-purpose flour
1 pound zucchini, sliced
oil, for deep-frying
salt and ground black pepper
fresh thyme sprigs, to garnish

**To serve**
lettuce leaves
watercress sprigs
slices of seeded bread

**1** Heat the oil in a pan. Add the onion and fry over low heat, stirring occasionally, for 2–3 minutes. Add the chile, then stir in the chili powder and cook for 30 seconds.

**2** Add the canned tomatoes. Crumble in the stock cube and stir in the water. Cover and cook for 10 minutes, then leave the sauce over very low heat until needed. Check for seasoning.

**3** Pour the milk into a shallow dish and spread out the flour in another dish. Dip the zucchini slices in the milk, then into the flour, until well-coated.

**4** Heat the oil for deep-frying to 350°F or until a cube of bread, added to the oil, browns in 45–60 seconds. Add the zucchini, in batches, and deep-fry for 3–4 minutes, until crisp. Drain on paper towels.

**5** Place two or three lettuce leaves on each serving plate. Add a few sprigs of watercress and fan out the bread slices to one side. Lightly mix the deep-fried zucchini into the sauce, then spoon some onto each plate. Garnish with the thyme sprigs and serve immediately.

# Turkish-style New Potato Casserole

A one-pot dish that's both easy to make and delicious—who could ask for more?

**Serves 4**

4 tablespoons olive oil
1 large onion, chopped
2 small–medium eggplant, cut into small cubes
4 zucchini, cut into small chunks
1 green bell pepper, seeded and chopped
1 red or yellow bell pepper, seeded and chopped
1 cup fresh or frozen peas
4 ounces green beans
1 pound new potatoes, cubed

½ teaspoon cinnamon
½ teaspoon ground cumin
1 teaspoon paprika
4–5 tomatoes, halved, seeded and chopped
14-ounce can chopped tomatoes
2 tablespoons chopped fresh parsley
3–4 garlic cloves, crushed
1½ cups vegetable stock
salt and ground black pepper
black olives and fresh parsley, to garnish

**1** Preheat the oven to 375°F. Heat 3 tablespoons of the oil in a heavy pan. Add the onion and fry over medium heat, stirring occasionally, for 5–7 minutes, until golden.

**2** Add the eggplant, sauté for about 3 minutes, then add the zucchini, peppers, peas, beans and potatoes. Stir in the cinnamon, cumin and paprika and season to taste with salt and pepper. Continue to cook for 3 minutes, stirring constantly. Transfer to a shallow ovenproof dish.

**3** Mix the fresh and canned tomatoes in a bowl. Stir in the parsley, garlic and the remaining olive oil.

**4** Pour the stock on the eggplant mixture, and spoon the prepared tomato mixture on top.

**5** Cover with aluminum foil and bake for 30–45 minutes, until the vegetables are tender. Serve immediately, garnished with black olives and parsley.

# Spicy Potato Strudel

Take a tasty mixture of vegetables in a spicy, creamy sauce and wrap in crisp phyllo pastry for a stylish and satisfying main course.

**Serves 4**

5 tablespoons butter
1 onion, chopped
2 carrots, coarsely grated
1 zucchini, chopped
12 ounces firm potatoes, finely chopped

2 teaspoons mild curry paste
½ teaspoon dried thyme
⅔ cup of water
1 egg, beaten
2 tablespoons light cream
½ cup grated Cheddar cheese
8 sheets phyllo pastry, thawed if frozen
sesame seeds, for sprinkling
salt and ground black pepper
mâche, to garnish

**1** Melt 2 tablespoons of the butter in a large frying pan and cook the onion, carrots, zucchini and potatoes for 5 minutes, tossing them frequently so they cook evenly. Stir in the curry paste and continue to cook the vegetables, stirring frequently, for 1–2 more minutes.

**2** Add the thyme and water and season with salt and pepper to taste. Bring to a boil, then lower the heat and simmer for 10 minutes, until tender, stirring occasionally.

**3** Remove the pan from heat and put the mixture into a large bowl. When cool, mix in the egg, cream and cheese. Chill until ready to fill the phyllo pastry.

**4** Preheat the oven to 375°F. Melt the remaining butter. Lay out four sheets of phyllo pastry, slightly overlapping them to form a fairly large rectangle. Brush with some melted butter and fit the other sheets on top. Brush again.

**5** Spoon the filling along one long side, then roll up the pastry. Form it into a circle and set on a baking sheet. Brush again with the last of the butter and sprinkle on the sesame seeds. Bake for about 25 minutes, until golden and crisp. Let stand for 5 minutes before cutting. Garnish with mâche.

# Eggplant & Sweet Potato Stew

Inspired by Thai cooking, this has a tasty coconut sauce scented with fragrant lemongrass and ginger.

**Serves 6**

4 tablespoons peanut oil
1 pound baby eggplant, halved
8 ounces shallots
1 teaspoon fennel seeds,
   lightly crushed
4–5 garlic cloves,
   thinly sliced
5 teaspoons finely chopped fresh
   ginger root
2 cups vegetable stock
2 lemongrass stalks, outer layers
   discarded, finely chopped

½ cup cilantro, stems and leaves
   chopped separately
3 kaffir lime leaves, lightly bruised
2–3 small red chiles
3–4 tablespoons Thai green
   curry paste
1½ pounds sweet potatoes,
   peeled and cut into chunks
1⅔ cups coconut milk
½–1 teaspoon light brown sugar
1⅔ cups mushrooms,
   thickly sliced
juice of 1 lime
salt and ground black pepper
fresh basil leaves, to serve

**1** Heat half the oil in a wide pan and cook the eggplant, stirring occasionally, until lightly browned on all sides. Remove with a draining spoon and set aside. Slice four of the shallots and set them aside. Fry the remaining whole shallots in the oil remaining in the pan, until lightly browned. Set aside.

**2** Add the remaining oil to the pan and cook the sliced shallots, fennel seeds, garlic and ginger until soft. Add the stock, lemongrass, chopped cilantro stems and any roots, lime leaves and whole chiles. Cover and simmer over low heat for 5 minutes.

**3** Stir in 2 tablespoons of the curry paste and the sweet potatoes. Simmer for 10 minutes, then return the eggplant and shallots to the pan and cook for 5 more minutes. Stir in the coconut milk and sugar. Stir in the mushrooms and simmer for 5 minutes or until all the vegetables are cooked.

**4** Season and add more curry paste and lime juice to taste. Stir in the cilantro leaves, sprinkle on the basil leaves and serve.

# Thai Vegetable Curry

Making your own spice paste gives this curry an authentic flavor.

**Serves 4**

2 teaspoons vegetable oil
1⅔ cups coconut milk
1¼ cups vegetable stock
8 ounces new potatoes, halved
   if large
4½ ounces baby corn
1 teaspoon sugar
6 ounces broccoli florets
1 red bell pepper, seeded and
   sliced lengthwise
4 ounces spinach, tough stems
   removed and shredded
salt and ground black pepper
cooked jasmine rice, to serve
2 tablespoons chopped
   cilantro, to garnish

**For the spice paste**

1 fresh red chile, seeded
   and chopped
3 fresh green chiles, seeded
   and chopped
1 lemongrass stalk, outer layers
   discarded and finely chopped
2 shallots, chopped
finely grated zest of 1 lime
2 garlic cloves, chopped
1 teaspoon ground coriander
½ teaspoon ground cumin
½-inch piece fresh galangal or
   ginger root, finely chopped
2 tablespoons chopped cilantro

**1** First, make the spice paste. Place all the ingredients in a food processor or blender and process into a coarse paste.

**2** Heat the oil in a large, heavy pan and fry the spice paste for 1–2 minutes, stirring constantly. Add the coconut milk and stock, and bring to a boil.

**3** Lower the heat, add the potatoes and simmer gently for 15 minutes. Add the baby corn, season to taste with salt and black pepper and cook for 2 minutes. Stir in the sugar, broccoli and red pepper and cook for 2 more minutes, until the vegetables are tender.

**4** Stir in the shredded spinach and half the cilantro. Cook for 2 minutes. Serve over jasmine rice, garnished with the remaining chopped cilantro.

# Bell Peppers Filled with Spiced Vegetables

Indian spices season the potato and eggplant stuffing in these colorful baked bell peppers.

**Serves 6**
1 eggplant
2 tablespoons peanut oil, plus extra for brushing
6 large even-shaped red or yellow bell peppers
1 1/4 pounds waxy potatoes
1 small onion, chopped
4–5 garlic cloves, chopped
2-inch piece of fresh root ginger, chopped
1–2 fresh green chiles, seeded and chopped
7 tablespoons water
2 teaspoons cumin seeds
1 teaspoon kalonji seeds
1/2 teaspoon ground turmeric
1 teaspoon ground coriander
1 teaspoon ground toasted cumin seeds
pinch of cayenne pepper
about 2 tablespoons lemon juice
salt and ground black pepper
chopped cilantro, to garnish

**1** Preheat the oven to 450°F. Cut the eggplant in half lengthwise and score the skin. Brush a roasting pan lightly with oil. Put the eggplant halves, cut-side down, in the pan and bake for 20 minutes. Let cool.

**2** Cut the tops off the peppers and carefully scoop out and discard the seeds. Cut a thin slice off the bottom of the peppers, if necessary, so they stand upright. Bring a large saucepan of lightly salted water to a boil. Cook the peppers for 5–6 minutes. Lift out with a draining spoon and drain upside down in a colander.

**3** Bring the water back to a boil and cook the potatoes until just tender. Drain, cool and peel, then cut into 1/2-inch dice. Peel the eggplant and cut the flesh into similar dice.

**4** Put the chopped onion, garlic, ginger and green chiles in a food processor or blender with 4 tablespoons of the water and process to a purée.

**5** Heat half the oil in a large, deep, frying pan and stir-fry the eggplant until browned. Remove from the pan and set aside. Add the remaining oil to the pan and cook the potatoes until lightly browned. Remove from the pan and set aside.

**6** Dry-fry the cumin and kalonji seeds in a nonstick pan. When the seeds darken, add the turmeric, coriander and ground cumin. Cook for 15 seconds. Stir in the onion and garlic purée and fry, scraping the pan with a spatula, until it begins to brown.

**7** Add the potatoes and eggplant to the pan, and season with salt, pepper and cayenne. Add the remaining water and half the lemon juice and cook, stirring, until the liquid evaporates. Preheat the oven to 375°F.

**8** Place the peppers on a baking sheet and fill with the potato mixture. Brush lightly with oil and bake for 30–35 minutes, until the peppers are cooked. Let cool a little, then sprinkle with more lemon juice, garnish with the cilantro and serve.

# Mixed Vegetable Curry

A good all-around vegetable curry that goes well with most Indian dishes.

**Serves 4**
2 tablespoons oil
1/2 teaspoon black mustard seeds
1/2 teaspoon cumin seeds
1 onion, thinly sliced
2 curry leaves
1 fresh green chile, seeded and finely chopped
1-inch piece of fresh ginger root, grated
2 tablespoons curry paste
1 small cauliflower, broken into florets
1 large carrot, thickly sliced
4 ounces green beans, cut into short lengths
1/4 teaspoon ground turmeric
1/4 teaspoon hot chili powder
1/2 teaspoon salt
2 tomatoes, finely chopped
1/2 cup frozen peas, thawed
2/3 cup hot vegetable stock
fresh curry leaves, to garnish

**1** Heat the oil in a large saucepan and fry the mustard seeds and cumin seeds for 2 minutes, until they begin to splutter. Add the onion and the curry leaves and fry for 5 more minutes.

**2** Stir in the chile and ginger and fry for 2 minutes. Add the curry paste, mix well and fry for 3–4 minutes.

**3** Add the cauliflower, carrot and beans and cook for 4–5 minutes. Stir in the turmeric, chili powder, salt and tomatoes and cook for 2–3 minutes.

**4** Add the thawed peas and cook for 2–3 more minutes. Pour in the stock. Cover and simmer gently over low heat for 10–13 minutes, until all the vegetables are tender. Serve, garnished with the curry leaves.

## Cook's Tip
*Keep ginger root in the freezer, and it will be very easy to grate. There's no need to peel it first, and it will thaw on contact with any hot mixture.*

# Vegetable Kashmiri

A spicy yogurt sauce coats the vegetables in this aromatic curry.

**Serves 4**

2 teaspoons cumin seeds
8 black peppercorns
seeds from 2 green
  cardamom pods
2-inch piece of cinnamon stick
½ teaspoon grated nutmeg
3 tablespoons oil
1-inch piece of fresh ginger
  root, grated
1 fresh green chile, chopped
1 teaspoon chili powder
½ teaspoon salt
2 large potatoes, cut into chunks
8 ounces cauliflower, broken
  into florets
8 ounces okra, thickly sliced
⅔ cup plain yogurt
⅔ cup vegetable stock
toasted sliced almonds and
  cilantro sprigs, to garnish

**1** Grind the cumin seeds, peppercorns, cardamom seeds, cinnamon stick and nutmeg into a fine powder, using a spice grinder or a mortar and pestle.

**2** Heat the oil in a large saucepan and stir-fry the ginger and fresh chile for 2 minutes. Add the chili powder, salt and ground spice mixture and fry for 2–3 minutes, stirring constantly to prevent the spices from sticking.

**3** Stir in the potatoes until coated, cover, and cook over low heat for 10 minutes, stirring occasionally. Add the cauliflower and okra and cook for 5 minutes.

**4** Add the yogurt and stock. Bring to a boil, then lower the heat. Cover and simmer for 20 minutes or until all the vegetables are tender. Spoon onto a platter, garnish with toasted almonds and cilantro sprigs, and serve.

> **Cook's Tip**
> An electric coffee grinder will make short work of preparing whole spices. Don't use it for anything else, though.

# Masala Okra

Okra, or "ladies fingers," are a popular vegetable in India, where they are known as bhindi. In this recipe they are stir-fried with spices.

**Serves 4**

1 pound okra
½ teaspoon ground turmeric
1 teaspoon mild chili powder
1 tablespoon ground cumin
1 tablespoon ground coriander
¼ teaspoon salt
¼ teaspoon sugar
1 tablespoon lemon juice
1 tablespoon dry,
  shredded coconut
2 tablespoons chopped cilantro
3 tablespoons vegetable oil
½ teaspoon cumin seeds
½ teaspoon black mustard seeds
chopped fresh tomatoes,
  to garnish
poppadums, to serve

**1** Wash, dry and trim the okra. In a bowl, mix the turmeric, chili powder, cumin, ground coriander, salt, sugar, lemon juice, coconut and cilantro.

**2** Heat the oil in a large, heavy frying pan. Add the cumin seeds and mustard seeds and fry over low heat, stirring occasionally, for about 2 minutes or until they begin to splutter and give off their aroma.

**3** Stir in the spice and coconut mixture and fry for 2 more minutes. Add the okra, cover, and cook over low heat for about 10 minutes or until tender.

**4** Spoon into a serving bowl, garnish with chopped fresh tomatoes and serve with poppadums.

> **Cook's Tips**
> • When buying okra, choose firm, brightly colored pods that are less than 4 inches long. They should snap cleanly. Avoid any that are soft or browning at the edges or tips.
> • Prepare okra by washing, drying and carefully cutting off the stem without breaking the seed pod.

## Curried Mushrooms

This is a delicious way of cooking mushrooms. The mixture would make a tasty filling for samosas.

**Serves 4**
2 tablespoons vegetable oil
1/2 teaspoon cumin seeds
1/4 teaspoon black peppercorns
4 green cardamom pods
1/4 teaspoon ground turmeric
1 onion, finely chopped
1 teaspoon ground cumin

1 teaspoon ground coriander
1/2 teaspoon garam masala
1 fresh green chile, finely chopped
2 garlic cloves, crushed
1-inch piece of fresh ginger root, grated
14-ounce can chopped tomatoes
1/4 teaspoon salt
6 cups button mushrooms, halved
chopped cilantro, to garnish

1 Heat the oil in a large saucepan. Add the cumin seeds, peppercorns, cardamom pods and turmeric and fry over low heat, stirring occasionally, for 2–3 minutes.

2 Add the onion and fry for about 5 minutes, stirring occasionally, until golden. Stir in the cumin, ground coriander and garam masala and fry for 2 more minutes.

3 Add the chile, garlic and ginger and fry for 2–3 minutes, stirring constantly to prevent the spices from sticking to the pan. Stir in the tomatoes and salt. Bring to a boil, then simmer for 5 minutes.

4 Add the mushrooms. Cover and simmer over low heat for 10 minutes. Spoon into a serving dish and remove and discard the cardamom pods. Garnish with chopped cilantro and serve immediately.

**Variation**
*This recipe would work well with any small, firm mushrooms, such as chestnut mushrooms or their pink or white equivalents, called champignons de Paris.*

## Fava bean & Cauliflower Curry

A tasty mid-week curry, this is especially good with basmati rice, baby poppadums and cucumber and yogurt raita.

**Serves 4**
2 garlic cloves, chopped
1-inch piece of fresh ginger root
1 fresh green chile, seeded and chopped
1 tablespoon vegetable oil
2 tablespoons ghee or butter
1 onion, sliced
1 large potato, chopped

1 tablespoon mild or hot curry powder
1 medium cauliflower, cut into small florets
2 1/2 cups vegetable stock
2 tablespoons creamed coconut
10-ounce can fava beans
juice of 1/2 lemon (optional)
salt and ground black pepper
chopped cilantro or parsley, to garnish
cooked white basmati rice, to serve

1 Put the garlic, ginger, chile and oil in a food processor and process until the mixture forms a smooth paste.

2 Heat the ghee or butter in a large, heavy pan. Add the onion and potato and fry over low heat, stirring occasionally, for about 5 minutes, until the onion is soft and pale golden. Stir in the spice paste and curry powder. Cook, stirring constantly, for 1 more minute.

3 Stir in the cauliflower florets, then pour in the stock. Bring to a boil over medium heat and mix in the creamed coconut, stirring until it melts.

4 Season well with salt and pepper, then lower the heat, cover and simmer for 10 minutes.

5 Add the fava beans, with the can juices, stir gently to mix and cook, uncovered, for 10 more minutes.

6 Check the seasoning and add a good squeeze of lemon juice if desired. Spoon into a serving bowl, garnish with cilantro or parsley, and serve immediately with basmati rice.

# Eggplant Curry

A simple and delicious way of cooking eggplant which makes sure their full flavor is retained.

**Serves 4**

2 large eggplant, about
  1 pound each
3 tablespoons vegetable oil
1/2 teaspoon black mustard seeds
1 bunch scallions, finely chopped
1 1/2 cups button mushrooms,
  halved
2 garlic cloves, crushed
1 fresh red chile, finely chopped

1/2 teaspoon mild chili powder
1 teaspoon ground cumin
1 teaspoon ground coriander
1/4 teaspoon ground turmeric
1 teaspoon salt
14-ounce can chopped tomatoes
1 tablespoon chopped cilantro
cilantro sprig, to garnish

**1** Preheat the oven to 400°F. Brush both of the eggplant with 1 tablespoon of the oil. Prick them with a fork and place in a roasting pan. Bake for 30–35 minutes, until soft.

**2** Meanwhile, heat the remaining oil in a large pan and fry the mustard seeds for 2 minutes, until they begin to splutter. Add the scallions, mushrooms, garlic and fresh chile and fry for about 5 minutes. Stir in the ground spices and salt and fry for 3–4 minutes. Add the tomatoes and simmer for 5 minutes.

**3** Cut each of the eggplant in half lengthwise and scoop out the soft flesh into a bowl. Mash the flesh roughly.

**4** Add the mashed eggplant and cilantro to the saucepan. Bring to a boil, then simmer for 5 minutes, or until the sauce thickens. Serve, garnished with a cilantro sprig.

> **Cook's Tip**
> *If you want to omit the oil, wrap the eggplant in aluminum foil and bake for 1 hour.*

# Aloo Gobi

Cauliflower and potatoes are coated in classic Indian spices in this dish.

**Serves 4**

1 pound potatoes, cut into
  1-inch chunks
2 tablespoons vegetable oil
1 teaspoon cumin seeds
1 fresh green chile, finely chopped
1 pound cauliflower, broken
  into florets

1 teaspoon ground coriander
1 teaspoon ground cumin
1/4 teaspoon chili powder
1/2 teaspoon ground turmeric
1/2 teaspoon salt
chopped cilantro, to garnish
tomato and onion salad and lime
  pickle, to serve

**1** Bring a large pan of lightly salted water to a boil and cook the potatoes for 10 minutes. Drain well and set aside.

**2** Heat the oil in a heavy, deep frying pan. Add the cumin seeds and fry over low heat, stirring occasionally, for 2 minutes, until they begin to splutter. Add the chile and fry for 1 more minute.

**3** Toss in the cauliflower florets. Stir well to coat them all over with the spice mixture. Continue to stir-fry, over low to medium heat for 5 more minutes.

**4** Add the potatoes, ground coriander, cumin, chili powder, turmeric and salt. Cook for 7–10 minutes or until the vegetables are tender.

**5** Spoon into a warmed serving dish, garnish with chopped cilantro and serve immediately with the tomato and onion salad and lime pickle.

> **Variation**
> *Try using sweet potatoes instead of ordinary potatoes for a curry with a sweeter flavor.*

# Aloo Saag

Potatoes, spinach and spices are the main ingredients in this authentic curried vegetable dish.

**Serves 4**

1 pound fresh young
  spinach leaves
2 tablespoons vegetable oil
1 teaspoon black mustard seeds
1 onion, thinly sliced
2 garlic cloves, crushed
1-inch piece of fresh ginger root,
  finely chopped
1 ½ pounds potatoes, cut into
  1-inch chunks
1 teaspoon mild chili powder
1 teaspoon salt
½ cup water

**1** Bring a large pan of lightly salted water to a boil and blanch the spinach leaves for 3–4 minutes. Drain thoroughly and set aside. When the spinach is cool enough to handle, use your hands to squeeze out any remaining liquid.

**2** Heat the oil in a large saucepan. Add the mustard seeds and fry over low heat, stirring occasionally, for 2 minutes or until they begin to splutter.

**3** Add the onion, garlic and ginger. Fry for 5 minutes, stirring constantly, then add the potatoes, chili powder, salt and water. Stir well and cook for 8 minutes.

**4** Stir in the spinach. Cover and simmer for 10–15 minutes or until the potatoes are tender. Spoon onto a warmed serving dish and serve immediately.

---

**Cook's Tips**
• *Use a waxy variety of potato for this dish, such as Ausonia, Spunta, Maris Bard or Morag, so the pieces do not break up during cooking.*
• *To make certain that the spinach is completely dry after it has been blanched and drained, you can put it in a clean dish towel, roll up tightly and then squeeze gently to remove the excess liquid.*

---

# Cumin-spiced Zucchini & Spinach

Tender chunks of marrow with spinach in a creamy, cumin-flavored sauce.

**Serves 2**

½ zucchini, about 1 pound
2 tablespoons vegetable oil
2 teaspoons cumin seeds
1 small fresh red chile, seeded
  and finely chopped
2 tablespoons water
2 ounces fresh young spinach
  leaves, torn into pieces
6 tablespoons light cream
salt and ground black pepper
boiled rice or naan,
  to serve

**1** Peel the zucchini and cut it in half. Scoop out and discard the seeds. Cut the flesh into cubes.

**2** Heat the oil in a large, heavy frying pan. Add the cumin seeds and the chopped chile. Cook over low heat, stirring occasionally, for 1 minute.

**3** Add the zucchini and water to the pan. Cover with aluminum foil or a lid and simmer gently, stirring occasionally, for 8 minutes, until the zucchini is just tender. Remove the foil cover or lid and cook for about 2 more minutes, or until most of the water has evaporated.

**4** Add the spinach to the marrow, with just the water that clings to the leaves after washing and draining. Replace the cover and cook gently for 1 minute.

**5** Stir in the cream and cook over high heat for 2 minutes. Season to taste and serve with rice or naan.

---

**Cook's Tip**
*Be careful when handling chiles, as the juice can burn sensitive skin. Wear rubber gloves to protect your hands or wash your hands very thoroughly after preparation.*

---

# Zucchini Curry

Next time you have a glut of zucchini in the garden, treat yourself to this colorful curry.

**Serves 4**

3 tablespoons vegetable oil
$^1\!/_2$ teaspoon cumin seeds
$^1\!/_2$ teaspoon mustard seeds
1 onion, thinly sliced
2 garlic cloves, crushed
$^1\!/_4$ teaspoon ground turmeric
$^1\!/_4$ teaspoon mild chili powder
1 teaspoon ground coriander
1 teaspoon ground cumin
$^1\!/_2$ teaspoon salt
1$^1\!/_2$ pounds zucchini, cut in
   $^1\!/_2$-inch slices
1 tablespoon tomato paste
14-ounce can chopped tomatoes
$^2\!/_3$ cup water
1 tablespoon chopped cilantro
1 teaspoon garam masala

**1** Heat the oil in a large, heavy pan. Add the cumin seeds and mustard seeds and fry over low heat, stirring occasionally, for 2 minutes, until they begin to splutter.

**2** Add the onion and garlic and fry, stirring occasionally, for about 5 minutes, until softened.

**3** Stir in the turmeric, chili powder, ground coriander, ground cumin and salt. Cook, stirring constantly, for 2–3 minutes.

**4** Add the sliced zucchini, all at once, and cook for 5 minutes. Meanwhile, mix the tomato paste, chopped tomatoes and water in a bowl.

**5** Add the tomato mixture to the pan, stir well and simmer for 10 minutes, until the sauce thickens. Stir in the cilantro and garam masala, then cook for 5 more minutes, until the zucchini are tender. Serve immediately.

## Variation
*This curry is also delicious made with other summer squash, such as patty pans.*

# Corn & Pea Curry

Chunks of corn on the cob not only look interesting in this unusual curry, they taste pretty good too!

**Serves 4**

6 pieces of frozen corn on the cob
3 tablespoons vegetable oil
$^1\!/_2$ teaspoon cumin seeds
1 onion, finely chopped
2 garlic cloves, crushed
1 fresh green chile, finely chopped
1 tablespoon curry paste
1 teaspoon ground coriander
1 teaspoon ground cumin
$^1\!/_4$ teaspoon ground turmeric
$^1\!/_2$ teaspoon salt
$^1\!/_2$ teaspoon sugar
14-ounce can
   chopped tomatoes
1 tablespoon tomato paste
$^2\!/_3$ cup water
1 cup frozen peas, thawed
2 tablespoons chopped cilantro

**1** Cut each piece of corn in half crosswise to make 12 equal pieces in total. Bring a large saucepan of water to a boil and cook the corn pieces for 10–12 minutes. Drain well.

**2** Heat the oil in a large pan. Add the cumin seeds and fry over low heat, stirring occasionally, for about 2 minutes or until they begin to splutter. Add the onion, garlic and chile and fry for 5–6 minutes, until the onions are golden.

**3** Stir in the curry paste and fry for 2 minutes. Stir in the remaining spices, salt and sugar and fry for 2–3 minutes.

**4** Add the chopped tomatoes, tomato paste and water and simmer for 5 minutes or until the sauce thickens. Add the peas and cook for 5 more minutes.

**5** Add the pieces of corn and the cilantro. Cook for 6–8 minutes or until the corn and peas are tender.

## Cook's Tip
*Use fresh corn on the cob when it is in season. Do not salt the water or the corn will become tough.*

# Vegetable Korma

The blending of spices is an ancient art in India. Here the aim is to produce a subtle, aromatic curry rather than an assault on the senses.

**Serves 4**

1/4 cup butter

2 onions, sliced

2 garlic cloves, crushed

1-inch piece of fresh ginger root, grated

1 teaspoon ground cumin

1 tablespoon ground coriander

6 cardamom pods

2-inch piece of cinnamon stick

1 teaspoon ground turmeric

1 fresh red chile, seeded and finely chopped

1 potato, cut into 1-inch cubes

1 small eggplant, chopped

1 1/2 cups mushrooms, thickly sliced

3/4 cup water

4 ounces green beans, cut into short lengths

4 tablespoons plain yogurt

2/3 cup heavy cream

1 teaspoon garam masala

salt and ground black pepper

cilantro sprigs, to garnish

poppadums, to serve

**1** Melt the butter in a heavy pan and cook the onions for 5 minutes, until soft. Add the garlic and ginger and cook for 2 minutes, then stir in the cumin, ground coriander, cardamoms, cinnamon stick, turmeric and chile. Stir-fry for 30 seconds.

**2** Add the potato, eggplant, mushrooms and water. Cover the pan, bring to a boil, then lower the heat and simmer for 15 minutes. Add the beans and cook, uncovered, for 5 minutes.

**3** With a draining spoon, remove the vegetables to a warmed serving dish and keep hot. Boil the cooking liquid until it reduces a little. Season with salt and pepper, then stir in the yogurt, cream and garam masala. Pour the sauce over the vegetables and garnish with cilantro. Serve with poppadums.

> **Variation**
> *Any combination of vegetables can be used for this korma, including carrots, cauliflower, broccoli, peas and chickpeas.*

# Tofu & Green Bean Red Curry

This Thai curry is simple and quick to make.

**Serves 4–6**

2 1/2 cups coconut milk

1 tablespoon red curry paste

3 tablespoons vegetarian "oyster" sauce (mushroom-based)

2 teaspoons sugar

1 1/2 cups button mushrooms

4 ounces green beans, trimmed

6 ounces firm tofu (bean curd), cut into 3/4-inch cubes

4 kaffir lime leaves, torn

2 fresh red chiles, sliced

cilantro leaves, to garnish

**1** Pour about one-third of the coconut milk into a pan. Cook until it starts to separate and an oily sheen appears.

**2** Stir in the curry paste, "oyster" sauce and sugar, then add the mushrooms. Stir and cook for 1 minute. Stir in the rest of the coconut milk and bring to a boil. Add the green beans and cubes of tofu and simmer gently for 4–5 more minutes. Stir in the kaffir lime leaves and sliced chiles. Serve immediately, garnished with the cilantro leaves.

# Tofu with Chiles

This is quick, easy and deliciously spicy.

**Serves 4**

1 pound tofu (bean curd), diced

1 tablespoon dark soy sauce

4 fresh red Thai chiles

3 garlic cloves

2 tablespoons vegetable oil

2 tablespoons light soy sauce

2 tablespoons vegetarian "oyster" sauce (mushroom-based)

1 tablespoon sugar

fresh Thai basil leaves, to garnish

**1** Mix the tofu and dark soy sauce in a bowl and set aside to marinate for 10 minutes.

**2** Meanwhile, pound the chiles and garlic together to a paste. Heat the oil in a wok and stir-fry the spice paste and tofu for 1 minute. Stir in the remaining ingredients and stir-fry for another 2 minutes. Serve, garnished with the basil leaves.

## Stir-fried Tofu & Bean Sprouts

Tofu (bean curd) is a boon
to the busy vegetarian cook,
providing plenty of protein
in this simple stir-fry.

**Serves 4**

8 ounces firm tofu (bean curd)
peanut oil, for deep-frying
6 ounces medium egg noodles
1 tablespoon sesame oil
1 teaspoon cornstarch
2 teaspoons dark soy sauce

1 tablespoon Chinese rice wine
1 teaspoon sugar
6–8 scallions, cut diagonally into
   1-inch lengths
3 garlic cloves, sliced
1 fresh green chile, seeded
   and sliced
4 ounces bok choy leaves,
   coarsely shredded
1 cup bean sprouts
1/2 cup cashews, toasted

**1** Drain the tofu and pat it dry with paper towels. Cut it
into 1-inch cubes. Half-fill a wok with peanut oil and
heat to 350°F or until a cube of day-old bread browns in
30–60 seconds. Deep-fry the tofu cubes, in batches, for
1–2 minutes, until golden and crisp. Remove the cubes with a
draining spoon' and drain them on paper towels. Carefully pour
all but 2 tablespoons of the oil from the wok.

**2** Bring a large pan of water to a boil, add the noodles and
remove the pan from heat. Cover and let stand for about
4 minutes, until the noodles are just tender. Drain, rinse under
cold water and drain again. Toss in 2 teaspoons of the sesame
oil and set aside.

**3** In a bowl, blend together the cornstarch, soy sauce, rice wine,
sugar and the remaining sesame oil.

**4** Reheat the 2 tablespoons of peanut oil in the wok. Add the
scallions, garlic, chile, bok choy and bean sprouts and stir-fry for
1–2 minutes.

**5** Add the tofu cubes, together with the noodles and sauce.
Cook, stirring, for about 1 minute, until thoroughly mixed and
heated through. Transfer to a warmed serving dish, sprinkle on
the cashews and serve immediately.

## Peanut Noodles

Add any of your favorite
vegetables to this quick and
easy recipe and increase the
number of chiles, if you can
take the heat!

**Serves 4**

7 ounces medium egg noodles
2 tablespoons olive oil
2 garlic cloves, crushed
1 large onion, roughly chopped
1 red bell pepper, seeded and
   roughly chopped
1 yellow bell pepper, seeded and
   roughly chopped
12 ounces zucchini,
   roughly chopped

1 1/4 cups roasted unsalted
   peanuts, roughly chopped
snipped fresh chives, to garnish

**For the dressing**

4 tablespoons good-quality
   olive oil
grated zest and juice of 1 lemon
1 fresh red chile, seeded and
   finely chopped
3 tablespoons snipped
   fresh chives
1–2 tablespoons balsamic vinegar
salt and ground black pepper

**1** Bring a large pan of water to a boil, add the noodles and
remove the pan from heat. Cover and let stand for about
4 minutes, until the noodles are tender. Drain, rinse under cold
water and drain again.

**2** Heat the olive oil in a wok. Add the garlic and onion and stir-
fry for 3–4 minutes, until the onion is beginning to soften. Add
the red and yellow peppers and the zucchini and stir-fry for
3–4 minutes, until crisp-tender. Add the peanuts and cook for
1 more minute.

**3** Make the dressing. In a pitcher, whisk together the olive oil,
grated lemon zest and 3 tablespoons of the lemon juice. Add
the chile and chives and whisk in balsamic vinegar to taste.
Season well with salt and pepper.

**4** Add the noodles to the vegetables and toss over the heat to
heat through. Add the dressing and stir to coat. Transfer to a
warmed serving dish and serve immediately, garnished with
snipped chives.

# Kitchiri

This is the Indian original that inspired the classic British breakfast dish, kedgeree. Made with basmati rice and small tasty lentils, this will make an ample supper or brunch dish.

**Serves 4**

²⁄₃ cup Indian masoor dhal or
   continental green lentils
¹⁄₄ cup ghee or butter
2 tablespoons sunflower oil
1 onion, chopped
1 garlic clove, crushed

generous 1 cup basmati rice
2 teaspoons ground coriander
2 teaspoons cumin seeds
2 cloves
3 cardamom pods
2 bay leaves
1 cinnamon stick
4 cups vegetable stock
2 tablespoons tomato paste
3 tablespoons chopped cilantro
   or parsley
salt and ground black pepper

**1** Put the dhal or lentils in a bowl. Pour in boiling water to cover and let soak for 30 minutes. Meanwhile, bring a pan of water to a boil. Drain the soaked dhal or lentils and add to the pan. Cook for 10 minutes. Drain once more and set aside.

**2** Heat the ghee or butter and oil in a large saucepan and fry the onion and garlic for about 5 minutes.

**3** Add the rice, stir well to coat the grains, then stir in the spices. Cook gently for 1–2 minutes, then add the lentils, stock, tomato paste and seasoning.

**4** Bring to a boil, lower the heat, cover and simmer for 20 minutes, until the stock has been absorbed. Stir in the cilantro or parsley and check the seasoning. Remove and discard the cinnamon stick and bay leaf and serve.

**Cook's Tip**
*In summer, it is worth growing cilantro in a pot, as it has an inimitable flavor and adds authenticity to many ethnic dishes.*

# Parsnip & Eggplant Biryani

It always seems such a humble vegetable, yet the parsnip has a superb flavor and brings a touch of sweetness to spicy dishes such as this one.

**Serves 4–6**

1 small eggplant, sliced
1¹⁄₄ cups basmati rice
3 onions
2 garlic cloves, roughly chopped
1-inch piece of fresh ginger
   root, peeled
3 tablespoons water
about 4 tablespoons vegetable oil

1¹⁄₂ cups unsalted cashews
¹⁄₄ cup golden raisins
1 red bell pepper, seeded
   and sliced
3 parsnips, chopped
1 teaspoon ground cumin
1 teaspoon ground coriander
¹⁄₂ teaspoon mild chili powder
¹⁄₂ cup plain yogurt
1¹⁄₄ cups vegetable stock
2 tablespoons butter
salt
cilantro sprigs and wedges of
   hard-boiled egg, to garnish

**1** Layer the eggplant slices in a colander, sprinkling each layer with salt. Let drain in the sink for 30 minutes. Rinse, pat dry with paper towels and cut into bite-size pieces.

**2** Soak the rice in a bowl of cold water while you cook the vegetables. Roughly chop one onion and put it in a food processor or blender with the garlic and ginger. Add the water and process into a paste.

**3** Thinly slice the remaining onions. Heat 3 tablespoons of the oil in a large flameproof casserole. Add the onion slices and fry over low heat, stirring occasionally, for about 10 minutes, until deep golden brown. Remove and drain. Add one-quarter of the cashews to the pan and stir-fry for 2 minutes. Add the golden raisins and fry until they swell. Remove and drain.

**4** Add the eggplant and red pepper to the casserole and stir-fry for 4–5 minutes. Drain on paper towels. Add the parsnips to the casserole and fry for 4–5 minutes. Stir in the remaining cashews and fry for 1 minute. Transfer to a plate with the eggplant and pepper.

**5** Add the remaining 1 tablespoon of oil to the casserole. Add the onion paste. Cook, stirring constantly, for 4–5 minutes. Stir in the cumin, ground coriander and chili powder. Cook, stirring, for 1 minute, then lower the heat and add the yogurt.

**6** Stir in the stock, parsnips, eggplant and peppers. Bring to a boil, then lower the heat, cover and simmer for 30–40 minutes, until the parsnips are tender.

**7** Preheat the oven to 300°F. Drain the rice and cook it in salted boiling water for 6 minutes. Drain, then pile in a mound on top of the spiced vegetables. Make a hole from the top to the base using the handle of a wooden spoon.

**8** Sprinkle the reserved fried onions, cashews and golden raisins on the rice and dot with the butter. Cover with a aluminum foil lid. Bake for 35–40 minutes, then spoon onto a warmed serving dish and garnish with the cilantro sprigs and egg.

# Fried Rice

This is a great way to use leftover cooked rice. It not only looks colorful, but also tastes delicious.

**Serves 4–6**

4 tablespoons oil
4 ounces shallots, halved and
  thinly sliced
3 garlic cloves, crushed
1 fresh red chile, seeded and
  finely chopped
6 scallions, finely chopped
1 red bell pepper, seeded and
  finely chopped
8 ounces white cabbage,
  finely shredded
6 ounces cucumber,
  finely chopped
½ cup frozen peas, thawed
3 eggs, beaten
1 teaspoon tomato paste
2 tablespoons freshly squeezed
  lime juice
¼ teaspoon Tabasco sauce
6 cups very cold cooked
  white rice
1 cup cashews, roughly chopped
about 2 tablespoons
  chopped cilantro, plus extra
  to garnish
salt and ground black pepper

**1** Heat the oil in a wok. Add the shallots and cook, stirring frequently, until very crisp and golden. Remove with a draining spoon and drain well on paper towels.

**2** Add the garlic and chile and cook for 1 minute. Add the scallions and red pepper and cook for 3–4 minutes or until beginning to soften. Add the cabbage, cucumber and peas and cook for 2 more minutes.

**3** Make a gap and add the beaten eggs. Scramble the eggs, stirring occasionally, then stir them into the vegetables.

**4** Stir in the tomato paste, lime juice and Tabasco. Add the rice, cashews and cilantro, with plenty of seasoning. Toss over high heat for 3–4 minutes, until the rice is piping hot. Serve garnished with the crisp shallots and cilantro.

# Egyptian Rice with Lentils

Two important staple foods come together in this simple but tasty Middle-Eastern dish, which owes its warm flavor to the inclusion of ground cumin and cinnamon.

**Serves 6**

1½ cups large brown lentils,
  soaked overnight
  in water
2 large onions
3 tablespoons olive oil
1 tablespoon ground cumin
½ teaspoon ground cinnamon
generous 1 cup long-grain rice
salt and ground black pepper
flat-leaf parsley, to garnish

**1** Drain the lentils and put them in a large pan. Add enough water to cover them by 2 inches. Bring to a boil, lower the heat, cover and simmer for 40 minutes–1½ hours or until tender. Drain thoroughly.

**2** Finely chop one onion, and slice the other. Heat 1 tablespoon of the oil in a pan. Add the chopped onion and fry over low heat, stirring occasionally, for 5 minutes, until soft. Add the lentils, cumin and cinnamon. Stir well and season to taste with salt and pepper.

**3** Measure the volume of rice and add it, with the same volume of water, to the lentil mixture. Cover and simmer for about 20 minutes, until both the rice and lentils are tender.

**4** Heat the remaining oil in a frying pan and cook the sliced onion for about 15 minutes, until very dark brown. Put the rice mixture into a serving bowl, sprinkle with the sliced onion and serve hot or cold, garnished with flat-leaf parsley.

**Cook's Tip**
Use two 14-ounce cans of cooked lentils, if you prefer. Simply add them to the fried chopped onion in Step 2.

# Lentil Dhal with Roasted Garlic

This spicy lentil dhal makes a comforting, starchy meal when served with boiled rice or Indian breads and a vegetable dish.

**Serves 4–6**

1 head of garlic
2 tablespoons extra virgin olive oil, plus extra for brushing
3 tablespoons ghee or butter
1 onion, chopped
2 fresh green chiles, seeded and chopped
1 tablespoon chopped fresh ginger root
1 cup yellow or red split lentils
3¾ cups water
1 teaspoon ground cumin
1 teaspoon ground coriander
2 tomatoes, peeled and diced
a little lemon juice
salt and ground black pepper
2–3 tablespoons cilantro sprigs, to garnish

**For the spice mix**

2 tablespoons peanut oil
4–5 shallots, sliced
2 garlic cloves, thinly sliced
1 tablespoon ghee or butter
1 teaspoon cumin seeds
1 teaspoon mustard seeds
3–4 small dried red chiles
8–10 fresh curry leaves

**1** Preheat the oven to 350°F. Place the garlic in an oiled roasting pan and roast it whole for 30 minutes.

**2** Meanwhile, melt the ghee or butter in a large pan. Add the onion, fresh chiles and ginger and cook over low heat, stirring occasionally, for 10 minutes, until golden.

**3** Stir in the lentils and water. Bring to a boil, then lower the heat and partially cover the pan. Simmer, stirring occasionally, for about 35 minutes, until the mixture looks like a very thick soup.

**4** When the garlic is soft and tender, remove it from the oven and let it cool slightly. Cut off the top third and, holding the garlic over a bowl, dig out the flesh from each clove so that it drops into the bowl. Mash it into a paste with the oil.

**5** Stir the roasted garlic purée, cumin and ground coriander into the lentil mixture and season with salt and pepper to taste. Cook for 10 minutes, uncovered, stirring frequently. Stir in the diced tomatoes, then adjust the seasoning, adding a little lemon juice to taste.

**6** For the spice mix, heat the oil in a small, heavy pan and fry the shallots until crisp and browned. Add the garlic and cook until it colors slightly. Remove the mixture from the pan and set it aside.

**7** Melt the ghee or butter in the same pan and fry the cumin and mustard seeds until the mustard seeds pop. Stir in the dried chiles, curry leaves and the shallot mixture, then swirl the hot mixture into the cooked dhal. Garnish with the cilantro sprigs and serve immediately.

> **Cook's Tip**
> Do not be alarmed by the amount of garlic; when roasted, it acquires a mild and mellow flavor.

# Tomato & Lentil Dhal with Toasted Almonds

Richly flavored with spices, coconut milk and tomatoes, this lentil dish is good enough to serve as part of a celebration supper.

**Serves 4**

2 tablespoons vegetable oil
1 large onion, finely chopped
3 garlic cloves, chopped
1 carrot, diced
2 teaspoons cumin seeds
2 teaspoons yellow mustard seeds
1-inch piece of fresh ginger root, grated
2 teaspoons ground turmeric
1 teaspoon mild chili powder
1 teaspoon garam masala
1 cup red split lentils
1⅔ cups water
1⅔ cups coconut milk
5 tomatoes, peeled, seeded and chopped
juice of 2 limes
4 tablespoons chopped cilantro
salt and ground black pepper
¼ cup sliced almonds, toasted, to serve

**1** Heat the oil in a large, heavy pan. Sauté the onion over low heat, stirring occasionally, for 5 minutes, until softened. Add the garlic, carrot, cumin and mustard seeds and ginger. Cook for 5 minutes, stirring constantly, until the seeds begin to pop and the carrot softens slightly.

**2** Stir in the ground turmeric, chili powder and garam masala, and cook for 1 minute or until the flavors begin to mingle, stirring to prevent the spices from burning.

**3** Add the lentils, water, coconut milk and tomatoes, and season well with salt and pepper. Bring to a boil, then lower the heat, cover and simmer, for about 15 minutes, stirring occasionally to prevent the lentils from sticking.

**4** Stir in the lime juice and 3 tablespoons of the cilantro and check the seasoning. Cook for 10–15 more minutes, until the lentils are tender. Spoon into a warmed serving dish and sprinkle with the remaining cilantro and the toasted almonds. Serve immediately.

# Egg & Lentil Curry

Hard-boiled eggs combine well with all pulses.

**Serves 4**
scant ½ cup green lentils
3 cups vegetable stock
6 eggs
2 tablespoons vegetable oil
3 cloves
¼ teaspoon black peppercorns
1 onion, finely chopped
2 fresh green chiles,
   finely chopped

2 garlic cloves, crushed
1-inch piece of fresh ginger
   root, chopped
2 tablespoons curry paste
14-ounce can chopped tomatoes
½ teaspoon sugar
¾ cup water
½ teaspoon garam masala
roughly chopped parsley,
   to garnish

**1** Put the lentils in a large, heavy pan and add the stock. Bring to a boil, cover, lower the heat and simmer for about 30 minutes or until the lentils are soft. Drain and set aside.

**2** Cook the eggs in boiling water for 10 minutes. Cool slightly, then shell and cut in half lengthwise.

**3** Heat the oil in a large frying pan and fry the cloves and peppercorns for 2 minutes. Add the onion, chiles, garlic and ginger and cook for 5–6 minutes, stirring frequently.

**4** Stir in the curry paste and fry for 2 minutes, stirring constantly. Add the tomatoes, sugar and water and simmer, stirring occasionally, for 5 minutes, until the sauce thickens.

**5** Add the boiled eggs, lentils and garam masala. Cover and simmer for 10 more minutes, then serve, garnished with parsley.

**Cook's Tip**
*As soon as the eggs are hard-boiled, lift them out of the water and plunge them into cold water. This prevents a dark ring from forming around the yolks.*

# Lentils with Fried Spices

If you've got a saucepan and a frying pan, you can cook this classic Indian dish. It is ideal for hungry students.

**Serves 4–6**
½ cup split red lentils
¼ cup yellow split peas
1½ cups water
4 fresh green chiles
1 teaspoon ground turmeric
1 large onion, sliced

14-ounce can chopped tomatoes
4 tablespoons vegetable oil
½ teaspoon mustard seeds
½ teaspoon cumin seeds
1 garlic clove, crushed
6 curry leaves
2 dried red chiles
¼ teaspoon asafoetida
salt
deep-fried onions, to garnish

**1** Combine the lentils and split peas in a heavy pan and add the water, chiles, turmeric and onion slices. Bring to a boil. Lower the heat, cover and simmer for about 30 minutes or until the lentils are soft and the water has evaporated.

**2** Mash the lentils with the back of a spoon. When almost smooth, add the tomatoes and season with salt to taste. Mix well. If necessary, thin the mixture with hot water.

**3** Heat the oil in a frying pan and add the mustard and cumin seeds, garlic and curry leaves. Crumble in the dried chiles and stir in the asafoetida. Fry over low heat, stirring constantly, until the garlic browns.

**4** Pour the oil and spices onto the lentils and cover the pan. After 5 minutes, mix well, garnish with the deep-fried onions and serve immediately.

**Cook's Tip**
*If you buy lentils loose, pick through them carefully and remove any small stones. Wash them thoroughly under cold running water. It is not necessary to soak the lentils, but if you soak the brown ones, it will speed up the cooking process.*

# Spinach Dhal

Yellow split peas cook down to a creamy consistency, which combines well with the spinach in this delicious, lightly spiced dish.

**Serves 4**

¾ cup chana dhal or yellow
   split peas
¾ cup water
1 tablespoon vegetable oil
¼ teaspoon black mustard seeds
1 onion, thinly sliced

2 garlic cloves, crushed
1-inch piece of fresh ginger
   root, grated
1 fresh red chile, finely chopped
10 ounces frozen spinach, thawed
   and drained
¼ teaspoon mild chili powder
½ teaspoon ground coriander
½ teaspoon garam masala
salt

**1** Wash the chana dhal or split peas in several changes of cold water. Put into a bowl and pour in plenty of water to cover. Let soak for 30 minutes.

**2** Drain the pulses and put them in a large pan with the measured water. Bring to a boil, lower the heat, cover and simmer for 20–25 minutes, until soft.

**3** Meanwhile, heat the oil in a large, heavy frying pan and fry the mustard seeds over low heat for 2 minutes, until they begin to splutter.

**4** Add the onion, garlic, ginger and chile to the pan and fry, stirring occasionally, for 5–6 minutes or until the onion has softened but not colored.

**5** Add the spinach and cook for about 10 minutes or until the spinach is dry and the liquid has been absorbed. Stir in the chili powder, ground coriander and garam masala and season to taste with salt. Cook for 2–3 minutes.

**6** Drain the chana dhal or split peas, add them to the spinach mixture and cook for about 5 minutes. Transfer to a warmed serving dish and serve immediately.

# Madras Sambal

There are many variations of this everyday Indian dish, which can be served solo but is often presented as part of a meal.

**Serves 4**

1 cup toovar dhal or red
   split lentils
2½ cups water
½ teaspoon ground turmeric
2 large potatoes, cut into
   1-inch chunks
2 tablespoons vegetable oil

½ teaspoon black mustard seeds
¼ teaspoon fenugreek seeds
4 curry leaves
1 onion, thinly sliced
4 ounces green beans, cut into
   short lengths
½ teaspoon mild chili powder
1 tablespoon lemon juice
4 tablespoons dry,
   shredded coconut
salt
toasted coconut, to garnish
chutney, to serve

**1** Wash the toovar dhal or lentils in several changes of water. Place in a heavy saucepan with the measured water and the turmeric. Bring to a boil, then lower the heat and simmer, covered, for 20–30 minutes, until the lentils are soft.

**2** Meanwhile, bring a large pan of lightly salted water to a boil. Add the potatoes and boil for 10 minutes. Drain well.

**3** Heat the oil in a large, deep frying pan and fry the seeds and curry leaves for 2–3 minutes, until the seeds begin to splutter. Add the onion and the beans and fry for 7–8 minutes. Stir in the potatoes and cook for 2 more minutes.

**4** Drain any free liquid from the lentils, then stir them into the vegetables with the chili powder, lemon juice and salt. Simmer for 2 minutes. Stir in the coconut and simmer for 5 minutes. Garnish with toasted coconut and serve with chutney.

**Cook's Tip**
*Toovar dhal are split yellow pigeon peas. Look for these pulses at Indian groceries.*

# Hot-&-Sour Chickpeas

If you visit India, you will find bowls of this tasty snack food on sale from stalls on the street.

**Serves 4**

3 tablespoons vegetable oil
2 onions, very finely chopped
2 tomatoes, peeled and
   finely chopped
1 tablespoon ground coriander
1 tablespoon ground cumin
1 teaspoon ground fenugreek

1 teaspoon ground cinnamon
2 14-ounce cans
   chickpeas, drained
1½ cups vegetable stock
1–2 fresh hot green chiles, seeded
   and thinly sliced
1-inch piece of fresh ginger
   root, grated
4 tablespoons lemon juice
salt
1 tablespoon chopped cilantro,
   to garnish

**1** Heat the oil in a large flameproof casserole. Reserve about 2 tablespoons of the chopped onions and fry the remainder, stirring frequently, for 4–5 minutes, until tinged with brown.

**2** Add the tomatoes and continue cooking over medium-low heat for 5–6 minutes, until soft. Stir frequently, mashing the tomatoes to a pulp.

**3** Stir in the ground spices. Cook for 30 seconds, then add the chickpeas and vegetable stock. Season with salt, cover and simmer very gently for 15–20 minutes, stirring occasionally and adding water if the mixture becomes too dry.

**4** Meanwhile, mix the reserved onion with the chile, ginger and lemon juice. Just before serving, stir this mixture into the chickpeas, with more salt, if needed, and garnish with cilantro.

> **Cook's Tip**
> In India, dried chickpeas would be used. If you want to follow suit, soak 1½ cups dried chickpeas overnight in water, then drain them and boil them in fresh water for 1–1¼ hours, until tender.

# Masala Chana

Tamarind gives this dish a deliciously tangy flavor.

**Serves 4**

2 ounces pressed tamarind
½ cup boiling water
2 tablespoons vegetable oil
½ teaspoon cumin seeds
1 onion, finely chopped
2 garlic cloves, crushed
1-inch piece of fresh ginger
   root, grated
1 fresh green chile, finely chopped

1 teaspoon ground cumin
1 teaspoon ground coriander
¼ teaspoon ground turmeric
½ teaspoon salt
2 tomatoes, peeled and
   finely chopped
2 14-ounce cans
   chickpeas, drained
½ teaspoon garam masala
chopped fresh chiles and chopped
   onion, to garnish

**1** Break up the tamarind and soak in the boiling water for about 15 minutes. Rub the mixture through a sieve into a bowl, discarding what remains in the sieve.

**2** Heat the oil in a large, heavy pan and fry the cumin seeds for 2 minutes, until they splutter. Add the onion, garlic, ginger and chile and fry over low heat, stirring occasionally, for 5 minutes, until the onion has softened.

**3** Stir in the ground cumin, ground coriander, turmeric and salt and fry for 3–4 minutes. Add the tomatoes and tamarind pulp. Mix thoroughly, bring to a boil, then lower the heat and simmer for 5 minutes.

**4** Add the chickpeas and stir in the garam masala. Cover and simmer for about 15 minutes. Spoon into a serving dish, garnish with the chopped chiles and onion, and serve.

> **Cook's Tip**
> Peeled, seeded tamarind pods compressed into bricks are sold at Indian grocers. Break off as much as you need and soak it as described in the recipe.

# Spicy Chickpeas with Fresh Ginger

Here's another excellent chickpea recipe, this time with ginger, scallions and fresh mint.

**Serves 4–6**

2 tablespoons vegetable oil
1 small onion, chopped
1 1/2-inch piece of fresh ginger root, finely chopped
2 garlic cloves, finely chopped
1/4 teaspoon ground turmeric
1 pound tomatoes, peeled, seeded and chopped
2 14-ounce cans chickpeas, drained
2 tablespoons chopped cilantro
2 teaspoons garam masala
salt and ground black pepper
cilantro sprigs, to garnish

**For the raita**

2/3 cup plain yogurt
2 scallions, finely chopped
1 teaspoon roasted cumin seeds
2 tablespoons chopped fresh mint
pinch of cayenne pepper

**1** Heat the oil in a large pan. Add the onion and fry over low heat, stirring occasionally, for 2–3 minutes. Add the ginger, garlic and turmeric. Fry for a few seconds more.

**2** Stir in the tomatoes and chickpeas and season with salt and pepper to taste. Bring to a boil, then simmer for 10–15 minutes, until the mixture is reduced to a thick sauce.

**3** Meanwhile, make the raita. Mix the yogurt, scallions, roasted cumin seeds, mint and cayenne pepper in a small serving bowl. Set aside.

**4** Just before the end of cooking, stir the chopped cilantro and garam masala into the chickpea mixture. Serve immediately, garnished with cilantro sprigs and accompanied by the raita.

> **Variation**
> *Try this with drained canned beans, if desired. Lima beans make an interesting alternative to chickpeas.*

# Curried Spinach & Chickpeas

Serve this with yogurt and naan for a complete, satisfying and very tasty meal.

**Serves 6**

2 tablespoons vegetable oil
2 garlic cloves, crushed
1 onion, roughly chopped
2 tablespoons medium curry paste
1 tablespoon black mustard seeds
1 pound potatoes, diced
2 cups water
1 pound frozen leaf spinach, thawed
14-ounce can chickpeas, drained
8 ounces Halloumi cheese, cubed
1 tablespoon freshly squeezed lime juice
salt and ground black pepper
cilantro sprigs, to garnish

**1** Heat the oil in a large, heavy pan. Add the garlic and onion and fry over medium heat, stirring occasionally, for about 5 minutes. Stir in the curry paste and mustard seeds and cook the mixture for 1 minute.

**2** Add the diced potatoes and pour in the measured water. Bring to a boil and cook gently, stirring occasionally, for 20–25 minutes, until the potatoes are almost tender and most of the liquid has evaporated.

**3** Meanwhile, place the thawed spinach in a sieve and press out as much liquid as possible. Chop it roughly, then stir it into the potato mixture, with the chickpeas. Cook for 5 minutes, or until the potatoes are tender, stirring frequently.

**4** Stir in the cheese cubes and lime juice, season to taste with salt and pepper and serve immediately, garnished with sprigs of cilantro.

> **Cook's Tip**
> *In India, paneer, rather than Halloumi, would be used. This cheese is made at home by curdling boiled milk with vinegar or lemon juice, straining the curds and then pressing them with a weight for a short while.*

# Parsnips & Chickpeas in an Aromatic Paste

The sweet flavor of parsnips goes very well with the spices in this special-occasion stew.

**Serves 4**

scant 1 cup dried chickpeas, soaked overnight
7 garlic cloves, finely chopped
1 small onion, chopped
2-inch piece of fresh ginger root, chopped
2 fresh green chiles, seeded and finely chopped
2¹⁄₂ cups water
2 tablespoons peanut oil
1 teaspoon cumin seeds
2 teaspoons ground coriander seeds
1 teaspoon ground turmeric
¹⁄₂–1 teaspoon mild chili powder
¹⁄₂ cup cashews, toasted and ground
2 tomatoes, peeled and chopped
2 pounds parsnips, cut into chunks
1 teaspoon ground roasted cumin seeds
juice of 1 lime
salt and ground black pepper
cilantro leaves and toasted cashews, to serve

**1** Drain the chickpeas and put them in a heavy pan. Cover with cold water and bring to a boil. Boil vigorously for 10 minutes, then lower the heat to a steady boil and cook for 1–1¹⁄₂ hours or until tender.

**2** Set 2 teaspoons of the garlic aside. Place the remaining garlic in a food processor or blender with the onion, ginger and half the fresh chiles. Add 5 tablespoons of the water and process into a smooth paste.

**3** Heat the oil in a large, deep frying pan and cook the cumin seeds for 30 seconds. Stir in the coriander seeds, turmeric, chili powder and the ground cashews.

**4** Add the ginger and chili paste and cook, stirring frequently, until the water begins to evaporate. Add the tomatoes and stir-fry until the mixture begins to turn red-brown in color.

**5** Drain the chickpeas and stir them into tomato mixture with the parsnips. Pour in the remaining water. Add 1 teaspoon salt and plenty of black pepper. Bring to a boil, stir well, then simmer, uncovered, for 15–20 minutes, until the parsnips are completely tender.

**6** Reduce the liquid, if necessary, by boiling fiercely until the sauce is thick. Add the ground roasted cumin with lime juice to taste. Stir in the reserved garlic and chile, and cook for a final 1–2 minutes. Sprinkle on the cilantro leaves and toasted cashews and serve immediately.

### Cook's Tip
*Dried chickpeas are used here, but they do demand some forethought, as they require soaking. For an impromptu meal, use two cans of chickpeas, adding them when the parsnips have been cooking for about 5 minutes.*

# Eggplant & Chickpea Ragoût

The perfect dish for a winter supper party, this combines two hearty main ingredients with a blend of warming spices.

**Serves 4**

3 large eggplant, cubed
scant 1 cup dried chickpeas, soaked overnight
3 tablespoons olive oil
3 garlic cloves, chopped
2 large onions, chopped
¹⁄₂ teaspoon ground cumin
¹⁄₂ teaspoon ground cinnamon
¹⁄₂ teaspoon ground coriander
3 14-ounce cans chopped tomatoes
salt and ground black pepper
cooked rice, to serve

**For the garnish**
2 tablespoons olive oil
1 onion, sliced
1 garlic clove, sliced
cilantro sprigs

**1** Put the eggplant cubes in a colander, sprinkling each layer with salt. Stand in the sink for 30 minutes, then rinse very well. Drain thoroughly and pat dry with paper towels.

**2** Drain the chickpeas and put them in a pan with enough water to cover. Bring to a boil. Boil vigorously for 10 minutes, then lower the heat and simmer for 1–1¹⁄₄ hours or until tender. Drain.

**3** Heat the oil in a large, heavy pan. Add the garlic and onions and fry over low heat, stirring occasionally, for 5 minutes, until softened.

**4** Add the cumin, cinnamon and ground coriander and cook, stirring constantly, for a few seconds. Stir in the eggplant until coated with the spice mixture. Cook for 5 minutes.

**5** Add the tomatoes and chickpeas and season to taste with salt and pepper. Cover and simmer for 20 minutes.

**6** Make the garnish. Heat the oil in a frying pan. When it is very hot, add the sliced onion and garlic and fry, stirring frequently until golden and crisp. Serve the ragoût with rice, topped with the onion and garlic and garnished with cilantro.

# Curried Kidney Beans

This is a very popular Punjabi-style dish. It also tastes good when made with lima beans.

**Serves 4**

2 tablespoons vegetable oil
1/2 teaspoon cumin seeds
1 onion, thinly sliced
1 fresh green chile, finely chopped
2 garlic cloves, crushed
1-inch piece of fresh ginger
    root, grated
2 tablespoons curry paste
1 teaspoon ground cumin
1 teaspoon ground coriander
1/2 teaspoon mild chili powder
14-ounce can chopped tomatoes
2 14-ounce cans red kidney
    beans, drained and rinsed
2 tablespoons chopped cilantro
salt and ground black pepper

**1** Heat the oil in a large, heavy frying pan. Add the cumin seeds and fry for 2 minutes, until they begin to splutter.

**2** Add the onion, chile, garlic and ginger and fry over low heat, stirring occasionally, for 5 minutes, until the onion has softened.

**3** Stir in the curry paste, cumin, ground coriander, chili powder and salt to taste and cook for 5 minutes.

**4** Add the tomatoes and simmer for 5 minutes. Add the beans and cilantro, reserving a little for the garnish. Cover and cook for 15 minutes, stirring in a little water if necessary.

**5** Taste the mixture and add salt and pepper, if needed. Garnish with the remaining chopped cilantro and serve.

> **Cook's Tip**
> *If you prefer to use dried red kidney beans, soak 1 1/4 cups overnight in cold water, then drain and put in a pan with plenty of cold water. Bring to a boil and boil vigorously for 10 minutes, then lower the heat slightly and cook for 1–1 1/4 hours, until soft.*

# Mixed Bean Curry

When your stock of dried beans is running low, mix the remains of several packages to make this marvellous curry. Start early, as the beans will need to soak overnight.

**Serves 4**

1/3 cup dried red kidney beans
1/3 cup dried black-eyed peas
1/3 cup dried haricot beans
1/3 cup dried flageolet beans
2 tablespoons vegetable oil
1 teaspoon cumin seeds
1 teaspoon black mustard seeds
1 onion, finely chopped
2 garlic cloves, crushed
1-inch piece of fresh ginger
    root, grated
2 fresh green chiles,
    finely chopped
2 tablespoons curry paste
1/2 teaspoon salt
14-ounce can chopped tomatoes
2 tablespoons tomato paste
1 cup water
2 tablespoons chopped cilantro,
    plus extra to garnish

**1** Mix the beans in a large bowl. Add enough cold water to cover and soak overnight.

**2** Drain the beans and put them into a large, heavy pan with at least double the volume of cold water. Bring to a boil and boil vigorously for 10 minutes. Lower the heat, cover and simmer for 1–1 1/2 hours or until all the beans are soft.

**3** Heat the oil in a large pan and fry the cumin and mustard seeds for 2 minutes, until they splutter. Add the onion, garlic, ginger and chiles and fry over low heat, stirring occasionally, for 5 minutes, until the onion has softened.

**4** Stir in the curry paste. Fry for 2–3 more minutes, stirring constantly, then add the salt. Add the tomatoes, tomato paste and the measured water, mix well and simmer for 5 minutes.

**5** Add the drained beans and the cilantro. Cover and simmer for 30 minutes, until the sauce thickens. Garnish with the extra cilantro and serve immediately.

# Dry Mung Dhal with Zucchini

Most dhal dishes are quite runny, but this one has a bit of texture—thanks mainly to the zucchini.

**Serves 4–6**

¾ cup mung dhal
½ teaspoon ground turmeric
1¼ cups water
2 tablespoons vegetable oil
1 large onion, thinly sliced
2 garlic cloves, crushed
2 fresh green chiles, chopped
½ teaspoon mustard seeds
½ teaspoon cumin seeds
¼ teaspoon asafoetida
a few cilantro and mint
    leaves, chopped
6–8 curry leaves
½ teaspoon sugar
7-ounce can tomatoes, drained
    and chopped
8 ounces zucchini, diced
salt
4 tablespoons lemon juice

**1** Soak the mung dhal in water to cover for about 4 hours. Drain thoroughly, then put into a heavy pan.

**2** Add the turmeric and measured water. Bring to a boil, then lower the heat. Cover and simmer for 15 minutes, until the dhal is cooked but not mushy. Drain, reserving the cooking liquid.

**3** Heat the oil in a frying pan and add all the remaining ingredients, except the lemon juice. Cover and cook, stirring occasionally, until the zucchini are almost tender.

**4** Fold in the mung dhal and lemon juice. If the dish is too dry, add a little of the reserved cooking liquid. Reheat and serve.

### Cook's Tips

• Mung dhal, also known as green gram, is one of those pulses most likely to be found at an Indian or ethnic food stores. It consists of split mung beans, which have been hulled.
• Asafoetida is made from the resinous sap of a rather foul-smelling fennel plant. When dried and powdered, it gives an onion flavor to Indian and Middle Eastern dishes and is also considered to aid digestion.

# Mung Beans with Potatoes

One of the quicker-cooking pulses, mung beans are very easy to use.

**Serves 4**

¾ cup mung beans
3 cups water
2 potatoes, cut into
    ¾-inch chunks
2 tablespoons vegetable oil
½ teaspoon cumin seeds
1 fresh green chile, finely chopped
1 garlic clove, crushed
1-inch piece of fresh ginger root,
    finely chopped
¼ teaspoon ground turmeric
½ teaspoon mild chili powder
1 teaspoon salt
1 teaspoon sugar
4 curry leaves, plus extra
    to garnish
5 tomatoes, peeled and
    finely chopped
1 tablespoon tomato paste

**1** Put the beans in a saucepan and add the water. Bring to a boil, then lower the heat and simmer for 30 minutes, until soft. Drain and set aside.

**2** Meanwhile, par-boil the potatoes in a separate pan of boiling water for 10 minutes. Drain and set aside.

**3** Heat the oil in a large, heavy pan and fry the cumin seeds until they splutter. Add the chile, garlic and ginger and fry over low heat, stirring frequently, for 3–4 minutes.

**4** Stir in the turmeric, chili powder, salt and sugar. Cook for 2 minutes, stirring constantly to prevent the mixture from sticking to the pan.

**5** Add the curry leaves, tomatoes and tomato paste and simmer for 5 minutes, until the sauce thickens. Stir in the mung beans and potatoes and reheat. Spoon onto a serving platter or dish, garnish with the extra curry leaves and serve.

### Cook's Tip

Unlike many other pulses, mung beans do not require soaking before they are cooked.

# Red Bean Chili

White wine and soy sauce may not be standard ingredients in chili, but they give this spicy bean dish a depth of flavor unmatched by more mundane mixtures.

**Serves 4**

2 tablespoons vegetable oil
1 onion, chopped
14-ounce can chopped tomatoes
2 garlic cloves, crushed
1¼ cups white wine
about 1¼ cups vegetable stock
½ cup red split lentils

2 fresh thyme sprigs or
    1 teaspoon dried thyme
2 teaspoons ground cumin
3 tablespoons dark soy sauce
½ fresh hot chile, seeded and
    finely chopped
1 teaspoon allspice
8-ounce can red kidney beans,
    drained and rinsed
2 teaspoons sugar
salt
boiled rice and corn, to serve

**1** Heat the oil in a large, heavy pan. Add the onion and fry over low heat, stirring occasionally for about 5 minutes, until slightly softened.

**2** Add the tomatoes and garlic, cook for 10 minutes, then stir in the wine and stock. Bring to a boil.

**3** Add the lentils, thyme, cumin, soy sauce, chile and allspice. Cover, then simmer for 40 minutes or until the lentils are cooked, stirring occasionally and adding more water if the lentils begin to dry out.

**4** Stir in the kidney beans and sugar and continue cooking for 10 minutes, adding a little extra stock or water if the mixture is becoming too dry. Season to taste with salt and serve hot with boiled rice and corn.

> **Cook's Tip**
> If you have a taste for very hot, spicy food, do not seed the chile before chopping it.

# Chili with Basmati Rice

Red kidney beans, tomatoes and chili make a great combination. Serve with pasta or pita bread instead of rice, if you prefer.

**Serves 4**

1¾ cups basmati rice
2 tablespoons olive oil
1 large onion, chopped
1 garlic clove, crushed

1 tablespoon hot chili powder
1 tablespoon all-purpose flour
1 tablespoon tomato paste
14-ounce can chopped tomatoes
14-ounce can red kidney beans,
    drained and rinsed
⅔ cup hot vegetable stock
salt and ground black pepper
chopped fresh parsley, to garnish

**1** Rinse the rice several times in cold water. If there is sufficient time, let it soak for about 30 minutes in the water used for the final rinse.

**2** Bring a large pan of water to a boil. Drain the rice, then cook it in the water for 10–12 minutes, until tender.

**3** Meanwhile, heat the oil in a heavy frying pan. Add the onion and garlic and cook over low heat, stirring occasionally, for 2 minutes. Stir in the chili powder and flour. Cook, stirring frequently, for 2 minutes.

**4** Stir in the tomato paste, tomatoes, beans and hot vegetable stock. Cover and cook for 12 minutes, stirring occasionally.

**5** Taste the mixture and stir in salt and pepper, if needed. Drain the rice and serve immediately, with the chili beans, sprinkled with a little chopped fresh parsley.

> **Cook's Tip**
> Basmati is generally considered to be the long-grain rice with the finest flavor and texture. However, if you prefer to use another type, including brown rice, there is, of course, no reason why you shouldn't.

# Mixed Vegetable Stir-fry

Serve this stir-fry with rice or noodles.

**Serves 4**

1 tablespoon vegetable oil
1 teaspoon toasted sesame oil
1 garlic clove, chopped
1-inch piece of fresh ginger root, finely chopped

8 ounces baby carrots
12 ounces broccoli florets
6 ounces asparagus tips
2 scallions, cut diagonally
6 ounces collard greens, shredded
2 tablespoons light soy sauce
1 tablespoon apple juice
1 tablespoon sesame seeds, toasted

**1** Heat the oils in a wok and sauté the garlic over low heat for 2 minutes. Raise the heat, add the ginger, carrots, broccoli and asparagus and stir-fry for 4 minutes. Add the cut scallions and collard greens and stir-fry for 2 more minutes.

**2** Drizzle on the soy sauce and apple juice and toss over the heat for 1–2 minutes, until the vegetables are crisp-tender. Sprinkle the sesame seeds on top and serve.

# Mixed Cabbage Stir-fry

Use three or four different types of cabbage, including bok choy.

**Serves 4**

1 tablespoon vegetable oil
1 garlic clove, chopped
1-inch piece of fresh ginger root, finely chopped

1 pound mixed cabbage leaves, finely shredded
2 teaspoons light soy sauce
1 teaspoon honey
1 tablespoon sesame seeds, toasted

**1** Heat the oil in a wok and sauté the garlic over low heat for 2 minutes. Raise the heat and add the ginger and shredded cabbage. Stir-fry for 4 minutes.
**2** Drizzle on the soy sauce and honey and toss over the heat for 1–2 minutes. Sprinkle with the sesame seeds and serve.

# Braised Eggplant & Zucchini

Fresh red chiles add a flicker of fire to a dish that is simple, spicy and quite sensational. If you don't like your food quite so hot, use mild chiles or even sweet red bell peppers.

**Serves 4**

1 eggplant, about 12 ounces
2 small zucchini
1 tablespoon vegetable oil

2 garlic cloves, finely chopped
2 fresh red chiles, seeded and finely chopped
1 small onion, diced
1 tablespoon black bean sauce
1 tablespoon dark soy sauce
3 tablespoons water
salt

**1** Trim the eggplant and slice it in half lengthwise, then cut it across into ½-inch slices. Layer the slices in a colander, sprinkling each layer with salt. Leave the colander in the sink for about 20 minutes, so the liquid that is drawn from the eggplant drains out.

**2** Meanwhile, roll cut each zucchini by slicing off one end diagonally, then rolling the zucchini through 180° and taking off another diagonal slice to form a triangular wedge. Make more wedges of zucchini in the same way.

**3** Rinse the eggplant slices well under cold running water, drain and dry thoroughly on paper towels.

**4** Heat the oil in a preheated wok. Add the finely chopped garlic, chopped chiles and diced onion and stir-fry over medium heat for 2–3 minutes. Stir in the black bean sauce, coating the onions well.

**5** Lower the heat and add the eggplant slices. Stir-fry for 2 minutes, sprinkling on a little water, if necessary, to prevent them from burning.

**6** Stir in the zucchini, soy sauce and measured water. Cook, stirring occasionally, for 5 minutes. Serve hot.

## Braised Tofu with Mushrooms

The mushrooms flavor the tofu (bean curd) to make this the perfect low-fat vegetarian main course.

**Serves 4**
12 ounces firm tofu (bean curd)
$1/2$ teaspoon sesame oil
2 teaspoons light soy sauce
1 tablespoon vegetable oil
2 garlic cloves, finely chopped
$1/2$ teaspoon grated fresh
  ginger root
$1^1/2$ cups shiitake mushrooms,
  stems removed
2 cups oyster mushrooms
$1^1/2$ cups drained, canned
  straw mushrooms
$1^1/2$ cups button mushrooms,
  cut in half
1 tablespoon Chinese rice wine or
  medium-dry sherry
1 tablespoon dark soy sauce
6 tablespoons vegetable stock
1 teaspoon cornstarch
1 tablespoon water
salt and ground white pepper
2 scallions, shredded,
  to garnish

**1** Put the tofu in a dish and sprinkle with the sesame oil, light soy sauce and a large pinch of pepper. Let marinate for 10 minutes, then drain and cut into $1 \times {}^1/2$-inch pieces, using a sharp knife.

**2** Heat the vegetable oil in a wok. Add the garlic and ginger and stir-fry over low heat for a few seconds. Raise the heat, add all the mushrooms and stir-fry for 2 minutes.

**3** Stir in the Chinese rice wine or sherry, soy sauce and stock and season with salt and pepper to taste. Toss over the heat for about 4 minutes.

**4** Mix the cornstarch into a paste with the water. Stir the mixture into the wok and cook, stirring constantly, until thickened.

**5** Carefully add the pieces of tofu, toss gently to coat thoroughly and simmer for 2 minutes.

**6** Transfer the stir-fry to a large, warmed serving dish and sprinkle the shredded scallions on top to garnish. Serve immediately.

## Red-cooked Tofu with Chinese Mushrooms

Red-cooked is a term used for Chinese dishes cooked with dark soy sauce.

**Serves 2–4**
6 dried Chinese mushrooms
8 ounces firm tofu (bean curd)
3 tablespoons dark soy sauce
2 tablespoons Chinese rice wine
  or medium-dry sherry
2 teaspoons dark brown sugar
1 garlic clove, crushed
1 tablespoon grated fresh
  ginger root
$1/2$ teaspoon Chinese five-
  spice powder
pinch of ground roasted
  Szechuan peppercorns
1 teaspoon cornstarch
2 tablespoons peanut oil
5–6 scallions, sliced into
  short lengths
small fresh basil leaves, to garnish
cooked rice noodles, to serve

**1** Soak the dried Chinese mushrooms in warm water for 20–30 minutes, until soft.

**2** Meanwhile, cut the tofu into 1-inch cubes. Place in a shallow dish. Combine the soy sauce, rice wine or sherry, sugar, garlic, ginger, five-spice powder and Szechuan pepper. Pour this onto the tofu, toss lightly and marinate for 10 minutes. Drain, reserve the marinade and stir in the cornstarch.

**3** Drain the mushrooms, reserving 6 tablespoons of the soaking liquid. Strain this into the cornstarch mixture, mix well and set aside. Squeeze out any excess liquid from the mushrooms, remove the tough stems and slice the caps.

**4** Heat the oil in a wok and fry the tofu for 2–3 minutes, until golden. Remove it with a draining spoon and set aside.

**5** Add the mushrooms and the white parts of the scallions to the wok and stir-fry for 2 minutes. Pour in the cornstarch mixture and stir for 1 minute, until the mixture thickens. Return the tofu to the wok with the green parts of the scallions. Simmer for 1–2 minutes. Serve immediately with basil leaves and rice noodles.

## Harvest Vegetable & Lentil Casserole

In autumn, thoughts turn to hearty, satisfying food. This sustaining, yet low-fat dish is an ideal choice.

**Serves 6**

1 tablespoon sunflower oil
2 leeks, sliced
1 garlic clove, crushed
4 celery stalks, chopped
2 carrots, sliced
2 parsnips, diced
1 sweet potato, diced
8 ounces rutabaga, diced

¾ cup whole brown or
   green lentils
1 pound tomatoes, peeled, seeded
   and chopped
1 tablespoon chopped
   fresh thyme
1 tablespoon chopped
   fresh marjoram
3¾ cups vegetable stock
1 tablespoon cornstarch
3 tablespoons water
salt and ground black pepper
fresh thyme sprigs, to garnish

**1** Preheat the oven to 350°F. Heat the oil in a large flameproof casserole. Add the leeks, garlic and celery and cook over low heat, stirring occasionally, for 3 minutes, until the onion is beginning to soften.

**2** Add the carrots, parsnips, sweet potato, rutabaga, lentils, tomatoes, herbs and stock. Stir well and season with salt and pepper to taste. Bring to a boil, stirring occasionally.

**3** Cover the casserole, put it in the oven and bake for about 50 minutes, until the vegetables and lentils are tender, stirring the vegetable mixture once or twice.

**4** Remove the casserole from the oven. Blend the cornstarch with the water in a small bowl. Stir the mixture into the casserole and heat it gently on top of the stove, stirring continuously, until the mixture boils and thickens. Lower the heat and simmer gently for 2 minutes, stirring.

**5** Spoon onto warmed serving plates or into bowls, garnish with the thyme sprigs and serve.

## Mushroom & Fennel Stew

Delicious flavors permeate this unusual dish which makes the most of dried and fresh mushrooms.

**Serves 4**

2 cups dried shiitake mushrooms
2 tablespoons olive oil
12 shallots, peeled and left whole
1 small head of fennel,
   roughly chopped

3 cups button mushrooms, halved
1¼ cups dry cider
2 large pieces sun-dried tomatoes
   in oil, drained and sliced
2 tablespoons sun-dried
   tomato paste
1 bay leaf
chopped fresh parsley, to garnish

**1** Place the dried mushrooms in a bowl. Pour in boiling water to cover and set aside for 20–30 minutes. Drain, reserving the liquid. Discard the stalks and chop the mushrooms into pieces.

**2** Heat the oil in a flameproof casserole. Add the shallots and fennel and sauté over low heat, stirring occasionally, for 10 minutes or until the mixture has softened and the shallots are lightly browned.

**3** Add the button mushrooms and fry for 2–3 minutes, then stir in the shiitake mushrooms and fry for 1 more minute.

**4** Pour in the cider and stir in the sun-dried tomatoes and sun-dried tomato paste. Add the bay leaf. Bring to a boil, then lower the heat, cover the casserole and simmer gently for about 30 minutes.

**5** If the mixture seems dry, stir in the reserved liquid from the soaked mushrooms. Reheat briefly, then remove the bay leaf and serve, sprinkled with plenty of chopped parsley.

> **Cook's Tip**
> Dried mushrooms swell up a great deal after soaking, so a little goes a long way in terms of both flavor and quantity.

# Stir-fried Vegetables with Cashews

This versatile stir-fry recipe will accommodate most other combinations of vegetables—you do not have to use the selection suggested here.

**Serves 4**
2 medium carrots
1 medium red bell pepper, seeded
1 medium green bell pepper, seeded
2 zucchini
4 ounces green beans, halved
1 medium bunch of scallions
1 tablespoon virgin olive oil
4–6 curry leaves
1/2 teaspoon white cumin seeds
4 dried red chiles
10–12 cashews
1 teaspoon salt
2 tablespoons lemon juice
fresh mint leaves, to garnish

**1** Prepare the vegetables: cut the carrots, peppers and zucchini into matchsticks, halve the beans and chop the scallions. Set aside.

**2** Heat the oil in a wok and stir-fry the curry leaves, cumin seeds and dried chiles for 1 minute.

**3** Add the vegetables and nuts and toss them over the heat for 3–4 minutes. Add the salt and lemon juice. Continue to stir and toss over the heat for 2 more minutes or until the vegetables are crisp-tender.

**4** Transfer to a warmed serving dish. Remove the dried chiles, if you like. Serve immediately, garnished with mint leaves.

> **Cook's Tips**
> • When making any of the stir-fries in this section, it is a good idea to use a nonstick wok to minimize the amount of oil needed. However, it cannot be heated to the same high temperature as a conventional wok.
> • You can reduce the fat content still more by using a light oil cooking spray instead of the olive oil.

# Carrot & Cauliflower Stir-fry

There's plenty of crunch in this tasty, quick-cooking supper dish, which is high in fiber but very low in fat.

**Serves 4**
1 tablespoon olive oil
1 bay leaf
2 cloves
1 small cinnamon stick
2 cardamom pods
3 black peppercorns
1 teaspoon salt
2 large carrots, cut into thin batons
1 small cauliflower, broken into florets
1/2 cup frozen peas
2 teaspoons lemon juice
1 tablespoon chopped cilantro
cilantro leaves, to garnish

**1** Heat the oil in a wok and add the bay leaf, cloves, cinnamon stick, cardamoms and peppercorns. Stir-fry over medium heat for 30–35 seconds, then add the salt.

**2** Add the carrot and cauliflower and stir-fry for 3–5 minutes. Add the peas, lemon juice and chopped cilantro and cook for 2–3 more minutes. Serve, garnished with the cilantro leaves.

# Broccoli Stir-fry

Ginger and orange make this quick stir-fry deliciously tangy and flavorful.

**Serves 4**
1 1/2 pounds broccoli, broken into florets
2 slices fresh ginger root
juice of 1 orange
2 teaspoons cornstarch
1/2 teaspoon sugar
4 tablespoons water
1 tablespoon olive oil
1 garlic clove, thinly sliced
matchstick strips of orange zest, soaked in cold water

**1** Slice the broccoli stems and cut the ginger into matchsticks. Mix the orange juice with the cornstarch, sugar and water.
**2** Heat the oil in a wok. Stir-fry the stems for 2 minutes. Add the ginger, garlic and florets and stir-fry for 3 minutes. Stir in the orange mixture until thickened. Toss in the zest and serve.

# Mushrooms in a Creamy Garlic Sauce

Low-fat and virtually fat-free fromage frais are real finds for anyone who is trying to limit the amount of fat he or she consumes. It gives this stir-fry a deceptively creamy taste.

**Serves 4**

1 tablespoon olive oil
1 bay leaf
3 garlic cloves, roughly chopped
2 fresh green chiles, seeded
   and chopped

$4^{1}/_{2}$ cups button mushrooms,
   halved
2–3 tablespoons vegetable stock
1 cup low-fat fromage frais
1 tablespoon chopped fresh mint
1 tablespoon chopped cilantro
1 teaspoon salt
fresh mint and cilantro leaves,
   to garnish

**1** Heat the oil in a wok, add the bay leaf, garlic and chiles and cook for about 1 minute.

**2** Add the mushrooms and moisten them with the stock. Cook over high heat, stirring constantly, for 3–5 minutes, until the stock has been absorbed.

**3** Remove the wok from heat and stir in the fromage frais, mint, cilantro and salt. Return the wok to the heat and cook, stirring constantly, for 2 minutes, until heated through. Transfer to a warmed serving dish. Garnish with the mint and cilantro leaves and serve immediately.

**Cook's Tip**
*All kinds of mushrooms will absorb an astonishing amount of fat, as anyone who has fried them in butter or oil will appreciate. Try using a well-flavored, homemade vegetable stock instead; the mushrooms will cook beautifully and will remain juicy.*

# Corn & Cauliflower

This quick and tasty vegetable dish is easily made with frozen corn.

**Serves 4**

1 tablespoon corn oil
4 curry leaves
$^{1}/_{4}$ teaspoon onion seeds

2 medium onions, diced
1 fresh red chile, seeded
   and diced
1 cup frozen corn kernels
$^{1}/_{2}$ small cauliflower, cut into
   small florets
6 fresh mint leaves

**1** Heat the oil in a wok. Add the curry leaves and the onion seeds and stir-fry for about 30 seconds.

**2** Add the onions and stir-fry for 5–8 minutes, until golden brown. Stir in the chile, corn and cauliflower and stir-fry for 5–8 minutes.

**3** Finally, add the mint leaves, and serve immediately.

# Glazed Snow Peas & Bell Peppers

A delectable sauce coats the crisp-tender vegetables in this simple stir-fry.

**Serves 2–4**

1 teaspoon cornstarch
2 teaspoons dry sherry
1 tablespoon soy sauce

6 tablespoons vegetable stock
1 tablespoon sweet chili sauce
1 tablespoon sunflower oil
2 red bell peppers, seeded
   and sliced
1 cup snow peas

**1** Mix the cornstarch to a paste with the sherry. Stir in the soy sauce, stock and chili sauce.

**2** Heat the oil in a wok and stir-fry the pepper slices and snow peas for 2–3 minutes, until crisp-tender.

**3** Stir in the cornstarch mixture and toss over the heat for 1–2 minutes, until the vegetables are glistening and the sauce is hot. Serve immediately.

# Potatoes with Eggplant

Using baby vegetables adds to the attractiveness and the flavor of this dish.

**Serves 4**

10–12 baby potatoes, unpeeled
1 tablespoon corn oil
2 medium onions, sliced
4–6 curry leaves
1/2 teaspoon onion seeds
1 teaspoon crushed coriander seeds
1 teaspoon cumin seeds
1 medium red bell pepper, seeded and sliced
1 teaspoon grated fresh ginger root
1 teaspoon crushed garlic
1 teaspoon crushed dried red chiles
1 tablespoon chopped fresh fenugreek
6 small eggplant, cut in quarters
1 teaspoon chopped cilantro
1 tablespoon low-fat plain yogurt
cilantro leaves, to garnish

**1** Bring a pan of water to a boil, add the potatoes and cook them for about 20 minutes, until just soft. Drain and set aside.

**2** Heat the oil in a wok and fry the onions, curry leaves, onion seeds, crushed coriander seeds and cumin seeds until the onions are pale golden brown.

**3** Add the pepper strips, ginger, garlic, crushed chiles and fenugreek, followed by the eggplant and potatoes. Stir everything together and cover with a lid. Lower the heat and cook for 5–7 minutes.

**4** Remove the lid and add the cilantro. Stir in the yogurt. Serve garnished with the cilantro leaves.

**Cook's Tip**
*To prevent curdling, it is always best to whisk the yogurt before adding it to a hot dish. If using more of yogurt than is called for this recipe, stabilize it with 1 teaspoon cornstarch before adding it to a hot dish.*

# Green Beans with Corn

Frozen green beans are useful for this, as they cook quickly. This dish is a colorful side dish.

**Serves 4**

1 tablespoon sunflower oil
1/4 teaspoon mustard seeds
1 medium red onion, diced
1/3 cup frozen corn kernels
1/3 cup drained canned red kidney beans, rinsed
6 ounces frozen green beans
1 fresh red chile, seeded and diced
1 garlic clove, chopped
1-inch piece of fresh ginger root, finely chopped
1 tablespoon chopped cilantro
1 teaspoon salt
1 tomato, seeded and diced, to garnish

**1** Heat the oil in a wok. Add the mustard seeds and onion and fry over low heat, stirring occasionally, for about 2 minutes, until the seeds begin to pop and give off their aroma and the onion is beginning to soften.

**2** Add the corn, kidney beans and green beans. Toss over the heat for 3–5 minutes, until the frozen vegetables have thawed and the beans are crisp-tender.

**3** Add the chile, garlic, ginger, cilantro and salt and toss over the heat for 2–3 minutes.

**4** Remove the wok from heat. Transfer the mixture to a warmed serving dish and garnish with the diced tomato.

**Cook's Tip**
*Strictly speaking, Balti dishes such as these are cooked in a karahi or Balti pan, which is similar to a wok and available in a range of sizes and materials. It is possible to stir-fry in an ordinary frying pan, as long as it is quite deep, but the heat is not distributed evenly. In Pakistan, the food is often served directly from the karahi, which is placed on a special stand on the table.*

# Mushroom & Okra Curry

This simple but delicious curry is served with a fresh gingery mango relish.

**Serves 4**

4 garlic cloves, roughly chopped
1-inch piece of fresh ginger root, roughly chopped
1–2 fresh red chiles, seeded and chopped
¾ cup cold water
1 tablespoon sunflower oil
1 teaspoon coriander seeds
1 teaspoon cumin seeds
1 teaspoon ground cumin
seeds from 2 green cardamom pods, ground
pinch of ground turmeric
14-ounce can chopped tomatoes
6 cups mushrooms, quartered if large

8 ounces okra, trimmed and cut into ½-inch slices
2 tablespoons chopped cilantro
cooked basmati rice, to serve

**For the mango relish**

1 large ripe mango, about 1¼ pounds
1 small garlic clove, crushed
1 onion, finely chopped
2 teaspoons grated fresh ginger root
1 fresh red chile, seeded and finely chopped
pinch of sugar
pinch of salt

**1** First, make the relish. Peel the mango and cut the flesh from the pit. Mash it in a bowl or pulse it in a food processor. Stir in the rest of the relish ingredients. Set aside.

**2** Put the garlic, ginger, chiles and 3 tablespoons of the water into a blender and blend until smooth.

**3** Heat the oil in a large pan. Add the coriander and cumin seeds and let them sizzle for a few seconds. Add the ground cumin, cardamom and turmeric and cook for 1 minute. Add the paste from the blender, the tomatoes, the remaining water, the mushrooms and okra. Stir and bring to a boil. Lower the heat, cover, and simmer for 5 minutes.

**4** Uncover and cook for 10 more minutes, until the okra is tender. Stir in the cilantro and serve with the relish and rice.

# Bengali-style Vegetables

Many curries need to be cooked slowly if their full flavor is to be realized. This one is very quick and easy, thanks to spices that rapidly release their properties.

**Serves 4**

½ cauliflower, broken into florets
1 large potato, peeled and cut into 1-inch dice
4 ounces green beans, trimmed
2 zucchini, halved lengthwise and sliced
2 fresh green chiles, seeded and chopped

1-inch piece of fresh ginger root, finely chopped
½ cup plain yogurt
2 teaspoons ground coriander
½ teaspoon ground turmeric
2 tablespoons ghee or clarified butter
½ teaspoon garam masala
1 teaspoon cumin seeds
2 teaspoons sugar
pinch of ground cloves
pinch of ground cinnamon
pinch of ground cardamom
salt and ground black pepper

**1** Bring a large pan of lightly salted water to a boil. Add the cauliflower and potato and cook for 5 minutes. Add the beans and zucchini and cook for 2–3 more minutes.

**2** Drain the vegetables and put them into a bowl. Add the chiles, ginger, yogurt, ground coriander and turmeric. Season with plenty of salt and pepper and mix well.

**3** Heat the ghee in a large frying pan. Add the vegetable mixture and cook over high heat for 2 minutes, stirring.

**4** Stir in the garam masala and whole cumin seeds and fry for 2 minutes. Stir in the sugar and the remaining spices. Cook for about 1 minute or until all the liquid has evaporated. Serve.

**Cook's Tip**
*To clarify butter, melt ¼ cup butter in a small pan. Remove from heat and leave for 5 minutes. Pour off the clear yellow clarified butter, leaving the sediment in the pan.*

# Spinach with Mushrooms & Red Bell Pepper

This is a wonderful way to cook three tasty and nutritious vegetables. Serve the stir-fry very hot, with freshly made chapatis.

**Serves 4**

1 pound fresh or frozen spinach
2 tablespoons corn oil
2 onions, diced
6–8 curry leaves
1/4 teaspoon onion seeds
1 teaspoon crushed garlic
1 teaspoon grated fresh
  ginger root
1 teaspoon mild chili powder
1 teaspoon salt
1 1/2 teaspoons ground coriander
1 large red bell pepper, seeded
  and sliced
1 1/2 cups mushrooms,
  roughly chopped
1 cup low-fat fromage frais
2 tablespoons cilantro leaves

**1** Blanch the fresh spinach briefly in boiling water and drain thoroughly. Thaw the frozen spinach, then drain. Set aside.

**2** Heat the oil in a wok. Add the onions, curry leaves and onion seeds and fry, stirring occasionally, for 1–2 minutes. Add the garlic, ginger, chili powder, salt and ground coriander. Stir-fry for 2–3 more minutes.

**3** Add half the red bell pepper slices and all the mushrooms and continue to stir-fry for 2–3 minutes.

**4** Add the spinach and stir-fry for 4–6 minutes. Finally, stir in the fromage frais and half the cilantro, followed by the remaining red bell pepper slices. Fry over medium heat, stirring constantly, for 2–3 more minutes before serving, garnished with the remaining cilantro.

> **Variation**
> For a spicier dish, add one finely chopped fresh red chile with the pepper slices in step 3.

# Rice Noodles with Vegetable Chili Sauce

A mixture of fresh and canned ingredients, this is a very versatile dish.

**Serves 4**

1 tablespoon sunflower oil
1 onion, chopped
2 garlic cloves, crushed
1 fresh red chile, seeded and
  finely chopped
1 red bell pepper, seeded
  and diced
2 carrots, finely chopped
1 1/2 cups baby corn, halved
8-ounce can sliced bamboo
  shoots, drained and rinsed
14-ounce can red kidney beans,
  drained and rinsed
1 1/4 cups passata or
  sieved tomatoes
1 tablespoon soy sauce
1 teaspoon ground coriander
9 ounces rice noodles
2 tablespoons chopped cilantro
salt and ground black pepper
fresh parsley sprigs, to garnish

**1** Heat the oil in a large pan and fry the onion, garlic, chile and red bell pepper, stirring occasionally, for 5 minutes. Stir in the carrots, corn, bamboo shoots, kidney beans, passata or sieved tomatoes, soy sauce and ground coriander. Bring to a boil, then lower the heat, cover and simmer gently, stirring occasionally, for 30 minutes, until the vegetables are tender. Season with salt and pepper to taste.

**2** Meanwhile, bring a large pan of water to a boil, add the noodles and remove the pan from heat. Cover and let stand for about 4 minutes, until the noodles are just tender. Drain thoroughly, rinse with boiling water and drain again.

**3** Stir the cilantro into the sauce. Spoon the noodles into bowls, top with the sauce, garnish with parsley and serve.

> **Cook's Tip**
> Rice noodles are specified here, but you can use any type of noodles or even spaghetti.

# Penne with Artichokes

The sauce for this pasta dish is garlicky and richly flavored. It would make the perfect first course for a dinner party during the globe artichoke season.

**Serves 6**
juice of ½ lemon
2 globe artichokes
1 tablespoon olive oil
1 small fennel bulb, thinly sliced, with feathery tops reserved
1 onion, finely chopped
4 garlic cloves, finely chopped
a handful of fresh flat-leaf parsley, roughly chopped
14-ounce can chopped Italian plum tomatoes
⅔ cup dry white wine
3 cups dried penne
2 teaspoons capers, chopped
salt and ground black pepper
freshly grated Parmesan cheese, to serve

1 Fill a bowl with cold water and add the lemon juice. Cut off the artichoke stems, then pull off and discard the outer leaves. Cut off the tops of the pale inner leaves so that the bottom remains. Cut this in half lengthwise, then prise out and discard the hairy choke. Cut the artichokes lengthwise into ¼-inch slices, adding these to the bowl of acidulated water.

2 Bring a large pan of salted water to a boil, add the artichokes and boil them for 5 minutes. Drain and set aside.

3 Heat the oil in a large frying pan and cook the fennel, onion, garlic and parsley over low heat for about 10 minutes, until the fennel has softened and is lightly colored. Add the tomatoes and wine, with salt and pepper to taste. Bring to a boil, stirring, then simmer for 10–15 minutes. Stir in the artichokes, replace the lid and simmer for 10 more minutes.

4 Meanwhile, bring a pan of lightly salted water to a boil and cook the pasta for about 12 minutes, until it is al dente.

5 Drain the pasta and return it to the clean pan. Stir the capers into the sauce, pour it onto the pasta and toss well. Serve immediately, garnished with the reserved fennel fronds. Pass grated Parmesan separately.

# Conchiglie with Roasted Vegetables

Nothing could be simpler— or more delicious—than tossing freshly cooked pasta with roasted vegetables.

**Serves 4**
1 small eggplant
2 tablespoons extra virgin olive oil, plus extra for brushing
1 red bell pepper, seeded and cut into ½-inch squares
1 yellow or orange pepper, seeded and cut into ½-inch squares
2 zucchini, roughly diced
1 tablespoon chopped fresh flat-leaf parsley
1 teaspoon dried oregano
9 ounces baby Italian plum tomatoes, halved lengthwise
2 garlic cloves, roughly chopped
3 cups dried conchiglie
salt and ground black pepper
4–6 fresh herb flowers, to garnish

1 Preheat the oven to 450°F. Cut the eggplant in half and score the cut-sides deeply. Brush a roasting pan lightly with oil and place the eggplant on it, cut-sides down. Roast for 15 minutes. Remove the eggplant from the oven and lower the temperature to 375°F.

2 Cut the eggplant halves into chunks and return them to the roasting pan. Add the peppers and zucchini.

3 Pour the olive oil onto the vegetables and sprinkle with the herbs and salt and pepper to taste. Stir well. Roast for about 30 minutes, stirring twice. Stir in the tomatoes and garlic, then roast for 20 more minutes, stirring once or twice.

4 Meanwhile, bring a large pan of lightly salted water to a boil and cook the pasta for about 12 minutes or until it is al dente.

5 Drain the pasta and put it into a warmed bowl. Add the roasted vegetables and toss well. Garnish with herb flowers.

**Cook's Tip**
*Roasting the eggplant first releases some of its liquid and also makes it less likely to absorb fat.*

# Rigatoni with Winter Tomato Sauce

In winter, when fresh
tomatoes are not at their
best, Italians use canned
tomatoes to make this
superb sauce, which is
particularly good with
chunky pasta shapes.

**Serves 6–8**
2 tablespoons olive oil
1 garlic clove, thinly sliced
1 onion, finely chopped
1 carrot, finely chopped
1 celery stalk, finely chopped
a few leaves each fresh
    basil, thyme and oregano
    or marjoram

2 14-ounce cans chopped Italian
    plum tomatoes
1 tablespoon sun-dried
    tomato paste
1 teaspoon sugar
about 6 tablespoons dry red or
    white wine (optional)
3 cups dried rigatoni
salt and ground black pepper
chopped fresh mixed herbs,
    such as thyme and basil, to
    garnish (optional)
coarsely shaved Parmesan
    cheese, to serve

**1** Heat the olive oil in a medium saucepan, add the garlic slices
and stir over very low heat for 1–2 minutes.

**2** Add the onion, carrot, celery, basil, thyme and oregano
or marjoram. Cook over low heat, stirring frequently, for
5–7 minutes, until all the vegetables have softened and are
lightly colored.

**3** Add the canned tomatoes, tomato paste and sugar, then stir
in the wine, if using. Season with salt and pepper to taste. Bring
to a boil, stirring constantly, then lower the heat and simmer for
about 45 minutes, stirring occasionally.

**4** Meanwhile, bring a large pan of lightly salted water to a boil
and cook the pasta for 12 minutes or until *al dente*. Drain it and
put it into a warmed bowl.

**5** Pour the sauce on the rigatoni and toss well. If desired,
garnish with extra chopped herbs. Serve immediately, with
shavings of Parmesan passed separately.

# Whole-wheat Pasta with Caraway Cabbage

Cabbage and Brussels
sprouts are the perfect
partners for pasta in this
healthy dish.

**Serves 6**
2 tablespoons olive oil
3 onions, roughly
    chopped
1²⁄₃ cups vegetable stock

12 ounces round white cabbage,
    roughly chopped
12 ounces Brussels sprouts,
    trimmed and halved
2 teaspoons caraway seeds
1 tablespoon chopped fresh dill
1³⁄₄ cups fresh or dried
    whole-wheat pasta spirals
salt and ground black pepper
fresh dill sprigs, to garnish

**1** Heat the oil in a large saucepan. Add the onions and fry over
low heat, stirring occasionally, for 10 minutes, until softened and
golden in color. If they start to stick to the pan, moisten them
with a little of the stock.

**2** Add the chopped cabbage and Brussels sprouts and cook for
2–3 minutes, then stir in the caraway seeds and chopped dill.
Pour in the remaining stock and season with salt and pepper to
taste. Cover and simmer for 5–10 minutes, until the cabbage
and sprouts are crisp-tender.

**3** Meanwhile, bring a pan of lightly salted water to a boil and
cook the pasta for 12 minutes or until *al dente*.

**4** Drain the pasta, put it into a warmed bowl and add the
cabbage mixture. Toss lightly, adjust the seasoning, if necessary,
and serve immediately, garnished with dill.

---

**Cook's Tips**
• *If tiny baby Brussels sprouts are available, they can be used
whole for this dish.*
• *Not only do caraway seeds complement the flavor of
cabbage, they also make it more digestible.*

---

# Tagliatelle with Pea Sauce, Asparagus & Fava Beans

A creamy pea sauce provides a wonderful contrast to the crunchy young vegetables.

**Serves 4**
1 tablespoon olive oil
1 garlic clove, crushed
6 scallions, sliced
2 cups frozen peas, thawed
2 tablespoons chopped fresh
  sage, plus extra leaves
  to garnish
finely grated zest of 2 lemons
1³/₄ cups vegetable stock
12 ounces fresh young asparagus,
  trimmed and cut into
  2-inch lengths
2 cups frozen fava beans, thawed
2 cups fresh or dried tagliatelle
4 tablespoons low-fat
  yogurt, whisked

**1** Heat the oil in a pan. Add the garlic and scallions and fry over low heat, stirring occasionally, for 2–3 minutes, until softened, but not colored.

**2** Add the peas, sage, lemon zest and stock. Stir in one-third of the asparagus stalks. Bring to a boil, lower the heat and simmer for 10 minutes, until tender. Process in a blender until smooth, then scrape into a saucepan.

**3** Pop the fava beans out of their skins and set them aside. Bring a large pan of water to a boil, add the remaining asparagus and blanch for 2 minutes. Transfer the asparagus pieces to a colander with a draining spoon and set aside.

**4** Bring the water in the pan back to a boil, add the tagliatelle and cook for about 10 minutes, until it is *al dente*.

**5** Meanwhile, add the cooked asparagus and shelled beans to the sauce and reheat. Off the heat, stir the yogurt into the sauce. Drain the pasta and divide among four warmed plates. Top the pasta with the sauce. Garnish with a few extra sage

# Mushroom Bolognese

A quick—and exceedingly tasty—vegetarian version of the classic Italian meat dish.

**Serves 4**
1 tablespoon olive oil
1 onion, chopped
1 garlic clove, crushed
6 cups mushrooms, quartered
1 tablespoon tomato paste
14-ounce can chopped tomatoes
1 tablespoon chopped
  fresh oregano
1 pound fresh pasta
salt and ground black pepper
chopped fresh oregano, to garnish
Parmesan cheese,
  to serve (optional)

**1** Heat the oil in a large pan. Add the chopped onion and garlic and fry over low heat, stirring occasionally, for 2–3 minutes, until just beginning to soften.

**2** Add the mushrooms to the pan and cook over high heat, stirring occasionally, for 3–4 minutes.

**3** Stir in the tomato paste, chopped tomatoes and oregano. Lower the heat, cover and cook for 5 minutes.

**4** Meanwhile, bring a large pan of lightly salted water to a boil. Cook the pasta for 2–3 minutes, until *al dente*.

**5** Season the mushroom sauce to taste with salt and pepper. Drain the pasta, put it into a bowl and add the mushroom mixture. Toss thoroughly to mix. Serve in individual bowls. Add a sprinkling of extra oregano and top with shavings of fresh Parmesan cheese, if desired.

---

**Cook's Tips**
• If you prefer to use dried pasta, make it the first thing that you cook. It will take 10–12 minutes, during which time you can make the mushroom sauce.
• This dish is even more delicious if you use wild mushrooms, such as cèpes, oysters and chanterelles.

---

# Vegetable & Macaroni Casserole

A tasty change from macaroni and cheese, this dish is great for a family meal.

**Serves 6**

2 cups whole-wheat macaroni
scant 2 cups vegetable stock
8 ounces leeks, sliced
8 ounces broccoli florets
4 tablespoons low-fat spread
$\frac{1}{2}$ cup whole-wheat flour
$2\frac{1}{2}$ cups skim milk
1 cup grated low-fat aged
   Cheddar cheese
1 teaspoon prepared
   English mustard
12-ounce can corn
   kernels, drained
$\frac{1}{2}$ cup fresh whole-wheat
   bread crumbs
2 tablespoons chopped
   fresh parsley
2 tomatoes, cut into eighths
salt and ground black pepper

**1** Preheat the oven to 400°F. Bring a large pan of lightly salted water to a boil and cook the macaroni for 8–10 minutes, until *al dente.*

**2** Meanwhile, heat the stock in a separate pan and cook the leeks for 8 minutes. Add the broccoli florets and cook for 2 more minutes. Drain, reserving 1¼ cups of the vegetable stock.

**3** Put the low-fat spread, flour and milk in a saucepan. Add the reserved stock. Heat gently, whisking constantly, until the sauce comes to a boil and has thickened. Simmer gently for 3 minutes, stirring constantly.

**4** Remove the pan from heat, stir in two-thirds of the cheese, then add the macaroni, leeks, broccoli, mustard and corn. Mix well and season with salt and pepper to taste. Transfer the mixture to an ovenproof dish.

**5** Mix the remaining cheese, bread crumbs and parsley and sprinkle the mixture on the surface. Arrange the tomatoes on top and then bake for 30–40 minutes, until the topping is golden brown and bubbling.

# Spinach & Hazelnut Lasagne

Using low-fat fromage frais instead of a white sauce makes this a healthy version of a popular vegetarian dish, and spinach and hazelnuts provide variations on the usual themes.

**Serves 4**

2 pounds fresh spinach
1¼ cups vegetable stock
1 medium onion, finely chopped
1 garlic clove, crushed
$\frac{3}{4}$ cup hazelnuts
2 tablespoons chopped fresh basil
6 sheets no pre-cook lasagne
14-ounce can chopped tomatoes
scant 1 cup low-fat fromage frais
salt and ground black pepper
chopped hazelnuts and chopped
   fresh parsley, to garnish

**1** Preheat the oven to 400°F. Wash the spinach and place it in a pan with just the water that is still clinging to the leaves. Cover and cook over a fairly high heat for about 2 minutes, until the spinach has wilted. Drain well and set aside until needed.

**2** Heat 2 tablespoons of the stock in a large pan. Add the onion and garlic, bring to a boil, then simmer until softened. Stir in the spinach, hazelnuts and basil.

**3** In a large ovenproof dish, make layers of the spinach, lasagne and tomatoes. Season each layer with salt and pepper to taste. Pour in the remaining stock. Spread the fromage frais evenly on top.

**4** Bake the lasagne for about 45 minutes or until golden brown. Serve hot, garnished with lines of hazelnuts and chopped fresh parsley.

**Cook's Tip**
*The flavor of hazelnuts is improved if they are roasted. Place them on a baking sheet and bake in a medium oven or under a hot broiler until light golden.*

# Zucchini, Corn & Plum Tomato Whole-wheat Pizza

This tasty whole-wheat pizza has a colorful topping. It is good hot or cold.

**Serves 6**

2 cups whole-wheat flour
pinch of salt
2 teaspoons baking powder
4 tablespoons margarine
⅔ cup skim milk
2 tablespoons tomato paste
2 teaspoons dried herbes de Provence
2 teaspoons olive oil
1 onion, sliced

1 garlic clove, crushed
2 small zucchini, sliced
1½ cups mushrooms, sliced
⅔ cup frozen corn kernels
2 plum tomatoes, sliced
½ cup grated low-fat Red Leicester cheese
½ cup grated low-fat mozzarella cheese
salt and ground black pepper
fresh basil sprigs, to garnish

**1** Preheat the oven to 425°F. Line a baking sheet with nonstick baking parchment. Put the flour, salt and baking powder in a bowl and rub in the margarine until the mixture resembles bread crumbs. Add enough milk to form a soft dough and knead lightly. Roll the dough out on a lightly floured surface, into a round about 10 inches in diameter.

**2** Place the dough on the prepared baking sheet and pinch the edges to make a rim. Spread the tomato paste on the crust and sprinkle the herbs on top.

**3** Heat the oil in a frying pan and cook the onion, garlic, zucchini and mushrooms gently for 10 minutes, stirring occasionally. Spread the vegetable mixture on the pizza crust, sprinkle on the corn and season to taste with salt and pepper. Arrange the tomato slices on top.

**4** Mix the cheeses and sprinkle on the pizza. Bake for 25–30 minutes, until cooked and golden brown. Serve the pizza hot or cold in slices, garnished with basil sprigs.

# Low-fat Calzone

Like pizza, calzone conjures up an image of sheer indulgence in terms of its fat content, but here's one you can eat with a completely clear conscience.

**Makes 4**

4 cups all-purpose flour
pinch of salt
1 envelope active dry yeast
about 1½ cups warm water

**For the filling**

1 teaspoon olive oil, plus extra for greasing
1 medium red onion, thinly sliced
3 medium zucchini, total weight about 12 ounces, sliced
2 large tomatoes, diced
5 ounces low-fat mozzarella cheese, diced
1 tablespoon chopped fresh oregano, plus extra sprigs, to garnish
skim milk, to glaze
salt and ground black pepper

**1** Sift the flour and salt into a bowl and stir in the yeast. Stir in just enough warm water to mix into a soft dough. Knead for about 5 minutes, until smooth.

**2** Return to the clean bowl, cover with plastic wrap and set in a warm place for about 1 hour or until doubled in bulk.

**3** Meanwhile, make the filling. Heat the oil. Add the onion and zucchini and fry over low heat, stirring occasionally, for 3–4 minutes, until softened but not colored. Remove from heat and add the tomatoes, cheese and oregano, then season with salt and pepper to taste.

**4** Preheat the oven to 425°F. Knead the dough lightly and divide into four pieces. Roll out each piece on a floured surface into an 8-inch round. Place one-quarter of the filling on one half of each round.

**5** Brush the edges of each round with milk and fold the dough over to enclose the filling. Press the edges together firmly to seal. Brush each calzone with milk to glaze.

**6** Bake on a lightly oiled baking sheet for 15–20 minutes. Serve.

# Polenta with Baked Tomatoes & Olives

A staple of northern Italy, polenta is a nourishing, filling food, served here with a delicious fresh tomato and olive topping.

**Serves 4–6**

9 cups water
4½ cups quick-cook polenta
2 teaspoons olive oil, plus extra for greasing
12 large ripe plum tomatoes, sliced
4 garlic cloves, thinly sliced
2 tablespoons chopped fresh oregano or marjoram
1 cup pitted black olives
salt and ground black pepper

**1** Pour the water into a large saucepan and bring it to a boil. Add the polenta, whisking constantly, and continue to whisk while simmering for 5 minutes.

**2** Remove the pan from heat and pour the polenta into a 13 x 9-inch jelly roll pan. Smooth the surface level and let cool.

**3** Preheat the oven to 350°F. When the polenta is cool and set, stamp out 12 rounds with a 3-inch round cookie cutter. Lay them so that they overlap slightly in a lightly oiled ovenproof dish.

**4** Layer the tomatoes, garlic, fresh herbs and olives on top of the polenta, seasoning the layers with salt and pepper to taste as you go. Drizzle with the olive oil, and bake, uncovered, for 30–35 minutes. Serve immediately.

**Cook's Tip**
*Olive oil contains a high proportion of monounsaturated fats—the "good" fats—as well as vitamin A. It is a healthy choice, as it helps to lower levels of blood cholesterol and is a useful part of a low-fat diet.*

# Potato Gnocchi with Hazelnut Sauce

These delicate potato dumplings are dressed with a light creamy-tasting hazelnut sauce.

**Serves 4**

1½ pounds large potatoes
1 cup all-purpose flour, plus extra for dusting

**For the hazelnut sauce**

1 cup hazelnuts, roasted
1 garlic clove, roughly chopped
½ teaspoon grated lemon zest
½ teaspoon lemon juice
2 tablespoons sunflower oil
scant ¾ cup low-fat fromage blanc
salt and ground black pepper

**1** Make the sauce. Put just over half of the hazelnuts in a food processor or blender with the garlic, grated lemon zest and juice. Process until coarsely chopped. With the motor running, gradually add the oil until the mixture is smooth. Spoon into a heatproof bowl and mix in the fromage blanc. Season to taste.

**2** Put the potatoes in a pan of cold water. Bring to a boil and cook for 20–25 minutes. Drain well. When cool enough to handle, peel them and pass through a food mill into a bowl.

**3** Add the flour, a little at a time, until the mixture is smooth and slightly sticky. Add salt to taste. Roll out the mixture on a floured board to a long sausage ½ inch in diameter. Cut into ¾-inch lengths. Roll one piece at a time on a floured fork to make the characteristic ridges. Flip onto a floured plate or tray.

**4** Bring a large pan of water to a boil and drop in about 20 gnocchi at a time. They will rise to the surface. Cook for 10–15 seconds, then lift them out with a draining spoon. Drop into a dish and keep hot. Continue with the rest of the gnocchi.

**5** To heat the sauce, place the bowl over a pan of simmering water and heat gently, being careful not to let it curdle. Pour the sauce onto the gnocchi. Roughly chop the remaining hazelnuts, scatter them on top and serve.

# Spring Vegetable Omelet

This resembles a Spanish omelet in that it is not flipped, but finished off under the broiler. Packed with tender vegetables, it makes a very tasty light lunch.

**Serves 4**
$^1/_2$ cup fresh asparagus tips
2 ounces collard greens, shredded
1 tablespoon sunflower oil
1 onion, sliced
6 ounces cooked new potatoes, halved or diced
2 tomatoes, chopped
6 eggs
1–2 tablespoons chopped fresh mixed herbs
salt and ground black pepper
salad, to serve

**1** Steam the asparagus tips and collard greens over a saucepan of boiling water for 5–10 minutes, until tender. Drain the vegetables and keep them warm.

**2** Heat the oil in a large frying pan, that can safely be used under the broiler. (Cover a wooden handle with aluminum foil to protect it.) Add the onion and cook over low heat, stirring occasionally, for 5–10 minutes, until softened.

**3** Add the new potatoes and cook, stirring constantly for 3 minutes. Stir in the tomatoes, asparagus and collard greens. Beat the eggs lightly with the herbs and season to taste with salt and pepper.

**4** Preheat the broiler. Pour the egg mixture onto the vegetables, then cook over low heat until the bottom of the omelet is golden brown. Slide the pan under the broiler and cook the omelet for 2–3 minutes, until the top is golden brown. Serve immediately, cut into wedges, with salad.

**Cook's Tip**
*Remember to use a low-fat dressing for the salad, such as cider vinegar and low-fat fromage frais.*

# Mushroom & Sunflower Seed Tart

Mushrooms, baby corn and spinach make a delectable filling for a tart.

**Serves 6**
1$^1/_2$ cups whole-wheat flour
6 tablespoons low-fat spread
1 tablespoon olive oil
6 ounces baby corn, each cut into 2–3 pieces
2 tablespoons sunflower seeds
3 cups mushrooms
3 ounces fresh spinach leaves, chopped
juice of 1 lemon
salt and ground black pepper
tomato salad, to serve

**1** Preheat the oven to 350°F. Sift the flour into a bowl, then add the bran from the sieve. Rub in the low-fat spread until the mixture resembles bread crumbs. Add enough water to make a firm dough.

**2** Roll out the dough on a lightly floured surface and line a 9-inch tart pan. Prick the crust, line it with aluminum foil and add a layer of baking beans. Bake blind for 15 minutes, then remove the foil and beans. Return the pastry shell to the oven and bake for 10 more minutes, or until the pastry is crisp and golden brown.

**3** Meanwhile, heat the oil in a heavy pan. Add the corn with the sunflower seeds and fry, stirring occasionally, for 5–8 minutes, until lightly browned all over.

**4** Add the mushrooms, lower the heat slightly and cook the mixture for 2–3 minutes. Stir in the chopped spinach, cover the pan and cook for 2–3 minutes.

**5** Sharpen the filling with a little lemon juice. Stir in salt and pepper to taste. Spoon into the shell.. Serve warm or cold, with a tomato salad.

**Cook's Tip**
*If the mushrooms are large, cut them in half or quarters.*

## Carrot Mousse with Mushroom Sauce

This impressive yet easy-to-make mousse makes healthy eating a pleasure.

**Serves 4**
about 12 ounces carrots, roughly chopped
1 small red bell pepper, seeded and roughly chopped
3 tablespoons vegetable stock
2 eggs, plus 1 egg white
½ cup Quark or low-fat cream cheese
1 tablespoon chopped fresh tarragon
salt and ground black pepper
fresh tarragon sprigs, to garnish
boiled rice and leeks, to serve

**For the mushroom sauce**
2 tablespoons low-fat spread
2¼ cups mushrooms, sliced
2 tablespoons all-purpose flour
1 cup skim milk

**1** Preheat the oven to 375°F. Line four dariole molds or ramekins with nonstick baking parchment. Put the carrots, red bell pepper and stock in a small pan and bring to a boil. Cover and cook for 5 minutes or until tender. Drain.

**2** Lightly beat the eggs and egg white. Mix with the Quark or cheese. Season to taste. Purée the cooked vegetables in a food processor or blender. Add the cheese mixture and process for a few more seconds, until smooth. Stir in the chopped tarragon.

**3** Divide the mixture among the molds or ramekins and cover with aluminum foil. Place in a roasting pan. Pour in boiling water to come halfway up the sides. Bake for 35 minutes, or until set.

**4** Make the sauce. Melt 1 tablespoon of the low-fat spread in a frying pan. Sauté the mushrooms for 5 minutes, until soft. Put the remaining low fat spread in a small pan and add the flour and milk. Cook over medium heat, stirring until the sauce thickens. Stir in the mushrooms and season to taste.

**5** Turn out each mousse onto a plate. Spoon on a little sauce and garnish with the tarragon. Serve, with rice and leeks.

# Spinach & Potato Galette

Creamy layers of potato, spinach and herbs make a warming supper dish.

**Serves 6**
2 pounds large potatoes, peeled
1 pound fresh spinach
2 eggs
1¾ cups low-fat cream cheese
1 tablespoon grainy mustard
2 ounces chopped fresh herbs (chives, parsley, chervil or sorrel)
salt and ground black pepper
salad, to serve

**1** Preheat the oven to 350°F. Line a deep 9-inch round cake pan with nonstick baking parchment.

**2** Place the potatoes in a large pan and cover with cold water. Bring to a boil and cook for 10 minutes. Drain well and let cool slightly before slicing thinly.

**3** Wash the spinach and place it in a large pan with only the water that still clings to the leaves. Cover and cook over low heat, stirring once, until the spinach has just wilted. Drain well in a sieve and squeeze out the excess moisture with your hands. Chop finely.

**4** Beat the eggs with the cream cheese and mustard, then stir in the chopped spinach and fresh herbs.

**5** Place a layer of the sliced potatoes in the lined pan, arranging them in concentric circles. Top with a spoonful of the cream cheese mixture and spread out.

**6** Continue layering, seasoning to taste with salt and pepper as you go, until all the potatoes and the cream cheese mixture have been used. Cover the cake pan with aluminum foil and place it in a roasting pan.

**7** Fill the roasting pan with enough boiling water to come halfway up the sides of the cake pan and cook for 45–50 minutes. Turn out onto a plate and serve hot or cold, with a salad of dressed leaves and tomatoes.

# Broccoli & Chestnut Terrine

Served hot or cold, this versatile terrine is equally suitable for a dinner party or a picnic.

**Serves 4–6**

1 pound broccoli, cut into
   small florets
8 ounces cooked chestnuts,
   roughly chopped
1 cup fresh whole-wheat
   bread crumbs
4 tablespoons low-fat
   plain yogurt
2 tablespoons freshly grated
   Parmesan cheese
freshly grated nutmeg
2 eggs, beaten
salt and ground black pepper
steamed new potatoes and
   dressed leaves, to serve

**1** Preheat the oven to 350°F. Line a 2-pound loaf pan with nonstick baking parchment.

**2** Blanch or steam the broccoli for 3–4 minutes, until just tender. Drain well. Reserve one-quarter of the florets (choosing the smallest ones) and chop the rest finely.

**3** Put the chestnuts in a bowl and stir in bread crumbs, yogurt and Parmesan. Season with nutmeg, salt and pepper to taste, then stir in the chopped broccoli, and the beaten eggs. Fold in the reserved broccoli florets.

**4** Spoon the broccoli mixture into the prepared pan and level the surface. Place the loaf pan in a roasting pan. Pour in boiling water to come halfway up the sides of the loaf pan. Bake for 20–25 minutes.

**5** Remove from the oven and invert onto a plate or tray. Serve in slices, with new potatoes and dressed leaves.

> **Cook's Tip**
> *To cook chestnuts, nick the shells, roast for about 5 minutes, peel and then steam or boil.*

# Ratatouille Crêpes

Pretty enough to serve for a dinner party, and packed with juicy vegetables, these pancakes are a tasty treat.

**Serves 4**

¾ cup all-purpose flour
¼ cup medium oats
1 egg, lightly beaten
1¼ cups skim milk
light oil cooking spray, for greasing
mixed salad, to serve

**For the filling**
1 large eggplant, cut into
   1-inch cubes
1 garlic clove, crushed
2 medium zucchini, sliced
1 green bell pepper, seeded
   and sliced
1 red bell pepper, seeded and sliced
5 tablespoons vegetable stock
7-ounce can chopped tomatoes
1 teaspoon cornstarch, mixed to
   a paste with 2 teaspoons water
salt and ground black pepper

**1** Sift the flour and a pinch of salt into a bowl. Stir in the oats. Make a well in the center, add the egg and half the milk and mix into a smooth batter. Gradually beat in the remaining milk. Cover the bowl and set aside for 30 minutes.

**2** Spray an 7-inch crêpe pan with cooking spray. Heat the pan, then pour in just enough batter to cover the bottom thinly. Cook the crêpe for 2–3 minutes, until set and the underside is golden brown. Flip over and cook for 1–2 more minutes. Slide the crêpes onto a plate lined with nonstick baking parchment. Make more crêpes in the same way, adding them to the stack and interleaving them with baking parchment. Keep warm.

**3** Make the filling. Put the eggplant cubes in a colander and sprinkle well with salt. Let drain in the sink for 30 minutes. Rinse thoroughly and drain again.

**4** Put the garlic, zucchini, peppers, stock and tomatoes into a large pan. Simmer, stirring occasionally, for 10 minutes. Add the eggplant and cook for 15 more minutes. Stir in the cornstarch paste and simmer for 2 minutes. Season to taste.

**5** Spoon the mixture into the middle of each crêpe. Fold them in half, then in half again to make cones. Serve with salad.

# Red Bell Pepper & Watercress Phyllo Purses

These crisp pastry purses have a delectable ricotta and vegetable filling. They are perfect for special occasion meals and dinner parties as they can be made in advance.

**Makes 8**

3 red bell peppers, halved
    and seeded
6 ounces watercress
$\frac{1}{2}$ cup low-fat ricotta cheese
blanched almonds, toasted
    and chopped
8 sheets of phyllo pastry, thawed
    if frozen
2 tablespoons olive oil
salt and ground black pepper
frisée salad, to serve

**1** Preheat the oven to 375°F. Place the pepper halves, skin-side up, on a broiler pan and broil until the skins have blistered and charred. Transfer to a bowl and cover with crumpled paper towels. Let cool slightly, then rub off the skins and chop the flesh roughly.

**2** Put the peppers and watercress in a food processor and pulse until coarsely chopped. Spoon into a bowl and stir in the ricotta and almonds. Season with salt and pepper to taste.

**3** Working with one sheet of phyllo pastry at a time and keeping the others covered, cut out two 7-inch squares and two 2-inch squares from each sheet. Brush one large square with a little olive oil and top it with a second large square at an angle of 45 degrees to form a star shape.

**4** Place one of the small squares in the center of the star shape, brush lightly with oil and top with a second small square. Set this aside, covered with plastic wrap, and make more layered pastry shapes in the same way.

**5** Divide the red bell pepper mixture among the pastries. Bring the edges of each together to form a purse shape and twist to seal. Place the purses on a lightly greased baking sheet and cook for 25–30 minutes, until golden. Serve with a frisée salad.

# Cheese, Onion & Mushroom Tart

A tasty savory tart makes great picnic fare and is also ideal for family suppers.

**Serves 6**

$1\frac{1}{2}$ cups whole-wheat flour, plus
    extra for dusting
6 tablespoons low-fat
    polyunsaturated margarine
1 onion, sliced
1 leek, sliced
$2\frac{1}{4}$ cups mushrooms, chopped
2 tablespoons vegetable stock
2 eggs
$\frac{2}{3}$ cup skim milk
$\frac{2}{3}$ cup frozen corn kernels
2 tablespoons snipped
    fresh chives
1 tablespoon chopped
    fresh parsley
$\frac{3}{4}$ cup finely grated low-fat aged
    Cheddar cheese
salt and ground black pepper
chives, to garnish

**1** Sift the flour and a pinch of salt into a bowl. Add the margarine and rub in with your fingertips until the mixture resembles fine bread crumbs, then add enough cold water to make a soft dough. Wrap and chill for 30 minutes.

**2** Mix the onion, leek, mushrooms and vegetable stock in a saucepan. Bring to a boil, then cover and cook over low heat for 10 minutes, until the vegetables are just tender. Drain well and set aside.

**3** Preheat the oven to 400°F. Roll out the pastry on a lightly floured surface and line an 8-inch tart pan. Place on a baking sheet. Using a draining spoon, spread the vegetable mixture in the pastry shell.

**4** Beat the eggs and milk together in a pitcher. Add the corn, snipped chives, parsley and cheese and mix well. Season to taste with salt and pepper.

**5** Pour the mixture over the vegetables. Bake for 20 minutes, then reduce the oven temperature to 350°F, and cook for 30 more minutes, until the filling is set and lightly browned. Garnish with chives and serve warm or cold in slices.

# Wild Rice Rösti with Carrot & Orange Purée

Rösti is a traditional dish from Switzerland. This variation has the extra nuttiness of wild rice.

**Serves 6**

1/3 cup wild rice
2 pounds large potatoes
2 tablespoons walnut oil

1 teaspoon yellow mustard seeds
1 onion, finely chopped
2 tablespoons fresh thyme leaves
salt and ground black pepper
broccoli and green beans, to serve

**For the purée**

1 large orange
12 ounces carrots, chopped

**1** Make the purée. Pare two large strips of zest from the orange and put them in a pan with the carrots. Cover with cold water and bring to a boil. Cook for 10 minutes or until the carrots are tender. Drain well and discard the zest. Squeeze the orange and put 4 tablespoons of the juice in a blender or food processor with the carrots. Process into a purée.

**2** Place the wild rice in a clean pan and cover with water. Bring to a boil and cook for 30–40 minutes, until the rice is just starting to split but is still crunchy. Drain.

**3** Put the unpeeled potatoes in a large pan and cover with cold water. Bring to a boil and cook for 15 minutes. Drain well. When they are cool enough to handle, peel them and grate them coarsely into a large bowl. Add the cooked rice.

**4** Heat 1 tablespoon of the oil in a nonstick frying pan and stir in the mustard seeds. When they start to pop, add the onion and cook gently for 5 minutes, until softened. Add to the potato mixture, then stir in the thyme leaves. Season to taste.

**5** Heat the remaining oil in the frying pan and add the potato mixture. Press down well and cook for 10 minutes. Cover the pan with an inverted plate. Flip over, then slide the rösti back into the pan. Cook for 10 more minutes. Meanwhile, reheat the purée. Serve the rösti with broccoli, green beans and the purée.

# Mixed Mushroom & Parmesan Risotto

A brown rice risotto of mixed mushrooms, herbs and fresh Parmesan cheese, this is beautifully moist and full of flavor.

**Serves 4**

1/2 cup dried porcini mushrooms
2/3 cup hot water
1 tablespoon olive oil
4 shallots, finely chopped
2 garlic cloves, crushed

6 cups mixed cultivated and
  wild mushrooms, sliced
1 1/4 cups long-grain brown rice
3 3/4 cups hot vegetable stock
3 tablespoons chopped fresh
  flat-leaf parsley
4 tablespoons freshly grated
  Parmesan cheese
salt and ground black pepper

**1** Soak the porcini mushrooms in the hot water for 20 minutes. Heat the oil in a large, heavy pan. Add the shallots and garlic and cook over low heat, stirring occasionally, for about 5 minutes, until softened. Drain the porcini, reserving their liquid, and chop them roughly.

**2** Add all the mushrooms to the pan, with the strained porcini soaking liquid. Stir in the brown rice and one-third of the hot stock. (Keep the stock simmering in a pan.)

**3** Bring to a boil, lower the heat and simmer gently, stirring frequently, until all the liquid has been absorbed. Add a ladleful of hot stock and stir until it, too, has been absorbed.

**4** Continue in this way, adding a ladleful of hot stock at a time and stirring frequently, until the rice is cooked and creamy but still retains "bite" at the center of the grain. This should take about 35 minutes, and it may not be necessary to add all the vegetable stock.

**5** Season with plenty of salt and pepper, stir in the chopped parsley and grated Parmesan and transfer to a warmed serving dish. Serve immediately.

# Lentil Risotto with Vegetables

Although purists may blanch at the concept of adding lentils to a risotto, this actually works very well. The lentils benefit from soaking, but if you are in a hurry, use red split lentils, which don't need to be soaked.

**Serves 4**

generous 1 cup brown basmati rice, washed and drained
4 teaspoons sunflower oil
1 large onion, thinly sliced
2 garlic cloves, crushed
1 large carrot, cut into matchsticks
1/2 cup green or brown lentils, soaked and drained
1 teaspoon ground cumin
1 teaspoon ground cinnamon
20 black cardamom seeds
6 cloves
2 1/2 cups vegetable stock
2 bay leaves
2 celery stalks
1 large avocado
3 plum tomatoes
salt and ground black pepper
green salad, to serve

**1** Rinse the rice several times in cold water. If there is enough time, let it soak for 30 minutes in the water used for the final rinse. Drain well.

**2** Heat the oil in a large, heavy pan. Add the onion, garlic and carrot and fry over low heat, stirring occasionally, for 5–6 minutes, until the onion is softened.

**3** Add the drained rice and lentils, with the spices, and cook the mixture over low heat for 5 more minutes, stirring to prevent it from sticking to the pan.

**4** Pour in the stock. Add the bay leaves and bring to a boil, then lower the heat, cover the pan and simmer for 15 more minutes or until the liquid has been absorbed and the rice and lentils are tender.

**5** Meanwhile, chop the celery into half-rounds and dice the avocado and tomatoes. Add the fresh ingredients to the rice and lentils and mix well. Season to taste. Spoon into a large serving bowl and serve immediately with a green salad.

# Red Bell Pepper Risotto

Several different types of risotto rice are available, and it is worth experimenting to find the one your family prefers. Look out for arborio, carnaroli and Vialone Nano.

**Serves 6**

3 large red bell peppers
2 tablespoons olive oil
3 large garlic cloves, thinly sliced
1 1/2 14-ounce cans chopped tomatoes
2 bay leaves
2 1/2 cups arborio or other risotto rice
about 6 cups hot vegetable stock
6 fresh basil leaves, snipped
salt and ground black pepper

**1** Put the peppers in a broiler pan and broil until the skins are charred and blistered all over. Put them in a bowl, cover with crumpled paper towels and leave for 10 minutes. Peel off the skins, then slice the flesh, discarding the cores and seeds.

**2** Heat the oil in a wide, shallow pan. Add the garlic and tomatoes and cook over low heat, stirring occasionally, for 5 minutes. Stir in the pepper slices and bay leaves and cook for 15 more minutes.

**3** Stir the rice into the vegetable mixture and cook, stirring constantly, for 2 minutes, then add a ladleful of the hot stock. Cook, stirring constantly, until it has been absorbed. (Keep the stock simmering in a pan adjacent to the risotto.)

**4** Continue to add stock in this way, making sure that each addition has been absorbed before ladling in the next. When the rice is tender, season with salt and pepper to taste. Remove the pan from heat, cover and let stand for 10 minutes before stirring in the basil and serving.

**Variation**
*Both yellow and orange bell peppers are also suitable for this recipe, but green bell peppers are too acerbic.*

# Mushroom, Leek & Cashew Risotto

Because this risotto is made with brown rice instead of the traditional Italian arborio rice, it has a delicious nutty flavor and interesting texture.

**Serves 4**
1 1/3 cups long-grain brown rice
3 3/4 cups vegetable stock
1 tablespoon walnut or
    hazelnut oil
2 leeks, sliced
3 cups mixed wild or cultivated
    mushrooms, sliced
1/2 cup cashews
grated zest of 1 lemon
2 tablespoons chopped
    fresh thyme
scant 1/4 cup pumpkin seeds
salt and ground black pepper

**For the garnish**
fresh thyme leaves
lemon wedges

**1** Place the brown rice in a large pan, pour in the stock and bring to a boil over medium heat. Lower the heat and cook gently for about 30 minutes, until all the stock has been absorbed and the rice grains are tender.

**2** About 5 minutes before the rice will be ready, heat the oil in a large, heavy frying pan. Add the leeks and mushrooms and fry over low heat, stirring occasionally, for 3 minutes, until the leeks are softened.

**3** Add the cashews, grated lemon zest and chopped thyme to the vegetable mixture and cook over low heat, stirring frequently, for 1–2 more minutes. Season to taste with salt and pepper.

**4** Drain off any excess stock from the cooked rice and stir the rice into the vegetable mixture. Turn the mixture into a warmed serving dish. Sprinkle the pumpkin seeds on top and garnish with the fresh thyme sprigs and lemon wedges. Serve the risotto immediately.

# Risotto Primavera

Celebrate springtime with this quick and easy rice dish. Use organic vegetables, if possible, so that you can really savor the flavor.

**Serves 4**
9 ounces mixed spring vegetables
2 teaspoons olive oil
1 medium onion, sliced
1 1/4 cups risotto rice
1/2 teaspoon ground turmeric
about 2 1/2 cups vegetable stock
3 tablespoons chopped
    fresh parsley
salt and ground black pepper

**1** Prepare the vegetables according to type, cutting them to more or less the same size and leaving small ones whole so that they cook evenly.

**2** Heat the oil in a large, nonstick pan. Add the onion and fry over low heat, stirring occasionally, for 10 minutes, until softened and golden.

**3** Stir in the rice and cook, stirring constantly, for 1–2 minutes, until the grains are all coated with oil and glistening. Add the turmeric and cook, stirring constantly, for 1 minute, then add the vegetable stock. Season well with salt and pepper. Bring to a boil, then add the vegetables.

**4** Bring back to a boil, then lower the heat, cover and cook gently, stirring occasionally, for 20 minutes or until the rice is tender and most of the liquid has been absorbed. Add more stock if necessary.

**5** Stir in the parsley. Transfer the risotto to a warmed serving dish and serve immediately.

**Variation**
Use this risotto to stuff lightly broiled, halved red bell peppers, but chop the vegetables finely in step 1.

# Lemon & Herb Risotto Cake

This unusual rice dish can be served as a main course with a mixed salad or as a satisfying side dish. It's also good served cold and packs well for picnics.

**Serves 4**

light oil cooking spray
1 small leek, thinly sliced
2½ cups vegetable stock
generous 1 cup risotto rice
finely grated zest of 1 lemon
2 tablespoons chopped
   fresh chives
2 tablespoons chopped
   fresh parsley
¾ cup grated low-fat
   mozzarella cheese
salt and ground black pepper

**For the garnish**

fresh flat-leaf parsley sprigs
lemon wedges

**1** Preheat the oven to 400°F. Thinly coat an 8½-inch springform cake pan with light oil cooking spray and set aside.

**2** Put the slices of leek in a large pan with 3 tablespoons of the vegetable stock. Cook over medium heat, stirring occasionally, for about 5 minutes, until softened. Add the rice and the remaining stock.

**3** Bring to a boil. Lower the heat, cover the pan and simmer gently, stirring occasionally, for about 20 minutes or until all the liquid has been absorbed.

**4** Stir in the lemon zest, chives, chopped parsley and grated mozzarella and season with salt and pepper to taste. Spoon into the pan, cover with aluminum foil and bake for 30–35 minutes or until lightly browned. Turn out and cut into slices. Serve immediately, garnished with parsley and lemon wedges.

> **Cook's Tip**
> If you cannot obtain risotto rice, use short-grain rice—the type normally used for rice pudding—instead.

# Low-fat Vegetable Paella

A delicious change from the more traditional seafood- or chicken-based paella, this vegetarian version is full of flavor and includes plenty of healthy fiber.

**Serves 6**

1 onion, chopped
2 garlic cloves,
   crushed
8 ounces leeks, sliced
3 celery stalks, chopped
1 red bell pepper, seeded
   and sliced
2 zucchini, sliced
2¼ cups brown cap
   mushrooms, sliced
1½ cups frozen peas
2½ cups long-grain brown rice
14-ounce can cannellini beans,
   drained and rinsed
3¾ cups vegetable stock
4 tablespoons dry white wine
a few saffron threads
8 ounces cherry tomatoes, halved
3–4 tablespoons chopped fresh
   mixed herbs
salt and ground black pepper
lemon wedges, whole cherry
   tomatoes and celery leaves,
   to garnish

**1** Mix the onion, garlic, leeks, celery, red bell pepper, zucchini and mushrooms in a large, heavy pan or flameproof casserole. Add the peas, rice, cannellini beans, stock, wine and saffron. Bring to a boil over medium heat, stirring constantly, then lower the heat and simmer, stirring occasionally, for about 35 minutes, until almost all the liquid has been absorbed and the rice is tender.

**2** Stir in the tomatoes and chopped herbs, season to taste with salt and pepper and heat through for 1–2 minutes. Serve garnished with lemon wedges, tomatoes and celery leaves.

> **Cook's Tips**
> • Paella, which originated in Valencia, is not actually the name of the dish but the heavy, two-handled, cast-iron pan in which it is traditionally cooked.
> • Long-grain rice works very well in this recipe, but for a more authentic texture, try to obtain a Spanish rice, such as calasparra, or even use risotto rice.

# Vegetable Biryani

The most everyday ingredients can be transformed into an exotic dish with a bit of imagination and flair.

**Serves 4–6**
scant 1 cup long-grain rice
2 whole cloves
seeds of 2 cardamom pods
scant 2 cups vegetable stock
2 garlic cloves
1 small onion, roughly chopped
1 teaspoon cumin seeds
1 teaspoon ground coriander
1/2 teaspoon ground turmeric

1/2 teaspoon mild chili powder
1 large potato, peeled and cut into 1-inch cubes
2 carrots, sliced
1/2 cauliflower, broken into florets
2 ounces green beans, cut into short lengths
6 tablespoons water
2 tablespoons chopped cilantro
2 tablespoons freshly squeezed lime juice
salt and ground black pepper
cilantro sprigs, to garnish

**1** Put the rice, cloves and cardamom seeds into a large, heavy saucepan. Pour in the stock and bring to a boil, then lower the heat, cover and simmer for 20 minutes or until all the stock has been absorbed.

**2** Meanwhile, put the garlic, onion and remaining spices into a spice mill. Grind into a powder, then put into a bowl and stir in enough water to make a paste.

**3** Preheat the oven to 350°F. Spoon the spicy paste into a flameproof casserole and cook over low heat, stirring frequently, for 2 minutes.

**4** Add the vegetables and measured water. Cover and cook over low heat for 12 minutes, stirring occasionally. Add the chopped cilantro.

**5** Spoon the rice onto the vegetables. Sprinkle on the lime juice and season to taste. Cover and cook in the oven for 25 minutes or until the vegetables are tender. Fluff up the rice with a fork before serving. Garnish with cilantro sprigs.

# Tomato, Pistachio & Sesame Seed Pilaf

Nuts and seeds can really lift the flavor of a simple vegetable and rice dish. The spicing is subtle but essential in this tasty pilaf.

**Serves 4**
generous 1 cup brown basmati rice
2 1/2 cups vegetable stock

pinch of saffron threads soaked in 1 tablespoon boiling water
3 tomatoes, peeled and chopped
1 red bell pepper, seeded and finely diced
seeds from 4–5 cardamom pods
1/4 cup pistachios, roughly chopped
2 tablespoons sesame seeds, toasted
salt

**1** Rinse the rice several times in cold water. If there is enough time, let it soak for 30 minutes in the water used for the final rinse. Drain well.

**2** Drain the rice and put it into a large pan. Add the stock, saffron soaking liquid and a pinch of salt. Bring to a boil, then lower the heat, cover and simmer for 25 minutes.

**3** Add the tomatoes and red bell pepper to the rice. Stir in the cardamom seeds. Cook for 5–10 more minutes, until the rice is tender and all the liquid has been absorbed.

**4** Put the rice into a warmed serving dish and sprinkle the pistachios and sesame seeds on top. Serve.

### Variations
• You can substitute other nuts for the pistachios; unsalted peanuts, almonds and cashews all work well.
• To make a more substantial dish or to provide extra servings for unexpected guests, you can add either fresh or frozen finely chopped vegetables, such as carrots, peas and corn, with the tomatoes and peppers in step 3.

# Herbed Rice Pilaf

A pilaf is a popular type of rice dish, usually featuring spices and often including a mixture of vegetables for color and extra flavor. This delightful dish has lots of herbs.

**Serves 4**
scant 1 cup mixed brown basmati
    and wild rice
1 tablespoon olive oil
1 onion, chopped
1 garlic clove, crushed
1 teaspoon ground cumin
1 teaspoon ground turmeric
1/3 cup golden raisins
3 cups vegetable stock
3 tablespoons chopped fresh
    mixed herbs
salt and ground black pepper
fresh herb sprigs and
    1/4 cup chopped nuts,
    to garnish

**1** Rinse the rice mixture several times in cold water. If there is enough time, let it soak for 30 minutes in the water used for the final rinse. Drain well.

**2** Heat the oil in a large, heavy saucepan. Add the chopped onion and garlic and fry over low heat, stirring occasionally, for about 5 minutes, until the onion is softened but not colored.

**3** Stir in the ground cumin, turmeric and rice and cook over medium heat, stirring constantly, for about 1 minute, until the rice grains are well coated.

**4** Stir in the golden raisins and vegetable stock. Bring to a boil, stirring frequently. Lower the heat, cover and simmer, stirring occasionally to prevent the rice from sticking, for 20–25 minutes, until the rice is cooked and just tender and almost all the liquid has been absorbed.

**5** Stir in the chopped mixed herbs and season to taste with salt and pepper. Spoon the pilaf into a warmed serving dish and garnish with fresh herb sprigs and a sprinkling of chopped nuts. Serve immediately.

# Fried Rice with Mushrooms

Sesame oil adds a hint of nutty flavor to this tasty and substantial rice dish.

**Serves 4**
generous 1 cup long-grain rice
1 tablespoon vegetable oil
1 egg, lightly beaten
2 garlic cloves, crushed
2 1/4 cups button
    mushrooms, sliced
1 tablespoon light soy sauce
1/4 teaspoon salt
1/2 teaspoon sesame oil
cucumber matchsticks, to garnish

**1** Rinse the rice until the water runs clear, then drain it thoroughly. Place it in a saucepan. Measure the depth of the rice against your index finger, then bring the tip of your finger up to just above the surface of the rice and add cold water to the same depth above the rice as the rice depth.

**2** Bring the water to a boil. Stir, boil for a few minutes, then cover the pan. Lower the heat to a simmer and cook the rice gently for 5–8 minutes, until all the water has been absorbed. Remove the pan from heat and, without lifting the lid, leave for 10 more minutes.

**3** Meanwhile, heat 1 teaspoon of the vegetable oil in a nonstick frying pan or wok. Add the beaten egg and cook, stirring with chopsticks or a wooden spoon until lightly scrambled. Remove from the pan or wok and set aside.

**4** Heat the remaining vegetable oil in the pan or wok. Add the garlic and stir-fry for a few seconds, then add the mushrooms and stir-fry for 2 minutes, adding a little water, if needed, to prevent them from burning.

**5** Fork up the cooked rice. Add it to the pan or wok. Toss to mix with the mushrooms, then cook for about 4 minutes or until the rice is hot, stirring occasionally.

**6** Add the scrambled egg, soy sauce, salt and sesame oil. Cook for 1 minute to heat through. Serve immediately, garnished with the cucumber matchsticks.

# Eggplant & Chickpea Tagine

Spiced with coriander, cumin, cinnamon, turmeric and a dash of chili sauce, this Moroccan-style stew makes a filling supper dish.

**Serves 4**

1 small eggplant, cut into
   1/2-inch dice
2 zucchini, thickly sliced
2 tablespoons olive oil
1 large onion, sliced
2 garlic cloves, chopped
2 cups brown cap
   mushrooms, halved
1 tablespoon ground coriander

2 teaspoons cumin seeds
1 tablespoon ground cinnamon
2 teaspoons ground turmeric
8 ounces new potatoes, quartered
2 1/2 cups passata
1 tablespoon tomato paste
2/3 cup water
1 tablespoon chili sauce
8 dried apricots
14-ounce can chickpeas, drained
   and rinsed
salt and ground black pepper
1 tablespoon chopped cilantro,
   to garnish
rice, to serve

**1** Put the eggplant and zucchini in a colander, sprinkling salt over each layer. Let stand in the sink for 30 minutes. Rinse very well, drain and pat dry with paper towels.

**2** Preheat the broiler. Arrange the zucchini and eggplant on a baking sheet and toss in half the olive oil. Broil for 20 minutes, turning occasionally, until tender and golden.

**3** Meanwhile, heat the remaining oil in a large heavy pan and cook the onion and garlic until softened. Add the mushrooms and sauté for 3 minutes, until tender. Add the spices and stir over the heat for 1 more minute.

**4** Add the potatoes and cook for 3 minutes, stirring. Pour in the passata, tomato paste and water and cook for 10 minutes or until the sauce begins to thicken.

**5** Add the eggplant, zucchini, chili sauce, apricots and chickpeas. Season to taste with salt and pepper and cook, partially covered, for 10–15 minutes, until the potatoes are tender. Sprinkle with chopped cilantro and serve with rice.

# Purée of Lentils with Baked Eggs

This unusual dish makes an excellent vegetarian supper. If you prefer, and have one big enough, bake the purée and eggs in a single large ovenproof dish.

**Serves 4**

2 cups split red lentils
3 leeks, thinly sliced
2 teaspoons coriander seeds,
   finely crushed

1 tablespoon chopped cilantro
2 tablespoons chopped fresh mint
1 tablespoon red wine vinegar
4 cups vegetable stock
oil, for greasing
4 eggs
salt and ground black pepper
generous handful of fresh parsley,
   chopped, to garnish

**1** Put the lentils in a deep saucepan. Add the leeks, coriander seeds, cilantro, mint, vinegar and stock. Bring to a boil over medium heat. Lower the heat, cover and simmer for 30–40 minutes or until the lentils are cooked and have absorbed all the liquid.

**2** Preheat the oven to 350°F. Lightly grease four individual ovenproof dishes. Season the lentil mixture to taste with salt and pepper and mix thoroughly. Divide the mixture among the prepared dishes and spread out.

**3** Using the back of a tablespoon, make a fairly small depression in the center of the lentil mixture in each dish. Break an egg into each hollow. Season the eggs lightly with salt and pepper. Cover the dishes with aluminum foil and bake for 15–20 minutes or until the eggs are set. Sprinkle with plenty of chopped parsley and serve immediately.

**Variation**
*Put a 14-ounce can of unsweetened chestnut purée into a bowl and beat well until softened. Stir the purée into the lentil mixture in step 2, with a little extra vegetable stock if needed. Proceed as in the main recipe.*

# Bulghur & Lentil Pilaf

Many of the ingredients for this tasty, aromatic dish can be found in a well-stocked pantry.

**Serves 4**

1 teaspoon olive oil
1 large onion, thinly sliced
2 garlic cloves, crushed
1 teaspoon ground coriander
1 teaspoon ground cumin
1 teaspoon ground turmeric
1/2 teaspoon ground allspice
1 1/4 cups bulghur wheat
about 3 2/3 cups vegetable stock
1 1/2 cups button mushrooms, sliced
1/2 cup green lentils
salt and ground black pepper
cayenne pepper
fresh parsley sprigs, to garnish

**1** Heat the oil in a nonstick saucepan. Add the onion, garlic, ground coriander, cumin, turmeric and allspice and fry over low heat, stirring constantly, for 1 minute.

**2** Stir in the bulghur and cook, stirring constantly, for about 2 minutes, until lightly browned. Add the vegetable stock, mushrooms and lentils.

**3** Bring to a boil, cover, then simmer over very low heat for 25–30 minutes, until the bulghur and lentils are tender and all the liquid has been absorbed. Add more stock or water during cooking, if necessary.

**4** Season the mixture with salt, pepper and cayenne. Transfer to a warmed serving dish and serve, garnished with fresh parsley.

**Cook's Tips**
• Bulghur is very easy to cook and can be used in almost any way you would normally use rice—hot or cold. Some of the finer grades need hardly any cooking, so check the package instructions for cooking times.
• Green lentils keep their shape well during cooking, but, if you can find them, use Puy lentils, which not only retain their texture but have a distinctive and delicious flavor.

# Toor Dhal with Cherry Tomatoes

When cooked, toor dhal has a wonderfully rich texture, best appreciated if served with plain boiled rice. Fresh fenugreek leaves, available at Asian grocers, impart a stunning aroma.

**Serves 4**

1/2 cup toor dhal
3 tablespoons corn oil
1/4 teaspoon onion seeds
1 bunch scallions, roughly chopped
1 teaspoon crushed garlic
1/4 teaspoon ground turmeric
1 1/2 teaspoons grated fresh ginger root
1 teaspoon mild chili powder
2 tablespoons fresh fenugreek or spinach leaves
1 teaspoon salt
6–8 cherry tomatoes
2 tablespoons cilantro leaves
1/2 green bell pepper, seeded and sliced
1 tablespoon lemon juice
shredded scallion tops and cilantro leaves, to garnish

**1** Cook the dhal in a pan of boiling water, stirring frequently, until soft and mushy. Set aside.

**2** Heat the oil with the onion seeds in a nonstick wok. Add the dhal and stir-fry for about 3 minutes. Add the scallions, garlic, turmeric, ginger, chili powder, fenugreek or spinach leaves and salt and continue to stir-fry for 5–7 minutes.

**3** Pour in enough water to loosen the mixture. Stir and add the cherry tomatoes, cilantro, green bell pepper and lemon juice. Serve immediately, garnished with shredded scallion tops and cilantro leaves.

**Cook's Tip**
• Toor dhal, also known as red gram, consists of split pigeon peas. Ask for it at your local health-food store or Asian grocer. If it is not available, substitute green or brown lentils.

# Urad Dhal with Chiles

The creamy urad dhal used in this recipe needs to be soaked overnight, as this makes it easier to cook. Serve with freshly made chapatis or naan.

**Serves 4**

4 ounces urad dhal
2 teaspoons low-fat olive oil spread
2 teaspoons corn oil
1 bay leaf
2 onions, sliced
1 piece of cinnamon bark or stick
1 tablespoon shredded fresh ginger root
2 garlic cloves, peeled but left whole
2 fresh green chiles, seeded and sliced lengthwise
2 fresh red chiles, seeded and sliced lengthwise
1 tablespoon chopped fresh mint

**1** Place the dhal in a bowl and add enough cold water to cover. Set aside to soak overnight. Drain, put into a pan and pour in cold water to cover by about 1 inch. Bring to a boil and cook until the individual pulses are soft enough to break into two. Set aside.

**2** Heat the low-fat spread with the oil in a nonstick wok or large, heavy frying pan over medium heat. Add the bay leaf with the onions and cinnamon bark or stick.

**3** Add the shredded ginger, whole garlic cloves and half the green and red chiles.

**4** Drain almost all the water from the dhal. Add to the wok or frying pan, then stir in the remaining green and red chiles and the fresh mint. Heat through briefly, transfer to a warm serving dish and serve immediately.

**Cook's Tip**
*Urad dhal, a creamy white lentil with a dark hull, is just one of several different pulses familiar to Indian cooks, but lesser known in the West. It is worth getting to know, so look for an Asian grocer that stocks it.*

# Aromatic Chickpea & Spinach Curry

High in fiber, this flavorful curry tastes great and boosts vitality. Serve it with brown rice or naan and mango chutney.

**Serves 3–4**

1 tablespoon sunflower oil
1 large onion, finely chopped
2 garlic cloves, crushed
1-inch piece of fresh ginger root, finely chopped
1 fresh green chile, seeded and finely chopped
2 tablespoons medium curry paste
2 teaspoons ground cumin
1 teaspoon ground turmeric
8-ounce can chopped tomatoes
1 green or red bell pepper, seeded and chopped
1¼ cups vegetable stock
1 tablespoon tomato paste
1 pound fresh spinach
15-ounce can chickpeas, drained
3 tablespoons chopped cilantro
1 teaspoon garam masala (optional)
salt

**1** Heat the oil in a large pan and cook the onion, garlic, ginger and chile over low heat for about 5 minutes or until the onion has softened but not browned. Stir in the curry paste, cook for 1 minute, then stir in the cumin and turmeric. Stir over low heat for 1 more minute.

**2** Add the tomatoes and pepper and stir to coat with the spice mixture. Pour in the stock and stir in the tomato paste. Bring to a boil, lower the heat, cover and simmer for 15 minutes.

**3** Remove any coarse stems from the spinach, then rinse the leaves thoroughly, drain them and tear them into large pieces. Add them to the pan, in batches, adding more as each batch cooks down and wilts.

**4** Stir in the chickpeas, cover and cook gently for 5 more minutes. Add the cilantro, season with salt to taste and stir well. Spoon into a warmed bowl and sprinkle on the garam masala, if using. Serve immediately.

# Lemon & Ginger Spicy Beans

An extremely quick and delicious dish, made with canned beans for speed. You probably won't need extra salt, as canned beans tend to be already salted.

**Serves 4**
2-inch piece of fresh ginger root, roughly chopped
3 garlic cloves, roughly chopped
1 cup cold water
1 tablespoon sunflower oil
1 large onion, thinly sliced
1 fresh red chile, seeded and finely chopped
¼ teaspoon cayenne pepper
2 teaspoons ground cumin
1 teaspoon ground coriander
½ teaspoon ground turmeric
2 tablespoons lemon juice
3 tablespoons chopped cilantro
14-ounce can black-eyed peas, drained and rinsed
14-ounce can adzuki beans, drained and rinsed
14-ounce can haricot beans, drained and rinsed
ground black pepper
crusty bread, to serve

**1** Place the ginger, garlic and 4 tablespoons of the cold water in a blender and blend until smooth.

**2** Heat the oil in a pan. Add the onion and chile and cook over low heat, stirring occasionally, for 5 minutes, until softened. Add the cayenne, cumin, ground coriander and turmeric and stir-fry for 1 minute.

**3** Stir in the ginger and garlic paste and cook for 1 more minute. Pour in the remaining water, with the lemon juice and cilantro, stir well and bring to a boil. Cover the pan tightly and cook for 5 minutes.

**4** Add all the beans and cook for 10 minutes, until they are hot. Season with pepper and serve immediately with crusty bread.

**Variation**
*You can use almost any combination of canned beans—red kidney, pinto, cannellini, fava or lima beans, for example.*

# Vegetable Chili

This alternative to chili con carne is delicious served with brown rice.

**Serves 4**
2 onions, chopped
1 garlic clove, crushed
3 celery stalks, chopped
1 green bell pepper, seeded and diced
3 cups mushrooms, sliced
2 zucchini, diced
14-ounce can red kidney beans, drained and rinsed
14-ounce can chopped tomatoes
⅔ cup passata
2 tablespoons tomato paste
1 tablespoon ketchup
1 teaspoon hot chili powder
1 teaspoon ground cumin
1 teaspoon ground coriander
salt and ground black pepper
cilantro, to garnish
low-fat plain yogurt, dusted with cayenne, to serve

**1** Put the onions, garlic, celery, pepper, mushrooms and zucchini in a large saucepan and mix.

**2** Stir in the kidney beans, tomatoes, passata, tomato paste, ketchup and spices. Season to taste and mix well.

**3** Bring to a boil, then lower the heat, cover and simmer for 20–30 minutes, stirring occasionally, until the vegetables are tender. Garnish with cilantro sprigs. Serve with the yogurt, dusted with cayenne.

# Simple Red Beans

Make this when you want a quick snack and don't have much in the pantry or refrigerator.

**Serves 2**
1 tablespoon sunflower or peanut oil
1 onion or leek, finely chopped
1 red bell pepper or fresh red chile, seeded and sliced
1 garlic clove, crushed
1-inch piece of fresh ginger root, grated
14-ounce can red kidney beans, drained and rinsed
2 tablespoons tomato paste, thinned with 4 tablespoons water
generous dash of vegetarian Worcestershire sauce or Tabasco sauce
salt and ground black pepper
lime wedges, to serve

**1** Heat the oil in a heavy pan. Add the onion or leek with the pepper or chile and fry over low heat, stirring occasionally, for 3 minutes.

**2** Add the garlic and ginger and cook, stirring constantly, for 2 more minutes.

**3** Add the beans and tomato paste mixture, stir well and spike with vegetarian Worcestershire sauce or Tabasco. Heat for about 10 minutes, until the beans are piping hot. Season to taste with salt and pepper and serve with the lime wedges.

**Cook's Tip**
*If you have time to cook your own beans make extra as they freeze very well. There is no need to thaw them before use.*

## Jamaican Black Bean Stew

Molasses imparts a rich flavor to the spicy sauce, which includes black beans, vibrant red and yellow bell peppers and melting butternut squash.

**Serves 4**
1¼ cups dried black beans, soaked overnight in water to cover
1 bay leaf
1 teaspoon vegetable bouillon powder
1 tablespoon sunflower oil
1 large onion, chopped
1 garlic clove, chopped
1 teaspoon English mustard powder
1 tablespoon blackstrap molasses
2 tablespoons dark brown sugar
1 teaspoon dried thyme
½ teaspoon dried chile flakes
1 red bell pepper, seeded and diced
1 yellow bell pepper, seeded and diced
1½ pounds butternut squash, seeded and cut into ½-inch dice
salt and ground black pepper
fresh thyme sprigs, to garnish
cooked rice, to serve

**1** Drain the beans, rinse them well and drain them again. Place them in a large pan, cover with fresh water and add the bay leaf. Bring to a boil, then boil rapidly for 10 minutes. Lower the heat, cover, and simmer for 30 minutes, until tender.

**2** Drain the beans, reserving the cooking liquid in a large measuring cup. Stir in the bouillon powder, then add water to make 1⅔ cups. Preheat the oven to 350°F.

**3** Heat the oil in the pan. Add the onion and garlic and sauté over low heat, stirring occasionally, for about 5 minutes, until softened. Stir in the mustard powder, molasses, sugar, dried thyme and chile flakes. Cook for 1 minute, stirring.

**4** Stir in the black beans and reserved bouillon. Spoon the mixture into a flameproof casserole. Cover and bake for 25 minutes, then add the peppers and squash. Season to taste with salt and pepper and mix well. Replace the lid and bake for 45 more minutes, until the vegetables are tender. Serve immediately, garnished with thyme sprigs, accompanied by the rice.

## Sweet-&-Sour Bean Stew

An appetizing mixture of mixed beans and vegetables in a tasty sweet-and-sour sauce, topped with a golden potato crust.

**Serves 6**
1 pound potatoes
1 tablespoon olive oil
3 tablespoons low-fat spread
6 tablespoons whole-wheat flour
1¼ cups passata
⅔ cup unsweetened apple juice
4 tablespoons light brown sugar
4 tablespoons ketchup
4 tablespoons dry sherry
4 tablespoons cider vinegar
4 tablespoons light soy sauce
14-ounce can lima beans
14-ounce can red kidney beans
14-ounce can flageolet beans
14-ounce can chickpeas
6 ounces green beans, chopped and blanched
8 ounces shallots, sliced and blanched
3 cups mushrooms, sliced
1 tablespoon chopped fresh thyme
1 tablespoon chopped fresh marjoram
salt and ground black pepper
fresh herb sprigs, to garnish

**1** Preheat the oven to 400°F. Bring a pan of water to a boil and parboil the potatoes for 4 minutes. Drain well, toss in the oil to coat all over and set them aside.

**2** Mix the low-fat spread, flour, passata, apple juice, sugar, ketchup, sherry, vinegar and soy sauce in a saucepan. Heat gently, whisking continuously, until the sauce comes to a boil and thickens. Simmer gently for 3 minutes, stirring.

**3** Rinse and drain the canned pulses and add to the sauce with the remaining ingredients, except the herb garnish. Mix, then put into an ovenproof dish and level the surface.

**4** Arrange the potato slices on top, overlapping them slightly and covering the bean mixture completely.

**5** Cover with aluminum foil and bake for 40 minutes. Remove the foil and bake for 20 more minutes, until the potatoes have begun to brown around the edges. Serve, garnished with fresh herbs.

# Bean Feast

A medley of mushrooms, beans and tomatoes, this richly flavored dish is perfect for a casual party, as it can easily be doubled or tripled

**Serves 4**

1 tablespoon sunflower oil
2 onions, sliced
1 garlic clove, crushed
1 tablespoon red wine vinegar
14-ounce can chopped tomatoes
1 tablespoon tomato paste
1 tablespoon vegetarian
  Worcestershire sauce
1 tablespoon whole-grain mustard
1 tablespoon dark brown sugar
1 cup vegetable stock
14-ounce can red kidney
  beans, drained
14-ounce can cannellini
  beans, drained
1 bay leaf
1/2 cup raisins
3 cups mushrooms, chopped
salt and ground black pepper
chopped fresh parsley, to garnish
whole-wheat bread, to serve

**1** Heat the oil in a large saucepan or flameproof casserole. Add the onions and garlic and fry over low heat, stirring occasionally, for 10 minutes, until softened and golden.

**2** Add the red wine vinegar, tomatoes, tomato paste, vegetarian Worcestershire sauce, mustard and sugar, then stir in the vegetable stock. Mix thoroughly.

**3** Rinse and drain the canned beans and add them to the pan, with the bay leaf and raisins. Bring to a boil, then lower the heat and simmer for 10 minutes, stirring frequently.

**4** Add the mushrooms and simmer for 5 more minutes. Season with salt and pepper to taste. Transfer to a warmed dish, sprinkle with chopped parsley and serve with bread.

> **Cook's Tip**
> Wipe mushrooms clean with damp paper towels before using.

# Spicy Bean & Lentil Loaf

This appetizing high fiber savory loaf is ideal for picnics or packed lunches. It uses canned beans, so takes very little time to prepare.

**Serves 12**

2 teaspoons olive oil
1 onion, finely chopped
1 garlic clove, crushed
2 celery stalks, finely chopped
14-ounce can red kidney beans
14-ounce can lentils
1 egg
1 carrot, coarsely grated
1/2 cup hazelnuts,
  finely chopped
1/2 cup low-fat aged Cheddar
  cheese, finely grated
1 cup fresh whole-wheat
  bread crumbs
1 tablespoon tomato paste
1 tablespoon ketchup
1 teaspoon ground cumin
1 teaspoon ground coriander
1 teaspoon hot chili powder
salt and ground black pepper
salad and vegetables, to serve

**1** Preheat the oven to 350°F. Lightly grease a 2-pound loaf pan. Heat the oil in a saucepan, add the onion, garlic and celery and cook gently for 5 minutes, stirring occasionally. Remove the pan from heat and cool slightly.

**2** Rinse and drain the beans and lentils. Put them in a blender or food processor with the onion mixture and egg and process until smooth.

**3** Scrape the mixture into a bowl. Mix in the carrot, hazelnuts, Cheddar, bread crumbs, tomato paste, ketchup, cumin, coriander and chile. Season with salt and pepper to taste.

**4** Spoon the mixture into the prepared pan and level the surface. Bake for about 1 hour, then remove from the pan and serve hot or cold in slices, accompanied by salad and vegetables.

> **Cook's Tip**
> You'll find it easier to remove the loaf from the pan if you line it with nonstick baking parchment first.

# Wild Mushroom Gratin with Beaufort Cheese, New Potatoes & Walnuts

This is one of the simplest and most delicious ways of cooking mushrooms. Serve this dish as the Swiss do, with gherkins.

**Serves 4**

2 pounds small new or
   salad potatoes
¼ cup butter or
   4 tablespoons olive oil
4½ cups assorted wild and
   cultivated mushrooms,
   thinly sliced
6 ounces Beaufort or Fontina
   cheese, thinly sliced
½ cup broken walnuts, toasted
salt and ground black pepper
fresh flat-leaf parsley,
   roughly chopped, to garnish
12 gherkins, sliced, to serve

**1** Bring a large pan of lightly salted water to a boil over medium heat and cook the potatoes for about 20 minutes, until tender. Drain well and return them to the pan. Add a pat of butter or a splash of oil and cover to keep warm.

**2** Heat the remaining butter or olive oil in a heavy frying pan that can safely be used under the broiler. (Cover a wooden handle with aluminum foil to protect it.) Add the sliced mushrooms and fry over low heat, stirring occasionally, until their juices begin to run, then increase the heat and fry until most of the juices have been absorbed again. Season to taste with salt and pepper.

**3** Meanwhile, preheat the broiler. Arrange the slices of cheese on top of the mushrooms. Place the pan under the broiler and cook until the cheese is bubbly and golden brown.

**4** Sprinkle on the gratin with the toasted walnuts, garnish with parsley, and serve immediately with the buttered potatoes and sliced gherkins.

# Zucchini Fritters with Pistou

The sauce is the French equivalent of pesto. It provides a lovely contrast to these delicious fritters.

**Serves 4**

1 pound zucchini, trimmed
¾ cup all-purpose flour
1 egg, separated
1 tablespoon olive oil
5 tablespoons water
vegetable oil, for frying
salt and ground black pepper

**For the pistou**
½ cup fresh basil leaves
4 garlic cloves, roughly chopped
1 cup freshly grated
   Parmesan cheese
finely grated zest of 1 lemon
⅔ cup olive oil

**1** Start by making the pistou. Put the basil leaves and garlic in a mortar and crush with a pestle into a fairly fine paste. Work in the grated Parmesan and lemon zest. Gradually blend in the olive oil, a little at a time, until fully incorporated, then transfer the pistou to a small serving dish.

**2** Grate the zucchini into a sieve. Sprinkle with plenty of salt. Place the sieve over a bowl, leave for 1 hour, then rinse thoroughly. Drain, then dry well on paper towels.

**3** Sift the flour into a bowl and make a well in the center, then add the egg yolk, olive oil and water to the well. Whisk, gradually incorporating the surrounding flour to make a smooth batter. Season to taste with salt and pepper and set aside to rest for 30 minutes.

**4** Stir the zucchini into the batter. Whisk the egg white until stiff, then fold it into the batter.

**5** Heat the vegetable oil in a large, heavy frying pan. Add tablespoons of batter to the oil and fry for about 2 minutes, until golden. Lift the fritters out and drain well on paper towels. Keep warm while you are frying the remainder. Serve immediately with the sauce.

# Vegetable Rösti with Whiskey

A splash of Scotch whiskey turns a familiar favorite into a special occasion dish, which is perfect for a celebration lunch.

**Serves 4**

3 medium carrots, grated
1 celeriac, about
   10 ounces, grated
1 large potato, grated
2 medium parsnips, grated
3 tablespoons chopped
   fresh parsley
1 ½ cups mushrooms, chopped
½ cup grated Cheddar cheese
2 tablespoons whiskey
¼ cup butter
2 tablespoons olive oil
salt and ground black pepper
flat-leaf parsley and cherry
   tomatoes, to garnish

**1** Mix the grated vegetables with the chopped parsley in a large bowl. Season with salt and pepper. In another bowl, combine the mushrooms, grated cheese and whiskey.

**2** Heat the butter and most of the oil in a large, nonstick frying pan that can safely be used under the broiler. (Cover a wooden handle with aluminum foil to protect it.) Add half the vegetables and press down in an even layer. Cover with the cheese mixture and top with the remaining grated vegetables. Press down firmly.

**3** Cook over high heat for 5 minutes, then cover, lower the heat and cook for about 10 more minutes or until the vegetables are soft.

**4** Meanwhile, preheat the broiler. Brush the top of the rösti with the remaining oil, slide the pan under the broiler and cook until the topping is golden brown. Serve in generous wedges, garnished with the parsley and cherry tomatoes.

> **Variation**
> Instead of cooking the rösti on top of the stove, press the mixture into an ovenproof dish and cook in a hot oven for 40 minutes.

# Potato Cakes with Goat Cheese

Broiled goat cheese makes a tangy topping for these herbed potato cakes.

**Serves 2–4**

1 pound floury potatoes
2 teaspoons chopped fresh thyme
1 garlic clove, crushed
2 scallions, white and green parts,
   finely chopped
2 tablespoons olive oil
¼ cup butter
2 2½ ounces firm
   goat cheeses
salt and ground black pepper
fresh thyme sprigs, to garnish
salad greens, tossed in walnut
   dressing, to serve

**1** Peel the potatoes, then grate them coarsely into a colander. Using your hands, squeeze out as much of the thick starchy liquid as possible, then put them into a bowl and mix them with the chopped thyme, garlic and scallions. Season well with salt and pepper. Preheat the oven to 250°F.

**2** Heat half the oil and butter in a nonstick frying pan. Add two large spoonfuls of the potato mixture (about half the mixture), spacing them well apart, and press down firmly with a spatula. Cook for 3–4 minutes on each side, until golden.

**3** Remove the potato cakes from the pan, drain on paper towels and keep them warm in the oven. Heat the remaining oil and butter and use the remaining mixture to make two more potato cakes.

**4** Preheat the broiler. Cut each goat cheese in half horizontally and place one half, cut-side up, on each potato cake. Broil for 2–3 minutes, until lightly golden. Serve, garnished with the fresh thyme sprigs, on individual plates, surrounded by the dressed salad greens.

> **Cook's Tip**
> These potato cakes make great party snacks. Make them half the size and serve warm on a large platter.

# Layered Vegetable Terrine

With its green outer layer, this spinach, pepper and potato terrine looks very pretty.

**Serves 6**

3 red bell peppers, halved
 and seeded
I pound waxy potatoes,
 peeled and halved
I medium zucchini,
 sliced lengthwise
4 ounces spinach
 leaves, trimmed
2 tablespoons butter
pinch of freshly grated nutmeg
I cup grated Cheddar cheese
salt and ground black pepper
torn lettuce leaves and tomato
 wedges, to serve

**1** Place the pepper halves, skin-side up, on a broiler pan and broil until the skins have blistered and charred. Transfer to a bowl, cover with crumpled paper towels and let cool.

**2** Meanwhile, bring a pan of lightly salted water to a boil. Cook the potatoes for 15 minutes. Drain and set aside. Bring a separate pan of water to a boil and add the zucchini slices. Blanch them for 1 minute, then lift out with a draining spoon. Add the spinach to the boiling water, blanch for a few seconds, then drain and pat dry on paper towels.

**3** Preheat the oven to 350°F. Line the bottom and sides of a 2-pound loaf pan with the spinach, overlapping the leaves slightly. Slice the potatoes thinly. Lay one-third of them over the bottom of the pan, dot with a little butter and season with salt, pepper and nutmeg. Sprinkle on some cheese.

**4** Peel the peppers, leaving the halves intact. Arrange half of them on top of the potatoes. Sprinkle with a little cheese and add a layer of zucchini. Lay another third of the potatoes on top with the remaining peppers and more cheese, seasoning as you go. Top with the final layer of potatoes and sprinkle on any remaining cheese. Fold over the spinach leaves. Cover with aluminum foil.

**5** Place the loaf pan in a roasting pan and pour in boiling water to come halfway up the sides. Bake for about 1 hour. Turn out the terrine and serve sliced, with lettuce and tomatoes.

# Zucchini, Mushroom & Pesto Panino

Packed with delectable vegetables, cheese and pesto, this is certain to impress. It is easy to transport, slices beautifully and tastes very good indeed.

**Serves 6**

I medium loaf country-style bread
2 tablespoons olive oil
3 zucchini, sliced lengthwise
3½ cups brown cap mushrooms,
 thickly sliced
I garlic clove, chopped
I teaspoon dried oregano
3 tablespoons pesto
9 ounces Taleggio cheese, sliced
2 cups green salad greens
salt and ground black pepper

**1** Slice off the top third of the bread and invert it on a board. Remove most of the crumb from the inside of both the lid and bottom, leaving a shell about ½ inch thick.

**2** Brush a ridged broiler pan with oil and broil the zucchini until they are tender and browned.

**3** Meanwhile, heat the remaining oil in a frying pan and fry the mushrooms, garlic and oregano for 3 minutes. Season well.

**4** Arrange half the zucchini in the bottom of the hollow loaf, then spread with half the pesto. Top with half the cheese and salad greens and all the mushroom mixture. Add one more layer each of the remaining cheese, salad greens and zucchini. Spread the rest of the pesto on the inside of the bread lid and place it on top.

**5** Press the lid down gently, wrap the bread in plastic wrap and let cool. Chill overnight. Serve cut into wedges.

**Cook's Tip**
*The zucchini can be grilled on a barbecue.*

# Summer Herb Ricotta Tart

Made without pastry, this delicate tart, infused with aromatic herbs, is ideal for a light lunch.

**Serves 4**

olive oil, for greasing
   and glazing
3 1/2 cups ricotta cheese
1 cup freshly grated
   Parmesan cheese
3 eggs, separated
4 tablespoons torn fresh
   basil leaves

4 tablespoons snipped
   fresh chives
3 tablespoons fresh
   oregano leaves
1/2 teaspoon salt
1/2 teaspoon paprika
ground black pepper
fresh herb leaves, to garnish

**For the black olive purée**

3 1/2 cups pitted black olives,
   rinsed and halved
5 garlic cloves, crushed
1/3 cup olive oil

**1** Preheat the oven to 350°F. Lightly grease a 9-inch springform cake pan with oil. Mix the ricotta, Parmesan and egg yolks in a food processor. Add the fresh herbs, with the salt, and a little pepper. Process until smooth and creamy, then scrape into a bowl.

**2** Whisk the egg whites in a large bowl until they form soft peaks. Gently fold the egg whites into the ricotta mixture. Spoon the mixture into the prepared pan and smooth the surface with a spatula.

**3** Bake for 1 hour and 20 minutes or until the flan has risen and the top is golden. Remove from the oven and brush lightly with olive oil, then sprinkle with paprika. Let the flan cool before removing it from the pan.

**4** Make the olive purée. Set aside a few olives for garnishing, if desired. Place the remainder in a food processor, add the garlic and process until finely chopped. With the motor running, gradually add the olive oil through the feeder tube, until the mixture forms a coarse paste. Transfer it to a serving bowl. Garnish the flan with the herb leaves. Serve with the olive purée.

# Wild Mushroom Brioche with Orange Butter Sauce

A butter-rich brioche, ribboned with a mushroom duxelles would make an impressive centerpiece for a sophisticated dinner party.

**Serves 4**

1 teaspoon active dry yeast
3 tablespoons milk, at
   room temperature
3 1/2 cups bread flour
1 teaspoon salt
1 tablespoon sugar
3 eggs
finely grated zest of 1/2 lemon
scant 1 cup butter, diced

**For the filling**

1/4 cup butter
2 shallots, chopped
4 cups assorted wild and
   cultivated mushrooms,
   roughly chopped
1/2 garlic clove, crushed
5 tablespoons chopped
   fresh parsley
salt and ground black pepper

**For the sauce**

2 tablespoons frozen
   concentrated orange juice
3/4 cup butter, diced
cayenne pepper

**1** Dissolve the yeast in the milk, add 1 cup of the flour and mix to form a dough. Fill a large bowl with lukewarm water, then place the bowl of dough in the water. Set aside for 30 minutes.

**2** Place the remaining flour in a food processor fitted with the dough blade. Add the salt, sugar, eggs, lemon zest and the risen dough and process briefly to mix. Add the butter, in small pieces, and process until the dough is silky smooth and very slack. Wrap it in plastic wrap and chill for 2 hours, until firm.

**3** Make the filling. Melt the butter in a large, heavy frying pan. Add the shallots and fry over low heat, stirring occasionally, until softened but not browned.

**4** Add the mushrooms and garlic and fry, stirring occasionally, until the juices begin to run. Increase the heat to medium to reduce the moisture. When dry, put the mixture into a bowl, add the parsley and season to taste with salt and pepper.

**5** Grease and line a 2-pound loaf pan. Roll out the dough to a 6 x 12-inch rectangle. Spoon the cooked mushroom mixture on the dough and roll up to make a fat sausage. Drop this into the loaf pan, cover with a damp dish towel and set aside in a warm place for 50 minutes or until the dough has risen above the level of the rim.

**6** Preheat the oven to 375°F, then bake the brioche for 40 minutes.

**7** Meanwhile, make the sauce. Place the orange juice concentrate in a heatproof glass bowl and heat by standing in a pan of simmering water. Off the heat, gradually whisk in the butter until creamy. Season to taste with cayenne pepper, cover and keep warm. When the brioche is cooked, turn it out, slice thickly and serve with the sauce.

# Roasted Winter Squash

Winter squash has a sweet, subtle flavor that contrasts well with black olives and sun-dried tomatoes. The rice adds substance and texture.

**Serves 2–4**

4 whole winter squashes
2 cups cooked white
   long-grain rice
4 pieces sun-dried tomatoes, in
   oil, drained and chopped, plus
   2 tablespoons oil from the jar
½ cup pitted black
   olives, chopped
1 tablespoon chopped fresh basil
   leaves, plus fresh basil sprigs,
   to serve
4 tablespoons soft goat cheese
tzatziki, to serve

**1** Preheat the oven to 350°F. Trim off the bottom of each squash, slice off the top, scoop out the seeds with a spoon and discard.

**2** Mix the rice, sun-dried tomatoes, olives, basil and cheese in a bowl. Stir in half the oil from the jar.

**3** Use a little of the remaining oil to grease a shallow ovenproof dish that is just large enough to hold the squash side by side. Divide the rice mixture among the squash and place them in the dish. Drizzle on any remaining oil.

**4** Cover with aluminum foil and bake for 45–50 minutes, until tender. Garnish with basil sprigs. Serve with tzatziki.

---

**Cook's Tip**

2 cups cooked rice is the equivalent of a generous ⅓ cup raw rice.

---

**Variations**

• If you don't like olives, use raisins instead.
• Acorn squash in this dish is especially good. Serve half an acorn squash per person.

# Stuffed Vegetables

Cooking for friends is fun when there are colorful dishes such as this with its interesting selection of different vegetables

**Serves 4**

3 tablespoons olive oil, plus extra
   for greasing
1 eggplant
1 green bell pepper
2 beefsteak tomatoes
1 onion, chopped
2 garlic clove, crushed
1½ cups button
   mushrooms, chopped
1 carrot, grated
2 cups cooked white
   long-grain rice
1 tablespoon chopped fresh dill
scant ½ cup feta
   cheese, crumbled
1 cup pine nuts,
   lightly toasted
2 tablespoons currants
salt and ground black pepper

**1** Preheat the oven to 375°F. Lightly grease a shallow ovenproof dish. Cut the eggplant in half, through the stem, and scoop out the flesh from each half to leave two hollow "boats." Dice the eggplant flesh. Cut the pepper in half lengthwise and remove the seeds.

**2** Cut off the tops from the tomatoes and hollow out the centers. Chop the flesh and add it to the diced eggplant. Drain the tomatoes upside down on paper towels.

**3** Bring a pan of water to a boil, add the eggplant halves and blanch for 3 minutes. Add the pepper halves and blanch for 3 more minutes. Drain, then place all the vegetables, hollow side up, in the prepared dish.

**4** Heat 2 tablespoons of the oil in a pan and fry the onion and garlic for about 5 minutes. Stir in the diced eggplant and tomato mixture with the mushrooms and carrot. Cover, cook for 5 minutes, until softened, then mix in the rice, dill, feta, pine nuts and currants. Season to taste with salt and pepper.

**5** Divide the mixture among the vegetable shells, drizzle on the remaining olive oil and bake for 20 minutes, until the topping has browned. Serve hot or cold.

# Kohlrabi Stuffed with Bell Peppers

If you haven't sampled kohlrabi, or have eaten it only in stews where its flavor is lost, do try this delectable dish.

**Serves 4**

4 small kohlrabi, about
    6 ounces each
about 1²/₃ cups hot
    vegetable stock

1 tablespoon sunflower oil
1 onion, chopped
1 small red bell pepper, seeded
    and sliced
1 small green bell pepper, seeded
    and sliced
salt and ground black pepper

**1** Preheat the oven to 350°F. Trim the kohlrabi. Arrange them in a single layer in the bottom of an ovenproof dish.

**2** Pour over the hot stock to come about halfway up the kohlrabi. Cover and braise in the oven for about 30 minutes, until tender. Transfer to a plate, reserving the stock, and let cool. Leave the oven on.

**3** Heat the sunflower oil in a large, heavy frying pan. Add the onion and fry over low heat, stirring occasionally, for 3–4 minutes, until softened. Add the red and green bell pepper slices and cook, stirring occasionally, for 2–3 more minutes, until the onion is lightly browned.

**4** Add the reserved vegetable stock and season to taste with salt and pepper, then simmer, uncovered, until most of the stock has evaporated.

**5** Scoop out the flesh from the kohlrabi and chop it roughly. Stir the flesh into the onion and pepper mixture, taste and adjust the seasoning, if necessary. Arrange the shells in a shallow ovenproof dish.

**6** Spoon the filling into the kohlrabi shells. Place in the oven for about 10 minutes to heat through, then serve.

# Cabbage Roulades with Lemon Sauce

Cabbage or chard leaves, filled with a rice and red lentil stuffing, and served with a light egg and lemon sauce make a light and tasty main course.

**Serves 4–6**

12 large cabbage or chard leaves,
    stems removed
2 tablespoons sunflower oil
1 onion, chopped
1 large carrot, grated
1¹/₂ cups sliced mushrooms
2¹/₂ cups vegetable stock

generous ¹/₂ cup long-grain rice
4 tablespoons red lentils
1 teaspoon dried oregano
3¹/₂ ounces cream cheese
    with garlic
¹/₄ cup all-purpose flour
juice of 1 lemon
3 eggs, beaten
salt and ground black pepper

**1** Bring a large pan of lightly salted water to a boil. Add the cabbage or chard leaves, in batches if necessary, and blanch briefly until they are just beginning to wilt. Drain thoroughly, reserving the cooking water. Pat the leaves dry with paper towels and set aside.

**2** Heat the oil in a large pan. Add the onion, carrot and mushrooms and fry over low heat, stirring occasionally, for 5 minutes, until the onion is softened but not colored.

**3** Pour the stock into the pan, then stir in the rice, lentils and oregano. Bring to a boil over medium heat. Cover, lower the heat and simmer gently for 15 minutes. Remove the pan from heat and stir in the cheese. Season to taste.

**4** Preheat the oven to 375°F. Lay each leaf in turn on a board, rib side down, and spoon a little of the filling onto the stem end. Fold in the sides and roll up.

**5** Place the roulades in a small roasting pan, seam-side down, and pour in the reserved cabbage water. Cover with aluminum foil and bake for 30–45 minutes, until the leaves are tender. Lift out the roulades with a draining spoon and place them on a warmed serving dish. Reserve the cooking liquid. Keep the roulades warm while you make the sauce.

**6** Strain 2¹/₂ cups of the cooking liquid into a pan and bring to a boil. Blend the flour into a paste with a little cold water and whisk into the boiling liquid, together with the lemon juice.

**7** Beat the eggs with about 4 tablespoons of the hot liquid in a heatproof pitcher. Gradually pour the mixture back into the pan of thickened liquid, whisking constantly. Continue to whisk over very low heat until smooth and thick. Do not let the sauce boil or it will curdle.

**8** Serve the roulades with some of the sauce poured on and the rest passed separately.

# Festive Lentil & Nut Loaf

For a special celebration, serve this with all the trimmings, including a vegetarian gravy. Garnish it with fresh cranberries and flat-leaf parsley for a really festive effect.

**Serves 6–8**
1/2 cup red lentils
1 cup hazelnuts
1 cup walnuts
1 large carrot
2 celery stalks
1 large onion
1 1/2 cups mushrooms
1/4 cup butter, plus extra
    for greasing
2 teaspoons mild curry powder
2 tablespoons ketchup
2 tablespoons vegetarian
    Worcestershire sauce
1 egg, beaten
2 teaspoons salt
4 tablespoons chopped
    fresh parsley
2/3 cup water

**1** Put the lentils in a bowl and add enough cold water to cover. Set aside for 1 hour to soak. Grind the nuts in a food processor until quite fine but not too smooth. Put the nuts into a large bowl. Coarsely chop the carrot, celery, onion and mushrooms, add them to the food processor and process until finely chopped.

**2** Heat the butter in a saucepan. Add the vegetables and fry gently over low heat, stirring occasionally, for 5 minutes. Stir in the curry powder and cook for 1 more minute. Remove from heat and set aside cool.

**3** Drain the soaked lentils and stir them into the ground nuts. Add the vegetables, ketchup, vegetarian Worcestershire sauce, egg, salt, parsley and water.

**4** Preheat the oven to 375°F. Grease a 2 1/4-pound loaf pan and line with waxed paper or a sheet of aluminum foil. Press the mixture into the pan.

**5** Bake for 1–1 1/4 hours, until just firm, covering the top with foil if it starts to burn. Let stand for 15 minutes before you turn it out and peel off the paper. It will be fairly soft when cut.

# Mushroom & Mixed Nut Loaf

The seed topping on this loaf, visible when you turn it out, looks very attractive and is a good contrast to the tender loaf.

**Serves 4**
2 tablespoons sunflower oil, plus
    extra for greasing
3 tablespoons sunflower seeds
3 tablespoons sesame seeds
1 onion, roughly chopped
2 celery stalks, roughly chopped
1 green bell pepper, seeded
    and chopped
3 cups mixed mushrooms,
    chopped
1 garlic clove, crushed
2 cups fresh whole-wheat
    bread crumbs
1 cup chopped mixed nuts
1/3 cup golden raisins
small piece of fresh ginger root,
    finely chopped
2 teaspoons coriander
    seeds, crushed
2 tablespoons light soy sauce
1 egg, beaten
salt and ground black pepper
celery and cilantro leaves,
    to garnish
tomato sauce, to serve

**1** Brush a 1 1/2-pound loaf pan with sunflower oil and line with waxed paper. Sprinkle the sunflower and sesame seeds evenly on the bottom.

**2** Preheat the oven to 375°F. Heat the oil in a large frying pan. Add the onion, celery, green bell pepper, mushrooms and garlic and fry over low heat, stirring occasionally, for about 5 minutes, until the onion has softened but not colored. Remove the pan from heat and set aside.

**3** Mix the bread crumbs and nuts in a large bowl. Add the contents of the frying pan, then stir in the golden raisins, ginger, coriander seeds and soy sauce. Bind with the egg, then season to taste with salt and pepper.

**4** Press the mixture evenly into the prepared pan and bake for 45 minutes. Loosen the sides of the loaf with a knife, then let cool for 2–3 minutes. Turn out onto a serving dish and garnish with the celery and cilantro leaves. Serve immediately with the tomato sauce.

# Fonduta

Fondues are coming back into fashion. They are perfect for casual entertaining. This variation is rich and tasty.

**Serves 4**
9 ounces Fontina or Gruyère
   cheese, diced
1 cup milk
1 tablespoon butter
2 eggs, lightly beaten
ground black pepper
1 loaf ciabatta or focaccia, cut in
   large cubes, to serve

**1** Put the cheese in a bowl, pour in the milk and let soak for 2–3 hours. Transfer to a double boiler or a heatproof bowl set over a pan of simmering water.

**2** Add the butter and eggs and cook gently, stirring until the cheese has melted and the sauce is smooth and thick, with the consistency of custard. Remove from heat and season with pepper. Transfer to a serving dish and serve immediately with the bread.

# Dutch Fondue

This is an amazingly easy yet delicious supper dish.

**Serves 4**
1 cup white wine
1 tablespoon lemon juice
1 pound Gouda cheese, grated
1 tablespoon cornstarch
2 tablespoons water
2 tablespoons gin
ground black pepper
cauliflower florets, carrot batons,
   endive leaves and bread cubes,
   to serve

**1** Bring the wine and lemon juice to a boil in a pan over low heat. Gradually stir in the cheese until melted.
**2** Mix the cornstarch and water into a paste and stir into the fondue. Bring to a boil, stirring constantly, add the gin and season with pepper.
**3** Transfer to a fondue pan. Serve with the vegetables and bread.

# Leek Soufflé

Some people think a soufflé is a tricky dish for a dinner party, but it is really quite easy.

**Serves 2–3**
3 tablespoons butter, plus extra
   for greasing
1 tablespoon sunflower oil
2 leeks, thinly sliced
about 1 1/4 cups milk
1/4 cup all-purpose flour
4 eggs, separated
3/4 cup grated Gruyère or
   Emmenthal cheese
salt and ground black pepper

**1** Preheat the oven to 350°F. Butter a 5-cup soufflé dish. Heat the oil and 1 tablespoon of the butter in a small pan and fry the leeks gently, stirring occasionally, for 4–5 minutes, until soft but not brown.

**2** Stir in the milk and bring to a boil. Cover, then simmer for 4–5 minutes, until the leeks are tender. Drain, reserving the liquid. Set the leeks aside and strain the liquid into a measuring cup. Add extra milk to make it up to 1 1/4 cups.

**3** Melt the remaining butter in a pan, stir in the flour and cook for 1 minute. Gradually add the milk, whisking constantly, until the mixture boils and thickens into a smooth sauce.

**4** Remove it from heat. Cool slightly, then beat in the egg yolks, cheese and reserved leeks. Season to taste.

**5** Whisk the egg whites until stiff. Using a large metal spoon, fold them into the leek and egg mixture. Pour into the prepared soufflé dish and bake for about 30 minutes, until golden and puffy. Serve immediately.

### Cook's Tip
*Everything except whisking the egg whites can be done in advance. Finish making the soufflé when your guests arrive, and half an hour later you'll be sitting down to a superb light meal.*

# Classic Cheese Soufflé

A melt-in-your-mouth cheese soufflé is one of the most delightful light lunches imaginable. All you need to go with it is salad and a glass of good wine.

**Serves 2–3**
1/4 cup butter
2–3 tablespoons fine, dried bread crumbs
5 tablespoons all-purpose flour
pinch of cayenne pepper
1/2 teaspoon English mustard powder
1 cup milk
1/2 cup grated aged Cheddar cheese
1/3 cup freshly grated Parmesan cheese
4 eggs, separated, plus 1 egg white
salt and ground black pepper

**1** Preheat the oven to 375°F. Melt 1 tablespoon of the butter and grease a 5-cup soufflé dish. Coat the inside of the dish with the bread crumbs.

**2** Melt the remaining butter in a saucepan, stir in the flour, cayenne and mustard powder and cook for 1 minute. Gradually add the milk, whisking constantly, until the mixture boils and thickens into a smooth sauce. Simmer the sauce for 1–2 minutes, then remove from heat and whisk in the Cheddar, half the Parmesan and seasoning. Cool a little, then beat in the egg yolks.

**3** Whisk the egg whites into soft, glossy peaks. Add a few spoonfuls to the sauce to lighten it. Beat well, then gently fold in the rest of the whites.

**4** Pour the mixture into the prepared soufflé dish, level the surface and sprinkle on the remaining Parmesan. Place the dish on a baking sheet and bake for about 25 minutes, until the soufflé has risen and is golden brown. Serve immediately.

**Cook's Tip**
To help the soufflé rise evenly, run your finger around the inside rim of the dish before baking.

# Spinach & Wild Mushroom Soufflé

A variety of wild mushrooms combine especially well with eggs and spinach in this sensational soufflé.

**Serves 4**
1/4 cup butter, plus extra for greasing
2 tablespoons freshly grated Parmesan cheese
8 ounces fresh spinach leaves
1 garlic clove, crushed
2 1/4 cups assorted wild mushrooms, chopped
scant 1 cup milk
1/4 cup all-purpose flour
6 eggs, separated
pinch of freshly grated nutmeg
salt and ground black pepper

**1** Preheat the oven to 375°F. Butter a 3 3/4-cup soufflé dish, paying particular attention to the sides. Sprinkle with a little of the cheese. Set aside.

**2** Steam the spinach over medium heat for 3–4 minutes. Cool under cold running water, then drain. Press out as much liquid as you can with the back of a large spoon, squeeze with your hands and then chop finely.

**3** Melt the 1/4 cup butter in a pan and gently soften the garlic and mushrooms. Increase the heat and cook until the mixture is quite dry. Add the spinach and transfer to a bowl. Cover and keep warm.

**4** Measure 3 tablespoons of the milk into a bowl and stir in the flour and egg yolks. Bring the remaining milk to a boil, whisk it into the egg and flour mixture until smooth, then pour the mixture back into the pan and whisk over the heat until the sauce thickens. Stir in the spinach mixture. Season to taste with salt, pepper and grated nutmeg.

**5** Whisk the egg whites to form soft peaks. Stir a spoonful into the spinach mixture to lighten it, then fold in the rest.

**6** Pour the mixture into the soufflé dish, level the surface, sprinkle on the remaining cheese and bake for about 25 minutes, until well risen and golden. Serve immediately.

# Celeriac & Blue Cheese Roulade

Celeriac adds a subtle flavor to this attractive dish. Be sure to roll up the roulade while it is still warm and pliable.

**Serves 6**
1 tablespoon butter
8 ounces cooked spinach, drained and chopped
²/₃ cup light cream
4 large eggs, separated
4 tablespoons freshly grated Parmesan cheese
pinch of freshly grated nutmeg
salt and ground black pepper

**For the filling**
1 large celeriac, about 8 ounces
lemon juice, to taste
3 ounces St. Agur cheese
½ cup fromage frais

**1** Preheat the oven to 400°F. Line a 13 × 9-inch jelly roll pan with nonstick baking parchment.

**2** Melt the butter in a pan and add the spinach. Cook gently until all the liquid has evaporated, stirring frequently. Off the heat, stir in the cream, egg yolks, Parmesan and nutmeg. Season to taste with salt and pepper.

**3** Whisk the egg whites until stiff, fold them gently into the spinach mixture and then spoon into the prepared pan. Spread the mixture evenly and smooth the surface.

**4** Bake for 10–15 minutes, until the roulade is firm to the touch and lightly golden on top. Carefully turn out onto a sheet of nonstick baking parchment and peel away the lining paper. Roll it up with the paper inside and let cool slightly.

**5** Make the filling. Peel the celeriac, grate it into a bowl and sprinkle well with lemon juice. Blend the blue cheese and fromage frais together and mix with the celeriac. Season with a little black pepper.

**6** Carefully unroll the roulade, spread the filling evenly on the surface and roll up again. Serve immediately, cut into slices, or wrap loosely and chill in the refrigerator.

# Twice-baked Spinach, Mushroom & Goat Cheese Roulade

A roulade is really a jelly roll soufflé. Because it has air trapped inside, it magically rises again on reheating and becomes quite crisp on the outside. This is an impressive dinner-party dish.

**Serves 4**
²/₃ cup butter, plus extra, or greasing
½ cup all-purpose flour
1¼ cups milk
3³/₄ ounces chèvre (goat cheese), chopped
½ cup freshly grated Parmesan cheese, plus extra for sprinkling
4 eggs, separated
3 cups fresh shiitake mushrooms, stalks discarded, sliced
10 ounces young spinach leaves, wilted
3 tablespoons crème fraîche
salt and ground black pepper

**1** Preheat the oven to 375°F. Line a 12 × 8-inch jelly roll pan with nonstick baking parchment, making sure that the paper rises well above the sides of the pan. Grease lightly with butter.

**2** Melt ¼ cup of the butter in a large, heavy saucepan. Stir in the flour and cook over low heat, stirring constantly, for 1 minute, then gradually whisk in the milk. Bring the mixture to a boil, whisking constantly, and continue cooking, whisking constantly, until the mixture thickens into a smooth sauce.

**3** Simmer for 2 minutes, then mix in the chèvre and half the Parmesan. Cool for 5 minutes, then beat in the egg yolks and plenty of salt and pepper.

**4** Whisk the egg whites until they form soft peaks. Stir a spoonful of the egg whites into the chèvre mixture to lighten it, then fold in the remainder. Spoon the mixture into the prepared pan, spread gently with a palette knife to level, then bake for 15–17 minutes, until the top feels just firm.

**5** Remove the roulade from the oven and cool for a few minutes, then invert it onto a sheet of nonstick baking parchment dusted with the remaining Parmesan. Carefully remove and discard the lining paper. Roll the roulade up with the baking parchment inside and let cool completely.

**6** Make the filling. Melt the remaining butter in a heavy frying pan and set aside 2 tablespoons. Add the mushrooms to the pan and fry over low heat, stirring occasionally, for about 3 minutes. Stir in the spinach and heat through briefly. Drain well, then stir in the crème fraîche. Season to taste with salt and pepper, then set aside cool.

**7** Preheat the oven to 375°F. Carefully unroll the roulade and spread the filling on the surface. Roll it up again and place, seam-side down, in an ovenproof dish. Brush with the reserved melted butter and sprinkle on the remaining Parmesan. Bake for 15 minutes or until risen and golden brown. Serve immediately.

# Leek Roulade with Cheese, Walnuts & Bell Peppers

This is surprisingly easy to prepare and is a good main course.

**Serves 4–6**

4 tablespoons butter, plus extra
    for greasing
2 tablespoons fine dried
    white bread crumbs
1 cup freshly grated
    Parmesan cheese
2 leeks, thinly sliced
6 tablespoons all-purpose flour
1 cup milk
1 teaspoon Dijon mustard
about ½ teaspoon freshly
    grated nutmeg

2 large eggs, separated, plus
    1 egg white
½ teaspoon cream of tartar
salt and ground black pepper

**For the filling**

2 large red bell peppers, halved
    and seeded
1½ cups ricotta cheese
¾ cup walnuts, chopped
4 scallions, finely chopped
½ cup fresh basil leaves

**1** Preheat the oven to 375°F. Grease a 12 x 9-inch jelly roll pan and line it with baking parchment. Sprinkle the bread crumbs and 2 tablespoons of the Parmesan evenly on the paper.

**2** Melt the butter in a saucepan and fry the leeks gently for 5 minutes, until softened but not browned. Stir in the flour and cook for 1 minute, stirring. Add the milk, whisking constantly until the mixture boils and thickens.

**3** Stir in the mustard and nutmeg and season. Reserve 2–3 tablespoons of the remaining Parmesan, then stir the rest into the sauce. Cool slightly, then beat in the egg yolks.

**4** Whisk the egg whites and cream of tartar until stiff. Stir 2–3 spoonfuls of the egg white into the leek mixture to lighten it, then carefully fold in the rest.

**5** Pour the mixture into the pan and level the surface. Bake for 15–18 minutes, until risen and just firm.

**6** Make the filling. Broil the peppers, skin-side facing up, until black and blistered. Place in a bowl, cover with crumpled paper towels and leave for 10 minutes. Peel off the skin and cut the peppers into long strips.

**7** Beat the cheese with the walnuts and scallions. Chop half the basil and beat it into the mixture. Season to taste.

**8** Scatter a large sheet of baking parchment with the remaining Parmesan. Turn the roulade out onto it. Strip off the lining paper and cool slightly. Spread on the cheese mixture and top with the red bell pepper strips. Tear the remaining basil leaves and sprinkle them on top.

**9** Using the paper as a guide, roll up the roulade and roll it onto a serving platter. Serve warm or cold.

# Crêpes with Butternut Squash Filling

These melt-in-you-mouth crêpes are wonderful served with a green salad and a rich tomato sauce.

**Serves 4**

1 cup all-purpose flour
scant ½ cup polenta
    or cornmeal
½ teaspoon mild chili powder
2 large eggs, beaten
scant 2 cups milk
2 tablespoons butter, melted
vegetable oil, for greasing
salt and ground black pepper

**For the filling**

3 tablespoons olive oil
3½ cups seeded and diced
    butternut squash
pinch of dried red chile flakes
2 large leeks, thickly sliced
½ teaspoon chopped
    fresh thyme
3 heads endive, thickly sliced
4 ounces goat cheese, cubed
¾ cup walnuts,
    roughly chopped
2 tablespoons chopped fresh
    parsley, plus extra to garnish
3 tablespoons freshly grated
    Parmesan cheese

**1** Mix the flour, polenta, chili powder and a pinch of salt and make a well in the center. Add the eggs and a little of the milk. Whisk, gradually incorporating the flour mixture and adding enough milk to make a creamy batter. Set aside for 1 hour.

**2** Whisk the melted butter into the batter. Heat a lightly greased crêpe pan. Pour in about 4 tablespoons of the batter, cook for 2–3 minutes, turn over and cook for 1–2 minutes, then slide out. Make more crêpes in the same way.

**3** Make the filling. Heat 2 tablespoons of the oil in a frying pan and cook the squash, stirring frequently, for 10 minutes. Stir in the chile flakes, leeks and thyme and cook for 5 minutes. Add the endive and cook, stirring frequently, for 4–5 minutes. Cool, then stir in the goat cheese, walnuts and parsley. Season well.

**4** Preheat the oven to 400°F. Lightly grease an ovenproof dish. Stuff each crêpe with 2–3 tablespoons of the filling and place in the dish. Sprinkle on the Parmesan and drizzle on the remaining olive oil. Bake for 10–15 minutes, until the cheese is bubbling and the crêpes are hot.

# Baked Herb Crêpes

A spinach, cheese and pine nut filling turns crêpes into party food.

**Serves 4**
1 cup chopped fresh herbs
1 tablespoon sunflower oil, plus
    extra for frying and greasing
1/2 cup milk
3 eggs
1/4 cup all-purpose flour

**For the sauce**
2 tablespoons olive oil
1 small onion, chopped
2 garlic cloves, crushed

14-ounce can chopped tomatoes
pinch of light brown sugar

**For the filling**
1 pound fresh spinach, cooked
    and drained
3/4 cup ricotta cheese
1 ounce pine nuts, toasted
5 pieces of sun-dried tomato in
    oil, drained and chopped
4 egg whites
2 tablespoons shredded
    fresh basil
salt and ground black pepper

**1** Process the herbs and oil in a food processor until smooth. Add the milk, eggs and flour, with a pinch of salt. Process again until smooth. Let rest for 30 minutes.

**2** Heat a lightly greased crêpe pan. Pour in one-eighth of the batter. Cook for 2 minutes, turn over and cook for 1–2 more minutes. Slide the crêpe out of the pan. Make seven more crêpes.

**3** Make the sauce. Heat the oil in a small pan, and cook the onion and garlic gently for 5 minutes. Add the tomatoes and sugar and cook for about 10 minutes, until thickened. Purée in a blender or food processor, then sieve into a pan and set aside.

**4** Mix all the filling ingredients except the egg whites, seasoning with salt and pepper. Whisk the egg whites until stiff. Stir one-third into the spinach mixture, then fold in the rest.

**5** Preheat the oven to 375°F. Place one crêpe at a time on a lightly oiled baking sheet, add a spoonful of filling and fold into quarters. Bake for 12 minutes, until set. Reheat the sauce and serve with the crêpes.

# Moroccan Crêpes

An unusual and tasty dish that is sure to please a crowd.

**Serves 4–6**
1 tablespoon olive oil
1 large onion, chopped
9 ounces fresh spinach leaves
14-ounce can chickpeas
2 zucchini, grated
2 tablespoons chopped cilantro
2 eggs, beaten
salt and ground
    black pepper
cilantro leaves, to garnish

**For the pancakes**
1 1/4 cups all-purpose flour
1 egg
about 1 1/2 cups milk
5 tablespoons water
1 tablespoon sunflower oil, plus
    extra for greasing

**For the sauce**
2 tablespoons butter
2 tablespoons all-purpose flour
about 1 1/4 cups milk

**1** Make the batter by blending the flour, egg, milk and water until smooth in a blender. Stir in the oil and a pinch of salt. Heat a lightly greased frying pan and ladle in about one-eighth of the batter. Cook for 2–3 minutes, without turning, then slide the crêpe out of the pan. Make seven more crêpes.

**2** Heat the olive oil in a small pan and fry the onion until soft. Set aside. Wash the spinach, place it in a pan and cook until wilted, shaking the pan occasionally. Chop the spinach roughly.

**3** Drain the chickpeas, place in a bowl of cold water and rub them until the skins float to the surface. Drain the chickpeas and mash roughly with a fork. Add the onion, zucchini, spinach and cilantro. Stir in the eggs, season and mix well.

**4** Preheat the oven to 350°F. Place the pancakes, cooked-side up, on a board and spoon the filling down the centers. Roll up and place in a large oiled ovenproof dish. Make the sauce. Melt the butter in a pan, stir in the flour and cook for 1 minute. Gradually whisk in the milk until the mixture boils. Season and pour onto the crêpes. Bake for 15 minutes, until golden. Serve garnished with the cilantro leaves.

# Artichoke & Leek Crêpes

Fill thin crêpes with a mouthwatering soufflé mixture of Jerusalem artichokes and leeks.

**Serves 4**
1 cup all-purpose flour
pinch of salt
1 egg
1¼ cups milk
vegetable oil, for greasing
fresh flat-leaf parsley, to garnish

**For the filling**
¼ cup butter
1 pound Jerusalem
    artichokes, diced
1 large leek, thinly sliced
2 tablespoons self-rising flour
2 tablespoons light cream
¾ cup grated aged
    Cheddar cheese
2 tablespoons chopped
    fresh parsley
freshly grated nutmeg
2 eggs, separated
salt and ground black pepper

**1** Make the batter by blending the flour, salt, egg and milk into a smooth batter in a blender or food processor. Heat a lightly greased frying pan and add one-eighth of the batter. Cook for 2–3 minutes, then turn over and cook the other side for 2 minutes. Slide the crêpe out of the pan. Make seven more crêpes in the same way.

**2** Make the filling. Melt the butter in a pan, add the artichokes and leek, cover and cook gently for about 12 minutes, until very soft. Mash with the back of a wooden spoon. Season well.

**3** Stir the flour into the vegetables and cook for 1 minute. Take the pan off the heat and beat in the cream, cheese, parsley and nutmeg to taste. Cool, then add the egg yolks.

**4** Preheat the oven to 375°F. Lightly grease a small ovenproof dish. Whisk the egg whites into soft peaks and carefully fold them into the leek and artichoke mixture.

**5** Fold each crêpe in fourths, hold the top open and spoon the mixture into the center. Arrange the crêpes in the prepared dish with the filling facing up, if possible. Bake for 15 minutes, until risen and golden. Serve immediately, garnished with parsley.

# Roast Asparagus Crêpes

Roast asparagus is truly delicious—good enough to eat just as it is. However, for a really splendid dish, try this simple recipe.

**Serves 3**
1½ cups all-purpose flour
2 eggs
1½ cups milk
vegetable oil, for frying

**For the filling**
6–8 tablespoons olive oil
1 pound fresh asparagus
¾ cup mascarpone cheese
4 tablespoons light cream
⅓ cup freshly grated
    Parmesan cheese
sea salt

**1** Make the crêpe batter by blending the flour, eggs, milk and a pinch of salt in a blender or food processor.

**2** Heat an 8-inch frying pan, grease it lightly with vegetable oil and add one-sixth of the batter to make a crêpe. Cook for 2–3 minutes, then turn over and cook the other side until golden. Slide out of the pan and set aside. Cook five more crêpes in the same way.

**3** Preheat the oven to 350°F. Lightly grease a large, shallow ovenproof dish. Arrange the asparagus in a single layer in the dish, trickle on the remaining olive oil and gently shake the dish to coat each asparagus spear.

**4** Sprinkle the asparagus with a little sea salt, then roast for 8–12 minutes, until tender.

**5** Mix the mascarpone with the cream and Parmesan, beating well to combine, and spread a generous tablespoonful of the mixture on each crêpe, reserving little for the topping. Preheat the broiler.

**6** Divide the asparagus spears among the crêpes, roll up and arrange in a single layer in an ovenproof dish. Spoon on the remaining cheese mixture and broil for 4–5 minutes, until heated through and golden brown. Serve immediately.

# Garganelli with Asparagus & Cream

A great recipe for late spring, when bunches of fresh young asparagus are on sale everywhere.

**Serves 4**
1 bunch fresh young asparagus, about 10 ounces
3 cups dried garganelli
2 tablespoons butter
1 cup heavy cream
2 tablespoons dry white wine
1 1/3 cups freshly grated Parmesan cheese
2 tablespoons chopped fresh mixed herbs
salt and ground black pepper

**1** With your fingers, snap off and discard the woody ends of the asparagus. Cut off the tips and set them aside. Cut the stalks diagonally into pieces that are about the same length and shape as the garganelli.

**2** Bring a large pan of lightly salted water to a boil and blanch the asparagus stalks for 1 minute. Add the tips and blanch for 1 more minute. Transfer to a colander with a draining spoon. Rinse under cold water, drain again and set aside.

**3** Bring the water in the pan back to a boil, add the pasta and cook until it is *al dente*. Meanwhile, mix the butter and cream in a pan, season to taste and bring to a boil. Simmer for a few minutes, until the cream thickens, then add the asparagus, wine and about half the grated Parmesan. Taste for seasoning and leave over low heat.

**4** Drain the cooked pasta and put it into a warmed bowl. Pour on the sauce, sprinkle with the fresh herbs and toss well. Serve immediately, topped with the remaining grated Parmesan.

> **Cook's Tip**
> *When buying asparagus, look for thin, unwrinkled stalks, which will be sweet and tender. The buds should be tight and the stalks should be an even color.*

# Fusilli with Wild Mushrooms

A very rich dish with an earthy flavor and lots of garlic, this makes an ideal main course, especially if it is followed by a crisp green salad in the French manner.

**Serves 4**
1/2 10-ounce jar wild mushrooms in olive oil
2 tablespoons butter
3 cups fresh wild mushrooms, sliced if large
1 teaspoon each finely chopped fresh thyme, marjoram or oregano, plus extra herbs, to garnish
4 garlic cloves, crushed
3 cups fresh or dried fusilli
1 cup heavy cream
salt and ground black pepper

**1** Drain about 1 tablespoon of the oil from the jar of wild mushrooms into a large, heavy frying pan. Slice or chop the bottled mushrooms into bite-size pieces, if they are large.

**2** Add the butter to the oil in the pan and place over low heat until sizzling. Add the bottled and the fresh mushrooms, the chopped herbs and the garlic. Season with salt and pepper to taste. Cook over low heat, stirring occasionally, for about 10 minutes, until the fresh mushrooms are soft and tender.

**3** Bring a large saucepan of lightly salted water to a boil and cook the pasta until it is *al dente*.

**4** Meanwhile, increase the heat under the pan of mushrooms to medium and toss the mixture until all the excess liquid has been cooked.

**5** Pour in the cream and bring to a boil, stirring constantly, then taste and add more salt and pepper if needed.

**6** Drain the pasta and put it into a warmed serving bowl. Pour the mushroom sauce on the pasta and toss thoroughly to mix. Serve the fusilli immediately, sprinkled with extra fresh herbs to garnish.

# Tagliarini with White Truffle

There is nothing quite like the fragrance and flavor of rare Italian white truffles.

**Serves 4**

. 12 ounces fresh tagliarini
6 tablespoons butter, diced
4 tablespoons freshly grated Parmesan cheese
freshly grated nutmeg
1 small white truffle, about 1–1½ ounces
salt and ground black pepper

**1** Bring a large pan of lightly salted water to a boil and cook the pasta until it is *al dente*. Immediately, drain it well and put it into a large, warmed bowl.

**2** Add the diced butter, grated Parmesan and a little freshly grated nutmeg. Season with salt and pepper to taste. Toss well until all the strands are coated in melted butter.

**3** Divide the pasta equally among four warmed, individual bowls and shave paper-thin slivers of the white truffle on top. Serve immediately.

# Farfalle with Dolcelatte Cream

Sweet and simple, this sauce has a light nutty tang from the blue cheese.

**Serves 4**

3 cups dried farfalle
6 ounces dolcelatte cheese, diced
⅓ cup heavy cream
2 teaspoons chopped fresh sage
salt and ground black pepper
fresh sage leaves, to garnish

**1** Bring a large pan of lightly salted water to a boil and cook the pasta until it is *al dente*.
**2** Meanwhile, melt the cheese with the heavy cream in a pan, stirring frequently.
**3** Drain the pasta and return to the pan. Pour in the sauce with the chopped sage and toss to coat. Serve garnished with sage.

# Sardinian Ravioli

With their unusual mashed potato and mint filling, these ravioli are certainly special.

**Serves 4–6**

1 batch Pasta Dough
all-purpose flour, for dusting
¼ cup butter
⅔ cup freshly grated Pecorino cheese

*For the filling*

14 ounces potatoes, diced
generous ⅔ cup grated aged Pecorino cheese
3 ounces soft fresh Pecorino cheese
1 egg yolk
leaves from 1 large bunch fresh mint, chopped
good pinch of saffron powder
salt and ground black pepper

**1** Make the filling. Bring a pan of lightly salted water to a boil and cook the potatoes for 15–20 minutes or until soft. Drain, put into a bowl, then mash until smooth. Cool, then stir in the cheeses, egg yolk, mint, saffron and salt and pepper to taste.

**2** Using a pasta machine, roll out one-quarter of the pasta into a 36-inch strip. Cut the strip into two 18-inch lengths.

**3** With a fluted 4-inch cookie cutter, cut out 4–5 discs from one of the strips. Using a heaping teaspoon, put a mound of filling on one side of each disk. Brush a little water around the edge of each disk, then fold the plain side of the disk over the filling to make a half-moon shape. Pleat the curved edge to seal.

**4** Put the ravioli on floured dish towels, sprinkle with flour and let dry. Repeat the process with the remaining dough to make 32–40 ravioli altogether.

**5** Preheat the oven to 375°F. Bring a large pan of lightly salted water to a boil and cook the ravioli for 4–5 minutes. Meanwhile, melt the butter in a small pan.

**6** Drain the ravioli, transfer to a large ovenproof dish and pour on the melted butter. Sprinkle with the grated Pecorino and bake for 10–15 minutes, until golden and bubbly. Let stand for 5 minutes before serving.

# Broiled Polenta with Caramelized Onions

Slices of broiled polenta topped with caramelized onions and bubbling Taleggio cheese are extremely tasty.

**Serves 4**

3³⁄₄ cups water
I teaspoon salt
generous I cup polenta
  or cornmeal
¹⁄₃ cup freshly grated
  Parmesan cheese

I teaspoon chopped fresh thyme
6 tablespoons olive oil
I¹⁄₂ pounds onions, halved
  and sliced
2 garlic cloves, chopped
a few fresh thyme sprigs
I teaspoon light brown sugar
2 tablespoons balsamic vinegar
2 heads radicchio, cut into thick
  slices or wedges
8 ounces Taleggio cheese, sliced
salt and ground black pepper

**I** Pour the water into a large saucepan, add the salt and bring to a boil. Adjust to a simmer. Stirring constantly, add the polenta in a steady stream, then bring to a boil. Immediately, reduce the heat to the lowest setting and cook, stirring frequently, for 30–40 minutes, until thick and smooth.

**2** Beat in the Parmesan and chopped thyme, then put the mixture on a large tray. Spread evenly, then let set.

**3** Heat 2 tablespoons of the oil in a frying pan and cook the onions over very low heat for 15 minutes, stirring occasionally. Add the garlic and some thyme sprigs. Cook for 10 more minutes, until golden and very soft. Add the sugar and half the vinegar. Season to taste. Cook for 10 minutes, until browned.

**4** Preheat the broiler. Thickly slice the polenta and brush with a little oil, then broil until crusty and lightly browned. Turn over. Add the radicchio to the broiler pan, season and brush with a little oil. Broil for 5 minutes, until the polenta and radicchio are browned. Drizzle a little vinegar over the radicchio.

**5** Heap the onions on the polenta. Sprinkle on the cheese and thyme sprigs. Broil until the cheese is bubbling. Serve immediately.

# Layered Polenta Casserole

When you are entertaining, it's good to serve something a little out of the ordinary. This combination of polenta, tomatoes, spinach and beans fits the bill very well.

**Serves 6**

8 cups water
I teaspoon salt
3 cups fine polenta or cornmeal
olive oil, for greasing and brushing
¹⁄₃ cup freshly grated
  Parmesan cheese
salt and ground black pepper

**For the tomato sauce**
I tablespoon olive oil
2 garlic cloves, chopped

I4-ounce can chopped tomatoes
I tablespoon chopped fresh sage
¹⁄₂ teaspoon light brown sugar
7-ounce can cannellini beans,
  drained and rinsed

**For the spinach sauce**
9 ounces spinach, tough
  stems removed
²⁄₃ cup light cream
4 ounces Gorgonzola
  cheese, cubed
large pinch of freshly
  grated nutmeg

**I** Pour the water into a large, heavy pan and add the salt. Bring to a boil. Remove the pan from heat and gradually whisk in the polenta.

**2** Return the pan to the heat and simmer over low heat, stirring constantly, for 15–20 minutes, until the polenta is thick and comes away from the side of the pan. Remove the pan from heat.

**3** Season the polenta to taste with pepper, then spoon it onto a wet work surface and spread it out evenly with a wet spatula until it is about ¹⁄₂ inch thick. Let cool for about I hour, or until set.

**4** Preheat the oven to 375°F. To make the tomato sauce, heat the oil in a pan, then fry the garlic for I minute. Add the tomatoes, sage and sugar and season to taste with salt and pepper. Simmer, stirring occasionally, for 10 minutes, until slightly reduced. Stir in the beans and cook for 2 more minutes.

**5** Meanwhile, wash the spinach thoroughly and place in a large pan with only the water that clings to the leaves. Cover the pan tightly and cook over medium heat, stirring occasionally, for about 3 minutes or until tender. Drain in a colander, squeezing out as much water as possible.

**6** Put the cream, cheese and nutmeg in a small pan. Bring to a boil over medium heat, stir in the spinach and season to taste with salt and pepper. Lower the heat and simmer gently, stirring frequently, until slightly thickened.

**7** Cut the polenta into triangles, then place a layer of polenta in an oiled deep ovenproof dish. Spoon on the tomato sauce, then top with another layer of polenta. Cover with the spinach sauce and then the remaining polenta triangles. Brush with olive oil, sprinkle with Parmesan and bake for 35–40 minutes. Brown the top under a broiler before serving, if desired.

# Gnocchi with Gorgonzola Sauce

A simple potato dough is used to make these ridged dumplings, which are delicious with a creamy cheese sauce.

**Serves 4**
I pound potatoes, unpeeled
I large egg
about I cup all-purpose flour

salt and ground black pepper
fresh thyme sprigs, to garnish
4 tablespoons freshly shaved
   Parmesan cheese, to serve

**For the sauce**
4 ounces Gorgonzola cheese
4 tablespoons heavy cream
I tablespoon chopped
   fresh thyme

**I** Put the potatoes in a pan of cold water. Bring to a boil, add salt and cook the potatoes for about 20 minutes, until tender. Drain and, when cool enough to handle, remove the skins.

**2** Put the potatoes into a sieve placed over a mixing bowl. Press through with the back of a spoon. Season, then beat in the egg. Add the flour, a little at a time, stirring after each addition until you have a smooth dough. (You may not need all the flour.)

**3** Knead the dough on a floured surface for 3 minutes, adding more flour if necessary, until smooth, soft and no longer sticky.

**4** Divide the dough into six equal pieces. Gently roll each piece between floured hands into a 1-inch wide log shape that is 6 inches long. Cut each log into six equal pieces, then gently roll each piece in the flour. Form into gnocchi by gently pressing each piece with the tines of a fork to leave ridges in the dough.

**5** Bring a large pan of water to a boil. Drop in the gnocchi, about 12 at a time. After about 2 minutes, they will rise to the surface. Cook for 4–5 more minutes, then lift out with a draining spoon. Drain and keep hot while you cook the rest.

**6** Make the sauce. Place the Gorgonzola, cream and thyme in a large frying pan and heat gently until the cheese melts to a thick, creamy consistency. Add the drained gnocchi and toss well to combine. Garnish with thyme and serve with Parmesan.

# Semolina & Pesto Gnocchi

These gnocchi are cooked rounds of semolina paste, which are brushed with melted butter, topped with cheese and baked. They taste wonderful with a homemade tomato sauce.

**Serves 4–6**
3 cups milk
I ½ cups semolina
3 tablespoons pesto sauce

4 tablespoons finely chopped
   sun-dried tomatoes, patted
   dry if oily
¼ cup butter, plus extra
   for greasing
I cup freshly grated
   Pecorino cheese
2 eggs, beaten
freshly grated nutmeg
salt and ground black pepper
fresh basil sprigs, to garnish
tomato sauce, to serve

**I** Heat the milk in a large nonstick saucepan. When it is on the point of boiling, sprinkle in the semolina, stirring constantly until the mixture is smooth and very thick. Lower the heat and simmer for 2 minutes.

**2** Remove the pan from heat and stir in the pesto and sun-dried tomatoes, with half the butter and half the Pecorino. Beat in the eggs, with nutmeg, salt and pepper to taste. Spoon onto a clean shallow ovenproof dish or pan to a depth of ½ inch and level the surface. Let cool, then chill.

**3** Preheat the oven to 375°F. Lightly grease a shallow ovenproof dish. Using a I ½-inch cookie cutter, stamp out as many rounds as possible from the semolina paste.

**4** Place the leftover semolina paste on the bottom of the greased dish and arrange the rounds on top in overlapping circles. Melt the remaining butter and brush it on the gnocchi. Sprinkle on the remaining Pecorino. Bake for 30–40 minutes, until golden. Garnish with the basil and serve with the tomato sauce.

---

**Variation**
*Use Parmesan instead of Pecorino, if desired.*

# Pumpkin Gnocchi with Chanterelle Cream

Very much a gourmet dish, this is perfect for occasions when you really want to impress your guests.

**Serves 4**

1 pound peeled
   pumpkin, chopped
1 pound potatoes, unpeeled
2 egg yolks
1³⁄₄ cups all-purpose flour, plus
   extra for dredging
pinch of ground allspice
¹⁄₄ teaspoon ground cinnamon
pinch of freshly grated nutmeg

finely grated zest of ¹⁄₂ orange
²⁄₃ cup freshly grated
   Parmesan cheese
salt and ground black pepper

**For the sauce**

2 tablespoons olive oil
1 shallot, chopped
2 cups fresh chanterelles, sliced
²⁄₃ cup crème fraîche
a little milk or water
5 tablespoons chopped
   fresh parsley

**1** Preheat the oven to 350°F. Wrap the pumpkin in aluminum foil and bake for 30 minutes. Meanwhile, put the potatoes in a pan of cold water, add salt and bring to a boil. Cook for about 20 minutes, until tender. Drain, peel and set aside.

**2** Add the pumpkin to the potato and pass through a potato ricer. Alternatively, press through a sieve. Mix in the egg yolks, flour, spices, orange zest and seasoning to make a soft dough.

**3** Bring a pan of lightly salted water to a boil. Dredge a work surface with flour. Spoon the dough into a piping bag with a ¹⁄₂-inch plain nozzle. Pipe a 6-inch sausage on the surface. Roll in flour and cut into 1-inch pieces. Mark each lightly with a fork and cook for 3–4 minutes in the boiling water.

**4** Make the sauce. Heat the oil in a pan and fry the shallot until soft. Add the chanterelles and cook briefly, then stir in the crème fraîche. Simmer and add milk or water, if needed. Add the parsley and season. Transfer the gnocchi to bowls. Spoon all the sauce on top. Sprinkle on Parmesan and serve.

# Radicchio Pizza

A scone dough crust and an interesting radicchio, leek and tomato topping make this a quick and easy dish.

**Serves 2**

5 teaspoons olive oil, plus
   extra for greasing and dipping
¹⁄₂ 14-ounce can
   chopped tomatoes
2 garlic cloves, crushed
pinch of dried basil
2 leeks, sliced
3¹⁄₂ ounces radicchio,
   roughly chopped

¹⁄₄ cup freshly grated
   Parmesan cheese
4 ounces mozzarella
   cheese, sliced
10–12 pitted black olives
salt and ground black pepper
fresh basil leaves, to garnish

**For the dough**

2 cups self-rising flour, plus extra
   for dusting
¹⁄₂ teaspoon salt
¹⁄₄ cup butter
about ¹⁄₂ cup milk

**1** Preheat the oven to 425°F. Grease a baking sheet. Make the dough by mixing the flour and salt in a bowl, rubbing in the butter and gradually stirring in the milk. Roll the dough out on a lightly floured surface into a 10–11-inch round. Place this on the baking sheet.

**2** Put the tomatoes into a small pan. Stir in half the crushed garlic, together with the dried basil and a little seasoning. Simmer over medium heat until the mixture is thick and has reduced by about half.

**3** Heat the olive oil in a large frying pan and fry the leeks and remaining garlic until slightly softened. Add the radicchio and cook, stirring constantly, for 2–3 minutes, then cover and simmer gently for 5–10 minutes. Stir in the Parmesan cheese and season to taste with salt and pepper.

**4** Cover the crust bottom with the tomato mixture, then spoon the leek and radicchio mixture on top. Arrange the mozzarella slices on the vegetables and sprinkle on the olives. Dip a few basil leaves in olive oil and arrange them on top. Bake the pizza for 15–20 minutes, until the crust and top are golden brown.

# Spring Vegetable & Pine Nut Pizza

Here's a chance to practice your artistic skills. With its colorful topping of tender young vegetables, the pizza looks like an artist's palette, and it tastes wonderful.

**Serves 2–3**
10–12-inch pizza crust
3 tablespoons olive oil
1 garlic clove, crushed
4 scallions, sliced
2 zucchini, thinly sliced
1 leek, thinly sliced
4 ounces asparagus tips, sliced
1 tablespoon chopped
   fresh oregano

2 tablespoons pine nuts
½ cup grated mozzarella, cheese
2 tablespoons freshly grated
   Parmesan cheese
salt and ground black pepper

**For the tomato sauce**
1 tablespoon olive oil
1 onion, finely chopped
1 garlic clove, crushed
14-ounce can chopped tomatoes
1 tablespoon tomato paste
1 tablespoon chopped fresh herbs
pinch of sugar

**1** Make the tomato sauce. Heat the oil in a pan and fry the onion and garlic over low heat, stirring occasionally, for about 5 minutes, until softened but not browned. Add the remaining ingredients, stir well and simmer for 15–20 minutes, until the mixture is thick and flavorful.

**2** Preheat the oven to 425°F. Brush the pizza crust with 1 tablespoon of the olive oil, then spread the tomato sauce evenly on top to within ½ inch of the edge.

**3** Heat half the remaining olive oil in a frying pan and stir-fry the garlic, scallions, zucchini, leek and asparagus over medium heat for 3–5 minutes.

**4** Arrange the vegetables on the tomato sauce, then sprinkle the oregano and pine nuts on top.

**5** Mix the cheeses and sprinkle them on. Drizzle on the remaining olive oil and season well. Bake for 15–20 minutes, until crisp and golden. Serve immediately.

# Roasted Vegetable & Goat Cheese Pizza

This pizza incorporates the smoky flavors of roasted vegetables and the unique taste of goat cheese.

**Serves 3**
1 eggplant, cut into thick chunks
2 zucchini, sliced lengthwise
1 red bell pepper, quartered
   and seeded
1 yellow bell pepper, quartered
   and seeded

1 small red onion, cut into wedges
6 tablespoons olive oil
10–12-inch pizza crust
14-ounce can chopped tomatoes,
   well drained
4 ounces goat cheese, cubed
1 tablespoon fresh thyme
ground black pepper
green olive tapenade (see Cook's
   Tip), to serve

**1** Preheat the oven to 425°F. Place the vegetables in a roasting pan. Brush with 4 tablespoons of the oil. Roast for 30 minutes, until charred, turning the peppers once. Remove the vegetables but leave the oven on.

**2** Put the peppers in a bowl and cover with crumpled paper towels. When cool enough to handle, peel off the skins and cut the flesh into thick strips. Brush the pizza crust with half the remaining oil and spread on the drained tomatoes. Arrange the roasted vegetables on top of the pizza. Dot with the goat cheese and sprinkle on the thyme.

**3** Drizzle on the remaining oil and season. Bake for 15–20 minutes, until crisp. Spoon on the tapenade to serve.

---

**Cook's Tip**

*For vegetarian green olive tapenade, put 40 pitted green olives and 1 teaspoon capers in a food processor. Add four pieces of drained sun-dried tomatoes in oil, 1 teaspoon ground almonds, one chopped garlic clove and a pinch of ground cumin. Process briefly, add 4 tablespoons olive oil and process into a paste.*

---

# Wild Mushroom Pizzettes

Serve these extravagant pizzas as an appetizer for special guests, or make miniature versions for serving with glasses of champagne or cocktails.

**Serves 4**

3 tablespoons olive oil
4 1/2 cups fresh wild
   mushrooms, sliced
2 shallots, chopped
2 garlic cloves, finely chopped
2 tablespoons chopped fresh
   mixed thyme and
   flat-leaf parsley
1 batch pizza dough
scant 1/2 cup grated
   Gruyère cheese
2 tablespoons freshly grated
   Parmesan cheese
salt and ground black pepper

**1** Preheat the oven to 425°F. Heat 2 tablespoons of the oil in a frying pan. Add the mushrooms, shallots and garlic and fry over medium heat, stirring occasionally, until all the juices have evaporated.

**2** Stir in half the mixed herbs and season to taste with salt and pepper, then set aside cool.

**3** Divide the dough into four pieces and roll out each one on a lightly floured surface into a 5-inch circle. Place well apart on two greased baking sheets, then push up the dough edges on each to form a thin rim. Brush the pizza crusts with the remaining oil and top with the wild mushroom mixture, leaving a small rim all the way around.

**4** Mix the Gruyère and Parmesan cheeses, then sprinkle one-quarter of the mixture on each of the pizzettes. Bake for 15–20 minutes, until crisp and golden. Remove from the oven and sprinkle on the remaining herbs to serve.

**Cook's Tip**
*Fresh wild mushrooms add a distinctive flavor to the topping, but a mixture of cultivated mushrooms, such as shiitake, oyster and chestnut mushrooms would do just as well.*

# Feta, Pimiento & Pine Nut Pizzettes

Perk up a party with these tempting mini pizzas. They take only minutes to make, a short time to cook and will be eaten even quicker.

**Makes 24**

Double batch pizza dough
4 tablespoons olive oil
2 tablespoons vegetarian green
   olive tapenade
6 ounces feta cheese
1 large canned or bottled
   pimiento, drained
2 tablespoons chopped fresh thyme
2 tablespoons pine nuts
ground black pepper
fresh thyme sprigs, to garnish

**1** Preheat the oven to 425°F. Divide the pizza dough into 24 pieces and roll out each one on a lightly floured surface into a small oval, about 1/8 inch thick.

**2** Place well apart on greased baking sheets and prick all over with a fork. Brush with 2 tablespoons of the oil.

**3** Spread a thin layer of the tapenade on each oval and crumble on the feta. Cut the pimiento into thin strips and pile on top of the cheese.

**4** Sprinkle each pizzette with thyme and pine nuts. Drizzle on the remaining oil and grind on plenty of black pepper. Bake for 10–15 minutes, until crisp and golden. Garnish with thyme sprigs and serve immediately.

**Cook's Tip**
*Try to find sheep's milk feta, which has the best flavor.*

**Variations**
• *Substitute goat cheese for the feta.*
• *The tapenade can be made with pitted black rather than green olives, if you prefer.*

# Spinach & Ricotta Panzerotti

These make great party snacks for serving with drinks, or appetizers.

**Makes 20–24**
4 ounces frozen chopped spinach, thawed, drained and squeezed dry
1/4 cup ricotta cheese
2/3 cup freshly grated Parmesan cheese
good pinch of freshly grated nutmeg
Double batch pizza dough
all-purpose flour, for dusting
1 egg white, lightly beaten
oil for deep-frying
salt and ground black pepper

**1** Place the spinach, ricotta, Parmesan and nutmeg in a bowl. Season to taste with salt and pepper and beat well with a wooden spoon until smooth.

**2** Roll out the dough on a lightly floured surface to a thickness of about 1/8 inch. Using a 3-inch plain round cutter, stamp out 20–24 circles.

**3** Spread a teaspoon of spinach mixture on one half of each circle, then brush the edges of the dough with a little egg white, fold over the dough and press the edges firmly together to seal.

**4** Heat the oil in a large heavy pan or deep-fat fryer to 350°F or until a cube of day-old bread, added to the oil, browns in 45–60 seconds. Deep-fry the panzerotti, a few at a time, for 2–3 minutes, until golden. Drain on paper towels and serve immediately.

**Cook's Tips**
• Make sure the spinach is squeezed as dry as possible.
• It is important to ensure that oil for deep-frying is heated to the right temperature before adding the panzerotti.
• Do not crowd the pan, as this not only drastically lowers the temperature of the oil, but can also cause it to splash.
• Do serve these as soon as possible after frying, as they don't taste as good if left cool.

# Eggplant & Sun-dried Tomato Calzone

Eggplant, shallots and sun-dried tomatoes make an unusual filling for calzone—pizza "turnovers."

**Serves 2**
3 tablespoons olive oil
3 shallots, chopped
4 baby eggplant, cut into small cubes
1 garlic clove, chopped
6 pieces of sun-dried tomatoes in oil, drained and chopped
1/4 teaspoon dried red chile flakes
2 teaspoons chopped fresh thyme
1 batch pizza dough
flour, for dusting
3 ounces mozzarella, cubed
salt and ground black pepper
1–2 tablespoons freshly grated Parmesan cheese, to serve

**1** Preheat the oven to 425°F. Heat 2 tablespoons of the oil in a heavy frying pan. Add the shallots and fry over low heat, stirring occasionally, for 5 minutes, until softened but not browned.

**2** Add the eggplant, garlic, sun-dried tomatoes, chile flakes and thyme and season with salt and pepper to taste. Cook for 4–5 minutes, stirring frequently, until the eggplant is beginning to soften.

**3** Divide the dough in half and roll out each piece on a lightly floured surface into a 7-inch circle. Spread the eggplant mixture on half of each circle, leaving a 1-inch border, then sprinkle on the mozzarella.

**4** Dampen the edges with water, then fold the dough over to enclose the filling. Press the edges firmly together to seal. Place the calzones on two greased baking sheets.

**5** Brush with half the remaining oil and make a small hole in the top of each to let the steam to escape. Bake the calzone for 15–20 minutes, until golden. Remove from the oven and brush with the remaining olive oil. Sprinkle on the grated Parmesan and serve immediately.

# Parsnip & Pecan Gougères

These nutty puffs conceal a sweet parsnip center.

**Makes 18**
1/2 cup butter, plus extra
   for greasing
1 1/4 cups water
3/4 cup all-purpose flour
1/2 cup whole-wheat flour
3 eggs, beaten
2 tablespoons finely grated
   Cheddar cheese

*pinch of cayenne pepper*
*3/4 cup pecans, chopped*
*1 parsnip, cut into 3/4-inch pieces*
*1 tablespoon milk*
*2 teaspoons sesame seeds*
*fresh watercress sprigs, to garnish*
*Watercress & Arugula Sauce to*
   *serve (optional)*

**1** Preheat the oven to 400°F. Place the butter and water in a pan. Bring to a boil, then add both the flours. Beat vigorously until the mixture leaves the sides of the pan.

**2** Remove from heat and cool for 10 minutes. Beat in the eggs, a little at a time, until the mixture is shiny with a soft dropping consistency. Beat in the Cheddar, cayenne and pecans.

**3** Lightly grease a large baking sheet and drop 18 heaping tablespoons of the mixture on it. Place a piece of parsnip on each and top with another heaping tablespoon of the mixture.

**4** Brush the gougères with a little milk and sprinkle with sesame seeds. Bake for 25–30 minutes, until firm and golden. Garnish with the watercress. Serve with the watercress sauce, if you like.

---

**Cook's Tip**
*The secret of making successful choux pastry is to let the flour and butter mixture cool before beating in the eggs to prevent them from setting.*

---

# Watercress & Arugula Sauce

This fresh-tasting sauce can be served with either of these gougères and is also good with pasta.

**Serves 4**
*5 ounces watercress, trimmed*
*5 ounces arugula, trimmed*
*3/4 cup low-fat plain yogurt*
*freshly grated nutmeg*
*salt and ground black pepper*

**1** Bring a pan of water to a boil and blanch the watercress and arugula for 2–3 minutes. Drain, refresh under cold water, drain again and chop roughly.
**2** Place the watercress and arugula in a blender or food processor with the yogurt and process until smooth. Add a pinch of nutmeg and season to taste with salt and pepper.
**3** Just before serving, place in the top of a double boiler or in a heatproof bowl set over a pan of barely simmering water. Heat gently, being careful not to let the sauce curdle.

# Mushroom Gougère

A savory choux pastry ring makes a great main course dish that can be made ahead, then baked when needed.

**Serves 4**
*6 tablespoons butter*
*1 cup all-purpose flour*
*1/2 teaspoon salt*
*scant 1 cup water*
*3 eggs, beaten*
*3/4 cup diced Gruyère cheese*

**For the filling**
*3 tablespoons butter*
*1 small onion, sliced*
*1 carrot, coarsely grated*
*3 cups button mushrooms, sliced*
*1 teaspoon mild curry paste*
*1/4 cup all-purpose flour*
*1 1/4 cups milk*
*2 tablespoons chopped*
   *fresh parsley*
*2 tablespoons sliced almonds*
*salt and ground black pepper*

**1** Preheat the oven to 400°F. Use a little butter to grease a shallow 9-inch round ovenproof dish. Sift the flour and salt onto a sheet of waxed paper.

**2** Heat the remaining butter and water in a large saucepan until the butter just melts, then add all the flour. Beat vigorously until the mixture leaves the sides of the pan and forms a ball.

**3** Remove from heat and cool for 10 minutes. Beat in the eggs, a little at a time, until the mixture is shiny and soft enough to fall gently from a spoon.

**4** Stir in the cheese, then spoon the mixture around the sides of the ovenproof dish.

**5** Make the filling. Melt the butter in a pan and sauté the onion, carrot and mushrooms for 5 minutes. Stir in the curry paste, then the flour. Gradually add the milk, stirring until the mixture boils and thickens. Mix in the parsley, season to taste with salt and pepper, then pour into the center of the choux ring.

**6** Bake for 35–40 minutes, until risen and golden brown, sprinkling on the almonds for the last 5 minutes. Serve immediately.

# Party Purses

Phyllo "money bags" filled with creamy leeks are a very attractive dinner party treat.

**Serves 4**

1/2 cup butter
8 ounces leeks, trimmed and
    finely chopped
I cup cream cheese
I tablespoon finely chopped
    fresh dill
I tablespoon finely chopped
    fresh parsley
2 scallions, finely chopped
pinch of cayenne pepper
I garlic clove, finely chopped
I egg yolk
9 sheets phyllo pastry, thawed
    if frozen
salt and ground black pepper
lightly cooked leeks, to serve

**I** Preheat the oven to 400°F. Melt 2 tablespoons of the butter in a frying pan and fry the leeks for 4–5 minutes, until soft. Drain off any liquid.

**2** Put the cream cheese in a bowl and stir in the dill, parsley, scallions, cayenne and garlic. Stir in the egg yolk and leeks and season well. Melt the remaining butter.

**3** Place one sheet of phyllo pastry on a board, brush with a little of the melted butter and place another sheet on top. Brush again with butter and top with a third sheet of phyllo.

**4** Cut the layered phyllo into four squares and place 4 teaspoons of the cheese mixture in the center of each square. Gather up the edges into a "bag," twisting the top to seal. Repeat with the remaining phyllo to make 12 bags. Brush them with a little butter.

**5** Place the bags on a greased baking sheet and bake for 20–25 minutes, until golden brown. Serve on a bed of lightly cooked leeks.

---

**Cook's Tip**
*For an attractive effect, tie each bag with a strip of blanched leek before serving.*

---

# Ratatouille & Fontina Strudel

Mix a colorful jumble of ratatouille vegetables with chunks of creamy cheese, wrap in phyllo and bake for a summery party pastry.

**Serves 6**

I small eggplant, diced
3 tablespoons extra virgin
    olive oil
I onion, sliced
2 garlic cloves, crushed
I red bell pepper, seeded
    and sliced
I yellow bell pepper, seeded
    and sliced
2 zucchini, cut into small chunks
generous pinch of dried
    mixed herbs
2 tablespoons pine nuts
2 tablespoons raisins
8 phyllo pastry sheets, each about
    12 x 7 inches, thawed if frozen
1/4 cup butter, melted
4 1/2 ounces Fontina or Bel Paese
    cheese, cut into small cubes
salt and ground black pepper
dressed mixed salad, to serve

**I** Layer the eggplant in a colander, sprinkling each layer with salt. Drain for 20 minutes, then rinse, drain and pat dry.

**2** Heat the oil in a large frying pan and gently fry the onion, garlic, peppers and eggplant for about 10 minutes. Add the zucchini and herbs and season with salt and pepper to taste. Cook for 5 minutes, until softened. Cool to room temperature, then stir in the pine nuts and raisins.

**3** Preheat the oven to 350°F. To assemble the strudel, brush two sheets of phyllo pastry lightly with a little of the melted butter. Lay the phyllo sheets side by side, overlapping them by about 2 inches, to make a large rectangle.

**4** Cover with the remaining phyllo, in the same way, brushing each layer with a little of the melted butter. Spoon the vegetable mixture down one long side of the phyllo.

**5** Sprinkle on the cheese, then roll up to a long sausage. Transfer to a nonstick baking sheet and curl around to form a ring. Brush with the remaining melted butter and bake for 30 minutes, until golden. Cool for 10 minutes, then slice and serve with a mixed salad.

# Potato & Leek Phyllo Pie

This makes an attractive and unusual centerpiece for a vegetarian buffet.

**Serves 8**

1¾ pounds new potatoes, thinly sliced
6 tablespoons butter
14 ounces leeks, sliced
½ cup parsley, finely chopped
4 tablespoons chopped mixed fresh herbs
12 sheets phyllo pastry, thawed if frozen
5 ounces white Cheshire, Lancashire or Cantal cheese, sliced
2 garlic cloves, finely chopped
1 cup heavy cream
2 large egg yolks
salt and ground black pepper

**1** Preheat the oven to 375°F. Bring a saucepan of lightly salted water to a boil and cook the potato slices for 3–4 minutes. Drain carefully.

**2** Melt 2 tablespoons of the butter in a frying pan and fry the leeks gently, stirring occasionally, until softened. Remove from heat, season with pepper and stir in half the parsley and half the mixed herbs.

**3** Melt the remaining butter. Line a 9-inch round springform pan with six or seven sheets of phyllo, brushing each layer with butter. Let the edges of the pastry overhang the pan.

**4** Layer the potatoes, leeks and cheese in the pastry-lined pan, sprinkling a few herbs and the garlic between the layers. Season with a little salt and pepper. Flip the overhanging pastry over the filling and cover with two sheets of phyllo, tucking in the sides to fit and brushing with melted butter as before. Cover the pie loosely with aluminum foil and bake for 35 minutes.

**5** Meanwhile, beat the cream, egg yolks and remaining herbs together. Make a hole in the center of the pie and gradually pour in the eggs and cream. Arrange the remaining pastry on top, teasing it into swirls, then brush with melted butter. Reduce the oven temperature to 350°F and bake the pie for another 25–30 minutes. Let cool before serving.

# Spanakopitta

This popular spinach and phyllo pastry pie comes from Greece. There are several ways of making it, but feta or Kefalotiri cheese is inevitably included.

**Serves 6**

2¼ pounds fresh spinach
4 scallions, chopped
11 ounces feta or Kefalotiri cheese, crumbled or coarsely grated
2 large eggs, beaten
2 tablespoons chopped fresh parsley
1 tablespoon chopped fresh dill
about 8 phyllo pastry sheets, each about 12 x 7 inches, thawed if frozen
⅔ cup olive oil
ground black pepper

**1** Preheat the oven to 375°F. Break off any thick stems from the spinach, then wash the leaves and cook them in just the water that clings to the leaves in a heavy pan. As soon as they have wilted, drain them, refresh under cold water and drain again. Squeeze dry and chop roughly.

**2** Place the spinach in a bowl. Add the scallions and cheese, then pour in the eggs. Mix in the herbs and season the filling with pepper.

**3** Brush a phyllo sheet with oil and fit it into a 9-inch pie dish, letting it hang over the edge. Top with three or four more sheets; place these at different angles and brush each one with more oil to make a roughly shaped pie case.

**4** Spoon in the filling, then top with all but one of the remaining phyllo sheets. Brush each phyllo sheet with oil. Fold in the over-hanging phyllo to seal in the filling. Brush the reserved phyllo with oil and scrunch it on top of the pie.

**5** Brush the pie with oil. Sprinkle with a little water to stop the phyllo edges from curling, then place on a baking sheet. Bake for about 40 minutes, until golden and crisp. Cool the pie for 15 minutes before serving.

# Asparagus Phyllo Wraps

For a taste sensation, try tender asparagus spears wrapped in crisp phyllo pastry. The buttery herb sauce is a perfect partner.

### Serves 2

4 sheets of phyllo pastry, thawed
   if frozen
1/4 cup butter, melted
16 young asparagus
   spears, trimmed
salad greens, to garnish (optional)

### For the sauce

2 shallots, finely chopped
1 bay leaf
2/3 cup dry white wine
3/4 cup butter, softened
1 tablespoon chopped fresh herbs
salt and ground black pepper
snipped chives, to garnish

**1** Preheat the oven to 400°F. Keeping the rest of the phyllo covered with a damp dish towel, brush each sheet with melted butter and fold one corner down to the bottom edge to create a wedge shape.

**2** Lay four asparagus spears on top at the longest edge and roll up toward the shortest edge. Using the remaining phyllo and asparagus spears, make three more rolls in the same way.

**3** Lay the rolls on a greased baking sheet. Brush with the remaining melted butter. Bake the rolls for 8 minutes, until the pastry is golden.

**4** Meanwhile, make the sauce. Mix the shallots, bay leaf and wine in a pan. Cook over high heat until the wine is reduced to about 3–4 tablespoons.

**5** Strain the wine mixture into a bowl. Whisk in the butter, a little at a time, until the sauce is smooth and glossy.

**6** Stir in the herbs and add salt and pepper to taste. Return to the pan and warm through gently. Serve the rolls on individual plates with salad, if desired. Pass the butter sauce separately, with a few snipped chives on top.

# Asparagus & Ricotta Tart

The melt-in-your-mouth filling in this summery tart has a much more delicate texture than a quiche—and tastes absolutely wonderful.

### Serves 4

1 1/2 cups all-purpose flour, plus
   extra for dusting
6 tablespoons butter

### For the filling

8 ounces asparagus
2 eggs, beaten
1 cup ricotta cheese
2 tablespoons plain yogurt
1/2 cup freshly grated
   Parmesan cheese
salt and ground black pepper

**1** Preheat the oven to 400°F. Mix the flour and a pinch of salt in a bowl and rub in the butter with your fingertips or a pastry blender until the mixture resembles fine bread crumbs. Stir in enough cold water to form a smooth dough, and knead lightly on a floured surface.

**2** Roll out the pastry on a lightly floured surface and then use to line a 9-inch tart pan. Prick the dough all over with a fork. Bake for 10 minutes, until the pastry is pale but firm. Remove from the oven and reduce the temperature to 350°F.

**3** Make the filling. Snap the asparagus and discard the woody ends. Cut off the tips and chop the remaining stalks into 1-inch pieces. Bring a pan of water to a boil. Blanch the stalks for 1 minute, then add the asparagus tips. Simmer for 4–5 minutes, until almost tender, then drain and refresh under cold water. Drain again. Separate the chopped stalks from the asparagus tips.

**4** Beat the eggs, ricotta, yogurt and Parmesan in a bowl. Stir in the asparagus stalks, season to taste with salt and pepper and pour the mixture into the pastry shell.

**5** Arrange the asparagus tips on top, pressing them down slightly into the ricotta mixture. Bake for 35–40 minutes, until golden. Serve warm or cold.

# Leek & Onion Tartlets

Individual tartlets are easy to serve and look pretty on the plate when garnished with lettuce and tomato.

**Serves 6**
2 tablespoons butter
I onion, thinly sliced
½ teaspoon dried thyme
I pound leeks, thinly sliced
½ cup grated Gruyère or
    Emmenthal cheese
3 eggs

1¼ cups light cream
pinch of freshly grated nutmeg
salt and ground black pepper
lettuce, parsley and cherry
    tomatoes, to serve

**For the pastry**
1½ cups all-purpose flour
½ teaspoon salt
6 tablespoons cold butter
I egg yolk
2–3 tablespoons cold water

**I** Make the pastry. Sift the flour and salt into a bowl and rub in the butter until the mixture resembles fine bread crumbs. Make a well in the center. Add the egg yolk and water and, using a fork, mix lightly into a dough. Wrap and chill for 30 minutes.

**2** Lightly butter six 4-inch tartlet pans. On a lightly floured surface, roll out the dough thinly, cut into 5-inch rounds and line the pans. Prick the dough and chill for 30 minutes.

**3** Preheat the oven to 375°F. Line the tartlets with aluminum foil and fill with baking beans. Place on a baking sheet and bake for 6–8 minutes, until the edges are golden. Remove the foil and beans and bake for 2 more minutes. Transfer to a wire rack. Reduce the oven temperature to 350°F.

**4** Melt the butter in a frying pan and cook the onion with the thyme for 3–5 minutes, until softened. Add the leeks and cook for 10–12 minutes, until they are soft and tender. Divide the mixture among the pastry shells and sprinkle each with cheese.

**5** Beat the eggs with the cream, nutmeg and seasoning. Place the tartlets on a baking sheet and pour in the egg mixture. Bake for 20 minutes, until set. Cool slightly, then remove from the pans. Serve with lettuce, parsley and cherry tomatoes.

# Pissaladière

A Provençal classic, this is a delicious and colorful tart full of flavor. The classic version includes anchovies, but it is just as good without.

**Serves 6**
2 cups all-purpose flour
½ cup butter
I teaspoon dried mixed herbs
pinch of salt

**For the filling**
3 tablespoons olive oil
2 large onions, thinly sliced
2 garlic cloves, crushed
14-ounce can chopped tomatoes
I teaspoon sugar
leaves from small sprig of thyme
freshly grated nutmeg
¾ cup pitted black olives, sliced
2 tablespoons rinsed capers
salt and ground black pepper
chopped fresh parsley, to garnish

**I** Preheat the oven to 375°F. Put the flour in a bowl and rub in the butter until the mixture resembles fine bread crumbs, then stir in the herbs and salt. Mix into a firm dough with cold water.

**2** Roll out the pastry and line a 9-inch round tart pan. Line the pastry with nonstick baking parchment and add baking beans. Bake for 20 minutes, then lift out the paper and beans and bake for 5–7 more minutes. Let cool.

**3** Make the filling. Heat the oil in a frying pan and fry the onions and garlic gently for about 10 minutes, until quite soft. Stir in the tomatoes, sugar, thyme and nutmeg. Season and simmer for 10 minutes.

**4** Let the filling cool. Mix in the olives and capers, then spoon into the shell. Sprinkle with parsley and serve.

**Variation**
*To serve Pissaladière hot, top with grated cheese and broil until the cheese is golden and bubbling.*

# Cheese & Spinach Tart

This tart freezes well and can be reheated once it has been defrosted. It makes an excellent addition to a party buffet table.

**Serves 8**
2 cups all-purpose flour, plus extra
    for dusting
1/2 cup butter
1/2 teaspoon English
    mustard powder
1/2 teaspoon paprika
large pinch of salt
1 cup grated Cheddar cheese
3–4 tablespoons cold water

beaten egg, to glaze

**For the filling**
1 pound frozen spinach
1 onion, finely chopped
pinch of grated nutmeg
1 cup cottage cheese
2 large eggs
2/3 cup freshly grated
    Parmesan cheese
2/3 cup light cream
salt and ground black pepper

**1** Put the flour in a bowl and rub in the butter until the mixture resembles fine bread crumbs. Stir in the mustard powder, paprika, salt and cheese. Bind into a dough with the cold water. Knead until smooth, wrap and chill for 30 minutes.

**2** Make the filling. Put the spinach and onion in a pan, cover and cook gently until the spinach has thawed and the onion is tender. Increase the heat and stir until the mixture is dry. Season with salt, pepper and nutmeg. Spoon the spinach into a bowl and cool slightly. Add the remaining filling ingredients.

**3** Preheat the oven to 400°F. Cut one-third off the pastry and set it aside for the lid. On a lightly floured surface, roll out the rest and line a 9-inch loose-bottomed tart pan. Pour the filling into the shell.

**4** Roll out the reserved pastry and cut a lid with a lattice pastry cutter. Carefully open the lattice. With the help of a rolling pin, lay it on the flan. Press the edges together and neaten the seams. Brush the pastry lattice with egg to glaze. Bake for 35–40 minutes or until golden brown. Serve hot or cold.

# Wild Mushroom Pie

Wild mushrooms give this pie a really rich flavor.

**Serves 6**
2 cups all-purpose flour
1/2 teaspoon salt
1/2 cup butter
2 teaspoons lemon juice
2/3 cup ice water
beaten egg, to glaze

**For the filling**
2/3 cup butter
2 shallots, finely chopped
2 garlic cloves, crushed
6 cups mixed wild
    mushrooms, sliced
3 tablespoons chopped
    fresh parsley
2 tablespoons heavy cream
salt and ground black pepper

**1** Sift the flour and salt into a bowl. Rub in half the butter until the mixture resembles bread crumbs. Cut the remaining butter into cubes and put these in the refrigerator to chill. Add the lemon juice to the flour mixture with enough ice water to make a soft but not sticky dough. Cover and chill for 20 minutes.

**2** Roll the pastry out into a rectangle on a lightly floured surface. With a narrow end facing you, mark the dough horizontally into three equal sections. Arrange half the butter cubes on top two sections of the dough. Fold the bottom section up and the top section down. Seal the edges with a rolling pin. Give the dough a quarter turn and roll it out again. Mark it into thirds and dot with the remaining butter cubes in the same way. Chill for 20 minutes, then repeat the rolling, folding and chilling three times, without the butter.

**3** Make the filling. Melt the butter and fry the shallots and garlic until soft. Add the mushrooms and cook for 35–40 minutes. Drain off any excess liquid and stir in the remaining ingredients. Let cool. Preheat the oven to 450°F.

**4** Divide the pastry in half. Roll out one half and line a 9-inch round pan. Pile the filling into the center. Roll out the remaining pastry to a round large enough to cover the top. Brush the edge of the shell with water and then lay the second circle on top. Press the edges together and decorate the top. Brush with egg. Bake for 45 minutes or until the pastry is golden.

# Mediterranean One-crust Pie

This free-form pie encases a rich tomato, eggplant and kidney bean filling. If your pastry cracks, just patch it up—it adds to the pie's rustic character.

### Serves 4

1¼ pounds eggplant, cubed
1 red bell pepper
2 tablespoons olive oil, plus extra
    for greasing
1 large onion, finely chopped
1 zucchini, sliced
2 garlic cloves, crushed
1 tablespoon chopped fresh
    oregano or 1 teaspoon dried,
plus extra fresh oregano
    to garnish
7-ounce can red kidney beans,
    drained and rinsed
1 cup pitted black olives, rinsed
⅔ cup passata
beaten egg, for brushing
2 tablespoons semolina
salt and ground black pepper

### For the pastry

¾ cup white flour
¾ cup whole-wheat flour
6 tablespoons
    vegetable margarine
⅔ cup freshly grated
    Parmesan cheese

**1** Preheat the oven to 425°F. Make the pastry. Sift both types of flour into a large bowl and add the bran remaining in the sieve into the bowl. Rub in the margarine with a pastry blender or your fingertips until the mixture resembles fine bread crumbs, then stir in the grated Parmesan. Mix in enough cold water to form a soft dough. Shape into a ball, wrap and chill for 30 minutes.

**2** Place the eggplant cubes in a colander, sprinkle with salt, then let drain in the sink for about 30 minutes. Rinse well, drain and pat dry with paper towels.

**3** Meanwhile, broil the red bell pepper until blistered and charred all over. Put in a small bowl, cover with crumpled paper towels and let cool slightly. Rub off the skin, remove the core and seeds and dice the flesh. Set it aside.

**4** Heat the oil in a large, heavy frying pan. Add the onion and fry over low heat, stirring occasionally, for 5 minutes, until softened. Add the eggplant cubes and fry for about 5 minutes, until tender.

**5** Stir in the zucchini slices, garlic and oregano, and cook for another 5 minutes, stirring frequently. Add the kidney beans and olives, stir well to mix, then add the passata and diced red bell pepper. Season to taste with salt and pepper. Cook over medium heat, stirring occasionally, until heated through, then set aside cool.

**6** Roll out the pastry into a rough 12-inch round. Place on a lightly oiled baking sheet. Brush with some beaten egg, then sprinkle on the semolina, leaving a 1½-inch border. Spoon in the filling.

**7** Gather up the edges of the pastry to partly cover the filling—it should remain open in the middle. Brush with the remaining egg and bake for 30–35 minutes, until golden. Transfer to a warmed serving plate, garnish with oregano and serve.

# Chestnut, Stilton & Ale Pie

This hearty winter dish has a rich stout gravy and a herb pastry top.

### Serves 4

2 tablespoons sunflower oil
2 large onions, chopped
8 cups button mushrooms, halved
3 carrots, sliced
1 parsnip, thickly sliced
1 tablespoon chopped
    fresh thyme
2 bay leaves
1 cup stout
½ cup vegetable stock
1 teaspoon yeast extract
1 teaspoon dark brown sugar
3 cups drained canned
    chestnuts, halved
2 tablespoons cornstarch, mixed
    into a paste with 2 tablespoons
    cold water
5 ounces Stilton cheese, cubed
beaten egg, to glaze
salt and ground black pepper

### For the pastry

1 cup whole-wheat flour
a pinch of salt
¼ cup butter
1 tablespoon chopped
    fresh thyme

**1** Make the pastry. Put the flour and salt in a bowl. Rub in the butter until the mixture resembles fine bread crumbs. Add the thyme and enough water to form a soft dough. Knead it lightly, wrap and chill for 30 minutes.

**2** Make the filling. Heat the oil in a pan and fry the onions until softened. Add the mushrooms and cook for 3 minutes. Stir in the carrots, parsnip and herbs. Cover and cook for 3 minutes.

**3** Pour in the stout and stock then stir in the yeast extract and sugar. Simmer, covered, for 5 minutes. Add the chestnuts and season to taste. Stir in the cornstarch paste until the sauce thickens. Stir in the cheese and heat until melted, stirring.

**4** Preheat the oven to 425°F. Spoon the chestnut mixture into a 6-cup pie dish. Roll out the pastry to make a lid. Dampen the edges of the dish and cover with the pastry. Seal, trim and crimp the edges. Cut a small slit in the top of the pie and use any surplus pastry to make pastry leaves. Brush with egg, and bake for 30 minutes.

# Shallot & Garlic Tarte Tatin

Savory versions of the famous apple tarte tatin have been popular for some years. Here, caramelized shallots are baked beneath a layer of Parmesan pastry.

**Serves 4–6**

11 ounces puff pastry, thawed
    if frozen
¼ cup butter
1 cup freshly grated Parmesan
    cheese

**For the topping**

3 tablespoons butter
1¼ pounds shallots, peeled but
    left whole
12–16 large garlic cloves, peeled
    but left whole
1 tablespoon brown sugar
1 tablespoon balsamic vinegar
3 tablespoons water
1 teaspoon chopped fresh thyme
salt and ground black pepper

**1** Roll out the pastry into a rectangle. Spread the butter on it, leaving a 1-inch border. Sprinkle the Parmesan on top. Fold the bottom third of the pastry up to cover the middle and the top third down. Seal the edges, give a quarter turn and roll out into a rectangle, then fold as before. Chill for 30 minutes.

**2** Make the topping. Melt the butter in a 9–10-inch heavy frying pan that can safely be used in the oven. Add the shallots and garlic and cook until lightly browned all over.

**3** Sprinkle the sugar on top and increase the heat a little. Cook until the sugar begins to caramelize, then turn the shallots and garlic in the buttery juices. Add the vinegar, water and thyme and season to taste. Partially cover the pan and cook for 5–8 minutes, until the garlic cloves are just tender. Cool.

**4** Preheat the oven to 375°F. Roll out the pastry into a round slightly larger than the pan and lay it on the shallots and garlic. Tuck the pastry overlap down inside the pan, then prick the pastry with a sharp knife. Bake the tart for 25–35 minutes or until it is risen and golden.

**5** Cool for 5–10 minutes, then turn the tart out onto a serving platter. Serve, cut in wedges.

# Red Onion Tart with a Polenta Crust

Mild red onions go well with Fontina cheese and thyme in this tasty tart.

**Serves 5–6**

4 tablespoons olive oil
2¼ pounds red onions, thinly sliced
2–3 garlic cloves, thinly sliced
1 teaspoon chopped fresh thyme,
    plus a few whole sprigs
1 teaspoon dark brown sugar
2 teaspoons sherry vinegar

8 ounces Fontina cheese,
    thinly sliced
salt and ground black pepper

**For the pastry**

1 cup all-purpose flour
⅔ cup fine polenta
1 teaspoon dark brown sugar
1 teaspoon chopped fresh thyme
7 tablespoons butter
1 egg yolk
about 2 tablespoons ice water

**1** Make the pastry. Mix the flour and polenta in a bowl and add salt, pepper, the sugar and thyme. Rub in the butter until the mixture resembles bread crumbs. Beat the egg yolk with the water and use to bind the pastry, adding more water, if needed. Gather the dough into a ball, wrap and chill for 30–40 minutes.

**2** Heat 3 tablespoons of the oil in a frying pan. Add the onions, cover and cook gently, stirring occasionally, for 20–30 minutes.

**3** Add the garlic and chopped thyme. Cook, stirring occasionally, for 10 minutes. Increase the heat slightly, then add the sugar and sherry vinegar. Cook, uncovered, for 5–6 more minutes, until the onions start to caramelize slightly. Season to taste. Cool.

**4** Preheat the oven to 375°F. Roll out the pastry thinly and use to line a 10-inch loose-bottomed tart pan. Prick the pastry with a fork and support the sides with aluminum foil. Bake for 12–15 minutes, until lightly colored.

**5** Spread the onions on the pastry. Add the cheese and most of the thyme sprigs and season. Drizzle on the remaining oil, then bake for 15–20 minutes, until the cheese is bubbling. Serve immediately, garnished with thyme sprigs.

# Leek & Roquefort Tart with Walnut Pastry

Mild leeks go exceptionally well with the salty flavor of Roquefort cheese.

**Serves 4–6**
2 tablespoons butter
1 pound leeks (trimmed weight), sliced
6 ounces Roquefort cheese, sliced
2 large eggs
1 cup heavy cream

2 teaspoons chopped fresh tarragon
salt and ground black pepper

**For the pastry**
1½ cups all-purpose flour
1 teaspoon dark brown sugar
¼ cup butter
¾ cup walnuts, ground
1 tablespoon lemon juice
2 tablespoons ice water

**1** First, make the pastry: sift the flour and ½ teaspoon salt into a bowl. Add some pepper and the sugar. Rub in the butter until the mixture resembles bread crumbs, then stir in the ground walnuts. Bind with the lemon juice and ice water. Form the dough into a ball, wrap and chill for 30–40 minutes.

**2** Preheat the oven to 375°F. Roll out the pastry and line a 9-inch loose-bottomed tart pan. Protect the sides of the pastry with aluminum foil, prick the bottom with a fork and bake for 15 minutes. Remove the foil and bake for another 5–10 minutes, until just firm to the touch. Reduce the oven temperature to 350°F.

**3** Meanwhile, melt the butter in a pan, add the leeks, cover and cook for 10 minutes. Season with salt and pepper to taste, stir and cook for another 10 minutes. Cool.

**4** Arrange the leeks and slices of Roquefort in the pastry shell. Whisk the eggs with the cream and season with black pepper. Beat in the tarragon and pour the mixture into the tart.

**5** Bake for 30–40 minutes, until the filling has risen and browned and feels firm when gently touched. Let cool for 10 minutes before serving.

# Mushroom, Nut & Prune Jalousie

A stunning dish for Sunday lunch, this comprises a nutty filling in a pastry shell.

**Serves 6**
⅓ cup green lentils, rinsed
1 teaspoon vegetable bouillon powder
1 tablespoon sunflower oil
2 large leeks, sliced
2 garlic cloves, chopped
2 teaspoons dried mixed herbs

3 cups field mushrooms, finely chopped
¾ cup chopped mixed nuts
⅓ cup pitted prunes
½ cup fresh white bread crumbs
2 eggs, beaten
2 sheets pre-rolled puff pastry, total weight 15 ounces, thawed if frozen
all-purpose flour, for dusting
salt and ground black pepper

**1** Put the lentils in a pan and cover with cold water. Bring to a boil, lower the heat and stir in the bouillon powder. Partially cover and simmer for 20 minutes, until the lentils are tender.

**2** Heat the oil in a large, heavy frying pan and fry the leeks and garlic for 5 minutes, until softened. Add the herbs and mushrooms and cook for 5 more minutes. Transfer the mixture to a bowl. Stir in the nuts, prunes, bread crumbs and lentils.

**3** Preheat the oven to 425°F. Add two-thirds of the eggs to the filling mixture and season. Set aside cool.

**4** Meanwhile, unroll one pastry sheet. Cut off and discard a 1-inch border, then lay it on a dampened baking sheet. Unroll the second sheet, dust lightly with flour, then fold in half lengthwise. Make a series of cuts across the fold, ½ inch apart, leaving a 1-inch border around the edge of the pastry.

**5** Spoon the filling mixture evenly on the pastry bottom, leaving a 1-inch border. Dampen the edges of the bottom. Open out the folded pastry and lay it on top of the filling. Trim the edges, then press them together to seal. Crimp the edges. Brush the top with the remaining beaten egg and bake for 25–30 minutes, until golden. Cool slightly before serving.

## Puff Pastry Boxes filled with Spring Vegetables in Pernod Sauce

Pernod is the perfect companion for these tender vegetables in crisp pastry.

**Serves 4**
8 ounces puff pastry, thawed
   if frozen
1 tablespoon freshly grated
   Parmesan cheese, plus extra
1 tablespoon chopped
   fresh parsley
beaten egg, to glaze
1 cup fava beans
4 ounces baby carrots, scraped

8 scallions, sliced
generous ½ cup peas
½ cup snow peas
salt and ground black pepper
fresh dill sprigs, to garnish

**For the sauce**
7-ounce can chopped tomatoes
2 tablespoons butter
¼ cup all-purpose flour
pinch of sugar
3 tablespoons chopped fresh dill
1¼ cups water
1 tablespoon Pernod

**1** Preheat the oven to 425°F. Grease a baking sheet. Roll out the pastry. Sprinkle with Parmesan and parsley, fold and roll out, then cut out four 3 x 4-inch rectangles. Lift them onto the baking sheet. Cut an inner oblong ½ inch from the edge on each, cutting halfway through. Score criss-cross lines on top of the inner rectangles, brush with egg and bake for 12–15 minutes, until golden.

**2** Meanwhile, make the sauce. Press the tomatoes through a sieve into a pan, add the remaining ingredients and bring to a boil, stirring. Season, lower the heat and simmer until required.

**3** Bring a pan of salted water to a boil. Cook the beans for 8 minutes. Add the carrots, onions and peas, cook for 5 more minutes, then add the snow peas. Cook for 1 minute. Drain well.

**4** Cut out the inner pieces from the pastry boxes. Swirl a little sauce on to four plates. Half-fill each box with vegetables, spoon over some sauce, then top up with vegetables. Sprinkle with Parmesan and place on the plates. Garnish with dill and set the lids at an angle. Serve with the remaining sauce.

## Zucchini & Dill Tart

It is worth making your own pastry for this tart. Using a mixture of whole-wheat flour and self-rising white flour gives very good results.

**Serves 4**
1 cup whole-wheat flour
1 cup self-rising flour
½ cup chilled butter, diced
5 tablespoons ice water
fresh dill sprigs, to garnish

**For the filling**
1 tablespoon sunflower oil
3 zucchini, thinly sliced
2 egg yolks
⅔ cup heavy cream
1 garlic clove, crushed
1 tablespoon finely chopped
   fresh dill
salt and ground black pepper

**1** Mix the flours in a food processor. Add a pinch of salt and butter and pulse until the mixture resembles fine bread crumbs. Gradually add the water until the mixture forms a dough. Wrap and chill for 30 minutes.

**2** Preheat the oven to 400°F. Grease an 8-inch tart pan. Roll out the pastry and ease it into the pan. Prick the dough with a fork and bake for 10–15 minutes, until golden.

**3** Meanwhile, make the filling. Heat the oil in a frying pan and sauté the zucchini for 2–3 minutes, until lightly browned. Mix the egg yolks, cream, garlic and dill in a small bowl. Season to taste with salt and pepper.

**4** Layer the zucchini slices in concentric circles in the pastry shell. Pour in the cream mixture. Bake for 25–30 minutes or until the filling is firm and lightly golden. Cool in the pan, then transfer to a board or plate. Garnish with dill and serve.

> **Cook's Tip**
> If you don't have a food processor, rub the butter into the flour mixture by hand.

# Upside-down Vegetable Tart

This is a Mediterranean variation on the tarte tatin.

**Serves 2–4**

2 tablespoons sunflower oil
about 1 1/2 tablespoons olive oil
1 eggplant, sliced lengthwise
1 large red bell pepper, seeded
    and cut into long strips
5 tomatoes
2 red shallots, finely chopped
1–2 garlic cloves, crushed
2/3 cup white wine
2 teaspoons chopped fresh basil
2 cups long-grain rice
1/3 cup pitted black
    olives, chopped
12 ounces puff pastry, thawed
    if frozen
ground black pepper
mâche, to garnish

**1** Cook the rice. Preheat the oven to 375°F. Heat the sunflower oil with 1 tablespoon of the olive oil in a frying pan and fry the eggplant slices for 4–5 minutes on each side, until golden brown. Lift out and drain on paper towels.

**2** Add the red bell pepper to the pan, turning to coat. Cover and sweat over medium heat for 5–6 minutes, stirring occasionally, until soft and flecked with brown.

**3** Slice two of the tomatoes and set them aside. Plunge the remaining tomatoes briefly into boiling water, then peel, cut into quarters and remove the core and seeds. Chop them roughly.

**4** Heat the remaining oil in the frying pan. Fry the shallots and garlic until softened. Add the chopped tomatoes and cook for 3 minutes. Stir in the wine and basil, with pepper to taste. Bring to a boil, remove from heat and stir in the rice and olives.

**5** Arrange the tomatoes slices, eggplant slices and peppers in a single layer on the bottom of a heavy, 12-inch shallow ovenproof dish. Spread the rice mixture on top.

**6** Roll out the pastry into a circle slightly larger than the dish and place on top of the rice, tucking in the overlap. Bake for 25–30 minutes, until risen and golden. Cool slightly, then invert onto a large, warmed serving plate. Garnish with mâche.

# Greek Picnic Pie

Eggplant layered with spinach, feta and rice is a delicious filling for a pie.

**Serves 6**

13 ounces shortcrust pastry,
    thawed if frozen
3–4 tablespoons olive oil
1 large eggplant, sliced
    into rounds
1 onion, chopped
1 garlic clove, crushed
6 ounces spinach
4 eggs
3 ounces feta cheese
1/2 cup freshly grated
    Parmesan cheese
4 tablespoons plain yogurt
6 tablespoons milk
2 cups cooked long-grain rice
salt and ground black pepper

**1** Preheat the oven to 350°F. Roll out the pastry thinly and line a 10-inch tart pan. Prick the pastry all over and bake the unfilled shell in the oven for 10–12 minutes, until the pastry is pale golden.

**2** Heat 2–3 tablespoons of the oil in a frying pan and fry the eggplant slices for 6–8 minutes on each side, until golden. Lift out and drain on paper towels.

**3** Add the onion and garlic to the oil remaining in the pan and fry gently until soft, adding a little extra oil if necessary.

**4** Chop the spinach finely, by hand or in a food processor. Beat the eggs in a large mixing bowl, then add the spinach, feta, Parmesan, yogurt, milk and the onion mixture. Season well with salt and pepper and stir thoroughly.

**5** Spread the rice in an even layer on the bottom of the partially cooked pastry shell.. Reserve a few eggplant slices for the top, and arrange the rest in an even layer on the rice.

**6** Spoon the spinach and feta mixture on the eggplant and place the remaining eggplant slices on top. Bake for 30–40 minutes, until lightly browned. Serve the pie warm, or cool completely before transferring to a serving plate or wrapping and packing for a picnic.

# Risotto with Four Cheeses

This is a very rich dish. Serve it as an appetizer for a special dinner party—preferably with a light, dry, sparkling white wine.

**Serves 4**

3 tablespoons butter
I small onion, finely chopped
5 cups well-flavored
 vegetable stock
I¾ cups risotto rice
scant I cup dry white wine
½ cup grated Gruyère cheese
½ cup diced Taleggio cheese
½ cup diced Gorgonzola cheese
⅔ cup freshly grated
 Parmesan cheese
salt and ground black pepper
chopped fresh flat-leaf parsley,
 to garnish

**I** Melt the butter in a large, heavy saucepan. Add the onion and fry over low heat, stirring occasionally, for about 8 minutes, until softened and lightly browned. Pour the stock into another pan and heat it to the simmering point. Lower the heat so that the stock is barely simmering.

**2** Add the rice to the onion mixture, stir until all the grains start to swell and burst, then stir in the white wine. When most of it has been absorbed, pour in a little of the hot stock. Season with salt and pepper to taste. Stir over low heat until the stock has been absorbed.

**3** Gradually add the remaining stock, a little at a time, letting the rice absorb the liquid before adding more, and stirring constantly. After 20–25 minutes the rice will be *al dente* and the risotto creamy.

**4** Turn off the heat under the pan, then add the Gruyère, Taleggio, Gorgonzola and half the Parmesan cheese. Stir gently until the cheeses have melted, then taste and adjust the seasoning, if necessary. Spoon the risotto into a warmed serving bowl and garnish with parsley. Serve immediately and pass the remaining Parmesan separately.

# Risotto with Asparagus

Fresh farm asparagus is only in season for a short time. Make the most of it by inviting friends to share this elegant risotto.

**Serves 3–4**

8 ounces fresh asparagus
3 cups well-flavored
 vegetable stock
5 tablespoons butter
I small onion, finely chopped
I½ cups risotto rice
I cup freshly grated
 Parmesan cheese
salt and ground black pepper

**I** Snap the asparagus stalks and discard the woody ends. Bring a pan of water to a boil, add the asparagus and cook for 5 minutes. Drain, reserving the cooking water, refresh under cold water and drain well again. Cut the asparagus stalks diagonally into I½-inch pieces. Keep the tips separate from the rest of the stalks.

**2** Pour the stock into a pan and add a scant 2 cups of the reserved asparagus cooking water. Heat to the simmering point.

**3** Melt two-thirds of the butter in a large, heavy pan and fry the onion until soft and golden. Stir in all the asparagus except the tips. Cook for 2–3 minutes. Add the rice and cook for I–2 minutes, stirring to coat the grains with butter. Add a ladleful of the hot stock and stir until it has been absorbed.

**4** Gradually add the remaining hot stock, a little at a time, letting the rice absorb each addition before adding more and stirring constantly.

**5** After 15 minutes of adding stock, mix in the asparagus tips. Continue to cook as before, for 5–10 minutes, until the rice is *al dente* and the risotto is creamy.

**6** Off the heat, stir in the remaining butter and the Parmesan. Grind in a little black pepper and salt, if needed. Serve immediately.

# Porcini & Parmesan Risotto

The success of a good risotto depends on both the quality of the rice used and the technique. Add the stock gradually and stir constantly to create a creamy texture.

**Serves 4**

1 cup dried porcini mushrooms
²⁄₃ cup warm water
4 cups well-flavored
   vegetable stock
generous pinch of saffron threads
2 tablespoons olive oil
1 onion, finely chopped
1 garlic clove, crushed
1³⁄₄ cups risotto rice
²⁄₃ cup dry white wine
2 tablespoons butter
²⁄₃ cup freshly grated
   Parmesan cheese
salt and ground black pepper
pink and yellow oyster
   mushrooms, to serve (optional)

**1** Put the dried porcini in a bowl and pour in the warm water. Let soak for 20 minutes, then lift out the mushrooms with a slotted spoon. Filter the soaking water through a sieve lined with paper towels, then place it in a pan with the stock. Bring the liquid to a gentle simmer.

**2** Spoon about 3 tablespoons of the hot stock into a cup and stir in the saffron threads. Set aside. Finely chop the porcini. Heat the oil in a separate pan and lightly sauté the onion, garlic and mushrooms for 5 minutes. Add the rice and stir to coat the grains in oil. Cook for 2 minutes, stirring constantly. Season with salt and pepper.

**3** Pour in the white wine. Cook, stirring until it has been absorbed, then ladle in one-quarter of the stock. Cook, stirring, until that has been absorbed, then gradually add the remaining stock, a little at a time. Let the rice absorb each batch of liquid before adding more, and stir constantly.

**4** After about 20 minutes, when all the stock has been absorbed and the rice is *al dente*, stir in the butter, saffron water (with the strands) and half the Parmesan. Serve, sprinkled with the remaining Parmesan and with oyster mushrooms, if desired.

# Champagne Risotto

This may seem rather extravagant, but it makes a beautifully flavored risotto, perfect for a special celebratory dinner.

**Serves 3–4**

2 tablespoons butter
2 shallots, finely chopped
1¹⁄₂ cups risotto rice
¹⁄₂ bottle or
   1¹⁄₄ cups champagne
3 cups simmering light vegetable
   stock
²⁄₃ cup heavy cream
¹⁄₂ cup freshly grated
   Parmesan cheese
2 teaspoons very finely chopped
   fresh chervil
salt and ground black pepper
black truffle shavings, to
   garnish (optional)

**1** Melt the butter in a large, heavy pan. Add the shallots and fry over low heat, stirring occasionally, for 2–3 minutes, until softened. Add the rice and cook, stirring constantly, until the grains are coated in butter.

**2** Carefully pour in about two-thirds of the champagne so that it doesn't bubble over, and cook over high heat, stirring constantly, until all the liquid has been absorbed.

**3** Add the stock, a ladleful at a time, stirring constantly and making sure that each addition has been completely absorbed before adding more. The risotto should gradually become creamy and velvety, and all the stock should be absorbed.

**4** When the rice is tender but retains a bit of "bite," stir in the remaining champagne with the heavy cream and Parmesan. Adjust the seasoning. Remove from heat, cover and let stand for a few minutes. Stir in the chervil. If you want to enhance the flavor, garnish with a few truffle shavings.

## Cook's Tip
*When cooking a risotto of this caliber, it is especially important to use the correct type of rice. Carnaroli would be perfect.*

# Barley Risotto with Roasted Squash & Leeks

This is more like a nutty pilaf than a classic risotto. Sweet leeks and roasted squash are superb with pearl barley.

**Serves 4–5**

scant 1 cup pearl barley

1 butternut squash, peeled, seeded and cut into chunks

2 teaspoons chopped fresh thyme

4 tablespoons olive oil

2 tablespoons butter

4 leeks, cut diagonally into fairly thick slices

2 garlic cloves, finely chopped

2¼ cups chestnut mushrooms, sliced

2 carrots, coarsely grated

about ½ cup vegetable stock

2 tablespoons chopped fresh flat-leaf parsley

2 ounces Pecorino cheese, grated or shaved

3 tablespoons pumpkin seeds, toasted

salt and ground black pepper

**1** Rinse and drain the barley. Bring a pan of water to the simmering point, add the barley and half-cover. Cook for 35–45 minutes, or until tender. Drain. Preheat the oven to 400°F.

**2** Place the squash in a roasting pan with half the thyme. Season with pepper and toss with half the oil. Roast, stirring once, for 30–35 minutes, until tender and beginning to brown.

**3** Heat half the butter with the remaining oil in a large frying pan. Cook the leeks and garlic gently for 5 minutes. Add the mushrooms and remaining thyme, then cook until the liquid from the mushrooms evaporates and they begin to fry.

**4** Stir in the carrots and cook for 2 minutes, then add the barley and most of the stock. Season and partially cover. Cook for 5 minutes. Pour in the remaining stock if necessary. Stir in the parsley, the remaining butter and half the Pecorino, then the squash, with salt and pepper to taste. Serve, sprinkled with pumpkin seeds and the remaining Pecorino.

# Risotto-stuffed Eggplant with Spicy Tomato Sauce

Dramatic good looks, plenty of substance and an interesting flavor make eggplant an excellent choice when entertaining.

**Serves 4**

4 small eggplant

7 tablespoons olive oil

1 small onion, chopped

scant 1 cup risotto rice

3 cups hot vegetable stock

1 tablespoon white wine vinegar

⅓ cup freshly grated Parmesan cheese

2 tablespoons pine nuts

**For the tomato sauce**

1¼ cups thick passata or puréed tomatoes

1 teaspoon mild curry paste

pinch of salt

**1** Preheat the oven to 400°F. Cut the eggplant in half lengthwise, cross-hatch the flesh, then remove it with a small knife. Brush the shells with 2 tablespoons of the oil and place on a baking sheet, supported by crumpled aluminum foil. Bake for 6–8 minutes. Set aside.

**2** Chop the eggplant flesh. Heat the remaining oil in a large, heavy pan. Add the eggplant flesh and the onion and cook over low heat, stirring occasionally, for 3–4 minutes, until softened but not colored.

**3** Stir in the rice and stock, and let simmer, uncovered, for about 15 minutes. Add the vinegar.

**4** Increase the oven temperature to 450°F. Spoon the rice mixture into the eggplant skins, top with the cheese and pine nuts, return to the oven and brown for 5 minutes.

**5** Meanwhile, make the sauce. Mix the passata or puréed tomatoes with the curry paste in a small pan. Heat through and add salt to taste. Spoon the sauce onto four individual serving plates and arrange two eggplant halves on each one.

# Wild Rice with Broiled Vegetables

The mixture of wild rice and long-grain rice in this dish works very well, and makes an extremely tasty vegetarian meal.

**Serves 4**
generous 1 cup mixed wild and
   long-grain rice
1 large eggplant, thickly sliced
1 red bell pepper, seeded and cut
   into quarters
1 yellow bell pepper, seeded and
   cut into quarters
1 green bell pepper, seeded and
   cut into quarters

2 red onions, sliced
3 cups brown cap or
   shiitake mushrooms
2 small zucchini, cut in
   half lengthwise
olive oil, for brushing
2 tablespoons chopped fresh
   thyme, plus whole sprigs to
   garnish (optional)

**For the dressing**
6 tablespoons extra virgin olive oil
2 tablespoons balsamic vinegar
2 garlic cloves, crushed
salt and ground black pepper

**1** Put the wild and long-grain rice in a large pan of cold salted water. Bring to a boil, then lower the heat, cover and cook gently for 30–40 minutes (or according to the instructions on the package), until tender.

**2** Preheat the broiler. Make the dressing by whisking together the olive oil, vinegar and garlic in a bowl, then season to taste with salt and pepper.

**3** Arrange all the vegetables on a broiler pan. Brush with olive oil and broil for about 5 minutes.

**4** Turn over the vegetables, brush them with more olive oil and broil for 5–8 more minutes or until tender and beginning to char in places.

**5** Drain the rice, put into a bowl and toss in half the dressing. Spoon onto individual plates and arrange the vegetables on top. Pour on the remaining dressing, sprinkle on the chopped thyme and serve. Whole thyme sprigs can be used as a garnish, if desired.

# Zucchini Roulade

This is an impressive buffet supper or dinner party dish.

**Serves 6**
3 tablespoons butter
1/2 cup all-purpose flour
1 1/4 cups milk
4 eggs, separated
3 zucchini, grated
1/3 cup freshly grated Parmesan
   cheese, plus 2 tablespoons
   for sprinkling
salt and ground black pepper
herb and green leaf salad,
   to serve

**For the filling**
2/3 cup soft goat cheese
4 tablespoons fromage frais
2 cups cooked rice
1 tablespoon chopped mixed
   fresh herbs
1 tablespoon olive oil
1 tablespoon butter
generous 1 cup button
   mushrooms, very finely chopped

**1** Preheat the oven to 400°F. Line a 13 x 9-inch jelly roll pan with nonstick baking parchment.

**2** Melt the butter in a saucepan, stir in the flour and cook for 1–2 minutes, stirring. Gradually stir in the milk until the mixture forms a smooth sauce. Remove from heat and cool. Stir in the egg yolks, add the zucchini and the Parmesan and season.

**3** Whisk the egg whites until stiff, fold them into the zucchini mixture and scrape into the prepared pan. Spread evenly. Bake for 10–15 minutes, until firm and lightly golden. Carefully turn out onto a sheet of nonstick baking parchment sprinkled with 2 tablespoons grated Parmesan. Peel off the lining paper. Roll up the roulade, using the paper as a guide, and let it cool.

**4** To make the filling, mix the goat cheese, fromage frais, rice and herbs in a bowl. Season with salt and pepper. Heat the oil and butter in a small pan, and fry the mushrooms until soft.

**5** Unwrap the roulade, spread with the rice filling and lay the mushrooms along the center. Roll up again. Serve with an herb and green leaf salad.

# Californian Citrus Fried Rice

As with all fried rice dishes, the important thing here is to make sure the rice is cold. Add it after cooking all the other ingredients, and stir to heat it through.

**Serves 4–6**

4 eggs
2 teaspoons Japanese rice vinegar
2 tablespoons light soy sauce
about 3 tablespoons peanut oil
½ cup cashews
2 garlic cloves, crushed
6 scallions, diagonally sliced
2 small carrots, cut into
    matchstick strips
8 ounces asparagus, each spear
    cut diagonally into 4 pieces

2¼ cups button
    mushrooms, halved
2 tablespoons rice wine
2 tablespoons water
4 cups cooked white
    long-grain rice
about 2 teaspoons sesame oil
1 pink grapefruit or
    orange, segmented
strips of orange zest, to garnish

**For the hot dressing**

1 teaspoon grated orange zest
2 tablespoons Japanese rice wine
3 tablespoons vegetarian
    "oyster" sauce
2 tablespoons freshly squeezed
    pink grapefruit or orange juice
1 teaspoon medium chili sauce

**1** Beat the eggs with the vinegar and 2 teaspoons of the soy sauce. Heat 1 tablespoon of the oil in a wok and cook the eggs until lightly scrambled. Transfer to a plate and set aside.

**2** Add the cashews to the wok and stir-fry for 1–2 minutes. Set aside. Heat the remaining oil and add the garlic and scallions. Cook until the onions begin to soften, then add the carrots and stir-fry for 4 minutes.

**3** Add the asparagus and cook for 2–3 minutes, then stir in the mushrooms and stir-fry for another 1 minute. Stir in the rice wine, the remaining soy sauce and the water. Simmer for a few minutes until the vegetables are crisp-tender.

**4** Mix the ingredients for the dressing, then add to the wok and bring to a boil. Add the rice, scrambled eggs and cashews. Toss over low heat for 3–4 minutes. Stir in the sesame oil and the citrus segments. Garnish with the orange zest and serve.

# Provençal Rice

Colorful and bursting with flavor, this is a substantial lunch or supper dish.

**Serves 3–4**

2 onions
6 tablespoons olive oil
scant 1 cup brown long-grain rice
2 teaspoons mustard seeds
2 cups vegetable stock
1 large or 2 small red bell
    peppers, seeded and cut
    into chunks
1 small eggplant, cut into cubes
2–3 zucchini, sliced

about 12 cherry tomatoes
5–6 fresh basil leaves, torn
2 garlic cloves, finely chopped
4 tablespoons white wine
4 tablespoons passata
2 hard-boiled eggs, cut
    into wedges
8 stuffed green olives, sliced
1 tablespoon drained and
    rinsed capers
butter, to taste
sea salt and ground black pepper
garlic bread, to serve

**1** Preheat the oven to 400°F. Finely chop one onion. Heat 2 tablespoons of the oil in a pan and fry the chopped onion gently until softened.

**2** Add the rice and mustard seeds. Cook, stirring, for 2 minutes. Pour in the stock with a little salt. Bring to a boil, lower the heat, cover and simmer for 35 minutes, until the rice is tender.

**3** Meanwhile, cut the remaining onion into wedges. Put these in a roasting pan with the peppers, eggplant, zucchini and cherry tomatoes. Sprinkle on the torn basil leaves and chopped garlic. Pour on the remaining olive oil and sprinkle with sea salt and black pepper. Roast for 15–20 minutes, until the vegetables begin to char, stirring halfway through cooking. Reduce the oven temperature to 350°F.

**4** Spoon the rice into an earthenware casserole. Put the roasted vegetables on top, together with any vegetable juices from the roasting pan, then pour in the wine and passata. Arrange the egg wedges on top, with the sliced olives and capers. Dot with butter, cover and cook for 15–20 minutes, until heated through. Serve with garlic bread.

# Kedgeree of Oyster & Chanterelle Mushrooms

Special occasion breakfasts and brunches call for something a little out of the ordinary, such as this luxurious British dish.

**Serves 4**

2 tablespoons butter
1 onion, chopped
2 cups long-grain rice
1 small carrot, cut into
    matchstick strips
3¾ cups boiling vegetable stock
pinch of saffron threads

3 cups oyster and chanterelle
    mushrooms, trimmed
    and halved
1 floury potato, about 4 ounces,
    peeled and grated
scant 2 cups milk
½ vegetable stock cube
½ teaspoon curry paste
2 tablespoons heavy cream
4 hard-boiled eggs, quartered
4 tablespoons chopped
    fresh parsley, plus a whole sprig

**1** Melt the butter in a large saucepan. Add the onion and fry over low heat, stirring occasionally, for about 5 minutes, until softened but not colored.

**2** Spoon about half the softened onion into a medium pan and set it aside until needed.

**3** Add the rice, carrot and stock to the large pan, with the saffron. Heat to the simmering point and cook, uncovered, for 15 minutes. Remove the pan from heat, cover and let stand for 5 minutes.

**4** Add the oyster and chanterelle mushrooms to the smaller pan and mix them with the onion. Cook over low heat for a few minutes to soften. Stir in the grated potato, milk, stock cube, curry paste and cream and simmer for 15 minutes, until the potatoes have thickened the liquid.

**5** Fork the rice onto a warmed serving platter. Spoon the mushrooms and sauce into the center and garnish with the egg quarters and chopped parsley. Serve immediately.

# Pilaf with Saffron & Pickled Walnuts

Pickled walnuts have a warm, tangy flavor that is great in rice and bulghur wheat dishes. This Eastern Mediterranean pilaf is interesting enough to serve on its own.

**Serves 4**

1 teaspoon saffron threads
1 tablespoon boiling water
½ cup pine nuts
3 tablespoons olive oil
1 large onion, chopped
3 garlic cloves, crushed

¼ teaspoon ground allspice
2-inch piece of fresh ginger
    root, grated
generous 1 cup long-grain rice
1¼ cups vegetable stock
½ cup pickled walnuts, drained
    and roughly chopped
¼ cup raisins
3 tablespoons roughly chopped
    fresh parsley or cilantro, plus
    whole leaves, to garnish
salt and ground black pepper
plain yogurt, to serve

**1** Put the saffron in a bowl with the boiling water and let stand. Heat a large frying pan and dry-fry the pine nuts until they turn golden. Set them aside.

**2** Heat the oil in the pan and fry the onion, garlic and allspice for 3 minutes. Stir in the ginger and rice and cook for 1 minute.

**3** Add the stock and bring to a boil. Lower the heat, cover and simmer gently for 15 minutes, until the rice is just tender.

**4** Stir in the saffron and liquid, the pine nuts, pickled walnuts, raisins and parsley or cilantro. Season to taste with salt and pepper. Heat through gently for 2 minutes. Garnish with the parsley or cilantro leaves and serve with yogurt.

> **Variation**
> Use one small eggplant, chopped and fried in a little olive oil, instead of the pickled walnuts, if desired.

# Artichoke Rösti

A traditional Swiss dish, rösti is usually made from potatoes alone. The addition of Jerusalem artichokes provides a subtle variation on flavor.

**Serves 4–6**
1 pound potatoes
juice of 1 lemon
1 pound Jerusalem artichokes
about ¼ cup butter
salt

**1** Peel the potatoes and place them in a pan of lightly salted water. Bring to a boil and cook until barely tender—they will take 15–20 minutes.

**2** Meanwhile, fill a pan with cold water and add the lemon juice. Peel the Jerusalem artichokes and add them to the pan, with a pinch of salt. Bring to a boil and cook for about 5 minutes, until barely tender.

**3** Drain and cool both the potatoes and the artichokes, then grate them into a bowl. Mix them with your fingers, without breaking them up too much.

**4** Melt the butter in a large, heavy frying pan. Add the artichoke mixture, spreading it out with the back of a spoon. Cook over low heat for about 10 minutes.

**5** Invert the "cake" onto a plate and then slide back into the pan. Cook the underside for about 10 minutes, until golden. Serve immediately.

---

**Cook's Tips**
• If there is time, chill the cooled par-boiled potatoes and Jerusalem artichokes in the refrigerator for 15–30 minutes before peeling. This makes them easier to grate, and they will be less likely to break up.
• Jerusalem artichokes discolor very quickly once they have been peeled. Dropping them in a bowl of cold water acidulated with a little lemon juice or vinegar helps to prevent this.

---

# Brussels Sprouts with Chestnuts

Brussels sprouts braised with chestnuts are delicious at winter and at any time of year.

**Serves 4–6**
2–3 cups chestnuts
½ cup milk
5 cups small tender Brussels sprouts
2 tablespoons butter
1 shallot, finely chopped
2–3 tablespoons dry white wine or water

**1** Using a small knife, score a cross in the bottom of each chestnut. Bring a pan of water to a boil and cook them for 6–8 minutes. Remove from heat. Remove a few chestnuts from the pan with a draining spoon. Holding them in a dish towel, remove the outer shell with a knife, then peel off the inner skin. Repeat with the remaining chestnuts, a few at a time.

**2** Rinse the pan, return the peeled chestnuts to it and add the milk. Pour in enough water to cover the chestnuts completely. Simmer for 12–15 minutes, until the chestnuts are just tender. Drain and set aside.

**3** Trim the Brussels sprouts and score a cross in the bottom of each. Melt the butter in a large, heavy frying pan, and cook the chopped shallot until just softened. Add the Brussels sprouts and wine or water. Cover the pan and cook over medium heat for 6–8 minutes, shaking the pan occasionally, and adding a little more water if necessary.

**4** Add the poached chestnuts and toss gently to combine, then cover and cook for 3–5 more minutes, until the chestnuts and Brussels sprouts are tender. Serve immediately.

---

**Cook's Tip**
Fresh chestnuts have a wonderful texture and flavor, but bottled or canned unsweetened whole chestnuts are an adequate substitute.

---

# Fava Beans with Cream

Tiny new fava beans can be eaten raw with a little salt, just like radishes. More mature beans taste wonderful when cooked and skinned to reveal the bright green kernel inside.

**Serves 4–6**
1 pound shelled fava beans (from about 4¹⁄₂ pounds fava beans in the pod)
6 tablespoons crème fraîche or whipping cream
salt and ground black pepper
finely snipped chives, to garnish

**1** Bring a large pan of lightly salted water to a boil over medium heat. Add the beans. Bring the water back to a boil, then lower the heat slightly and cook the beans gently for about 8 minutes, until just tender. Drain and rinse under cold water, then drain again.

**2** To remove the skins, make a slit along one side of each bean with the tip of a sharp knife and then gently squeeze out the kernel with your fingers.

**3** Put the skinned beans in a pan with the crème fraîche or whipping cream, season with salt and pepper to taste, cover and heat through gently. Transfer to a warmed serving dish, sprinkle with the snipped chives and serve immediately.

> **Variation**
> If you can find them, fresh flageolet or lima beans may be served in the same way.

# Asparagus with Vermouth Sauce

Coating young asparagus spears with a vermouth and parsley sauce creates a sensational dish.

**Serves 4**
20 asparagus spears
1 teaspoon olive oil
²⁄₃ cup freshly grated Parmesan cheese
salt and ground black pepper

**For the sauce**
3 tablespoons dry white vermouth
1 cup well-flavored vegetable stock
1 tablespoon chopped fresh parsley
2 tablespoons chilled butter, cubed

**1** Brush the asparagus spears with olive oil and seasoning. Place on a broiler pan, sprinkle with the Parmesan and broil slowly, under a medium broiler, until the asparagus is just tender when pierced with the tip of a knife and lightly charred.
**2** Meanwhile, make the sauce. Pour the vermouth and stock into a saucepan. Boil over high heat until reduced by half. Stir in the parsley and season with salt and pepper.
**3** Lower the heat and stir in the chilled butter cubes, two at a time. Continue to stir over low heat until all the butter has melted and the sauce has thickened. Arrange the asparagus spears in a serving dish, pour on the sauce and serve immediately.

# String Beans with Garlic

Delicate and fresh-tasting flageolet beans and garlic add a distinct French flavor to this simple side dish.

**Serves 4**
1¹⁄₄ cups dried flageolet beans, soaked in cold water overnight and drained
1 tablespoon olive oil
2 tablespoons butter

1 onion, finely chopped
1–2 garlic cloves, crushed
3–4 tomatoes, peeled and chopped
12 ounces string beans, sliced
²⁄₃ cup white wine
²⁄₃ cup vegetable stock
2 tablespoons chopped fresh parsley
salt and ground black pepper

**1** Place the flageolet beans in a large saucepan of water, bring to a boil over medium heat, then lower the heat and simmer for 45 minutes–1 hour, until tender. Drain thoroughly and set aside.

**2** Heat the oil and butter in a large, heavy frying pan. Add the onion and garlic and fry over low heat, stirring occasionally, for 3–4 minutes, until soft.

**3** Add the chopped tomatoes to the pan and cook over low heat until they are soft.

**4** Stir the flageolet beans into the onion and tomato mixture, then add the string beans, wine and stock and season with a little salt. Stir well. Cover and simmer for 5–10 minutes, until the string beans are tender.

**5** Increase the heat to medium to reduce the liquid, then stir in the chopped parsley. Check the seasoning, adding a little more salt, if necessary, and pepper. Transfer to a warmed serving dish and serve immediately.

> **Cook's Tip**
> Flageolets are also known as green haricot beans.

# Zucchini in Citrus Sauce

Zucchini are so attractive, especially the brightly colored varieties, that their bland taste can sometimes be horribly disappointing. This spicy and piquant sauce ensures that will not be the case here.

**Serves 4**

12 ounces baby zucchini
4 scallions, finely sliced
1-inch piece of fresh ginger
  root, grated
2 tablespoons cider vinegar
1 tablespoon light soy sauce
1 teaspoon light brown sugar
3 tablespoons vegetable stock
finely grated zest and juice of
  1/2 lemon and 1/2 orange
1 teaspoon cornstarch
2 teaspoons water

**1** Bring a pan of lightly salted water to a boil. Add the zucchini, bring back to a boil and simmer for 3–4 minutes, until just tender.

**2** Meanwhile, combine the onions, ginger, vinegar, soy sauce, sugar, stock and orange and lemon juice and zest in a small pan. Bring to a boil, lower the heat and simmer for 2 minutes.

**3** Mix the cornstarch into a paste with the water, then stir the paste into the sauce. Bring to a boil, stirring constantly until the sauce has thickened.

**4** Drain the zucchini well and put them into a warmed serving dish. Spoon on the hot sauce. Shake the dish gently to coat the zucchini and serve immediately.

### Cook's Tip
*If you can't find baby zucchini—about 3 inches long—use larger ones, but cook them whole so that they don't absorb too much water and become soggy. Halve them lengthwise after cooking and then cut the halves into 4-inch lengths before coating them in the sauce.*

# Red Cabbage in Port & Red Wine

A sweet-and-sour, spicy red cabbage dish, with the added juiciness of pears and extra crunch of walnuts.

**Serves 6**

1 tablespoon walnut oil
1 onion, sliced
2 whole star anise
1 teaspoon ground cinnamon
pinch of ground cloves
1 pound red cabbage,
  finely shredded
2 tablespoons dark brown sugar
3 tablespoons red wine vinegar
1 1/4 cups red wine
2/3 cup port
2 pears, cut into 1/2-inch cubes
2/3 cup raisins
1 cup walnut halves
salt and ground black pepper

**1** Heat the oil in a large, heavy pan. Add the onion and cook over low heat, stirring occasionally, for about 5 minutes, until softened.

**2** Add the star anise, cinnamon, cloves and cabbage and cook for about 3 more minutes.

**3** Stir in the sugar, vinegar, red wine and port. Cover the pan and simmer gently for 10 minutes, stirring occasionally.

**4** Stir in the cubed pears and raisins and cook for 10 more minutes, without replacing the lid, or until the cabbage is tender. Season to taste with salt and pepper. Mix in the walnut halves and serve immediately.

### Cook's Tip
*The vinegar and wine help to preserve the beautiful color of the cabbage as well as adding to the flavor.*

### Variation
*Juniper berries taste wonderful with red cabbage. Omit the star anise and cinnamon and add 1 tablespoon juniper berries with the ground cloves.*

# Baked Cabbage

This healthy and economical dish uses the whole cabbage, including the flavorful core.

**Serves 4**

1 green or white cabbage, about
   1½ pounds
1 tablespoon light olive oil
2 tablespoons water
3–4 tablespoons
   vegetable stock
4 firm, ripe tomatoes, peeled
   and chopped
1 teaspoon mild chili powder
1 tablespoon chopped fresh
   parsley or fennel, to
   garnish (optional)

**For the topping**

3 firm ripe tomatoes, thinly sliced
1 tablespoon olive oil
salt and ground black pepper

**1** Preheat the oven to 350°F. Shred the leaves and the core of the cabbage finely. Heat the oil in a frying pan with the water and add the cabbage. Cover and cook over very low heat, to let the cabbage sweat, for 5–10 minutes. Stir occasionally.

**2** Pour in the vegetable stock, then stir in the tomatoes. Cook over low heat for another 10 minutes. Season with the chili powder and a little salt.

**3** Put the cabbage mixture into a large square ovenproof dish. Level the surface and arrange the sliced tomatoes on top. Brush with the oil, then sprinkle with salt and pepper to taste.

**4** Bake for 30–40 minutes or until the tomatoes are just starting to brown. Serve hot, with a little parsley or fennel sprinkled on top, if desired.

### Cook's Tips
*To vary the taste, add seeded, diced red or green bell peppers to the cabbage with the tomatoes. If you have a shallow flameproof casserole, you could cook the cabbage in it on the stove and then simply transfer the casserole to the oven.*

# Broccoli & Cauliflower with Cider & Apple Mint Sauce

The cider sauce is also ideal for other vegetables, such as celery or beans.

**Serves 4**

1 tablespoon olive oil
1 large onion, chopped
2 large carrots, chopped
1 large garlic clove
1 tablespoon dill seeds
4 large fresh apple mint sprigs
2 tablespoons all-purpose flour
1¼ cups dry cider
4 cups broccoli florets
4 cups cauliflower florets
2 tablespoons tamari
2 teaspoons mint jelly
salt

**1** Heat the olive oil in a large, heavy frying pan. Add the onion, carrots, garlic, dill seeds and apple mint leaves and cook over low heat, stirring occasionally, for about 5 minutes, until the vegetables are soft.

**2** Stir in the flour and cook, stirring constantly, for 1 minute, then stir in the cider. Bring to a boil, then simmer until the sauce looks glossy. Remove the pan from heat and set aside to cool slightly.

**3** Bring two small pans of lightly salted water to a boil and cook the broccoli and cauliflower separately until just tender.

**4** Meanwhile, pour the sauce into a food processor and add the tamari and mint jelly. Process into a fine purée.

**5** Drain the broccoli and cauliflower well and mix them in a warmed serving dish. Pour on the sauce, mix lightly to coat and serve immediately.

### Cook's Tip
*Tamari is a Japanese soy sauce. It is dark and thick and less salty than Chinese soy sauce.*

# Baked Fennel with a Crumb Crust

The delicate aniseed flavor of baked fennel makes it a very good accompaniment to pasta dishes and risottos.

**Serves 4**
3 fennel bulbs, cut lengthwise into quarters
2 tablespoons olive oil
1 cup day-old whole-grain bread crumbs
1 garlic clove, chopped
2 tablespoons chopped fresh flat-leaf parsley
salt and ground black pepper
fennel leaves, to garnish

**1** Bring a saucepan of lightly salted water to a boil over medium heat. Add the fennel quarters, bring back to a boil, then lower the heat and simmer for about 10 minutes or until just tender.

**2** Preheat the oven to 375°F. Drain the fennel and place the pieces in an ovenproof dish or roasting pan. Brush on half of the olive oil.

**3** Put the bread crumbs, garlic and parsley in a separate bowl and drizzle on the remaining olive oil. Season to taste with salt and pepper. Mix lightly, then sprinkle the mixture evenly over the fennel.

**4** Bake for 30 minutes or until the fennel is tender and the bread crumbs are crisp and golden. Serve hot, garnished with feathery fennel leaves.

**Variations**
• Add 4 tablespoons finely grated, strongly flavored cheese, such as aged Cheddar, Red Leicester or Parmesan, to the bread crumb topping.
• Add two or three cored and sliced red apples to the dish with the cooked fennel quarters.

# Spinach with Raisins & Pine Nuts

Wilted spinach benefits from a touch of sweetness, as this delicious Spanish dish amply illustrates.

**Serves 4**
1/3 cup raisins
1 thick slice crusty white bread
3 tablespoons olive oil
1/3 cup pine nuts
1 1/4 pounds young spinach leaves, stems removed
2 garlic cloves, crushed
salt and ground black pepper

**1** Put the raisins in a small bowl. Cover with boiling water and let soak for 10 minutes.

**2** Cut off the crusts from the bread and discard. Cut the bread into small cubes.

**3** Heat 2 tablespoons of the oil in a large, heavy frying pan. Add the bread cubes and fry over medium heat, stirring and turning frequently, until golden all over. Lift out with a draining spoon and drain well on paper towels.

**4** Add the remaining oil to the pan. When it is hot, fry the pine nuts until beginning to color. Add the spinach and garlic and cook quickly, turning the spinach until it has just wilted.

**5** Drain the raisins, toss them into the pan and season lightly with salt and black pepper. Transfer to a warmed serving dish. Sprinkle on the croutons and serve.

**Variation**
*Swiss chard can be used instead of the spinach, but will need to be cooked a little more.*

# Zucchini in Rich Tomato Sauce

Serve this colorful dish hot or cold. Cut the zucchini fairly thickly, so they stay slightly crunchy.

**Serves 4**
1 tablespoon olive oil
1 onion, chopped
1 garlic clove, chopped
4 zucchini, thickly sliced
14-ounce can chopped tomatoes, drained
2 tomatoes, peeled, seeded and chopped
1 teaspoon vegetable bouillon powder
1 tablespoon tomato paste
salt and ground black pepper

**1** Heat the oil in a heavy pan and sauté the onion and garlic until softened, stirring occasionally. Add the zucchini and cook for 5 more minutes.

**2** Add the canned and fresh tomatoes, then stir in the bouillon powder and tomato paste. Simmer for 10–15 minutes, until the sauce has thickened and the zucchini are just tender. Season to taste with salt and pepper and serve.

# Braised Leeks with Carrots

Sweet carrots and leeks go well together, especially when married with a little chopped mint, chervil or flat-leaf parsley.

**Serves 6**
5 tablespoons butter
1 1/2 pounds carrots, thickly sliced
2 bay leaves
1/2 teaspoon sugar
5 tablespoons water
1 1/2 pounds leeks, cut into 2-inch lengths
1/2 cup white wine
2 tablespoons chopped fresh mint
salt and ground black pepper

**1** Melt 2 tablespoons of the butter in a pan and cook the carrots gently for 4–5 minutes. Do not let them brown.

**2** Add the bay leaves, sugar and water. Season with salt and pepper to taste. Bring to a boil, cover tightly and cook for 10–15 minutes or until the carrots are tender, shaking the pan frequently to stop the carrots from sticking. Remove the lid, then boil until the juices have evaporated, leaving the carrots moist and glazed.

**3** Meanwhile, melt 2 tablespoons of the remaining butter in a pan that is wide enough to hold the leeks in a single layer. Add the leeks, stir to coat them in butter, then fry over low heat for 4–5 minutes, without letting them brown.

**4** Stir in the wine and half the mint, then season to taste. Heat until simmering, then cover and cook gently for 5–8 minutes or until the leeks are tender, but have not collapsed.

**5** Uncover the leeks and turn them in the buttery juices. Increase the heat, then boil the liquid rapidly until reduced to a few tablespoons.

**6** Add the carrots to the leeks and reheat them gently, then swirl in the remaining butter. Adjust the seasoning, if necessary. Transfer to a warmed serving dish and serve sprinkled with the remaining mint.

# Caramelized Shallots

Wonderful with well-flavored nut roasts or lentil loaves, these also taste good with other braised or roasted vegetables, such as chunks of butternut squash.

**Serves 4–6**
1/4 cup butter
1 1/4 pounds shallots or small onions, peeled, with root ends intact
1 tablespoon brown sugar
2 tablespoons red or white wine
2/3 cup vegetable stock
2–3 fresh bay leaves
salt and ground black pepper
fresh thyme sprigs, to garnish

**1** Melt the butter in a large frying pan and add the shallots or onions in a single layer. Fry over low heat, turning occasionally, for about 10 minutes, until lightly browned.

**2** Sprinkle the sugar on the shallots or onions and cook gently, turning them in the juices, until the sugar begins to caramelize. Add the red or white wine and let the mixture bubble for 4–5 minutes.

**3** Pour in the stock and add the bay leaves. Season with salt and pepper to taste. Cover and cook for 5 minutes, then remove the lid and cook until the liquid evaporates and the shallots are tender and glazed.

**4** Adjust the seasoning, if necessary, and spoon into a serving bowl. Garnish with the sprigs of thyme and serve.

**Variation**
*Shallots with Chestnuts: Cook the shallots as above, but toss in 2–3 cups partially cooked chestnuts just before adding the stock. Cook the two vegetables together for about 5–10 minutes, then serve sprinkled with plenty of chopped flat-leaf parsley.*

# Okra with Coriander & Tomatoes

When combined with tomatoes and mild spices, okra makes a very good side dish and is particularly good with potato strudel or a zucchini and dill tart.

**Serves 4**

1 pound tomatoes or 14-ounce
 can chopped tomatoes
1 pound fresh okra
3 tablespoons olive oil
2 onions, thinly sliced
2 teaspoons coriander
 seeds, crushed
3 garlic cloves, crushed
about $^1/_2$ teaspoon sugar
finely grated zest and juice
 of 1 lemon
salt and ground black pepper

**1** If using fresh tomatoes, cut a cross in the skin at the top of each one with a sharp knife, then plunge them into boiling water for 30 seconds. Drain and refresh in cold water. Peel off the skins and chop the flesh.

**2** With a sharp knife, trim off any stems from the okra and leave the pods whole. Avoid piercing the pods, or the sticky juice they contain will leak out.

**3** Heat the oil in a large, heavy frying pan. Add the onions with the coriander seeds and fry over medium heat, stirring occasionally, for 3–4 minutes, until the onions are softened and beginning to color.

**4** Add the okra and garlic and fry for 1 minute. Carefully stir in the tomatoes and sugar, without breaking up the okra, then lower the heat and simmer gently for about 20 minutes or until the okra is tender, stirring once or twice.

**5** Stir in the lemon zest and juice. Season to taste with salt and pepper. Taste the mixture and add a little more sugar, if necessary. Transfer to a warmed serving dish and serve immediately. Alternatively, set aside to cool and then serve at room temperature.

# Braised Lettuce & Peas

This dish is based on the traditional French way of braising peas with lettuce and scallions in butter.

**Serves 4**

$^1/_4$ cup butter
4 small heads lettuces,
 halved lengthwise
2 bunches scallions, trimmed
1 teaspoon sugar
$3^1/_2$ cups shelled peas (about
 $2^1/_4$ pounds in pods)
4 fresh mint sprigs
$^1/_2$ cup vegetable stock
1 tablespoon fresh mint leaves
salt and ground black pepper

**1** Melt half the butter in a wide, heavy saucepan over low heat. Add the lettuces and scallions. Turn the vegetables in the butter, then sprinkle in the sugar, $^1/_2$ teaspoon salt and plenty of black pepper. Cover, and cook very gently for 5 minutes, stirring once.

**2** Add the peas and mint sprigs. Turn the peas in the buttery juices and pour in the stock, then cover and cook over low heat for 5 more minutes. Uncover and increase the heat to reduce the liquid to a few tablespoons.

**3** Stir in the remaining butter and adjust the seasoning, if necessary. Transfer to a warmed serving dish and sprinkle with the mint leaves. Serve immediately.

### Variations
• Braise about eight baby carrots with the lettuce.
• Use 1 head lettuce, shredding it coarsely, and omit the mint. Toward the end of cooking, stir in about 5 ounces arugula (preferably the stronger-flavored wild arugula) and cook briefly until the leaves are just wilted.
• Any of the smaller Romaine-type lettuces, such as Sucrine and Winter Density, would work well in this recipe.
• For a different flavor, omit the mint and season with freshly grated nutmeg to taste.

# Celeriac Gratin

It may not look very attractive, but celeriac has a delicious sweet and nutty flavor, which is accentuated in this dish by the addition of Emmenthal cheese.

**Serves 4**
juice of $\frac{1}{2}$ lemon
1 pound celeriac
2 tablespoons butter
1 small onion, finely chopped
2 tablespoons all-purpose flour
1$\frac{1}{4}$ cups milk
$\frac{1}{4}$ cup grated Emmenthal cheese
1 tablespoon capers, rinsed
  and drained
salt and cayenne pepper

1 Preheat the oven to 375°F. Fill a pan with water and add the lemon juice. Peel the celeriac and cut it into $\frac{1}{4}$-inch slices, immediately adding them to the pan of acidulated water. This prevents them from discoloring.

2 Bring the water to a boil, then lower the heat and simmer the celeriac for 10–12 minutes, until just tender. Drain the celeriac and arrange the slices, overlapping them slightly, in a shallow ovenproof dish.

3 Melt the butter in a small pan. Add the onion and fry over low heat, stirring occasionally, for 5 minutes, until soft but not browned. Stir in the flour, cook for 1 minute and then gradually add the milk, stirring constantly until the mixture thickens, to make a smooth sauce.

4 Stir in the grated cheese and capers and season with salt and cayenne to taste. Pour the mixture onto the celeriac. Bake for 15–20 minutes, until the top is golden brown.

**Variation**
For a less strongly flavored dish, alternate the layers of celeriac with potato. Slice the potato, cook until almost tender, then drain well before assembling the dish.

# Baked Bell Peppers & Tomatoes

The juices from this vegetable medley are absolutely delicious, so serve it with a pasta or rice dish or just crusty bread to soak them up.

**Serves 8**
2 red bell peppers, seeded
2 yellow bell peppers, seeded
1 red onion, sliced
2 garlic cloves, halved
6 plum tomatoes, quartered
$\frac{1}{4}$ cup black olives
1 teaspoon light brown sugar
3 tablespoons sherry
3–4 fresh rosemary sprigs
2 tablespoons olive oil
salt and ground black pepper

1 Preheat the oven to 400°F. Cut each pepper into 12 strips and place them in a large roasting pan. Add the onion, garlic, tomatoes and olives.

2 Sprinkle on the sugar, then drizzle on the sherry. Season well, cover with aluminum foil and bake for 45 minutes.

3 Remove the foil from the pan and stir the mixture well. Add the rosemary sprigs.

4 Drizzle on the olive oil. Return the pan to the oven and roast for 30 more minutes, until the vegetables are tender. Serve hot.

**Cook's Tip**
For the best flavor, buy tomatoes on the vine, if possible.

**Variation**
Use four or five well-flavored beef tomatoes instead of plum tomatoes, if you prefer. Cut them into thick wedges instead of quarters.

# Corn with Jalapeños & Cheese

When you tire of plain corn on the cob, try this creamy vegetable dish, spiked with pickled chiles.

**Serves 6**

4 ears corn
¼ cup butter
1 small onion, finely chopped
⅔ cup drained pickled jalapeño chile slices
⅔ cup cream cheese
⅓ cup freshly grated Parmesan cheese, plus shavings, to garnish
salt and ground black pepper

**1** Strip the husks from the corn and pull off the silk. Place the ears in a bowl of water and use a vegetable brush to remove any remaining silk. Stand each ear in turn on a board and slice off the kernels, cutting as close to the cob as possible.

**2** Melt the butter in a saucepan, add the onion and fry, stirring occasionally, for 4–5 minutes, until softened and translucent.

**3** Add the corn kernels and cook for 4–5 minutes, until they are just tender. Chop the jalapeños finely and stir them into the corn mixture.

**4** Stir in the cream cheese and the grated Parmesan. Cook over low heat until both cheeses have melted and the corn kernels are coated in the mixture. Season to taste, put into a heated dish and serve, topped with shaved Parmesan.

---

**Variations**
• Whole cooked ears of corn may be dipped in cream, then sprinkled with crumbled fresh cheese.
• Put whole ears of corn in a shallow ovenproof dish and bake them in an oven preheated to 400°F for 30 minutes, until tender and golden. Pour on ½ cup sour cream or crème fraîche, then sprinkle the ears with 2 tablespoons freshly grated Parmesan cheese and serve. Alternatively broil the corn, brushed with butter, on a barbecue.

---

# Spiced Pumpkin with Tomato Salsa

Roasted pumpkin has a wonderful, rich flavor, especially when served with a salsa and a dollop of crème fraîche.

**Serves 6**

2¼ pounds pumpkin
¼ cup butter, melted
2 teaspoons hot chili sauce
½ teaspoon salt
½ teaspoon ground allspice
1 teaspoon ground cinnamon
chopped fresh herbs, to garnish
crème fraîche, to serve

*For the tomato salsa*

3 fresh serrano chiles
1 large onion, finely chopped
grated zest and juice of 2 limes, plus strips of lime zest, to garnish
8 ripe, firm tomatoes, peeled and diced
large bunch of cilantro, finely chopped
pinch of sugar

**1** Make the salsa about 3 hours in advance. Broil the chiles until the skins are blistered and charred. Place in a bowl, cover with crumpled paper towels and set aside for 20 minutes. Meanwhile, marinate the onion in the lime zest and juice.

**2** Add the tomatoes to the marinated onion. Peel the chiles, remove the core and seeds from each, then chop the flesh finely. Add it to the bowl with the cilantro and the sugar. Mix well, garnish with extra lime zest, cover and chill.

**3** Preheat the oven to 425°F. Cut the pumpkin into large pieces. Scoop out and discard the fiber and seeds, then put the pumpkin pieces in a roasting pan.

**4** Mix the melted butter and chili sauce and drizzle the mixture evenly on the pumpkin pieces. Mix the salt, allspice and cinnamon in a bowl. Sprinkle the mixture on the pumpkin.

**5** Roast for 30–40 minutes or until the pumpkin flesh yields when pressed gently. Transfer the pumpkin to a heated serving platter, garnish with the chopped herbs and serve with the salsa and crème fraîche.

# Roasted Mediterranean Vegetables with Pecorino

Eggplant, zucchini, bell peppers and tomatoes make a marvellous medley when roasted and served drizzled with fragrant olive oil. Shavings of sheep's milk Pecorino add the perfect finishing touch.

**Serves 4–6**
1 eggplant, sliced
2 zucchini, sliced
2 bell peppers (red or yellow or one of each), quartered and seeded
1 large onion, thickly sliced
2 large carrots, cut in sticks
4 firm plum tomatoes, halved
extra virgin olive oil, for brushing and sprinkling
3 tablespoons chopped fresh parsley
3 tablespoons pine nuts, lightly toasted
4-ounce piece of Pecorino cheese
salt and ground black pepper

**1** Layer the eggplant slices in a colander, sprinkling each layer with a little salt. Let drain over a sink for about 20 minutes, then rinse thoroughly under cold running water, drain well and pat dry with paper towels. Preheat the oven to 425°F.

**2** Spread out eggplant slices, zucchini, peppers, onion, carrots and tomatoes in one or two large roasting pans. Brush them lightly with olive oil and roast them for 20–30 minutes or until they are lightly browned and the skins on the peppers have begun to blister.

**3** Transfer the vegetables to a large serving platter. If desired, peel the peppers and discard the skins. Trickle on any vegetable juices from the pan and season to taste with salt and pepper. As the vegetables cool, sprinkle them with more olive oil. When they are at room temperature, mix in the fresh parsley and toasted pine nuts.

**4** Using a swivel vegetable peeler, shave the Pecorino and sprinkle the shavings on the vegetables.

# Lemony Vegetable Parcels

What could be prettier—or more convenient—than these handy packages of winter vegetables? They're guaranteed to brighten up even the dreariest day.

**Serves 4**
2 medium carrots, cubed
1 small rutabaga, cubed
1 large parsnip, cubed
1 leek, sliced
finely grated zest of ¹/₂ lemon
1 tablespoons lemon juice
1 tablespoons whole-grain mustard
1 teaspoon walnut or sunflower oil
salt and ground black pepper

**1** Preheat the oven to 375°F. Place the carrot, rutabaga and parsnip cubes in a large bowl, then add the sliced leek. Stir in the lemon zest and juice and the mustard. Season to taste with salt and pepper.

**2** Cut four 12-inch squares of nonstick baking parchment and brush them lightly with the oil. Divide the vegetable mixture among them. Roll up the paper from one side, then twist the ends firmly to seal.

**3** Transfer the parcels to a baking sheet and bake them for 50–55 minutes or until the vegetables are just tender.

**4** Serve on heated plates, opening each parcel slightly to reveal the contents.

---

**Cook's Tip**
*If you don't have any baking parchment, use waxed paper, but aluminum foil is not suitable for these parcels.*

---

**Variation**
*Substitute the same amount of curry or tikka paste for the mustard, and omit the lemon zest and juice.*

# Radicchio & Endive Gratin

Creamy béchamel sauce, with its delicate flavor, is the perfect foil for these bitter-tasting leaves.

**Serves 4**
oil, for greasing
2 heads radicchio
2 heads endive
4 pieces of sun-dried tomatoes in
    oil, drained and roughly

chopped, plus 2 tablespoons oil
    from the jar
2 tablespoons butter
1 tablespoon all-purpose flour
1 cup milk
pinch of freshly grated nutmeg
1/2 cup grated Emmenthal cheese
salt and ground black pepper
chopped fresh parsley, to garnish

**1** Preheat the oven to 350°F. Grease a 5-cup ovenproof dish. Trim the radicchio and endive and pull off and discard any damaged or wilted leaves. Quarter them lengthwise and arrange them in the dish.

**2** Sprinkle on the sun-dried tomatoes and brush the leaves liberally with the oil from the jar. Sprinkle with salt and pepper and cover with aluminum foil. Bake for 15 minutes, then remove the foil and bake for 10 more minutes, until the vegetables are soft.

**3** Meanwhile, make the sauce. Melt the butter in a small pan, stir in the flour and cook for 1 minute. Gradually add the milk, whisking until the sauce boils and thickens. Lower the heat and simmer for 2–3 minutes. Season to taste and add the nutmeg.

**4** Pour the sauce on the vegetables and sprinkle with the cheese. Bake for 20 more minutes, until the topping is golden. Serve immediately, garnished with parsley.

**Cook's Tip**
*In Italy radicchio and endive are often broiled on a barbecue. To do this, prepare the vegetables as above and brush with olive oil. Place the cut-sides down on the rack for 7–10 minutes, until browned. Turn and broil until the other side is browned.*

# Mixed Vegetables with Aromatic Seeds

A tantalizing aroma is the first indication of how tasty this vegetable medley will be. Fresh ginger and three different types of seeds create a wonderful flavor.

**Serves 4–6**
1 1/2 pounds small new potatoes
1 small cauliflower
6 ounces green beans

1 cup frozen peas
a small piece of fresh ginger root
2 tablespoons sunflower oil
2 teaspoons cumin seeds
2 teaspoons black mustard seeds
2 tablespoons sesame seeds
juice of 1 lemon
salt and ground black pepper

**1** Scrub the potatoes, but do not peel them. Cut the cauliflower into small florets, then trim and halve the green beans.

**2** Cook the vegetables in separate pans of lightly salted boiling water until tender, allowing 15–20 minutes for the potatoes, 8–10 minutes for the cauliflower and 4–5 minutes for the beans and peas. Drain thoroughly.

**3** Using a small, sharp knife, peel and finely chop the ginger.

**4** Heat the oil in a wide, shallow pan. Add the ginger and seeds. Cover the pan and fry until the seeds start to pop.

**5** Add the cooked vegetables and toss over the heat for another 2–3 minutes. Sprinkle on the lemon juice and season with pepper.

**Cook's Tip**
*Other vegetables could be used, such as zucchini, leeks or broccoli. Buy whatever looks freshest, and do not store vegetables for long periods, as their vitamin content, flavor and texture will deteriorate.*

# Baked Potato Wedges

This easy alternative to French fries tastes just as good and is much easier to cook. They also make very popular canapés to serve with pre-dinner drinks.

**Serves 4–6**

²⁄₃ cup olive oil

4 medium to large baking potatoes

1 teaspoon mixed dried herbs (optional)

sea salt flakes

mayonnaise, to serve

**1** Preheat the oven to the highest temperature; this is generally 475°F. Lightly oil a large shallow roasting pan and place it in the oven to get really hot while you are preparing the potatoes.

**2** Cut the potatoes in half lengthwise, then into long thin wedges, or thicker ones if you prefer. Brush each side lightly with olive oil.

**3** When the oven is really hot, remove the roasting pan carefully and scatter the potato wedges in it, spreading them out in a single layer on the hot oil.

**4** Sprinkle the potato wedges with the herbs and sea salt flakes and then roast for about 20 minutes or longer if they are thicker, turning once so that they brown evenly, until they are golden brown, crisp and lightly puffy. Remove from the oven, drain thoroughly on paper towels and serve with a dollop of mayonnaise.

---

**Variations**
• Sweet potatoes also make fine wedges. Prepare and roast as for regular potatoes, although you may find they do not take as long to cook.
• You can flavor the wedges with mild paprika instead of mixed herbs.
• Serve with lemon juice instead of mayonnaise.

---

# Mashed Garlic Sweet Potatoes

Orange-fleshed sweet potatoes not only look good; they taste delicious mashed with garlicky butter.

**Serves 4**

2 pounds sweet potatoes

3 tablespoons butter

3 garlic cloves, crushed

salt and ground black pepper

**1** Bring a large pan of lightly salted water to a boil. Add the sweet potatoes and cook for about 15 minutes or until tender. Drain very well, return to the pan and cover tightly.

**2** Melt the butter in a frying pan and sauté the garlic over low heat, stirring constantly, for 1–2 minutes, until light golden.

**3** Pour the garlic butter on the potatoes, season with salt and pepper, and mash until smooth and creamy. Serve immediately.

# Perfect Creamed Potatoes

Smooth mashed potatoes taste very good and are the ideal accompaniment for other vegetarian dishes.

**Serves 4**

2 pounds firm but not waxy potatoes, diced

3 tablespoons extra virgin olive oil

about 1²⁄₃ cup hot milk

freshly grated nutmeg

a few fresh basil leaves or parsley sprigs, chopped

salt and ground black pepper

fresh basil leaves, to garnish

**1** Put the potatoes in a pan of cold water and bring to a boil. Cook until just tender. Drain very well. Press the potatoes through a potato ricer or mash with a potato masher.

**2** Beat in the olive oil and enough hot milk to make a smooth, thick purée.

**3** Flavor to taste with the nutmeg and seasoning, then stir in the chopped fresh herbs. Spoon into a warm serving dish and serve immediately, garnished with the basil leaves.

# Potato Gratin

Baked potatoes layered with mustardy butter are perfect to serve with a green salad for supper, or as an accompaniment to a vegetable or nut loaf.

**Serves 4**
4 large potatoes, total weight
    about 2¼ pounds
2 tablespoons butter
1 tablespoon olive oil
2 large garlic cloves, crushed
2 tablespoons plain or herbed
    Dijon mustard
1 tablespoon lemon juice
1 tablespoon fresh thyme leaves,
    plus extra to garnish
4 tablespoons well-flavored
    vegetable stock
salt and ground black pepper

**1** Peel the potatoes and slice them thinly, using a knife or the slicing attachment on a food processor. Place the slices in a bowl of cold water to prevent them from discoloring.

**2** Preheat the oven to 400°F. Heat the butter and oil in a deep frying pan that can safely be used in the oven. Add the garlic and cook gently for 3 minutes, until light golden, stirring constantly. Stir in the mustard, lemon juice and thyme. Remove from heat and pour the mixture into a pitcher.

**3** Drain the potatoes and pat them dry with paper towels. Place a layer of potatoes in the frying pan, season and pour on one-third of the butter mixture. Place another layer of potatoes on top, season, and pour on another third of the butter mixture. Arrange a final layer of potatoes on top, pour on the remainder of the butter mixture and then the stock. Season and sprinkle with the extra thyme.

**4** Cover with nonstick baking parchment and bake for 1 hour. Remove the paper and bake for 15 more minutes, until golden.

> **Variation**
> *Any root vegetables can be used: try celery stalks, parsnips, carrots or a mixture.*

# Lyonnaise Potatoes

Two simple ingredients are prepared separately and then tossed together to create the perfect combination. These potatoes go very well with broiled beef tomatoes and lightly cooked green beans.

**Serves 6**
2 pounds floury potatoes,
    scrubbed but not peeled
vegetable oil, for shallow frying
2 tablespoons butter
1 tablespoon olive oil
2 medium onions, sliced into rings
sea salt
1 tablespoon chopped
    fresh parsley

**1** Bring a large pan of lightly salted water to a boil and cook the potatoes for 10 minutes. Drain them in a colander and let cool slightly. When the potatoes are cool enough to handle, peel them and slice them finely.

**2** Heat the vegetable oil in a large, heavy pan. Add half the potato slices and fry over low heat, turning occasionally, for about 10 minutes, until crisp. Remove from the pan with a draining spoon and drain on paper towels. Set aside and keep hot while you fry the remaining potato slices.

**3** Meanwhile, melt the butter with the olive oil in a frying pan. Add the onions and fry over low heat, stirring occasionally, for about 10 minutes, until golden. Drain on paper towels.

**4** Remove the second batch of potato slices with a draining spoon and drain on paper towels. Mix the two batches together in a warmed serving dish, toss with sea salt and carefully mix with the onions. Sprinkle with the parsley and serve.

> **Variation**
> *For garlic-flavored Lyonnaise potatoes, add about six unpeeled garlic cloves when you par-boil the potatoes in step 1. Then either leave them whole or squeeze out the flesh and spread it on the potatoes.*

# Potato Latkes

These traditional Jewish potato pancakes taste wonderful with apple sauce and sour cream.

**Serves 4**

2 medium floury potatoes
1 onion
1 large egg, beaten
2 tablespoons medium-ground
    matzo meal
vegetable oil, for frying
salt and ground black pepper

**1** Peel the potatoes and grate them coarsely. Grate the onion in the same way. Mix the potatoes and onion in a large colander in the sink, but do not rinse them. Press them down, squeezing out as much of the thick starchy liquid as possible. Put the potato mixture into a large bowl.

**2** Immediately stir in the beaten egg. Add the matzo meal, stirring gently to mix. Season with salt and plenty of pepper.

**3** Preheat the oven to 300°F. Pour oil to a depth of ½ inch into a heavy frying pan. Heat it until a small piece of day-old bread, added to the oil, sizzles. Take a spoonful of the potato mixture and lower it carefully into the oil. Continue adding spoonfuls, leaving space between each one.

**4** Flatten the pancakes slightly with the back of a spoon. Fry for a few minutes, until the latkes are golden brown on the underside, then turn them over carefully and continue frying until golden brown all over.

**5** Drain the latkes on paper towels, then transfer to an ovenproof serving dish and keep warm in the oven while frying the remainder. Serve hot.

> **Variation**
> *Try using equal amounts of potatoes and Jerusalem artichokes for a really distinct flavor.*

# New Potatoes with Shallot Butter

New potatoes are always a treat and are superb with this delicate butter.

**Serves 6**
1¼ pounds small new potatoes
2 tablespoons butter

3 shallots, finely chopped
2 garlic cloves, crushed
1 teaspoon chopped
    fresh tarragon
1 teaspoon chopped fresh chives
1 teaspoon chopped fresh parsley
salt and ground black pepper

**1** Bring a pan of lightly salted water to a boil. Add the potatoes and cook for 15–20 minutes, until just tender. Drain them well.

**2** Melt the butter in a large frying pan. Fry the shallots and garlic over low heat, stirring occasionally, for 5 minutes. Add the potatoes to the pan and mix with the shallot butter. Season to taste with salt and pepper. Cook, stirring constantly, until the potatoes are heated through.

**3** Transfer the potatoes to a warmed serving bowl. Sprinkle with the chopped herbs and serve immediately.

# New Potatoes with Sour Cream

This is a traditional Russian way of serving potatoes. The sour cream may be flavored with scallions, as here, or snipped fresh chives.

**Serves 6**
2 pounds new potatoes
⅔ cup sour cream
4 scallions, thinly sliced
salt and ground black pepper
1 tablespoon chopped fresh dill,
    to garnish

**1** Bring a pan of lightly salted water to a boil. Add the potatoes and cook for 15–20 minutes, until just tender. Drain.

**2** Mix the sour cream and scallions and season to taste with salt and pepper. Place the potatoes in a warm serving dish, add the cream mixture and toss lightly. Garnish with dill.

# Marquis Potatoes

Swirled potato nests filled with a tangy tomato mixture look wonderfully appetizing and taste superb. As a side dish, this recipe will serve six, but could also make a tasty lunch for two or three people.

**Makes 6 nests**

4 large floury potatoes, total
   weight about 2 pounds
1 tablespoons olive oil, plus extra
   for greasing
2 shallots, finely chopped
1 pound ripe tomatoes, peeled,
   seeded and diced
2 tablespoons butter
4 tablespoons milk
3 egg yolks
salt and ground black pepper
chopped fresh parsley, to garnish

**1** Peel the potatoes and cut them into small chunks. Put them in a pan of cold water. Add salt, bring to a boil and cook for 20 minutes or until very tender.

**2** Heat the olive oil in a large frying pan. Add the shallots and fry, stirring constantly, for 2 minutes.

**3** Add the diced tomatoes and fry over low heat, stirring occasionally, for 10 more minutes, until all the moisture has evaporated. Keep warm over low heat.

**4** Drain the potatoes in a colander, then return them to the pan so that they can dry off. Cool slightly, then mash with the butter, the milk and two of the egg yolks. Season to taste with salt and pepper.

**5** Preheat the broiler and grease a baking sheet. Spoon the potato mixture into a piping bag fitted with a medium star nozzle. Pipe six oval nests onto the baking sheet. Beat the remaining egg yolk with a little water and carefully brush on the potato. Broil for 5 minutes or until golden.

**6** Spoon the tomato mixture inside the nests and top with a little parsley. Serve them immediately.

# Gratin Dauphinois

This popular dish is a good alternative to traditional roast potatoes, particularly as it needs no last-minute attention.

**Serves 8**

butter, for greasing
3 1/2 pounds potatoes
2–3 garlic cloves, crushed

1 cup grated Cheddar cheese
1/2 teaspoon freshly
   grated nutmeg
2 1/2 cups milk
1 1/4 cups light cream
2 large eggs, beaten
salt and ground black pepper

**1** Preheat the oven to 350°F. Generously grease a 10-cup shallow ovenproof dish with butter. Peel the potatoes and slice them thinly.

**2** Layer the potatoes in the dish, with the garlic and two-thirds of the grated cheese. Season each layer with salt and pepper to taste and a little grated nutmeg.

**3** Whisk the milk, cream and eggs in a pitcher, then pour the mixture onto the potatoes. If necessary, prick the layered potatoes with a skewer so that the liquid goes all the way to the bottom of the dish.

**4** Sprinkle the remaining grated cheese on top and bake for 45–50 minutes or until golden brown. Test the potatoes with a sharp knife; they should be very tender. Serve immediately.

## Variations
• For a lower-fat version, substitute skim milk for the milk. Omit the cheese and cream and use 15 ounces fromage blanc instead.
• For gratin savoyarde, omit the milk, cream and eggs. Substitute Beaufort cheese for the Cheddar. Layer the potatoes with the cheese and butter, then pour in 3¾ cups vegetable stock. Bake as above.

# Caribbean Roasted Sweet Potatoes, Onions & Beets

An aromatic coconut, ginger and garlic paste makes a medley of root vegetables truly memorable.

**Serves 4**
2 tablespoons peanut oil
1 pound sweet potatoes, peeled
   and cut into thick strips
   or chunks
4 freshly cooked beets, peeled
   and cut into wedges
1 pound small red or yellow
   onions, halved
1 teaspoon coriander seeds,
   lightly crushed
3–4 small whole fresh red chiles
salt and ground black pepper
chopped cilantro, to garnish

**For the paste**
2 large garlic cloves, chopped
1–2 fresh green chiles, seeded
   and chopped
1 tablespoon chopped fresh
   ginger root
3 tablespoons chopped cilantro
5 tablespoons coconut milk
2 tablespoons peanut oil
grated zest of ½ lime
½ teaspoon light brown sugar

**1** Preheat the oven to 400°F. Make the paste. Process the garlic, chiles, ginger, cilantro and coconut milk in a food processor or blender. Scrape the paste into a small bowl and beat in the oil, lime zest and brown sugar.

**2** Heat the oil in a roasting pan in the oven for 5 minutes. Add the sweet potatoes, beets, onions and coriander seeds, tossing them in the hot oil. Roast for 10 minutes.

**3** Stir in the paste and the whole red chiles. Season to taste with salt and pepper and toss the vegetables to coat them thoroughly with the paste.

**4** Roast the vegetables for another 25–35 minutes or until the sweet potatoes and onions are fully cooked and tender. Stir occasionally to prevent the paste from sticking to the pan. Transfer to a warmed platter and serve immediately, sprinkled with a little chopped cilantro.

# Swiss Soufflé Potatoes

A fabulous combination of rich and satisfying ingredients—cheese, eggs, cream, butter and potatoes. This is perfect for cold-weather entertaining.

**Serves 4**
4 floury baking potatoes, total
   weight about 2 pounds
1 cup grated Gruyère cheese
½ cup herb butter
4 tablespoons heavy cream
2 eggs, separated
salt and ground black pepper
snipped fresh chives, to garnish
mayonnaise, to serve (optional)

**1** Preheat the oven to 425°F. Prick the potatoes all over with a fork. Bake for 1–1½ hours, until tender. Remove them from the oven and reduce the temperature to 350°F.

**2** Cut each potato in half and scoop out the flesh into a bowl. Place the potato shells on a baking sheet and return them to the oven to crisp up while you are making the filling.

**3** Mash the potato flesh, then add the Gruyère, herb butter, cream and egg yolks. Beat well until smooth, then taste and add salt and pepper if needed.

**4** Whisk the egg whites into stiff peaks, then carefully fold them into the potato mixture. Pile the mixture into the potato shells and bake for 20–25 minutes, until risen and golden brown.

**5** Transfer the potatoes to a warm serving dish, garnish with chives and serve with mayonnaise, if desired.

> **Cook's Tip**
> To make the herb butter, mix 3 tablespoons finely chopped fresh parsley and 2 teaspoons finely chopped fresh dill with ½ cup softened butter. Season with a little salt.

# Rice Pilaf with Whole Spices

This fragrant rice dish makes a perfect accompaniment to any Indian vegetarian dish.

**Serves 4**

2½ cups hot vegetable stock
generous pinch of saffron threads
1⅓ cups basmati rice
¼ cup butter
1 onion, chopped
1 garlic clove, crushed
½ cinnamon stick
6 green cardamom pods
1 bay leaf
⅓ cup golden raisins
1 tablespoon sunflower oil
½ cup cashews
naan and tomato and onion
   salad, to serve (optional)

**1** Pour the stock into a bowl and stir in the saffron threads. Set aside to infuse. Rinse the rice several times in cold water. If there is time, let it soak for 30 minutes in the water used for the final rinse.

**2** Heat the butter in a saucepan and fry the onion and garlic for 5 minutes. Stir in the cinnamon stick, cardamoms and bay leaf and cook for 2 minutes.

**3** Drain the rice thoroughly, add it to the pan and cook, stirring, for 2 more minutes. Pour in the saffron-flavored stock and add the golden raisins. Bring to a boil, stir, then lower the heat, cover and cook gently for about 10 minutes or until the rice is tender and all the liquid has been absorbed.

**4** Meanwhile, heat the oil in a frying pan and fry the cashews until browned. Drain well on paper towels. Sprinkle the cashews on the rice. Serve with naan and a tomato and onion salad, if desired.

**Cook's Tip**
*Don't be tempted to use black cardamoms in this dish. They are coarser and more strongly flavored than green cardamoms and are only used in dishes that are cooked for a long time.*

# Indonesian Coconut Rice

This way of cooking rice is very popular throughout all Southeast Asia.

**Serves 4–6**

1¾ cups Thai fragrant rice
14-fluid ounce can coconut milk
1¼ cups water
½ teaspoon ground coriander
2-inch piece of cinnamon stick
1 lemongrass stalk, bruised
1 bay leaf
salt
deep-fried onions (see Cook's Tip),
   to garnish

**1** Put the rice in a strainer and rinse thoroughly under cold water. Drain well, then put in a pan. Pour in the coconut milk and water. Add the coriander, cinnamon stick, lemongrass and bay leaf. Season with salt. Bring to a boil, then lower the heat, cover and simmer for 8–10 minutes.

**2** Lift the lid and check that all the liquid has been absorbed, then fork the rice through carefully, removing the cinnamon stick, lemongrass and bay leaf.

**3** Cover the pan with a tight-fitting lid and continue to cook over the lowest possible heat for 3–5 more minutes.

**4** Pile the rice onto a warm serving dish and serve garnished with the crisp, deep-fried onions.

**Cook's Tips**
• *Deep-fried onions are a traditional Indonesian garnish. You can buy them ready-prepared at Asian food stores, but they are easy to make at home. Slice 1 pound onions very thinly, then spread the slices in a single layer on paper towels. Let dry for at least 1 hour, preferably longer. Deep-fry in batches in hot oil until crisp and golden. Drain on paper towels and use immediately, or cool, then store in an airtight container.*
• *If you have access to a well-stocked Asian supermarket, substitute a pandan leaf for the bay leaf. Pull the tines of a fork through the leaf to release its flavor.*

# Tomato Rice

Proof positive that you don't need elaborate ingredients or complicated cooking methods to make a delicious dish.

**Serves 4**
2 cups basmati rice
2 tablespoons sunflower oil
1/2 teaspoon onion seeds
1 onion, sliced
2 tomatoes, chopped
1 orange or yellow bell pepper, seeded and sliced
1 teaspoon crushed fresh ginger root
1 garlic clove, crushed
1 teaspoon hot chili powder
1 potato, diced
1 1/2 teaspoons salt
3 cups water
2–3 tablespoons chopped cilantro

**1** Rinse the rice several times in cold water. If there is enough time, let it soak for about 30 minutes in the water used for the final rinse.

**2** Heat the oil in a large, heavy pan and fry the onion seeds for about 30 seconds, until they are giving off their aroma. Add the sliced onion and fry over low heat, stirring occasionally, for 5 minutes, then increase the heat slightly.

**3** Stir in the tomatoes, orange or yellow bell pepper, ginger, garlic, chili powder, diced potato and salt. Stir-fry over medium heat for about 5 more minutes.

**4** Drain the rice thoroughly. Add it to the pan, then stir for about 1 minute, until the grains are well coated in the spicy vegetable mixture.

**5** Pour in the water and bring it to a boil, then lower the heat, cover the pan with a tight-fitting lid and cook the rice for 12–15 minutes. Remove from heat, without lifting the lid, and let the rice stand for 5 minutes.

**6** Gently fork through the rice to fluff up the grains, stir in the chopped cilantro and transfer to a warmed serving dish. Serve immediately.

# Wild Rice Pilaf

Wild rice isn't a rice at all but is actually a type of wild grass. Call it what you will, it has a wonderful nutty flavor and makes a fine addition to this fruity, Middle-Eastern mixture.

**Serves 6**
1 cup wild rice
3 tablespoons butter
1/2 onion, finely chopped
1 cup long-grain rice
2 cups vegetable stock
3/4 cup sliced almonds
2/3 cup golden raisins
2 tablespoons chopped fresh parsley
salt and ground black pepper

**1** Bring a large pan of lightly salted water to a boil. Add the wild rice and 1 teaspoon salt. Lower the heat, cover and simmer gently for 45–60 minutes, until the rice is tender. Drain well.

**2** Meanwhile, melt 1 tablespoon of the butter in another pan and fry the onion until it is just softened. Stir in the long-grain rice and cook for 1 more minute.

**3** Stir in the stock and bring to a boil. Lower the heat, cover tightly and simmer gently for about 30 minutes, until the rice is tender and the liquid has been absorbed.

**4** Melt the remaining butter in a small pan. Add the almonds and cook until they are just golden. Set aside.

**5** Put both types of rice into a warmed serving dish and stir in the almonds, golden raisins and half the parsley. Adjust the seasoning if necessary. Sprinkle on the remaining parsley and serve.

> **Cook's Tip**
> Like all pilaf dishes, this one must be made with well-flavored stock. Make your own, if possible, and let it reduce so that the flavor intensifies.

# Minted Couscous Castles

These pretty little timbales are perfect for serving as part of a summer lunch. They're virtually fat-free, so you can indulge yourself with impunity.

**Makes 4**
1¼ cups couscous
2 cups boiling vegetable stock
1 tablespoon lemon juice
2 tomatoes, diced
2 tablespoons chopped fresh mint
vegetable oil, for brushing
salt and ground black pepper
fresh mint sprigs, to garnish

**1** Put the couscous in a bowl and pour in the boiling stock. Cover and let stand for 30 minutes, until all the stock has been absorbed and the grains are tender.

**2** Stir in the lemon juice with the tomatoes and chopped mint. Season to taste with salt and pepper.

**3** Brush the insides of four cups or individual molds lightly with oil. Spoon in the couscous mixture and pack down firmly. Chill for several hours.

**4** Invert the castles on a platter and serve cold, garnished with mint. Alternatively, cover and heat gently in a low oven, then turn out and serve hot.

### Cook's Tip
*Moroccan couscous, the kind most commonly seen in Western supermarkets, is produced in fairly small grains, whereas the grains of Israeli couscous are about the size of peppercorns, and Lebanese couscous resembles small chickpeas in appearance. All three types may be cooked in the slow, traditional manner. Only Moroccan couscous is produced in an "instant," ready-cooked form, but this is not immediately distinguishable from traditional couscous, so always check the instructions on the package.*

# Stir-fried Noodles with Bean Sprouts

A classic Chinese noodle dish that makes a great dish. In China, noodles are served at virtually every meal— even breakfast.

**Serves 4**
6 ounces dried egg noodles
1 tablespoon vegetable oil
1 garlic clove, finely chopped
1 small onion, halved and sliced
4 cups bean sprouts
1 small red bell pepper, seeded and cut into strips
1 small green bell pepper, seeded and cut into strips
½ teaspoon salt
¼ teaspoon ground white pepper
2 tablespoons light soy sauce

**1** Bring a large pan of water to a boil. Add the noodles and remove the pan from heat. Cover and let stand for about 4 minutes, until the noodles are just tender.

**2** Heat the oil in a wok. When it is very hot, add the garlic, stir briefly, then add the onion slices. Cook, stirring, for 1 minute, then add the bean sprouts and peppers. Stir-fry for 2–3 minutes.

**3** Drain the noodles thoroughly, then add them to the wok. Toss over the heat, using two spatulas or wooden spoons, for 2–3 minutes or until the ingredients are well mixed and have heated through.

**4** Add the salt, white pepper and soy sauce and stir thoroughly before serving the noodle mixture in heated bowls.

### Variations
*This is a useful, basic noodle dish that not only makes a good side dish, but can also be easily adapted to make a more substantial main course. For example, add carrot batons, quartered button mushrooms and snow peas with the bean sprouts and peppers in step 2, or ½ cucumber, cut into batons, with the vegetables in step 2 and 2 cups shredded spinach just before adding the noodles in step 3.*

# Warm Dressed Salad with Poached Eggs

Soft poached eggs, hot croutons and cool, crisp salad greens with a warm dressing make a lively and unusual combination.

**Serves 2**
½ small loaf whole-grain bread
3 tablespoons walnut oil
2 eggs

2 cups mixed salad greens
3 tablespoons extra virgin olive oil
2 garlic cloves, crushed
1 tablespoon balsamic or
   sherry vinegar
2-ounce piece of Parmesan
   cheese, shaved
ground black pepper (optional)

**1** Carefully cut off the crust from the bread and discard it. Cut the bread into 1-inch cubes.

**2** Heat the walnut oil in a large, heavy frying pan. Add the bread cubes and cook over low heat for about 5 minutes, turning and tossing the cubes occasionally, until they are crisp and golden brown all over.

**3** Bring a pan of water to a boil. Break each egg into a bowl, one at a time, and carefully slide each one into the water. Gently poach the eggs over low heat for about 4 minutes, until lightly cooked and the whites have just set.

**4** Meanwhile, divide the salad greens among two plates. Arrange the croutons on the leaves.

**5** Wipe the frying pan clean with paper towels. Heat the olive oil in the pan, add the garlic and vinegar, and cook over high heat for 1 minute. Pour the warm dressing on the salad on each plate.

**6** Lift out each poached egg, in turn, with a draining spoon and place one on top of each of the salads. Top with thin shavings of Parmesan and a little freshly ground black pepper, if desired. Serve immediately.

# Springtime Salad with Quail's Eggs

Enjoy some of the best early season garden vegetables in this crisp green salad. Quail's eggs add a touch of sophistication and elegance.

**Serves 4**
6 ounces fava beans
6 ounces fresh peas
6 ounces asparagus
6 ounces very small new
   potatoes, scrubbed

3 tablespoons good lemon
   mayonnaise (see Cook's Tip)
3 tablespoons sour cream or
   crème fraîche
½ bunch fresh mint, chopped,
   plus whole leaves for garnishing
8 quail's eggs, soft-boiled
   and peeled
salt and ground black pepper

**1** Cook the fava beans, peas, asparagus and new potatoes in separate pans of lightly salted boiling water until just tender. Drain, refresh under cold water and drain again.

**2** When the vegetables are cold, mix them lightly in a bowl.

**3** Mix the mayonnaise with the sour cream or crème fraîche and chopped mint in a pitcher. Stir in salt and pepper, if needed.

**4** Pour the dressing on the salad and toss to coat. Add the quail's eggs and whole mint leaves and toss very gently to mix. Serve immediately.

**Cook's Tip**
*To make your own lemon mayonnaise, combine two egg yolks, 1 teaspoon Dijon mustard, and the grated zest and juice of half a lemon in a blender or food processor. Add salt and pepper to taste. Process to combine. With the motor running, add about 1 cup mild olive oil (or a mixture of olive oil and sunflower oil) through the lid or feeder tube, until the mixture emulsifies. Trickle the oil in at first, then add it in a steady stream. For a glossy mayonnaise, beat in about 1 tablespoon boiling water at the end.*

# Leek & Broiled Bell Pepper Salad with Goat Cheese

This is a perfect dish for entertaining, as the salad actually benefits from being made in advance.

**Serves 6**

$1/2$-inch slices goat cheese
$3/4$ cup fine dry white
   bread crumbs
$1 1/2$ pounds young leeks
1 tablespoon olive oil
2 large red bell peppers, halved
   and seeded

few fresh thyme sprigs, chopped
vegetable oil, for shallow frying
3 tablespoons chopped fresh
   flat-leaf parsley
salt and ground black pepper

**For the dressing**

5 tablespoons extra virgin olive oil
1 small garlic clove,
   finely chopped
1 teaspoon Dijon mustard
1 tablespoon red wine vinegar

**1** Roll the cheese slices in the bread crumbs, pressing them in so that the cheese is well coated. Chill the cheese for 1 hour.

**2** Preheat the broiler. Bring a saucepan of lightly salted water to a boil and cook the leeks for 3–4 minutes. Drain, cut into 4-inch lengths and place in a bowl. Add the olive oil, toss to coat, then season to taste. Place the leeks on a broiler pan and broil for 3–4 minutes on each side.

**3** Set the leeks aside. Place the peppers on the broiler pan, skin-side up, and broil until blackened and blistered. Place them in a bowl, cover with crumpled paper towels and leave for 10 minutes. Rub off the skin and cut the flesh into strips. Place in a bowl and add the leeks, thyme and a little pepper.

**4** Make the dressing by shaking all the ingredients together in a jar, adding seasoning to taste. Pour the dressing on the leek mixture, cover and chill for several hours.

**5** Heat a little oil and fry the cheese until golden on both sides. Drain and cool, then cut into bite-size pieces. Toss the cheese and parsley into the salad and serve at room temperature.

# Squash Salad with Feta Cheese

This is especially good served with a grain or starchy salad, based on rice or couscous. The salad is best served warm or at room temperature, rather than chilled.

**Serves 4–6**

5 tablespoons olive oil
1 tablespoon balsamic vinegar,
   plus a little extra if needed
1 tablespoon sweet soy sauce
   (kecap manis)

12 ounces shallots, peeled but
   left whole
3 fresh red chiles, chopped
1 butternut squash, peeled,
   seeded and cut into chunks
1 teaspoon finely chopped
   fresh thyme
$1/2$ cup flat-leaf parsley
1 small garlic clove,
   finely chopped
$3/4$ cup walnuts, chopped
5 ounces feta cheese
salt and ground black pepper

**1** Preheat the oven to 400°F. Put the olive oil, balsamic vinegar and soy sauce in a large bowl and beat until thoroughly incorporated.

**2** Toss the shallots and two of the chiles in the oil mixture and put into a large, shallow roasting pan. Roast, uncovered, for about 25 minutes, stirring once or twice.

**3** Add the butternut squash and roast for 35–40 more minutes, stirring once, until the squash is tender and browned. Remove from the oven, stir in the chopped thyme and set the vegetables aside to cool.

**4** Chop the parsley and garlic together and mix with the walnuts. Seed and finely chop the remaining chile.

**5** Stir the parsley, garlic and walnut mixture into the cooled vegetables. Add the remaining chopped chile. Taste and season with salt and pepper, if necessary, and add a little extra balsamic vinegar. Crumble the feta and add it to the salad.

**6** Transfer to a serving dish and serve immediately, at room temperature, rather than chilled.

# Roasted Plum Tomato & Arugula Salad

This is a good side salad to accompany a cheese flan or a fresh herb pizza.

**Serves 4**

1 pound ripe baby Italian plum
   tomatoes, halved lengthwise
5 tablespoons extra virgin olive oil
2 garlic cloves, cut into thin slivers

2 cups dried pasta shapes
2 tablespoons balsamic vinegar
2 pieces sun-dried tomato in olive
   oil, drained and chopped
large pinch of sugar
1 handful arugula leaves
salt and ground black pepper

**1** Preheat the oven to 375°F. Arrange the halved tomatoes, cut-side up, in a roasting pan. Drizzle 2 tablespoons of the oil over them and sprinkle with the slivers of garlic and salt and pepper to taste. Roast for 20 minutes, turning once.

**2** Meanwhile, bring a large pan of lightly salted water to a boil and cook the pasta until it is *al dente*.

**3** Put the remaining oil in a large bowl with the vinegar, sun-dried tomatoes and sugar with salt and pepper to taste.

**4** Drain the pasta, add it to the bowl of dressing and toss to mix. Add the roasted tomatoes and mix gently.

**5** Just before serving, add the arugula leaves, toss lightly and taste for seasoning. Serve at room temperature or chilled.

**Variations**
• *If you are in a hurry and don't have time to roast the tomatoes, you can make the salad with halved raw tomatoes instead, but make sure that they are really ripe.*
• *If desired, add 5 ounces mozzarella cheese, drained and diced, with the arugula.*

# Broiled Bell Pepper Salad with Pesto

The ingredients of this colorful salad are simple and few, but the overall flavor is quite intense.

**Serves 4**

1 large red bell pepper, halved
   and seeded
1 large green bell pepper, halved
   and seeded
2¼ cups dried fusilli tricolore or
   other pasta shapes

1 handful fresh basil leaves
1 handful cilantro leaves
1 garlic clove
salt and ground black pepper

*For the dressing*
2 tablespoons bottled pesto
juice of ½ lemon
4 tablespoons extra virgin olive oil

**1** Place the red and green bell pepper halves, skin-side up, on a broiler pan and broil until the skins have blistered and are beginning to char. Transfer the peppers to a bowl, cover with crumpled paper towels and let cool slightly. When they are cool enough to handle, rub off the skins and discard.

**2** Bring a large pan of lightly salted water to a boil and cook the pasta until it is *al dente*.

**3** Meanwhile, whisk together the pesto, lemon juice and olive oil in a large bowl. Season to taste with salt and pepper.

**4** Drain the cooked pasta well and put it into the bowl of dressing. Toss thoroughly to mix and set aside to cool.

**5** Chop the pepper flesh and add it to the pasta. Put most of the basil and cilantro and all the garlic on a board and chop them. Add the herb mixture to the pasta and toss, then season to taste, if necessary, and serve, garnished with the herb leaves.

**Cook's Tip**
*Serve the salad at room temperature or lightly chilled, whichever you prefer.*

# Gado Gado

The peanut sauce on this traditional Indonesian salad owes its flavor to galangal, an aromatic rhizome that resembles ginger.

**Serves 4**
9 ounces white cabbage, shredded
4 carrots, cut into
   matchstick strips
4 celery stalks, cut into
   matchstick strips
4 cups bean sprouts
$^1/_2$ cucumber, cut into
   matchstick strips
fried onion, salted peanuts and
   sliced fresh chile, to garnish

**For the peanut sauce**
1 tablespoon vegetable oil
1 small onion, finely chopped
1 garlic clove, crushed
1 small piece galangal, grated
1 teaspoon ground cumin
$^1/_4$ teaspoon mild chili powder
1 teaspoon tamarind paste or
   freshly squeezed lime juice
4 tablespoons crunchy
   peanut butter
1 teaspoon light brown sugar

**1** Steam the cabbage, carrots and celery for 3–4 minutes, until just tender. Cool. Spread out the bean sprouts on a serving dish. Top with the cabbage, carrots, celery and cucumber.

**2** Make the sauce. Heat the oil in a saucepan, add the onion and garlic and cook gently for 5 minutes, until soft. Stir in the galangal, cumin and chili powder and cook for 1 more minute. Stir in the tamarind paste or lime juice, peanut butter and sugar.

**3** Heat gently, stirring occasionally and adding a little hot water, if necessary, to make a coating sauce. Spoon a little of the sauce on the vegetables and garnish with fried onions, peanuts and sliced chile. Pass the rest of the sauce separately.

> **Variations**
> As long as the sauce remains the same, the vegetables can be altered at the whim of the cook and the season.

# Couscous Salad

Couscous has become an extremely popular salad ingredient, and there are many variations on the classic theme. This salad comes from Morocco.

**Serves 4**
$1^2/_3$ cups couscous
$2^1/_4$ cups boiling vegetable stock
16–20 pitted black olives, halved
2 small zucchini, cut in
   matchstick strips
$^1/_4$ cup sliced almonds, toasted

4 tablespoons olive oil
1 tablespoon lemon juice
1 tablespoon chopped cilantro
1 tablespoon chopped
   fresh parsley
good pinch of ground cumin
good pinch of cayenne pepper
salt

**1** Place the couscous in a bowl and pour in the boiling stock. Stir with a fork, then set aside for 10 minutes for the stock to be absorbed. Fluff up with a fork.

**2** Add the olives, zucchini and almonds to the couscous and mix in gently.

**3** Whisk the olive oil, lemon juice, cilantro, parsley, cumin, cayenne and a pinch of salt in a pitcher. Pour the dressing on the salad and toss to mix.

> **Cook's Tip**
> This salad benefits from being made several hours ahead, so that the flavors can blend.

> **Variations**
> • You can substitute $^1/_2$ cucumber for the zucchini and pistachios for the almonds.
> • For extra heat, add a pinch of chili powder to the dressing.

# Tabbouleh

The classic bulghur salad, this remains a winner. Serve it with roasted or barbecued vegetables.

**Serves 4**
scant 1 cup bulghur
2½ cups water
3 scallions, finely chopped
2 large garlic cloves, crushed

4 firm tomatoes, peeled
  and chopped
6 tablespoons chopped
  fresh parsley
4 tablespoons chopped fresh mint
6 tablespoons fresh lemon juice
5 tablespoons extra virgin olive oil
salt and ground black pepper

**1** Place the bulghur in a bowl and pour in the water. Let soak for 20 minutes.

**2** Line a colander with a clean dish towel. Put the soaked bulghur into the center, let it drain, then gather up the sides of the dish towel and squeeze out any remaining liquid. Put the bulghur into a large bowl.

**3** Add the scallions, garlic, tomatoes, parsley and mint. Mix well, then pour over the lemon juice and olive oil. Season generously with salt and pepper, then toss so that all the ingredients are combined. Cover and chill in the refrigerator for several hours before serving.

# Ratatouille

Wonderfully versatile, ratatouille can be served hot or cold. Apart from being a good side dish, it makes an excellent filling for baked potatoes and warm tortillas and a good sauce for pasta.

**Serves 4–6**
4 tablespoons olive oil
2 large onions, chopped
2 garlic cloves, crushed

2 large eggplant, cut into
  large cubes
3 zucchini, thickly sliced
2 bell peppers (red and green),
  seeded and sliced
3 large tomatoes, peeled, seeded
  and chopped
1 tablespoon sun-dried tomato
  paste dissolved in
  2 tablespoons boiling water
2 tablespoons chopped cilantro
salt and ground black pepper

**1** Heat the oil in a large pan and fry the onions and garlic until softened. Add the eggplant and fry for 10 minutes, stirring frequently. Stir in the zucchini, peppers and tomatoes, with the diluted tomato paste and plenty of salt and pepper.
**2** Bring to a boil, then lower the heat and simmer for about 30 minutes, stirring occasionally and adding a little water if needed, until the vegetables are just tender. Stir in the cilantro and serve hot or cold.

> **Cook's Tip**
> If you have time, salt the eggplant cubes in a colander over the sink for 20 minutes. Rinse well and pat dry before using.

# Cracked Wheat Salad with Oranges & Almonds

The citrus flavors of lemon and orange really come through in this tasty salad, which can be made several hours before serving.

**Serves 4**
scant 1 cup bulghur
2½ cups water
1 small green bell pepper, seeded
  and diced
¼ cucumber, diced

½ cup chopped fresh mint
4 tablespoons sliced
  almonds, toasted
grated zest and juice of 1 lemon
2 seedless oranges
salt and ground black pepper
fresh mint sprigs, to garnish

**1** Place the bulghur in a bowl, pour in the water and let soak for 20 minutes.

**2** Line a colander with a clean dish towel. Put the soaked bulghur into the center, let it drain, then gather up the sides of the dish towel and squeeze out any remaining liquid. Put the bulghur into a large bowl.

**3** Add the green bell pepper, diced cucumber, mint, toasted almonds and grated lemon zest. Pour in the lemon juice and toss thoroughly to mix.

**4** Cut the zest from the oranges, then, working over a bowl to catch the juice, cut both oranges into neat segments. Add the segments and the juice to the bulghur mixture, then season to taste with salt and pepper and toss lightly. Garnish with the mint sprigs and serve.

> **Cook's Tip**
> Bulghur is also known as cracked wheat because the grains are cracked after hulling and steaming and before drying.

# Spanish Rice Salad

Ribbons of green and yellow bell pepper add color and flavor to this simple salad.

**Serves 6**

1½ cups white long-grain rice
1 bunch scallions, thinly sliced
1 green bell pepper, seeded and sliced
1 yellow bell pepper, seeded and sliced
3 tomatoes, peeled, seeded and chopped
2 tablespoons chopped cilantro

**For the dressing**

3 tablespoons mixed sunflower and olive oil
1 tablespoon rice vinegar
1 teaspoon Dijon mustard
salt and ground black pepper

**1** Bring a large pan of lightly salted water to a boil and cook the rice for 10–12 minutes, until tender but still slightly firm at the center of the grain. Do not overcook. Drain, rinse under cold water and drain again. Leave until cold.

**2** Place the rice in a large serving bowl. Add the scallions, peppers, tomatoes and cilantro.

**3** Make the dressing. Mix the oils, vinegar and mustard in a jar with a tight-fitting lid and season to taste with salt and pepper. Shake vigorously. Stir 4–5 tablespoons of the dressing into the rice and adjust the seasoning, if necessary.

**4** Cover and chill for about 1 hour before serving. Offer the remaining dressing separately.

> **Variations**
> • Cooked garden peas, cooked diced carrot and drained, canned corn can be added to this versatile salad.
> • This recipe works well with long-grain rice, but if you can obtain Spanish rice, it will be more authentic. It has a rounder grain, a little like risotto rice.

# Fruity Brown Rice Salad

An Asian-style dressing gives this colorful rice salad extra piquancy.

**Serves 4–6**

⅔ cup brown rice
1 small red bell pepper, seeded and diced
7-ounce can corn kernels, drained
3 tablespoons golden raisins
8-ounce can pineapple pieces in fruit juice
1 tablespoon light soy sauce
1 tablespoon sunflower oil
1 tablespoon hazelnut oil
1 garlic clove, crushed
1 teaspoon finely chopped fresh ginger root
salt and ground black pepper
4 scallions, diagonally sliced, to garnish

**1** Bring a large pan of lightly salted water to a boil and cook the brown rice for about 30 minutes or until it is just tender. Drain thoroughly, rinse under cold water and drain again. Set aside to cool.

**2** Put the rice into a bowl and add the red bell pepper, corn and golden raisins. Drain the pineapple pieces, reserving the juice, then add them to the rice mixture and toss lightly.

**3** Pour the reserved pineapple juice into a clean screw-top jar. Add the soy sauce, sunflower and hazelnut oils, garlic and chopped ginger root and season to taste with salt and pepper. Close the jar tightly and shake vigorously.

**4** Pour the dressing on the salad and toss well. Sprinkle scallions on top and serve.

> **Cook's Tips**
> • Hazelnut oil gives a distinctive flavor to any salad dressing and is especially good for leafy salads that need a bit of a lift. It is like olive oil, in that it contains mainly monounsaturated fats.
> • Brown rice is often mistakenly called whole-grain. In fact, the outer husk is completely inedible and is removed from all rice, but the bran layer is left intact on brown rice.

# Sesame Noodle Salad

Toasted sesame oil adds a nutty flavor to this salad, which is at its best when served warm.

**Serves 2–4**

9 ounces medium egg noodles
1 3/4 cups sugar snap peas or
   snow peas, sliced diagonally
2 carrots, cut into
   matchstick strips
2 tomatoes, seeded and diced
2 tablespoons chopped cilantro,
   plus cilantro sprigs, to garnish
1 tablespoon sesame seeds
3 scallions, shredded

**For the dressing**

2 teaspoons light soy sauce
2 tablespoons toasted sesame
   seed oil
1 tablespoon sunflower oil
1 1/2-inch piece of fresh ginger
   root, finely grated
1 garlic clove, crushed

**1** Bring a large pan of water to a boil, add the noodles and remove the pan from heat. Cover and let stand for about 4 minutes, until the noodles are just tender.

**2** Meanwhile, bring a second, smaller saucepan of water to a boil. Add the sugar snap peas or snow peas, bring back to a boil and cook for 2 minutes. Drain and refresh under cold water, then drain again.

**3** Make the dressing. Put the soy sauce, sesame seed and sunflower oils, ginger and garlic in a screw-top jar. Close tightly and shake vigorously to mix.

**4** Drain the noodles thoroughly and put them into a large bowl. Add the peas or snow peas, carrots, tomatoes and cilantro. Pour the dressing on top, and toss thoroughly with your hands to combine.

**5** Sprinkle the salad with the sesame seeds, top with the shredded scallions and cilantro sprigs and serve while the noodles are still warm.

# Japanese Salad

Delicate and refreshing, this is based on a mild-flavored, sweet-tasting seaweed, combined with radishes, cucumber and bean sprouts.

**Serves 4**

1/2 cup dried hijiki
1 1/4 cups radishes, sliced into very
   thin rounds
1 small cucumber, cut into
   thin sticks
1 1/2 cups bean sprouts

**For the dressing**

1 tablespoon sunflower oil
1 tablespoon toasted sesame oil
1 teaspoon light soy sauce
2 tablespoons rice vinegar or
   1 tablespoon wine vinegar
1 tablespoon mirin or dry sherry

**1** Place the hijiki in a bowl and add cold water to cover. Soak for 10–15 minutes, until it is rehydrated, then drain, rinse under cold running water and drain again. It should have almost tripled in volume.

**2** Place the hijiki in a saucepan of water. Bring to a boil, then lower the heat and simmer for about 30 minutes, or until tender. Drain well.

**3** Meanwhile, make the dressing. Place the sunflower and sesame oils, soy sauce, vinegar and mirin or sherry in a screw-top jar. Shake vigorously to combine.

**4** Arrange the hijiki in a shallow bowl or platter with the radishes, cucumber and bean sprouts. Pour on the dressing and toss lightly.

**Cook's Tip**
*Hijiki is a type of seaweed. A rich source of minerals, it comes from Japan, where it has a distinguished reputation for enhancing beauty and adding luster to hair. Look for hijiki at Asian food stores.*

# Fragrant Lentil & Spinach Salad

This earthy salad is great for a picnic or barbecue.

**Serves 6**
1 cup Puy lentils
1 fresh bay leaf
1 celery stalk
1 fresh thyme sprig
2 tablespoons olive oil
1 onion, finely sliced
2 teaspoons crushed toasted
  cumin seeds
14 ounces young
  spinach leaves

2–3 tablespoons chopped fresh
  parsley, plus a few extra sprigs
  for garnishing
salt and ground black pepper
toasted French bread, to serve

**For the dressing**
3 tablespoons extra virgin olive oil
1 teaspoon Dijon mustard
2–5 teaspoons red wine vinegar
1 small garlic clove,
  finely chopped
1/2 teaspoon finely grated
  lemon zest

**1** Rinse the lentils and place them in a large saucepan. Add water to cover. Tie the bay leaf, celery and thyme into a bundle and add to the pan, then bring to a boil. Lower the heat to a steady boil. Cook the lentils for 30–45 minutes, until just tender.

**2** Meanwhile, make the dressing. Mix the oil and mustard with 1 tablespoon of the vinegar. Add the garlic and lemon zest, and whisk to mix. Season well with salt and pepper.

**3** Drain the lentils and discard the herbs. Put them into a bowl, add most of the dressing and toss. Set aside and stir occasionally.

**4** Heat the oil in a pan and cook the onion for 4–5 minutes, until it starts to soften. Add the cumin and cook for 1 minute.

**5** Add the spinach and season to taste, then cover and cook for 2 minutes. Stir, then cook again briefly until wilted.

**6** Stir the spinach into the lentils and let the salad cool to room temperature. Stir in the remaining dressing and chopped parsley. Adjust the seasoning, adding more vinegar if necessary. Spoon onto a serving platter, sprinkle on some parsley sprigs, and serve at room temperature with toasted French bread.

# White Bean Salad with Roasted Red Bell Pepper Dressing

The speckled herb and red bell pepper dressing adds a wonderful colour contrast to this salad, which is best served warm.

**Serves 4**
1 large red bell pepper, halved
  and seeded
2 tablespoons olive oil

1 large garlic clove, crushed
1 cup fresh oregano leaves or
  flat-leaf parsley
2 teaspoons balsamic vinegar
3 cups drained canned flageolet
  beans, rinsed
1 1/2 cups drained canned
  cannellini beans, rinsed
salt and ground black pepper

**1** Preheat the broiler. Place the red bell pepper in a broiler pan and cook under medium heat until the skin is blistered and blackened all over. Place in a bowl and cover with crumpled paper towels. Set aside to cool slightly.

**2** When the pepper is cool enough to handle, rub off the skin. Carefully pull out the core and seeds, saving any juices, then dice the flesh.

**3** Heat the olive oil in a saucepan. Add the garlic and fry over low heat, stirring constantly, for 1 minute, until softened. Remove the pan from heat, then add the oregano or parsley. Stir in the diced red bell pepper and any reserved juices, then stir in the balsamic vinegar.

**4** Put the beans in a large bowl and pour on the dressing. Season to taste with salt and pepper, then stir gently until thoroughly combined. Serve immediately.

**Cook's Tip**
*Cannellini beans are always a creamy white, but flageolets may be green or white. The salad will look attractive either way, but if you prefer white beans, you could substitute haricots.*

# Sweet-&-Sour Artichoke Salad

This Italian salad combines spring vegetables with a deliciously piquant sauce called *agrodolce*.

**Serves 4**
juice of 1 lemon
6 small globe artichokes
2 tablespoons olive oil
2 medium onions,
   roughly chopped
1 cup fresh or frozen fava beans
   (shelled weight)

1¼ cups water
1½ cups fresh or frozen peas
   (shelled weight)
salt and ground black pepper
fresh mint leaves, to garnish

**For the sauce**
½ cup white wine vinegar
1 tablespoon sugar
a handful of fresh mint leaves,
   roughly torn

**1** Fill a bowl with cold water and add the lemon juice. Peel the outer leaves from the artichokes and discard them. Cut the artichokes into quarters and place them in the bowl of acidulated water to prevent them from discoloring.

**2** Heat the oil in a large, heavy pan. Add the onions and fry over low heat, stirring occasionally, until they are golden.

**3** Stir in the beans, then drain the artichokes and add them to the pan. Pour in the measured water. Bring the water to a boil, lower the heat, cover and cook for 10–15 minutes.

**4** Add the peas, season to taste with salt and pepper and cook for 5 more minutes, stirring occasionally, until the vegetables are tender. Drain them thoroughly, place them in a bowl, let cool, then cover and chill.

**5** Make the sauce. Mix all the ingredients in a small pan. Heat gently for 2–3 minutes, until the sugar has dissolved. Simmer for about another 5 minutes, stirring occasionally. Remove from heat and let cool.

**6** To serve, drizzle the sauce on the vegetables and garnish with the fresh mint leaves.

# Beet & Red Onion Salad

This salad looks especially attractive when it is made with a mixture of red and yellow beets.

**Serves 6**
1¼ pounds small beets
5 tablespoons water
4 tablespoons olive oil
scant 1 cup walnut halves
1 teaspoon sugar, plus a little
   extra for the dressing
2 tablespoons walnut oil
1 tablespoon sherry vinegar
1 teaspoon soy sauce

1 teaspoon grated orange zest
½ teaspoon ground roasted
   coriander seeds
1–2 teaspoons orange juice
1 red onion, halved and very
   thinly sliced
1–2 tablespoons chopped
   fresh fennel
3 ounces watercress or
   mizuna leaves
handful of baby red chard or beet
   leaves (optional)
salt and ground black pepper

**1** Preheat the oven to 350°F. Place the beets in an ovenproof dish in a single layer and add the water. Cover tightly and roast for 1–1½ hours or until they are just tender.

**2** Cool, then peel the beets. Slice or cut into strips and toss with 1 tablespoon of the olive oil in a bowl. Set aside.

**3** Heat 1 tablespoon of the remaining olive oil in a small frying pan. Fry the walnuts until starting to brown. Add the sugar and cook, stirring, until starting to caramelize. Season with pepper and ½ teaspoon salt, then put them on a plate to cool.

**4** In a pitcher, whisk together the remaining olive oil, the walnut oil, sherry vinegar, soy sauce, orange zest and coriander seeds. Season with salt and pepper and add a pinch of sugar. Whisk in orange juice to taste.

**5** Separate the red onion slices into half-rings and add them to the beets. Pour on the dressing and toss well. When ready to serve, toss the salad with the fennel, watercress or mizuna and red chard or beet leaves, if using. Transfer to individual bowls or plates and sprinkle on the caramelized nuts.

# Feta & Mint Potato Salad

The oddly named pink fir apple potatoes are perfect for this salad, and taste great with feta cheese, yogurt and fresh mint.

**Serves 4**
1¼ pounds pink fir
    apple potatoes
3½ ounces feta cheese, crumbled

**For the dressing**
1 cup plain yogurt
½ cup fresh mint leaves
2 tablespoons mayonnaise
salt and ground black pepper

**1** Steam the potatoes over a pan of boiling water for about 20 minutes, until tender.

**2** Meanwhile, make the dressing. Mix the yogurt and mint in a food processor and pulse until the mint leaves are finely chopped. Scrape the mixture into a small bowl, stir in the mayonnaise and season to taste with salt and pepper.

**3** Drain the potatoes well and put them into a large bowl. Spoon on the dressing and sprinkle the feta cheese on top. Serve immediately.

**Cook's Tip**
*Pink fir apple potatoes have a smooth waxy texture and retain their shape when cooked, making them ideal for salads. Charlotte, Belle de Fontenay and other special salad potatoes could be used instead.*

**Variations**
• *Crumbled Kefalotiri or young Manchego could be used instead of the feta.*
• *For a richer dressing, use Greek-style yogurt.*

# Baked Sweet Potato Salad

This salad has a truly tropical taste and is ideal served with Asian or Caribbean dishes.

**Serves 4–6**
2¼ pounds sweet potatoes
1 red bell pepper, seeded and
    finely diced
3 celery stalks, finely diced
¼ red skinned onion,
    finely chopped

1 fresh red chile, finely chopped
salt and ground black pepper
cilantro leaves, to garnish

**For the dressing**
3 tablespoons chopped cilantro
juice of 1 lime
⅔ cup plain yogurt

**1** Preheat the oven to 400°F. Wash the potatoes, pierce them all over with a fork and bake for about 40 minutes or until tender.

**2** Meanwhile, make the dressing. Whisk together the cilantro, lime juice and yogurt in a small bowl and season to taste with salt and pepper. Chill in the refrigerator while you prepare the remaining salad ingredients.

**3** In a large bowl, mix the diced red bell pepper, celery, chopped onion and chile.

**4** Remove the potatoes from the oven. As soon as they are cool enough to handle, peel them and cut them into cubes. Add them to the bowl. Drizzle on the dressing and toss carefully. Taste and adjust the seasoning, if necessary. Serve, garnished with cilantro leaves.

**Cook's Tip**
*It is generally thought that the seeds are the hottest part of a chile. In fact, they contain no capsaicin—the hot element—but it is intensely concentrated in the flesh surrounding them. Removing the seeds usually removes this extra hot flesh.*

# Broiled Onion & Eggplant Salad with Tahini

Deliciously smoky, this dish balances sweet and sharp flavors. It tastes good with crisp lettuce and sweet, sun-ripened tomatoes.

**Serves 6**

3 eggplant, cut into
　½-inch thick slices
1½ pounds onions, thickly sliced
5–6 tablespoons olive oil
3 tablespoons roughly chopped
　flat-leaf parsley
3 tablespoons pine nuts, toasted
salt and ground black pepper

**For the dressing**
2 garlic cloves, crushed
⅔ cup light tahini
juice of 1–2 lemons
3–4 tablespoons water

**1** Place the eggplant in a colander, sprinkling each layer generously with salt. Let stand in the sink for about 45 minutes, then rinse thoroughly under cold running water and pat dry with paper towels.

**2** Thread the onion slices onto skewers (soaked in cold water if wooden or bamboo), to keep them together.

**3** Heat a ridged cast-iron broiler pan. Brush the eggplant slices and onions with about 3 tablespoons of the oil and cook for 6–8 minutes on each side, brushing with more oil, as necessary. The vegetables should be browned and soft when cooked. The onions may need a little longer than the eggplant.

**4** Arrange the vegetables on a serving dish and season to taste with salt and pepper. Sprinkle on the remaining olive oil if they look a bit dry.

**5** To make the dressing, put the garlic and a pinch of salt in a mortar and crush with a pestle. Gradually work in the tahini. When it has been fully incorporated, gradually work in the juice of 1 lemon, then the water. Taste and add more lemon juice if you think the dressing needs it. Thin with more water, if necessary, so that the dressing is fairly runny.

**6** Drizzle the dressing on the salad and set aside for 30–60 minutes for the flavors to mingle. Sprinkle on the chopped parsley and pine nuts. Serve the salad at room temperature, not chilled.

**Cook's Tips**
• If you don't have a cast-iron grill pan, cook the vegetables under the broiler.
• Tahini is a thick, smooth, oily paste made from sesame seeds. It is available at Middle Eastern stores, whole-food stores and some supermarkets.

**Variation**
Use red, rather than yellow onions.

# Asian Salad

Ribboned vegetables and crisp bean sprouts look very attractive, and taste good together. Serve this salad with samosas or Thai tempeh cakes.

**Serves 4**

4 cups bean sprouts
1 cucumber
2 carrots
1 small daikon radish
1 small red onion, thinly sliced
1-inch piece of fresh ginger root,
　cut into thin matchsticks
1 small fresh red chile, seeded
　and thinly sliced
a handful of cilantro leaves or
　mint leaves

**For the Asian dressing**
1 tablespoon rice vinegar
1 tablespoon light soy sauce
2 teaspoons vegetarian "oyster"
　sauce, or to taste
1 garlic clove, finely chopped
1 tablespoon sesame oil
3 tablespoons peanut oil
2 tablespoons sesame seeds,
　lightly toasted

**1** Make the dressing. Put the vinegar, soy sauce, "oyster" sauce, garlic, sesame and peanut oils and sesame seeds in a screw-top jar. Close the lid tightly and shake vigorously.

**2** Wash the bean sprouts under cold running water and drain thoroughly in a colander.

**3** Peel the cucumber and cut it in half lengthwise. Scoop out the seeds with a teaspoon and discard. Using a vegetable peeler, peel the cucumber flesh into long ribbon strips. Peel the carrots and daikon radish into similar strips.

**4** Place the carrot, radish and cucumber strips in a large shallow serving dish. Add the bean sprouts, onion, ginger, chile and cilantro or mint and toss to mix. Pour on the dressing just before serving and toss lightly.

**Cook's Tip**
If you have difficulty tracking down the vegetarian version of oyster sauce, use more soy sauce instead.

# Avocado, Red Onion & Spinach Salad with Polenta Croutons

The simple lemon dressing gives a sharp tang to this sophisticated salad, while the croutons, with their crunchy golden exterior and soft center, add a contrast.

**Serves 4**
1 large red onion, cut into wedges
11 ounces ready-made polenta, cut into ½-inch cubes

olive oil, for brushing
8 ounces baby spinach leaves
1 avocado
1 teaspoon lemon juice

**For the dressing**
4 tablespoons extra virgin olive oil
juice of ½ lemon
salt and ground black pepper

1 Preheat the oven to 400°F. Place the onion wedges and polenta cubes on a lightly oiled baking sheet and bake for 25 minutes or until the onion is tender and the polenta is crisp and golden, turning everything frequently to prevent sticking. Let cool slightly.

2 Meanwhile, make the dressing. Place the olive oil and lemon juice in a screw-top jar. Add salt and pepper to taste, close the jar tightly and shake vigorously to combine.

3 Place the spinach in a serving bowl. Peel, pit and slice the avocado, then toss the slices in the lemon juice to prevent them from discoloring. Add them to the spinach with the onions.

4 Pour the dressing on the salad and toss gently. Sprinkle the polenta croutons on top or pass them separately.

**Cook's Tip**
If you can't find ready-made polenta, you can make your own using instant polenta grains. Simply cook 1 cup according to the instructions on the package, then pour into a tray and let cool and set.

# Watercress, Pear, Walnut & Roquefort Salad

Sharp-tasting blue Roquefort and peppery leaves are complemented in this salad by sweet fruit and crunchy nuts.

**Serves 4**
¾ cup shelled walnuts, halved
2 red Williams' pears
1 tablespoon lemon juice
1 large bunch watercress, about 5 ounces, tough stems removed

7 ounces Roquefort cheese, cut into chunks

**For the dressing**
3 tablespoons extra virgin olive oil
2 tablespoons lemon juice
½ teaspoon honey
1 teaspoon Dijon mustard
salt and ground black pepper

1 Toast the walnuts in a dry frying pan over low heat for about 2 minutes, until golden, tossing frequently to prevent them from burning.

2 Meanwhile, make the dressing. Put the olive oil, lemon juice, honey and mustard into a screw-top jar and season to taste with salt and pepper. Close the lid tightly and shake vigorously until thoroughly combined.

3 Core and slice the pears then toss them in the lemon juice to prevent them from discoloring. Place the slices in a bowl and add the watercress, walnuts and Roquefort. Pour the dressing onto the salad, toss well and serve immediately.

**Cook's Tip**
For a special dinner party, fan the pears on a bed of the dressed watercress. Cut the pears in half, remove the cores, then, keeping them intact at the top, slice them lengthwise. Brush them with lemon juice to prevent discoloration, then place one half, cut-side down, on each salad. Press down gently to fan the slices. Sprinkle on the toasted walnuts.

# Fattoush

This simple salad has been served for centuries in the Middle East. It has been adopted by restaurateurs all over the world, and you are as likely to encounter it in San Francisco as in Syria.

**Serves 4**

1 yellow or red bell pepper, seeded and sliced
1 large cucumber, roughly chopped
4–5 tomatoes, chopped
1 bunch scallions, sliced
2 tablespoons finely chopped fresh parsley
2 tablespoons finely chopped fresh mint
2 tablespoons finely chopped cilantro
2 garlic cloves, crushed
juice of 1½ lemons
3 tablespoons olive oil
salt and ground black pepper
2 pita breads

**1** Place the yellow or red bell pepper, cucumber and tomatoes in a large salad bowl. Add the scallions, with the finely chopped parsley, mint and cilantro.

**2** Make the dressing. Mix the garlic with the lemon juice in a pitcher. Gradually whisk in the olive oil, then season to taste with salt and black pepper. Pour the dressing over the salad and toss lightly to mix.

**3** Toast the pita bread, in a toaster or under a hot broiler until crisp. Serve with the salad.

---

**Cook's Tip**
*People either love or hate cilantro. If you hate it, omit it and double the amount of parsley.*

---

**Variation**
*If you prefer, make this salad in the traditional way. After toasting the pita breads until crisp, crush them in your hand and sprinkle on the salad before serving.*

---

# Radish, Mango & Apple Salad

Clean, crisp tastes and mellow flavors make this salad a good choice at any time, although it is at its best with fresh garden radishes in early summer.

**Serves 4**

10–15 radishes
1 apple
2 celery stalks, thinly sliced
1 small ripe mango
fresh dill sprigs, to garnish

**For the dressing**
½ cup low fat crème fraîche
2 teaspoons creamed horseradish
1 tablespoon chopped fresh dill
salt and ground black pepper

**1** Make the dressing by mixing the crème fraîche with the creamed horseradish and dill in a small pitcher. Season with a little salt and pepper.

**2** Trim the radishes, then slice them thinly. Place them in a bowl. Cut the apple into quarters, remove the core from each wedge, then slice the flesh thinly and add it to the bowl with the celery.

**3** Cut through the mango lengthwise either side of the pit. Leaving the skin on each section, cross-hatch the flesh, then bend it back so that the cubes stand proud of the skin. Slice them off with a small knife and add them to the bowl.

**4** Pour the dressing onto the vegetables and fruit and stir gently to coat. When ready to serve, spoon the salad into a salad bowl and garnish with the dill.

---

**Cook's Tip**
*Radishes are members of the mustard family and may be red or white, round or elongated. They vary considerably in their strength of flavor; small, slender French radishes are especially mild and sweet. Whatever type you are buying, look for small, firm, brightly colored specimens, with no sign of limpness.*

# Romanian Bell Pepper Salad

Try to locate authentic long
bell peppers for this salad.

**Serves 4**
8 long green and/or orange bell
   peppers, halved and seeded
1 garlic clove, crushed

4 tablespoons wine vinegar
5 tablespoons olive oil
4 tomatoes, sliced
1 red onion, thinly sliced
salt and ground black pepper
cilantro sprigs, to garnish
black bread, to serve

**1** Place the pepper halves, skin-side up, on a broiler pan and
broil until the skins have blistered and charred. Transfer to a
bowl and cover with crumpled paper towels. Let cool slightly,
then rub off the skins and cut each piece in half lengthwise.

**2** Mix the garlic and vinegar in a bowl, then whisk in the olive
oil. Arrange the peppers, tomatoes and onion on four serving
plates and pour on the garlic dressing. Season to taste with
salt and pepper, garnish with cilantro sprigs and serve with
black bread.

# Simple Bell Pepper Salad

Bell peppers are perfect for
making refreshing salads.

**Serves 4**
4 large mixed peppers, halved
   and seeded
4 tablespoons olive oil

1 medium onion, thinly sliced
2 garlic cloves, crushed
4 tomatoes, peeled and chopped
pinch of sugar
1 teaspoon lemon juice
salt and ground black pepper

**1** Place the peppers, skin-side up, on a broiler pan and broil
until blistered. Transfer to a bowl and cover with crumpled
paper towels. Cool slightly, then rub off the skins and slice thinly.
**2** Heat the oil and fry the onion and garlic until softened. Add
the peppers and tomatoes and fry for 10 more minutes.
**3** Remove from heat, stir in the sugar and lemon juice and
season. Let cool and serve at room temperature.

# Cucumber & Tomato Salad

Yogurt cools the dressing for
this salad; fresh chile spices it
up. The combination works
very well and is delicious
with fresh bread.

**Serves 4**
1 pound firm ripe tomatoes
1/2 cucumber
1 onion
1 small hot chile, seeded and
   chopped and snipped chives,
   to garnish
country bread or tomato toasts
   (see Cook's Tip), to serve

**For the dressing**
4 tablespoons olive oil
6 tablespoons plain yogurt
2 tablespoons chopped fresh
   parsley or snipped chives
1/2 teaspoon white wine vinegar
salt and ground black pepper

**1** Peel the tomatoes by first cutting a cross in the bottom of
each tomato. Place in a bowl and cover with boiling water for
1–2 minutes or until the skin starts to curl back from the
crosses. Drain, plunge into cold water and drain again. Peel, cut
the tomatoes into quarters, seed and chop.

**2** Chop the cucumber and onion into pieces that are the same
size as the tomatoes and put them all in a bowl.

**3** Make the dressing. Whisk together the oil, yogurt, parsley or
chives and vinegar in a bowl and season to taste with salt and
pepper. Pour onto the salad and toss all the ingredients
together. Sprinkle on black pepper and the chopped chile and
chives to garnish. Serve with crusty bread or tomato toasts.

---

**Cook's Tip**
*To make tomato toasts, cut a loaf of French bread diagonally
into thin slices. Mix a crushed garlic clove, a peeled and
chopped tomato and 2 tablespoons olive oil. Season. Spread on
the bread and bake at 425°F for 10 minutes.*

---

# Grated Beet & Celery Salad

Raw beets have a great crunchy texture. In this Russian salad, their flavor is brought out by marinating the beets in a cider dressing.

**Serves 4–6**
1 pound uncooked beets, peeled and grated
4 celery stalks, finely chopped

2 tablespoons apple juice
fresh herbs, to garnish

**For the dressing**
1 tablespoon cider vinegar
4 scallions, finely sliced
2 tablespoons chopped fresh parsley
3 tablespoons sunflower oil
salt and ground black pepper

**1** Toss the beets and celery with the apple juice in a bowl until well mixed.

**2** Make the dressing. Put the vinegar, scallions and parsley in a small bowl and whisk in the oil until well blended. Season with salt and pepper to taste, then stir half the dressing into the beet mixture.

**3** Drizzle the remaining dressing on the salad, cover it and chill for 2 hours. Garnish with fresh herbs and serve.

# Beet & Orange Salad

This is a classic combination for a refreshing salad.

**Serves 4**
1 small lettuce, shredded
8 cooked baby beets, halved
2 oranges, peeled and segmented

2 tablespoons orange juice
1 tablespoon lemon juice
2 tablespoons olive oil
1 teaspoon sugar
2 teaspoons snipped fresh chives, plus extra to garnish

**1** Place the lettuce on a serving plate and top with the beet and orange segments in a circle.
**2** Whisk together the remaining ingredients and pour onto the salad. Garnish with extra chives and serve.

# Fennel, Orange & Arugula Salad

This light and refreshing salad is ideal for serving with spicy or rich foods.

**Serves 4**
2 oranges
1 fennel bulb
2 cups arugula leaves
⅓ cup pitted black olives

**For the dressing**
1 tablespoon balsamic vinegar
1 small garlic clove, crushed
2 tablespoons extra virgin olive oil
salt and ground black pepper

**1** With a vegetable peeler, cut thin strips of zest from the oranges, leaving the pith behind. Cut the pieces into thin matchstick strips. Set them aside.

**2** Peel the oranges, removing all the white pith. Slice them into thin rounds and discard any seeds. Bring a small pan of water to a boil, add the strips of zest and cook for 2–3 minutes. Drain and dry on paper towels.

**3** Cut the fennel bulb in half lengthwise and slice across the bulb as thinly as possible, preferably in a food processor fitted with a slicing disk, or using a mandoline.

**4** Combine the orange rounds and fennel slices in a serving bowl and toss with the arugula leaves.

**5** Make the dressing. Mix the vinegar and garlic in a bowl. Whisk in the oil, then season with salt and pepper to taste. Pour the dressing onto the salad, toss well and let stand for a few minutes. Sprinkle with the black olives and garnish with the blanched strips of orange zest before serving.

**Cook's Tip**
*Although extra virgin olive oil is expensive, it is worth investing in it for salad dressings, as it has by far the best flavor.*

# Fruit & Nut Coleslaw

A delicious and nutritious mixture of crunchy vegetables, fruit and nuts, tossed together in a mayonnaise dressing.

**Serves 6**
8 ounces white cabbage
1 large carrot
¾ cup dried apricots
½ cup walnuts
½ cup hazelnuts
⅔ cup raisins
2 tablespoons chopped
   fresh parsley
7 tablespoons light mayonnaise
5 tablespoons plain yogurt
salt and ground black pepper
fresh chives, to garnish

**1** Finely shred the cabbage, coarsely grate the carrot and place both in a large mixing bowl.

**2** Roughly chop the dried apricots, walnuts and hazelnuts. Stir them into the cabbage and carrot mixture with the raisins and chopped parsley.

**3** In a separate bowl, mix the mayonnaise and yogurt and season to taste with salt and pepper.

**4** Add the mayonnaise mixture to the cabbage mixture and toss together to mix. Cover and set aside in a cool place for at least 30 minutes before serving, to let the flavors mingle. Garnish with a few fresh chives and serve.

---

**Variations**
• *For a salad that is lower in fat, use low-fat yogurt and reduced-calorie mayonnaise.*
• *Instead of walnuts and hazelnuts, use sliced almonds and chopped pistachios.*
• *Omit the dried apricots and add a cored and chopped, unpeeled apple.*
• *Substitute other dried fruit or a mixture for the apricots—try nectarines, peaches or prunes.*

---

# Panzanella

Open-textured, Italian-style bread is essential for this colorful Tuscan salad.

**Serves 6**
10 thick slices day-old Italian style
   bread, about 10 ounces
1 cucumber, peeled and cut
   into chunks
5 tomatoes, seeded and diced
1 large red onion, chopped
1 cup pitted black or green olives
20 fresh basil leaves, torn

**For the dressing**
4 tablespoons extra virgin olive oil
1 tablespoon red or white
   wine vinegar
salt and ground black pepper

**1** Soak the bread in water to cover for about 2 minutes, then lift it out and squeeze gently, first with your hands and then in a dish towel to remove any excess water.

**2** Make the dressing. Place the oil, vinegar and seasoning in a screw-top jar. Close the lid tightly and shake vigorously. Mix the cucumber, tomatoes, onion and olives in a bowl.

**3** Break the bread into chunks and add to the bowl with the basil. Pour the dressing on the salad, and toss before serving.

# Date, Orange & Carrot Salad

A simple oil-free dressing is perfect on this juicy salad.

**Serves 4**
1 head lettuce
2 carrots, finely grated
2 oranges, segmented
⅔ cup fresh dates, pitted and
   sliced lengthwise
2 tablespoons toasted almonds
2 tablespoons lemon juice
1 teaspoon sugar
¼ teaspoon salt
1 tablespoon orange flower water

**1** Spread out the lettuce leaves on a platter. Place the carrot in the center. Surround it with the oranges, dates and almonds.
**2** Mix the lemon juice, sugar, salt and orange flower water. Sprinkle on the salad and serve chilled.

# Caesar Salad

There are few dishes more famous than this popular combination of crisp lettuce leaves and Parmesan in a fresh egg dressing.

**Serves 4**
2 large garlic cloves, halved
3 tablespoons extra virgin olive oil
4 slices whole-wheat bread
1 small romaine lettuces
2-ounce piece of Parmesan cheese, shaved or coarsely grated

**For the dressing**
1 egg
2 teaspoons French mustard
1 teaspoon vegetarian Worcestershire sauce
2 tablespoons fresh lemon juice
2 tablespoons extra virgin olive oil
salt and ground black pepper

**1** Preheat the oven to 375°F. Rub the inside of a salad bowl with one of the half cloves of garlic.

**2** Heat the oil gently with the remaining garlic in a frying pan for 5 minutes, then remove and discard the garlic.

**3** Remove the crusts from the bread and cut the crumb into small cubes. Toss these in the garlic-flavored oil, making sure that they are well coated. Spread out the bread cubes on a baking sheet, and bake for about 10 minutes, until crisp. Remove from the oven, then let cool.

**4** Separate the lettuce leaves, wash and dry them and arrange in a shallow salad bowl. Chill until ready to serve.

**5** Make the dressing. Bring a small pan of water to a boil, lower the egg into the water and boil for 1 minute only. Crack it into a bowl. Use a teaspoon to scoop out and discard any softly set egg white. Using a balloon whisk, beat in the French mustard, Worcestershire sauce, lemon juice and olive oil, then season with salt and pepper to taste.

**6** Sprinkle the Parmesan on the salad and then drizzle the dressing. Sprinkle on the croutons. Take the salad to the table, toss lightly and serve immediately.

# Mixed Leaf & Herb Salad with Toasted Seeds

This simple salad is the perfect antidote to a rich, heavy meal, as it contains fresh herbs that can aid the digestion.

**Serves 4**
4 cups mixed salad greens
2 cups mixed salad herbs, such as cilantro, parsley, basil and arugula
2 tablespoons pumpkin seeds
2 tablespoons sunflower seeds

**For the dressing**
4 tablespoons extra virgin olive oil
1 tablespoon balsamic vinegar
$1/2$ teaspoon Dijon mustard
salt and ground black pepper

**1** Start by making the dressing. Combine the olive oil, balsamic vinegar and mustard in a screw-top jar. Add salt and pepper to taste. Close the jar tightly, then shake the dressing vigorously until well combined.

**2** Mix the salad and herb leaves in a large bowl.

**3** Toast the pumpkin and sunflower seeds in a dry frying pan over medium heat for 2 minutes, until golden, tossing frequently to prevent them from burning. Let the seeds cool slightly before sprinkling them on the salad.

**4** Pour the dressing on the salad and toss gently with your hands until the leaves are well coated. Serve immediately.

**Variations**
• *Balsamic vinegar adds a rich, sweet taste to the dressing, but red or white wine vinegar could be used instead.*
• *A few nasturtium flowers would look very pretty in this salad, as would borage flowers.*
• *Substitute your favorite seeds for those given here.*

# Split-Top Bread

As its name suggests, this bread is so called because of the center split. Some bakers mold the dough in two loaves, which join together when the dough is proved but retain the characteristic crack after baking.

**Makes I loaf**
5 cups bread flour, plus extra
   for dusting
2 teaspoons salt
½ ounce fresh yeast
1¼ cups lukewarm water
4 tablespoons lukewarm milk

**I** Lightly grease a 2-pound loaf pan. Sift the flour and salt into a bowl and make a well in the center. Mix the yeast with half the lukewarm water in a bowl, then stir in the remaining water.

**2** Pour the yeast mixture into the center of the flour. Gradually mix in enough of the surrounding flour to make a thick, smooth batter. Sprinkle a little more flour on the batter and set in a warm place for about 20 minutes, until bubbles appear in the batter. Add the milk and remaining flour; mix into a firm dough.

**3** Knead on a lightly floured surface for 10 minutes, until smooth and elastic. Place in a lightly oiled bowl, cover with lightly oiled plastic wrap and set aside in a warm place for 1–1¼ hours or until almost doubled in bulk.

**4** Punch down the dough, then shape it into a rectangle the length of the pan. Roll up lengthwise, tuck the ends under and place, seam-side down, in the pan. Cover and set in a warm spot to rise for 20–30 minutes or until almost doubled in size.

**5** Using a sharp knife, make one deep central slash the length of the bread; dust with flour. Leave for 10–15 minutes. Preheat the oven to 450°F.

**6** Bake for 15 minutes, then reduce the oven temperature to 400°F. Bake for 20–25 more minutes or until the bread is golden and sounds hollow when tapped on the bottom. Turn out onto a wire rack to cool.

# Wheat Bread

The dough for this quick and easy bread requires no kneading and takes only a minute to mix. The bread should stay moist for several days.

12 cups whole-wheat flour
1 tablespoon salt
1 tablespoon active dry yeast
1 tablespoon brown sugar
5 cups warm water (95–100°F)

**Makes 3 loaves**
oil, for greasing

**I** Thoroughly grease three loaf pans, each measuring about 8½ x 4½ x 2½ inches and set aside in a warm place. Sift the flour and salt into a large bowl and warm slightly to take off the chill.

**2** Stir in the dry yeast and sugar. Make a well in the center and pour in the water. Mix for about 1 minute, working the sides into the middle. The dough should be slippery.

**3** Divide among the prepared pans, cover with oiled plastic wrap and set in a warm place, for 30 minutes or until the dough has risen to within ½ inch of the top of the pans.

**4** Meanwhile, preheat the oven to 400°F. Bake for 40 minutes or until the loaves are crisp and sound hollow when tapped on the bottom. Cool on a wire rack.

---

**Cook's Tips**
• Most breads require a raising or leavening agent, and yeast is the most common, although there are a number of others.
• Active dry yeast is widely available. There is no need to mix it with liquid before adding it to the flour and other dry ingredients. Lukewarm liquid is then added.
• Ordinary dry yeast must be mixed with a little warm liquid, and sometimes with sugar as well. When it has dissolved and the mixture is frothy it can be added to the dried ingredients.

# Cottage Bread

Always an attractive bread, this makes a good centerpiece for a casual lunch or supper.

**Makes 1 large round loaf**

6 cups bread flour, plus extra
   for dusting
2 teaspoons salt
$^3/_4$ ounce fresh yeast
$1^2/_3$ cups lukewarm water
oil, for greasing

**1** Lightly grease two baking sheets. Sift the flour and salt into a large bowl and make a well in the center. Dissolve the yeast in $^2/_3$ cup of the water. Add to the flour, with the remaining water, and mix into a firm dough.

**2** Knead the dough on a lightly floured surface for 10 minutes. Place in a lightly oiled bowl, cover with lightly oiled plastic wrap and set in a warm place to rise for about 1 hour or until doubled in bulk.

**3** Punch down the dough on a lightly floured surface. Knead for 2–3 minutes, then divide the dough into two-thirds and one-third; shape each to a ball.

**4** Place the balls of dough on the prepared baking sheets. Cover with inverted bowls and set in a warm place to rise, for about 30 minutes.

**5** Gently flatten the top of the larger ball and cut a cross in the center, about 2 inches across. Brush with a little water and place the smaller ball on top. Make small cuts around each ball.

**6** Carefully press a hole through both balls, using the thumb and first two fingers of one hand. Cover with lightly oiled plastic wrap and let rest in a warm place for about 10 minutes.

**7** Heat the oven to 425°F and place the baking sheet on the lower shelf. The loaf will finish expanding as the oven heats up. Bake for 35–40 minutes or until golden brown and sounding hollow when tapped. Cool on a wire rack.

# Whole-wheat Bread with Seeds

This seeded loaf looks rustic and is great for picnics and other *al fresco* meals.

**Makes 4 rounds**

$^3/_4$ ounce fresh yeast
$1^1/_4$ cups lukewarm milk
1 teaspoon sugar
2 cups whole-wheat flour
2 cups bread flour, plus extra
   for dusting
1 teaspoon salt
$^1/_4$ cup chilled butter, cubed
1 egg, lightly beaten
oil, for greasing
2 tablespoons mixed seeds

**1** Mix the yeast with a little of the milk and the sugar until it dissolves to make a paste. Sift both types of flour and the salt into a large warmed mixing bowl. Rub in the butter until the mixture resembles bread crumbs.

**2** Add the yeast mixture, remaining milk and egg and mix into a fairly soft dough. Knead on a floured surface for 15 minutes. Place in a lightly oiled bowl, cover with lightly oiled plastic wrap and let rise in a warm place for at least 1 hour, until doubled in bulk.

**3** Punch down the dough and knead it for 10 minutes. Divide the dough into four pieces and shape them into flattish rounds. Place them on a floured baking sheet and let rise for about 15 more minutes.

**4** Preheat the oven to 400°F. Sprinkle the loaves with the mixed seeds. Bake for about 20 minutes, until golden and firm. Cool on wire racks.

**Cook's Tip**
*Fresh yeast is available at some food markets. $^1/_2$ ounce fresh yeast is the same as 1 tablespoon dried. Put it into a bowl and then mix with a little lukewarm liquid before adding to the dry ingredients.*

# Whole-grain Bread

Serve this delicious bread warm, so the house is infused with its welcoming fresh-baked aroma.

**Makes 1 round loaf**
4 cups whole-wheat
  flour plus extra
  for dusting
2 teaspoons salt
½ ounce fresh yeast

1¼ cups lukewarm water or milk
  and water mixed
oil, for greasing

**For the topping**
2 tablespoons water
½ teaspoon salt
wheat flakes or cracked wheat,
  to sprinkle

**1** Lightly flour a baking sheet. Sift the flour and salt into a large bowl. Place in a very low oven for 5 minutes to warm.

**2** Put the yeast into a small bowl and add a little of the water or milk mixture. Mix with a fork, then blend in the remaining liquid. Add the yeast mixture to the flour and mix to form a dough.

**3** Knead on a floured surface for about 10 minutes. Place in a lightly oiled bowl, cover with lightly oiled plastic wrap and set in a warm place for 1¼ hours or until doubled in bulk.

**4** Punch down the dough, knead it for 2–3 minutes, then roll it into a ball. Flatten it slightly so that it resembles a plump round cushion in appearance. Place on the prepared baking sheet, cover with an inverted bowl and set in a warm place to rise for 30–45 minutes.

**5** Preheat the oven to 450°F. Mix the water and salt for the topping and brush on the bread. Sprinkle with wheat flakes or cracked wheat.

**6** Bake for 15 minutes, then reduce the oven temperature to 400°F and bake for 20 more minutes or until the bread is firm to the touch and sounds hollow when tapped on the bottom. Cool on a wire rack.

# Irish Soda Bread

Traditional Irish soda bread can be prepared in minutes and is excellent served warm, with plenty of butter. You can use all white flour, if preferred, to create a bread with a finer texture.

**Makes 1 round loaf**
oil, for greasing
2 cups unbleached
  all-purpose flour

2 cups whole-wheat flour, plus
  extra for dusting
1 teaspoon salt
2 teaspoons baking soda
2 teaspoons cream of tartar
3 tablespoons butter
1 teaspoon sugar
1½–1⅔ cups buttermilk

**1** Preheat the oven to 375°F. Lightly grease a baking sheet and set aside. Sift both types of flour and the salt into a large bowl.

**2** Add the baking soda and cream of tartar, then rub in the butter. Stir in the sugar.

**3** Pour in enough buttermilk to mix into a soft dough. Do not over-mix or the bread will be heavy and tough. Shape into a round on a lightly floured surface.

**4** Place on the prepared baking sheet and mark a cross using a sharp knife, cutting deep into the dough.

**5** Dust lightly with whole-wheat flour and bake the loaf for 35–45 minutes or until well risen. The bread should sound hollow when tapped on the bottom. Cool slightly on a wire rack, but serve warm.

**Variations**
• Shape into two small loaves and bake for 25–30 minutes.
• Sour cream may be used instead of buttermilk, as both have a high lactic acid content and so react with the soda.

# Sour Rye Bread

You need to plan ahead to make this loaf, as the starter takes a day or two.

**Makes 2 loaves**

4 cups rye flour

4 cups white flour, plus extra
    for dusting

1 tablespoon salt

$^1/_4$-ounce envelope active
    dry yeast

2 tablespoons butter, softened

$2^1/_2$ cups warm water

oil, for greasing

1 tablespoon caraway seeds,
    for sprinkling

**For the sourdough starter**

4 tablespoons rye flour

3 tablespoons warm milk

**1** For the starter, mix the rye flour and milk in a small bowl. Cover with plastic wrap and set in a warm place for 1–2 days or until it smells pleasantly sour.

**2** Sift both types of flour and the salt into a large bowl and stir in the yeast. Make a well in the center and add the butter, water and sourdough starter. Mix into a soft dough.

**3** Knead the dough on a floured surface for 10 minutes. Put it in a clean bowl, cover with lightly oiled plastic wrap and set in a warm place to rise for 1 hour or until doubled in bulk.

**4** Knead for 1 minute. Divide the dough in half. Shape each piece into a 6-inch round. Place on greased baking sheets. Cover with oiled plastic wrap and let rise for 30 minutes.

**5** Preheat the oven to 400°F. Brush the loaves with water, sprinkle with caraway seeds and bake them for 35–40 minutes. The loaves should have browned and sound hollow when tapped on the bottom. Cool on a wire rack.

> **Cook's Tip**
> Sour rye bread keeps fresh for up to a week. This recipe can also be made without yeast, but it will be much denser.

# Pan de Cebada

This Spanish bread is perfect for serving with chilled soup or a healthy dip.

**Makes 1 large loaf**

**For the sourdough starter**

$1^1/_2$ cups cornmeal

scant $2^1/_2$ cups water

2 cups whole-wheat flour,
    plus extra

$^3/_4$ cup barley flour

oil, for greasing

**For the dough**

cornmeal, for dusting

$^3/_4$ ounce fresh yeast

3 tablespoons lukewarm water

2 cups whole-wheat flour

1 tablespoon salt

**1** In a pan, mix the cornmeal for the sourdough starter with half the water, then stir in the remainder. Stir over low heat until thickened. Transfer to a large bowl and set aside to cool. Mix in the whole-wheat and barley flours. Knead on a lightly floured surface for 5 minutes, then return the bowl, cover with lightly oiled plastic wrap and set in a warm place for 36 hours.

**2** Make the dough. Dust a baking sheet with cornmeal. In a small bowl, mix the yeast with the water, then add to the starter with the whole-wheat flour and salt and work into a dough. Knead on a lightly floured surface for 4–5 minutes.

**3** Put the dough in a lightly oiled bowl, cover with oiled plastic wrap and set in a warm place to rise for $1^1/_2$–2 hours.

**4** Punch down the dough, shape it into a plump round and sprinkle with a little cornmeal. Put it on the prepared baking sheet and cover with a large upturned bowl. Set in a warm place to rise, for about 1 hour or until almost doubled in bulk.

**5** Place an empty roasting pan in the bottom of the oven. Preheat the oven to 425°F. Pour $1^1/_4$ cups cold water into the pan. Lift the bowl off the bread and place the baking sheet in the oven. Bake for 10 minutes. Remove the pan of water, reduce the oven temperature to 375°F and bake the bread for 20 more minutes. Cool on a wire rack.

# Walnut Bread

This wholesome and delicious enriched whole-wheat bread is filled with walnuts. It is the perfect companion for cheese, and also tastes wonderful with salads.

**Makes 2 loaves**
*oil, for greasing*
*¼ cup butter*

*3 cups whole-wheat flour, plus extra or dusting*
*I cup bread flour*
*I tablespoon light brown sugar*
*I½ teaspoons salt*
*¾ ounce fresh yeast*
*generous I cup lukewarm milk*
*I½ cups walnut pieces*

**I** Lightly grease two baking sheets. Melt the butter in a small pan until it starts to turn brown, then set aside to cool. Mix the flours, sugar and salt in a large bowl and make a well in the center. Mix the yeast with half the milk. Add to the well with the remaining milk. Strain the cool butter into the liquids in the well and mix with your hand, gradually incorporating the surrounding flour to make a batter, then a moist dough.

**2** Knead for 6–8 minutes. Place in a lightly oiled bowl, cover with lightly oiled plastic wrap and set in a warm place to rise for I hour or until doubled in bulk.

**3** Gently punch down the dough on a lightly floured surface. Press or roll it flat, then sprinkle on the nuts, press them in and roll up the dough. Return it to the oiled bowl, re-cover and set, in a warm place for 30 minutes.

**4** Turn out onto a lightly floured surface, divide in half and shape each piece into a ball. Place on the baking sheets, cover with lightly oiled plastic wrap and set in a warm place to rise for 45 minutes or until doubled in bulk.

**5** Meanwhile, preheat the oven to 425°F. Using a sharp knife, slash the top of each loaf three times. Bake for about 35 minutes or until the loaves sound hollow when tapped on the bottom. Cool on a wire rack.

# Focaccia with Green Peppercorns & Rock Salt

There's something irresistible about a loaf of freshly baked focaccia with its dimpled surface and fabulous flavor.

**Makes I loaf**
*3 cups bread flour, plus extra for dusting*
*½ teaspoon salt*
*2 teaspoons active dry yeast*

*2 teaspoons drained green peppercorns in brine, lightly crushed*
*5 teaspoons fruity extra virgin olive oil*
*about I cup lukewarm water*
*4 teaspoons roughly crushed rock salt, for the topping*
*fresh basil leaves, to garnish*

**I** Sift the flour and salt into a mixing bowl. Stir in the yeast and peppercorns. Make a well in the center and add I tablespoon of the oil, with half the water. Mix, gradually incorporating the flour and adding more water to make a soft dough.

**2** Knead the dough on a lightly floured surface for 10 minutes. Return to the clean, lightly oiled bowl, cover with lightly oiled plastic wrap and set in a warm place until doubled in bulk.

**3** Punch down the dough and knead lightly for 2–3 minutes. Place on an oiled baking sheet and pat out to an oval. Cover with lightly oiled plastic wrap and set for 30 minutes.

**4** Preheat the oven to 375°F. Make a few dimples in the surface of the dough with your fingers. Drizzle on the remaining oil and sprinkle on the salt. Bake for 25–30 minutes, until pale gold. Sprinkle on basil leaves and serve warm.

> **Cook's Tip**
> *Kneading is a vital step in bread-making, as it develops the gluten in the flour. Press and stretch the dough, using the heel of your hand and turning the dough frequently.*

# Onion Focaccia

This pizza-like flat bread is characterized by its soft dimpled surface, sometimes dredged simply with coarse sea salt, or as here, with red onions.

**Makes 2 loaves**

6 cups all-purpose flour, plus extra
   for dusting
1/2 teaspoon salt
1/2 teaspoon sugar

1 tablespoon active dry yeast
4 tablespoons extra virgin olive oil,
   plus extra for greasing
scant 2 cups lukewarm water

**To finish**
2 red onions, thinly sliced
3 tablespoons extra virgin olive oil
1 tablespoon coarse salt

**1** Sift the flour, salt and sugar into a large bowl. Stir in the yeast, oil and water and mix into a dough using a round-bladed knife. Add a little extra water if the dough is dry.

**2** Knead on a lightly floured surface for about 10 minutes, then put the dough in a clean, lightly oiled bowl and cover with lightly oiled plastic wrap. Set in a warm place for about 1 hour, until doubled in bulk.

**3** Preheat the oven to 400°F. Place two 10-inch metal cake rings on baking sheets. Oil the insides of the rings and the baking sheets.

**4** Halve the dough and roll each piece into a 10-inch round. Press into the rings, cover each with a dampened dish towel and set for 30 minutes to rise.

**5** With your fingers, make dimples about 1 inch apart, in the dough. Cover and leave for 20 more minutes.

**6** To finish, sprinkle the surface of the two loaves with the sliced onions and drizzle on the olive oil. Sprinkle on the coarse salt, then a little cold water, to stop a crust from forming. Bake for about 25 minutes, sprinkling with water once during cooking. Cool on a wire rack.

# Ciabatta

This irregular-shaped Italian bread is made with a very wet dough flavored with olive oil; cooking produces a bread with holes and a wonderfully chewy crust.

**Makes 3 loaves**
**For the biga starter**
1/4 ounce fresh yeast
3/4–scant 1 cup lukewarm water
3 cups unbleached all-purpose
   flour, plus extra for dusting

**For the dough**
oil, for greasing
1/2 ounce fresh yeast
1 2/3 cups lukewarm water
4 tablespoons lukewarm milk
5 cups bread flour
2 teaspoons salt
3 tablespoons extra virgin olive oil

**1** Mix the yeast for the biga starter with a little of the water. Sift the flour into a large bowl. Gradually mix in the yeast mixture and add enough of the remaining water to form a firm dough.

**2** Knead the dough for about 5 minutes, until smooth and elastic. Return it to the bowl, cover with lightly oiled plastic wrap and set in a warm place for 12–15 hours or until the dough has risen and is starting to collapse.

**3** Sprinkle three baking sheets with flour. Mix the yeast for the dough with a little of the water until creamy, then mix in the remaining water. Gradually add this yeast mixture to the biga and mix them together.

**4** Mix in the milk, beating thoroughly with a wooden spoon. Using your hand, gradually beat in the flour, lifting the dough as you mix. Mixing the dough will take 15 minutes or more and form a very wet dough, impossible to knead on a work surface.

**5** Beat in the salt and olive oil. Cover with lightly oiled plastic wrap and let rise, in a warm place, for 1 1/2–2 hours or until doubled in bulk.

**6** Using a spoon, carefully put one-third of the dough at a time onto the prepared baking sheets, trying to avoid punching down the dough in the process.

**7** Using floured hands, shape into rough rectangular loaf shapes, about 1 inch thick. Flatten slightly with splayed fingers. Sprinkle with flour and let rise in a warm place for 30 minutes.

**8** Preheat the oven to 425°F. Bake the loaves for 25–30 minutes or until golden brown. The loaves should sound hollow when tapped on the bottom. Cool on a wire rack.

---

**Cook's Tip**
*Ciabatta is delicious served warm, but not hot.*

# Olive Bread

A mixture of olives com-
bined with olive oil make
this wonderful Italian bread.

**Makes 1 loaf**
*oil, for greasing*
*2½ cups bread flour, plus extra*
*½ cup whole-wheat flour*
*¼-ounce envelope active*
  *dry yeast*
*½ teaspoon salt*
*scant 1 cup lukewarm water*
*1 tablespoon extra virgin olive oil,*
  *plus extra for brushing*
*1 cup pitted black and green*
  *olives, coarsely chopped*

**1** Lightly grease a baking sheet. Mix the flours, yeast and salt together in a large bowl and make a well in the center.

**2** Add the water and oil to the well in the flour and mix into a soft dough. Knead on a lightly floured surface until smooth and elastic, then place in a lightly oiled bowl, cover with lightly oiled plastic wrap and set in a warm place to rise for 1 hour or until doubled in bulk.

**3** Punch down the dough on a lightly floured surface. Flatten it and sprinkle on the olives. Fold up and knead to distribute the olives. Let rest for 5 minutes, then shape into an oval loaf. Place on the prepared baking sheet.

**4** Make six deep cuts in the top of the loaf, and gently push the sections over. Cover with lightly oiled plastic wrap and set in a warm place to rise for 30–45 minutes or until doubled in size.

**5** Meanwhile, preheat the oven to 400°F. Brush the bread with olive oil and bake for 35 minutes. Cool on a wire rack.

> **Variation**
> *Increase the proportion of whole-wheat flour to make the bread more rustic.*

# Challah

With its braided shape, light texture and rich flavor, Challah is perfect for every special occasion, not just the Jewish Sabbath.

**Makes 1 large loaf**
*oil, for greasing*
*5 cups bread flour, plus extra*
*2 teaspoons salt*
*¾ ounce fresh yeast*
*scant 1 cup lukewarm water*
*2 tablespoons sugar*
*2 eggs*
*6 tablespoons butter, melted*

**For the topping**
*1 egg yolk*
*1 tablespoon water*
*2 teaspoons poppy seeds*

**1** Lightly grease a baking sheet. Sift the flour and salt into a bowl and make a well in the center. Mix the yeast with the water and sugar; add to the well with the eggs and melted butter. Gradually mix in the flour to form a soft dough.

**2** Knead on a lightly floured surface for 10 minutes. Place in a lightly oiled bowl, cover with lightly oiled plastic wrap and set in a warm place to rise for 1 hour or until doubled in bulk.

**3** Punch down, re-cover and let rise again in a warm place for about 1 hour. Punch down, turn out onto a lightly floured surface and knead gently. Divide into four equal pieces. Roll each piece into a rope about 18 inches long. Line them up next to each other. Pinch the ends together at one end.

**4** Starting from the right, lift the first rope over the second and the third over the fourth. Place the fourth rope between the first and second ropes. Repeat, starting from the right, and continue until braided. Tuck the ends under and place the loaf on the baking sheet. Cover with oiled plastic wrap and set in a warm place to rise for 30–45 minutes or until doubled in size.

**5** Preheat the oven to 400°F. Beat the egg yolk and water for the topping together. Gently brush the loaf with the mixture. Sprinkle on the poppy seeds and bake for 35–40 minutes, until deep golden brown. Cool on a wire rack.

# Dill Bread

The slightly aniseed flavor of fresh dill works well in this tasty bread enriched with cottage cheese.

**Makes 2 loaves**

7½ cups bread flour, plus extra
  for dusting
4 teaspoons active dry yeast
2 tablespoons sugar
4 teaspoons salt
2 cups lukewarm water
4 tablespoons light olive oil, plus
  extra for greasing
½ onion, chopped
a large bunch of fresh dill,
  finely chopped
2 eggs, lightly beaten
½ cup cottage cheese
milk, for glazing

**1** Mix 3 cups of the flour with the yeast, sugar and salt in a large bowl. Make a well in the center. Pour in the water. Beat, gradually incorporating the surrounding flour to make a smooth batter. Cover and set in a warm place to rise for 45 minutes.

**2** Meanwhile, heat 1 tablespoon of the oil in a small pan. Add the onion and fry over low heat, stirring occasionally, for 5 minutes, until soft. Set aside to cool.

**3** When the onion is cool, stir it into the risen batter. Stir in the dill, eggs, cottage cheese and remaining oil, then gradually add the remaining flour until the mixture forms a dough.

**4** Knead the dough on a floured surface for 10 minutes. Place in a bowl, cover with oiled plastic wrap and set in a warm place for 1–1½ hours, until doubled in bulk.

**5** Grease a large baking sheet. Cut the dough in half and shape into two rounds. Cover again and let rise for 30 minutes.

**6** Meanwhile, preheat the oven to 375°F. Score the top of each round, making a criss-cross pattern on the entire surface. Brush with the milk. Bake for about 50 minutes, until the loaves are golden brown and sound hollow when tapped on the bottom. Cool on wire racks.

# Russian Potato Bread

Another extremely attractive bread, this keeps very well, thanks to the mashed potatoes in the dough.

**Makes 1 loaf**
oil, for greasing
8 ounces potatoes, peeled
  and diced
3 cups bread flour
1 cup whole-wheat flour, plus
  extra for sprinkling
¼-ounce envelope active
  dry yeast
½ teaspoon caraway
  seeds, crushed
2 tablespoons butter
salt

**1** Lightly grease a baking sheet. Put the potatoes in a pan of lightly salted water and bring to a boil. Cook until tender, then drain, reserving ⅔ cup of the cooking water. Mash the potatoes and press them through a sieve into a bowl. Let cool.

**2** Mix both types of flour in a large bowl. Add the yeast, seeds and 2 teaspoons salt, then rub in the butter. Mix the reserved potato water and sieved potatoes. Gradually work this mixture into the flour mixture to form a soft dough.

**3** Knead on a lightly floured surface for 8–10 minutes. Place in a lightly oiled bowl, cover with lightly oiled plastic wrap and set in a warm place to rise for 1 hour or until doubled in bulk.

**4** Punch down the dough and knead it gently. Shape into a plump oval loaf, about 7 inches long. Place on the prepared baking sheet and sprinkle with a little whole-wheat flour.

**5** Cover the loaf with lightly oiled plastic wrap and set in a warm place for 30 minutes or until doubled in size. Meanwhile, preheat the oven to 400°F.

**6** Using a sharp knife, slash the top with 6–8 diagonal cuts to make a criss-cross effect. Bake for 30–35 minutes or until the bread is golden and sounds hollow when tapped on the bottom. Cool on a wire rack.

# Spiral Herb Bread

When cut, this loaf looks very pretty with its swirls of garlic and herbs. It tastes pretty good, too.

**Makes 2 loaves**

3 cups bread flour, plus extra
    for dusting
3 cups whole-wheat flour
2 ¼-ounce envelope active
    dry yeast
2½ cups lukewarm water

oil, for greasing
2 tablespoons butter
1 bunch of scallions,
    finely chopped
1 garlic clove, finely chopped
1 large bunch of fresh parsley,
    finely chopped
1 egg, lightly beaten
salt and ground black pepper
milk, for glazing

**1** Mix the flours in a large bowl. Stir in 1 tablespoon salt and the yeast. Make a well in the center and pour in the water. Beat, gradually incorporating the flour to make a rough dough.

**2** Knead the dough on a floured surface for 8–10 minutes. Return it to the bowl, cover with lightly oiled plastic wrap and set in a warm place to rise for 2 hours, until doubled in bulk.

**3** Meanwhile, melt the butter in a pan and cook the scallions and garlic over low heat, until softened. Season with salt and pepper, stir in the parsley and set aside.

**4** Grease two 9 x 5-inch bread pans. When the dough has risen, cut it in half, then roll each half into a 14 x 9-inch rectangle. Brush with the beaten egg and divide the herb mixture between them, spreading it just to the edges.

**5** Roll up each dough rectangle from a long side and pinch the short ends together to seal. Place in the pans, seam-side down. Cover and set in a warm place until the dough has risen above the rims of the pans.

**6** Preheat the oven to 375°F. Brush the loaves with milk and bake for 55 minutes, until they are golden and sound hollow when tapped on the bottom. Cool on a wire rack.

# Three-grain Twist

A mixture of grains gives this bread a delightful nutty flavor.

**Makes 1 loaf**
2 tablespoons malt extract
2 cups boiling water
2 cups bread flour, plus extra
    for dusting
1½ teaspoons salt
2 cups whole-wheat flour

2 cups rye flour
1 tablespoon active dry yeast
pinch of sugar
2 tablespoons linseed
scant 1 cup medium oats
3 tablespoons sunflower seeds
oil, for greasing

**1** Stir the malt extract into the boiling water. Let the mixture cool until it is lukewarm.

**2** Sift the white flour and salt into a mixing bowl and add the other flours. Stir in the yeast and sugar. Set aside 1 teaspoon of the linseed and add the rest to the flour mixture with the oats and sunflower seeds. Make a well in the center.

**3** Pour the malted water into the well and gradually mix in the flour to make a soft dough, adding extra water if necessary. Knead on a floured surface for about 5 minutes, then return to the clean bowl, cover with lightly oiled plastic wrap and set in a warm place to rise for about 2 hours, until doubled in bulk.

**4** Flour a baking sheet. Knead the dough again and divide it in half. Roll each half into a 12-inch long sausage. Twist them together, dampen the ends and press to seal. Lift the twist onto the prepared baking sheet. Brush it with water, sprinkle with the remaining linseed and cover loosely with a large plastic bag (ballooning it to trap the air inside). Set in a warm place until well risen. Preheat the oven to 425°F.

**5** Bake the loaf for 10 minutes, then reduce the oven temperature to 400°F and cook for 20 more minutes or until the bread sounds hollow when it is tapped underneath. Cool on a wire rack.

# Sweet Potato Bread with Cinnamon & Walnuts

Spicy and sweet, this tastes great with savory dishes and as a teabread, with cream cheese.

**Makes 1 loaf**
1 medium sweet potato
4 cups white flour, plus extra
   for dusting
1 teaspoon ground cinnamon
1 teaspoon active dry yeast
²⁄₃ cup walnut pieces
1¼ cups warmed milk
salt and ground black pepper
oil, for greasing

**1** Bring a pan of water to a boil and cook the sweet potato whole, without peeling, for 45 minutes or until tender. Meanwhile, sift the flour and cinnamon into a large bowl. Stir in the dry yeast.

**2** Drain the sweet potato, cool it in cold water, then peel it. Mash the flesh with a fork, then mix it into the dry ingredients with the nuts and some salt and pepper.

**3** Make a well in the center of the mixture and pour in the milk. Mix with a round-bladed knife into a rough dough, then knead on a floured surface for 5 minutes.

**4** Return the dough to a bowl and cover with oiled plastic wrap. Set in a warm place to rise for 1 hour or until doubled in bulk. Turn out the dough and punch it down to remove any air bubbles. Knead again for a few minutes.

**5** Grease a 2-pound loaf pan lightly with oil and line the bottom with nonstick baking parchment. Shape the dough to fit the pan. Cover with lightly oiled plastic wrap and set in a warm place for 1 hour or until doubled in size.

**6** Preheat the oven to 400°F. Bake the bread for 25 minutes. Turn it out and tap the bottom; if it sounds hollow the bread is cooked. Cool on a wire rack.

# Polenta & Bell Pepper Bread

Full of Mediterranean flavors, this satisfying, sunshine-colored bread is best eaten while it is still warm, drizzled with a little virgin olive oil.

**Makes 2 loaves**
scant 1½ cups polenta
1 teaspoon salt
3 cups bread flour, plus extra
   for dusting
1 teaspoon sugar
¼-ounce envelope active
   dry yeast
1 red bell pepper, roasted, peeled
   and diced
1 tablespoon olive oil, plus extra
   for greasing
1¼ cups lukewarm water

**1** Mix the polenta, salt, flour, sugar and yeast in a large bowl. Stir in the diced red pepper until it is evenly distributed, then make a well in the center of the mixture. Grease two loaf pans.

**2** Add the warm water and the oil to the well in the dry ingredients and mix into a soft dough. Knead for 10 minutes. Place in an oiled bowl, cover with oiled plastic wrap and set in a warm place to rise for 1 hour, until doubled in bulk.

**3** Punch down the dough, knead it lightly, then divide it in half. Shape each piece into an oblong and place in a pan. Cover with oiled plastic wrap and let rise for 45 minutes. Preheat the oven to 425°F.

**4** Bake for 30 minutes, until golden and the loaves sound hollow when tapped underneath. Leave in the pans for about 5 minutes, then cool on a wire rack.

**Cook's Tip**
*Broil the pepper until blistered and beginning to char, then place in a bowl, cover with paper towels and set aside until cool enough to peel.*

# Sun-dried Tomato Bread

This is one bread that absolutely everyone seems to love. Chopped onion and sun-dried tomatoes give it an excellent flavor.

**Makes 4 small loaves**
6 cups all-purpose flour, plus extra
    for dusting
2 teaspoons salt
2 tablespoons sugar

I ounce fresh yeast
1²/₃–2 cups lukewarm milk
I tablespoon tomato paste
³/₄ cup sun-dried tomatoes in oil,
    drained and chopped, plus
    5 tablespoons oil from the jar
5 tablespoons extra virgin olive oil,
    plus extra for greasing
I large onion, chopped

**I** Sift the flour, salt and sugar into a bowl and make a well in the center. Put the yeast into a bowl, mix with ²/₃ cup of the milk and pour into the well in the flour.

**2** Stir the tomato paste into the remaining milk, then add to the well in the flour, with the tomato oil and olive oil.

**3** Mix the liquid ingredients, and gradually incorporate the surrounding flour to make a dough. Knead on a floured surface for about 10 minutes, then return the dough to the clean bowl, cover with lightly oiled plastic wrap and let rise in a warm place for about 2 hours.

**4** Punch down the dough, and add the tomatoes and onion. Knead until evenly distributed. Shape into four rounds and place on two greased baking sheets. Cover each pair with a dish towel and let rise again for about 45 minutes.

**5** Preheat the oven to 375°F. Bake the bread for 45 minutes or until the loaves sound hollow when you tap them underneath. Cool on a wire rack.

### Cook's Tip
*Use a pair of sharp kitchen scissors to cut up the tomatoes.*

# Warm Herb Bread

This mouthwatering Italian-style bread, flavored with basil, rosemary, olive oil and sun-dried tomatoes, is absolutely delicious served warm with fresh salads.

**Makes 3 loaves**
12 cups bread flour, plus extra
    for dusting
I tablespoon salt
I teaspoon sugar
¹/₄-ounce envelope active
    dry yeast

about 3³/₄ cups lukewarm water
³/₄ cup sun-dried tomatoes in oil,
    drained and roughly chopped
²/₃ cup virgin olive oil, plus extra
    for greasing
5 tablespoons chopped mixed
    fresh basil and rosemary

**To finish**
extra virgin olive oil
rosemary leaves
sea salt flakes

**I** Sift the flour and salt into a bowl. Stir in the sugar and yeast. Make a well in the center and add the water, tomatoes, oil and herbs. Beat well, gradually incorporating the surrounding flour.

**2** As the mixture becomes stiffer, bring it together with your hands. Mix into a soft but not sticky dough, adding a little extra water if needed.

**3** Knead the dough on a lightly floured surface for about 10 minutes, then return it to the bowl, cover loosely with oiled plastic wrap and put in a warm place for 30–40 minutes or until doubled in bulk.

**4** Knead the dough again until smooth and elastic, then cut it into three pieces. Shape each into an oval loaf about 7 inches long and place each on an oiled baking sheet. Slash the top of each loaf in a criss-cross pattern. Cover loosely and set in a warm place for 15–20 minutes, until well risen.

**5** Preheat the oven to 425°F. Brush the loaves with a little olive oil and sprinkle on the rosemary leaves and salt flakes. Cook for about 25 minutes, until golden brown. The bottoms should sound hollow when tapped.

# Spicy Millet Bread

This is a delicious spicy bread with a golden crust. Cut into wedges and serve warm with a thick soup.

**Makes I loaf**
1/2 cup millet
5 1/2 cups unbleached all-purpose flour, plus extra for dusting
2 teaspoons salt
1/4-ounce envelope active dry yeast
I teaspoon sugar
I teaspoon dried chile flakes (optional)
2 tablespoons butter
I onion, roughly chopped
I tablespoon cumin seeds
I teaspoon ground turmeric

**I** Bring a scant I cup water to a boil in a small pan. Add the millet, cover and simmer gently for 20 minutes, until the grains are soft and the water has been absorbed. Remove from heat and let cool until just warm.

**2** Mix the flour, salt, yeast, sugar and chile flakes, if using, in a large bowl. Stir in the millet, then add 1 2/3 cups warm water and mix into a soft dough.

**3** Knead the dough on a floured surface for 10 minutes, then place it in an oiled bowl and cover with oiled plastic wrap. Set in a warm place for I hour or until doubled in bulk.

**4** Meanwhile, melt the butter in a heavy frying pan, and fry the onion until softened. Add the cumin seeds and turmeric, and fry for 5–8 more minutes, stirring constantly, until the cumin seeds begin to pop. Set aside.

**5** Punch down the dough, knead it briefly again and shape it into a round. Place the onion mixture in the middle of the dough and bring the sides over to cover it. Seal well. Place the loaf on an oiled baking sheet, seam-side down, cover with oiled plastic wrap and set in a warm place for 45 minutes, until doubled in size. Preheat the oven to 425°F.

**6** Bake the bread for 30 minutes, until golden. It should sound hollow when tapped underneath. Cool on a wire rack.

# Cheese & Zucchini Cluster Bread

This unusual bread owes its moistness to grated zucchini, and its depth of flavor to freshly grated Parmesan cheese.

**Makes I loaf**
4 zucchini, coarsely grated
6 cups bread flour
2 1/4-ounce envelope active dry yeast
2/3 cup freshly grated Parmesan cheese
2 tablespoons olive oil, plus extra for greasing
milk, to glaze
poppy seeds or sesame seeds, to sprinkle
salt and ground black pepper

**I** Put the grated zucchini into a colander and sprinkle with salt. Stand the colander in a sink for about 20 minutes to drain the juices, then rinse the zucchini thoroughly, drain again and pat dry with paper towels.

**2** Sift the flour into a large bowl and add the yeast, Parmesan, 1/2 teaspoon salt and pepper to taste. Stir in the oil and zucchini, then add enough lukewarm water to make a firm but still soft dough.

**3** Knead the dough for about 10 minutes, then return it to the bowl, cover with lightly oiled plastic wrap and set in a warm place for about I hour or until doubled in bulk.

**4** Lightly grease a deep 9-inch cake pan. Punch down the dough and knead it again. Divide it into eight pieces and roll into smooth balls. Fit these into the pan, placing one in the center and the remainder around the outside.

**5** Glaze the loaf with a little milk and sprinkle on the seeds. Cover lightly with oiled plastic wrap and let rise in a warm place until the balls of dough have doubled in size.

**6** Meanwhile, preheat the oven to 400°F. Bake the loaf for 35–45 minutes, until it is golden brown and sounds hollow when tapped on the bottom. Cool on a wire rack and eat as soon as possible.

## Syrian Onion Bread

These unusual small breads come from Syria and have a spicy topping spiked with fresh mint.

**Makes 8 breads**

4 cups bread flour, plus extra
1 teaspoon salt
3/4 ounce fresh yeast
scant 1 1/4 cups lukewarm water

oil, for greasing

**For the topping**
4 tablespoons finely
  chopped onion
1 teaspoon ground cumin
2 teaspoons ground coriander
2 teaspoons chopped fresh mint
2 tablespoons olive oil

**1** Lightly flour two baking sheets. Sift the flour and salt together into a large bowl and make a well in the center. Cream the yeast with a little of the water, then mix in the remainder.

**2** Add the yeast mixture to the center of the flour and mix into a firm dough. Knead on a lightly floured surface for 8–10 minutes, until smooth and elastic. Place in a lightly oiled bowl, cover with lightly oiled plastic wrap and set in a warm place for about 1 hour, until doubled in bulk.

**3** Punch down the dough and turn it out onto a lightly floured surface. Divide into eight equal pieces and roll each into a 5–6-inch round. Make the rounds slightly concave. Prick them all over and space well apart on the baking sheets. Cover with lightly oiled plastic wrap and let rise for 15–10 minutes.

**4** Meanwhile, preheat the oven to 400°F. Mix the chopped onion, ground cumin, ground coriander and chopped mint in a bowl. Brush the breads with the olive oil, sprinkle them evenly with the spicy onion mixture and bake for 15–20 minutes. Serve the onion breads warm.

> **Cook's Tip**
> If you don't have any fresh mint, add 1 tablespoon dried mint. Use the freeze-dried variety, if you can, as it has much more flavor.

## Scallion, Chive & Ricotta Bread

Ricotta cheese and chives make moist, well-flavored rolls or bread, both of which are excellent for serving with salads, especially ones that are based on rice or bulghur wheat.

**Makes 1 loaf or 16 rolls**

1/2 ounce fresh yeast
1 teaspoon sugar
1 1/6 cups lukewarm
  water

4 cups unbleached white flour,
  plus a little extra
1 1/2 teaspoons salt
1 large egg, beaten
1/2 cup ricotta cheese
2 tablespoons extra virgin olive oil,
  plus extra for greasing
1 bunch scallions, sliced
3 tablespoons snipped
  fresh chives
1 tablespoon milk
2 teaspoons poppy seeds
coarse sea salt

**1** Using a fork, mix the fresh yeast with the sugar and then gradually stir in 1/2 cup lukewarm water. Set aside in a warm place for 10 minutes.

**2** Sift the flour and salt into a warmed bowl. Make a well in the center and pour in the yeast liquid and the remaining lukewarm water. Reserve a little of the beaten egg, then add the remainder to the liquid in the bowl. Add the ricotta and mix all the ingredients to form a dough, adding a little more flour if the mixture is very sticky.

**3** Knead the dough on a floured work surface for 10 minutes, until smooth elastic, then return it to the bowl, cover with lightly oiled plastic wrap and set aside in a warm place for 1–2 hours, until doubled in bulk.

**4** Meanwhile, heat the oil in a small pan. Add the scallions and cook over low heat, stirring occasionally, for 3–4 minutes, until soft but not browned. Set aside to cool.

**5** Punch down the risen dough and knead in the onions, with any oil remaining in the pan. Add the chives. Shape the dough into rolls, a large loaf or a braid.

**6** Grease a baking sheet or loaf pan and place the rolls or bread in it. Cover with oiled plastic wrap and set in a warm place to rise for about 1 hour. Preheat the oven to 400°F.

**7** Beat the milk into the reserved beaten egg and use to glaze the rolls or loaf. Sprinkle on poppy seeds and a little coarse sea salt, then bake until golden and well risen. Rolls will need about 15 minutes, and a large loaf will require 30–40 minutes. Cool on a wire rack.

> **Cook's Tip**
> To make a braid, divide the dough into three equal sausage-shaped pieces about 16 inches long. Press them together at one end and then braid, pressing the ends together to seal when completed.

# French Baguettes

Baguettes are difficult to reproduce at home, as they require a very hot oven and steam. However, by using less yeast and a triple fermentation, you can produce a bread that looks and tastes better than when mass-produced.

**Makes 3 loaves**
5 cups bread flour, plus extra
1 cup all-purpose flour
2 teaspoons salt
1/2 ounce fresh yeast
2 1/4 cups lukewarm water

**1** Sift the flours and salt together into a bowl. Stir the yeast into the water in another bowl. Gradually beat in half the flour mixture to form a batter. Cover with plastic wrap and set aside for 3 hours or until almost tripled in size and starting to collapse.

**2** Beat in the remaining flour, a little at a time, with your hand. Knead on a lightly floured surface for 8–10 minutes to form a moist dough. Place in a lightly oiled bowl, cover with lightly oiled plastic wrap and let rise, in a warm place, for about 1 hour.

**3** Punch down the dough and divide it into three equal pieces. Shape each into a ball and then into a rectangle measuring 6 x 3 inches. Fold the bottom third of each up lengthwise and the top third down and press down. Seal the edges. Repeat two or three more times until each loaf is an oblong.

**4** Gently stretch each loaf lengthwise to 14 inches long. Pleat a floured dish towel on a baking sheet to make three molds so the loaves hold their shape. Cover with lightly oiled plastic wrap and set in a warm place for 45–60 minutes.

**5** Meanwhile, preheat the oven to 450°F. Roll the loaves onto a baking sheet, spaced well apart. Using a sharp knife, slash the top of each loaf several times with long diagonal slits. Place at the top of the oven, spray the inside of the oven with water and bake for 20–25 minutes or until golden. Spray the oven twice more during the first 5 minutes of baking. Cool on a wire rack. Eat on the day of baking.

# Cheese & Onion Herb Sticks

These tasty breads are very good with soup or salads. Use an extra-strong cheese to give plenty of flavor.

**Makes 2 sticks**
1 tablespoon sunflower oil, plus extra for greasing
1 red onion, chopped
4 cups white flour, plus extra for dusting
1 teaspoon salt
1 teaspoon dry mustard powder
2 teaspoons active dry yeast
pinch of sugar
3 tablespoons chopped mixed fresh herbs
3/4 cup grated low-fat Cheddar cheese
about 1 1/4 cups lukewarm water

**1** Heat the oil in a frying pan and fry the onion until well colored. Lightly grease two baking sheets.

**2** Sift the flour, salt and mustard into a mixing bowl. Add the dry yeast, sugar and herbs. Set aside 2 tablespoons of the cheese. Stir the rest into the flour mixture and make a well in the center. Add the lukewarm water, with the fried onions and oil, then gradually incorporate the flour and mix into a soft dough, adding extra water if necessary.

**3** Knead the dough on a floured surface for about 10 minutes. Return the dough to the clean bowl, cover with lightly oiled plastic wrap and set aside in a warm place to rise for about 1 hour, until doubled in bulk.

**4** Turn the dough onto a floured surface, knead it briefly, then divide the mixture in half and roll each piece into 12-inch long stick. Place each stick on a baking sheet and make diagonal cuts along the top.

**5** Sprinkle the sticks with the reserved cheese. Cover and set for 30 minutes, until well risen.

**6** Preheat the oven to 425°F. Bake the sticks for 25 minutes or until they sound hollow when they are tapped underneath. Cool on a wire rack.

# Pita Bread

Although you can buy pita breads at any grocery store, it is fun to bake your own. They are delicious filled with ratatouille, roasted Mediterranean vegetables or salad. Make sure the oven is hot, or they will not puff up.

**Makes 6**

2 cups bread flour, plus extra
1 teaspoon salt
½ ounce fresh yeast
scant ⅔ cup lukewarm water
3 teaspoons extra virgin olive oil

**1** Sift the flour and salt into a bowl. Dissolve the yeast in the water, then stir in 2 teaspoons of the olive oil and pour into a large bowl. Gradually beat in the flour to form a soft dough.

**2** Knead on a lightly floured surface for 10 minutes, then return to the clean bowl, cover with lightly oiled plastic wrap and set in a warm place to rise for about 1 hour or until doubled in bulk.

**3** Punch down the dough. On a lightly floured surface, divide it into six equal pieces and shape into balls. Cover with oiled plastic wrap and let rest for 5 minutes. Roll out each ball of dough into an oval, about ¼ inch thick and 6 inches long. Place on a floured dish towel and cover with lightly oiled plastic wrap. Let rise at room temperature for about 20–30 minutes.

**4** Meanwhile, preheat the oven to 450°F. Place three large baking sheets in the oven to heat.

**5** Place the breads on the baking sheets and bake for 4–6 minutes or until puffed up. Transfer to a wire rack to cool slightly, then cover them with a dish towel to keep them soft.

> **Variations**
> To make whole-wheat pita breads, replace half the bread flour with whole-wheat flour. You can also make smaller round pita breads, about 4 inches in diameter, to serve as snacks and for canapés.

# Spiced Naan

Traditionally, Indian naan is baked in a fiercely hot tandoori oven, but you can use a combination of a hot oven and a broiler.

**Makes 6**

4 cups all-purpose flour, plus extra
   for dusting
1 teaspoon baking powder
½ teaspoon salt
¼-ounce envelope active
   dry yeast
1 teaspoon sugar
1 teaspoon fennel seeds
2 teaspoons black onion seeds
1 teaspoon cumin seeds
⅔ cup lukewarm milk
2 tablespoons oil, plus extra
   for greasing and brushing
⅔ cup plain yogurt
1 egg, beaten

**1** Sift the flour, baking powder and salt into a mixing bowl. Stir in the yeast, sugar and seeds. Make a well in the center. Pour in the milk, oil, yogurt and beaten egg. Beat well, gradually incorporating the surrounding flour to make a dough.

**2** Knead the dough on a lightly floured surface for 10 minutes. Place in a lightly oiled bowl, cover with oiled plastic wrap and set in a warm place for about 1 hour, until doubled in bulk.

**3** Put a heavy baking sheet in the oven and preheat the oven to 475°F. Preheat the broiler. Knead the dough lightly again and divide it into six pieces. Cover five pieces. Roll out the sixth to a tear-drop shape, brush lightly with oil and slap onto the hot baking sheet. Repeat with the remaining five pieces.

**4** Bake the naan for 3 minutes, until puffed up, then place the baking sheet under the broiler for about 30 seconds to brown the naan lightly. Serve hot or warm.

> **Variation**
> Vary the spices used by adding chopped chile to the mixture, or sprinkling on poppy seeds before baking.

# Chapatis

These chewy, unleavened breads from India are the authentic accompaniment to spicy vegetarian dishes.

**Makes 6 chapatis**
1½ cups atta or whole-wheat flour, plus extra for dusting
½ teaspoon salt
scant ½ cup water
1 teaspoon vegetable oil, plus extra for greasing
melted ghee or butter, for brushing (optional)

**1** Sift the flour and salt into a bowl. Add the water and mix into a soft dough. Knead in the oil.

**2** Knead on a lightly floured surface for 5–6 minutes, until smooth. Place in a lightly oiled bowl, cover with a damp dish towel and let rest for 30 minutes. Turn out onto a floured surface. Divide the dough into six equal pieces. Shape each piece into a ball. Press the dough into a larger round with the palm of your hand, then roll into a 5-inch chapati. Stack, layered between plastic wrap, to keep moist.

**3** Heat a griddle or heavy frying pan over medium heat for a few minutes. Take one chapati, brush off any excess flour, and place on the griddle. Cook for 30–60 seconds, until the top begins to bubble and white specks appear on the underside.

**4** Turn the chapati over using a spatula and cook for 30 seconds more. Remove from the pan and keep warm, layered between a folded dish towel, while cooking the remaining chapatis. If desired, lightly brush the chapatis with melted ghee or butter immediately after cooking. Serve warm.

### Cook's Tip
*Atta or ata is a very fine whole-wheat flour, which is found only at Indian stores and supermarkets. It is sometimes simply labeled chapati flour.*

# Bagels

Bagels are great fun to make and taste wonderful with cream cheese, either on its own or with grilled eggplant or zucchini and fresh herbs.

**Makes 10 bagels**
oil, for greasing
3 cups bread flour, plus extra
2 teaspoons salt
¼-ounce envelope active dry yeast
1 teaspoon malt extract
scant 1 cup lukewarm water

**For poaching**
2½ quarts water
1 tablespoon malt extract

**For the topping**
1 egg white
2 teaspoons cold water
2 tablespoons poppy, sesame or caraway seeds, or a mixture

**1** Grease two baking sheets. Sift the flour and salt into a bowl. Stir in the yeast. Mix the malt extract and water, add to the flour and mix into a dough. Knead on a floured surface for 10 minutes. Place in a lightly oiled bowl, cover with lightly oiled plastic wrap and set in a warm place for about 1 hour or until doubled in bulk.

**2** Punch down, knead for 1 minute, then divide into 10 equal pieces. Shape into balls, cover with plastic wrap and let rest for 5 minutes. Gently flatten each ball and make a hole through the center. Place on a floured tray; re-cover and set in a warm place, for 10–20 minutes or until the rings begin to rise.

**3** Meanwhile, preheat the oven to 425°F. Place the water and malt extract for poaching in a large pan, bring to a boil, then reduce to a simmer. Poach two or three bagels at a time for about 1 minute. They will sink and then rise again when first added to the pan. Turn them over and poach the other side for 30 seconds. Remove and drain on a dish towel.

**4** Place five bagels on each baking sheet. Beat the egg white with the water and brush on the bagels. Sprinkle on the seeds. Bake for 25 minutes, until golden. Cool on a wire rack.

# Shaped Dinner Rolls

These rolls are the perfect choice for entertaining.

**Makes 12**
oil, for greasing
4 cups bread flour, plus extra
2 teaspoons salt
$^1/_2$ teaspoon sugar
$^1/_4$-ounce envelope active
    dry yeast
$^1/_4$ cup butter

1 cup lukewarm milk
1 egg, beaten

**For the topping**
1 egg yolk
1 tablespoon water
poppy seeds and sesame seeds,
    for sprinkling

**1** Grease two baking sheets. Sift the flour and salt into a bowl. Stir in the sugar and yeast. Rub in the butter. Add the milk and egg and mix into a dough. Knead on a lightly floured surface for 10 minutes. Place in a lightly oiled bowl, cover with oiled plastic wrap and set in a warm place for 1 hour, until doubled in bulk.

**2** Punch down the dough on a lightly floured surface and knead for 2–3 minutes. Divide into 12 equal pieces and make shapes.

**3 Braid:** divide a piece of dough into three sausages. Pinch together at one end, braid, then pinch the ends and tuck under.
**Trefoil:** make three balls from a piece of dough and fit them together in a triangular shape.
**Baton:** shape a piece of dough into an oblong. Slash the surface.
**Cottage roll:** divide a piece of dough into two-thirds and one-third and shape into two rounds. Place the small one on top of the large one and make a hole through the center.
**Knot:** shape a piece of dough into a rope and tie a single knot.

**4** Place the rolls on the baking sheets, cover with oiled plastic wrap and set in a warm place for 30 minutes, until doubled in bulk. Meanwhile, preheat the oven to 425°F.

**5** Mix the egg yolk and water and brush the rolls. Sprinkle some with poppy seeds and some with sesame seeds. Bake for 15–18 minutes or until golden. Cool on a wire rack.

# Panini All'olio

The Italians adore elaborately shaped rolls.

**Makes 16**
4 tablespoons extra virgin olive
    oil, plus extra for greasing
    and brushing

4 cups bread flour, plus extra
    for dusting
2 teaspoons salt
$^1/_2$ ounce fresh yeast
1 cup lukewarm water

**1** Lightly oil three baking sheets. Sift the flour and salt into a bowl. Mix the yeast with half of the water, then stir in the remainder. Add to the flour with the oil and mix into a dough.

**2** Knead the dough on a floured surface for 8–10 minutes. Place in a lightly oiled bowl, cover with lightly oiled plastic wrap and set in a warm place for about 1 hour or until the dough has almost doubled in bulk.

**3** Punch down on a lightly floured surface. Divide into 12 equal pieces and shape into rolls as described below.

**4 Tavalli (twisted spirals):** roll each piece of dough into a strip about 12 inches long and 1$^1/_2$ inches wide. Twist each strip into a loose spiral and join the ends of dough in a circle.
**Filoncini (finger-shaped rolls):** flatten each piece of dough into an oval and roll to about 9 inches long. Make it 2 inches wide at one end and 4 inches wide at the other. Roll up from the wider end, then stretch to 8–9 inches long. Cut in half.
**Carciofi (artichoke-shaped rolls):** shape each piece of dough into a ball.

**5** Place the rolls on the baking sheets. Brush with olive oil, cover with oiled plastic wrap and set in a warm place for 30 minutes. Meanwhile, preheat the oven to 400°F.

**6** To finish the carciofi, snip four or five $^1/_4$-inch deep cuts in a circle on top of each ball, then make five larger horizontal cuts around the sides. Bake the rolls for about 15 minutes. Cool on a wire rack.

# Tomato Breadsticks

Fresh, healthy and low in fat, these are delectable with dips. Make plenty, as they are very delicious.

**Makes 16**

2 cups all-purpose flour, plus extra
 for dusting
½ teaspoon salt
1½ teaspoons active
 dry yeast
1 teaspoon honey
2 teaspoons olive oil, plus extra
 about ⅔ cup lukewarm water
6 pieces of sun-dried tomatoes in
 olive oil, drained and chopped
1 tablespoon skim milk
2 teaspoons poppy seeds

**1** Place the flour, salt and yeast in a food processor. Add the honey and 1 teaspoon of the olive oil and, with the machine running, gradually pour in enough lukewarm water to make a dough. Process for 1 more minute.

**2** Knead the dough on a lightly floured surface for 3–4 minutes. Knead in the chopped sun-dried tomatoes. Form the dough into a ball and place in a lightly oiled bowl. Set aside to rise for 5 minutes.

**3** Preheat the oven to 300°F. Lightly brush a baking sheet with oil.

**4** Divide the dough into 16 pieces and roll each piece into a stick about 11 × ½ inches long. Place the breadsticks on the prepared baking sheet and set aside in a warm place to rise for 15 minutes.

**5** Brush the sticks with milk and sprinkle on poppy seeds. Bake for 30 minutes. Cool on a wire rack.

> **Cook's Tip**
> Flours vary in their absorbency, so you may not need all the water. Stop adding it as soon as soon as the dough starts to hold together.

# Whole-wheat Herb Triangles

Stuffed with salad and cheese, these make a good lunchtime snack.

**Makes 8**

2 cups whole-wheat flour, plus
 extra for dusting
1 cup bread flour
1 teaspoon salt
½ teaspoon baking soda
1 teaspoon cream of tartar
½ teaspoon chili powder
¼ cup soft margarine
4 tablespoons chopped mixed
 fresh herbs
1 cup skim milk
1 tablespoon sesame seeds

**1** Preheat the oven to 425°F. Lightly flour a baking sheet. Put the whole-wheat flour in a mixing bowl. Sift in the white flour, salt, baking soda, cream of tartar and chili powder, then rub in the soft margarine.

**2** Add the herbs and milk and mix quickly into a soft dough. Turn onto a lightly floured surface. Knead only very briefly or the dough will become tough.

**3** Roll out to a 9-inch round and place on the prepared baking sheet. Brush lightly with water and sprinkle evenly with the sesame seeds.

**4** Carefully cut the dough round into 8 wedges, separate them slightly and bake for 15–20 minutes. Cool briefly on a wire rack and serve warm.

> **Variations**
> • For cheese and herb triangles, add ½–1 cup grated Gruyère or Emmental cheese after rubbing in the margarine in step 1.
> • To make sun-dried tomato triangles, omit the fresh mixed herbs and replace them with 2 tablespoons drained chopped sun-dried tomatoes in oil. Add 1 tablespoon each mild paprika, chopped fresh parsley and chopped fresh marjoram with the milk in step 2.

# Brioche

Rich, yet light and airy, this is
a classic French bread.

**Makes I loaf**
3 cups bread flour, plus extra
   for dusting
$\frac{1}{2}$ teaspoon salt
$\frac{1}{2}$ ounce fresh yeast
4 tablespoons lukewarm milk

3 eggs, lightly beaten
$\frac{3}{4}$ cup butter, softened
2 tablespoons sugar
oil, for greasing

**For the glaze**
I egg yolk
I tablespoon milk

**I** Sift the flour and salt into a large bowl and make a well in the
center. Mix the yeast with the milk in a bowl, then add it to the
flour, with the eggs. Mix into a soft dough.

**2** Using your hand, beat the dough for 4–5 minutes. Cream the
butter and sugar together. Add the butter mixture to the dough
in small amounts, making sure it is incorporated before adding
more. Beat until smooth, shiny and elastic.

**3** Cover with lightly oiled plastic wrap and set in a warm place for
1½ hours or until the dough has doubled in bulk. Punch it down
lightly, cover again and put it in the refrigerator for 8–10 hours.

**4** Lightly grease a brioche mold. Turn the dough out onto a
lightly floured surface. Shape three-quarters of the dough into a
ball and put it in the mold. Shape the rest into an elongated
oval. Make a hole in the center of the large ball of dough.
Gently press a narrow end of the oval dough into the hole.

**5** Mix the egg yolk and milk for the glaze, and brush a little on
the brioche. Cover with lightly oiled plastic wrap and set in a
warm place, for 1½–2 hours or until the dough almost reaches
the top of the mold.

**6** Meanwhile, preheat the oven to 450°F. Brush the brioche
with the remaining glaze and bake for 10 minutes. Reduce the
oven temperature to 375°F and bake for 20–25 more minutes
or until golden. Cool on a wire rack.

# Croissants

Served with homemade
preserves, these melt-in-
your-mouth rolls are the
ultimate breakfast treat.

**Makes 18**
5 cups all-purpose flour, plus extra
   for dusting
1½ teaspoons salt

2 teaspoons sugar
I tablespoon active dry yeast
1⅓ cups lukewarm milk
oil, for greasing
I cup chilled butter
I egg, beaten with 2 teaspoons
   water, for the glaze

**I** Mix the flour, salt, sugar and yeast in a bowl. Add enough of
the milk to make a soft dough. Transfer to a clean bowl, cover
with lightly oiled plastic wrap and let rise for 1½ hours.

**2** Knead the dough until smooth. Wrap in waxed paper and
chill for 15 minutes. Meanwhile, divide the butter in half and roll
each half between two sheets of waxed paper to form a
6 x 4-inch rectangle.

**3** Roll out the dough on a floured surface to a 12 x 8-inch
rectangle. Place a sheet of butter in the center. Fold the
bottom third of dough over the butter, press to seal, then
place the remaining butter sheet on top. Fold on top third.
Turn the dough so the short side faces you. Roll it gently to a
12 x 8-inch rectangle. Fold in thirds as before, then wrap and
chill for 30 minutes. Repeat this process twice more, then wrap
and chill for at least 2 hours or overnight.

**4** Roll out the dough to a rectangle, about 13 inches wide. Cut
in half, then into 18 triangles, 6 inches high, with a 4-inch base.
Roll them slightly to stretch, then roll up from bottom to point.
Place on baking sheets, curving to make crescents. Cover with
lightly oiled plastic wrap and let rise for 1–1½ hours.

**5** Preheat the oven to 475°F. Brush the croissants with the egg
glaze and bake for 2 minutes. Lower the oven temperature to
375°F and bake them for 10–12 more minutes, until golden.
Serve warm.

# Cheese & Potato Scones

The addition of creamy mashed potatoes gives these whole-wheat scones a moist crumb and a crisp crust.

**Makes 9**

3 tablespoons butter, plus extra for greasing
1 cup whole-wheat flour, plus extra for dusting
1/2 teaspoon salt
4 teaspoons baking powder
2 eggs, beaten
4 tablespoons low-fat milk
1 1/3 cups cooked, mashed potatoes
3 tablespoons chopped fresh sage
1/2 cup grated aged Cheddar cheese
sesame seeds, for sprinkling

**1** Preheat the oven to 425°F. Grease a baking sheet. Sift the flour, salt and baking powder into a bowl. Rub in the butter, then mix in half the beaten eggs and all the milk. Add the mashed potatoes, sage and half the Cheddar, and mix into a soft dough.

**2** Knead the dough lightly on a floured surface until smooth. Roll it out to 3/4 inch thick, then stamp out nine scones using a 2 1/2-inch fluted cutter.

**3** Place the scones on the prepared baking sheet and brush the tops with the remaining beaten egg. Sprinkle the rest of the cheese and the sesame seeds on top and bake for 15 minutes, until golden. Cool on a wire rack.

> **Cook's Tip**
> Use a sharp cutter to avoid compressing the edges of the scones, which would prevent them from rising evenly.

> **Variations**
> • Use unbleached self-rising flour instead of whole-wheat flour and baking powder, if desired.
> • Fresh rosemary or basil can be used instead of the sage.

# Caramelized Onion & Walnut Scones

These are very good buttered and served with aged Cheddar or Lancashire cheese. They are also excellent with soup or a robust vegetable stew.

**Makes 10–12**

7 tablespoons butter
1 tablespoon olive oil
1 Spanish onion, chopped
1/2 teaspoon cumin seeds, lightly crushed, plus a few extra
1 2/3 cups self-rising flour, plus extra
1 teaspoon baking powder
1/4 cup oats
1 teaspoon light brown sugar
scant 1 cup chopped walnuts
1 teaspoon chopped fresh thyme
1/2–2/3 cup buttermilk
a little milk
salt and ground black pepper
coarse sea salt

**1** Melt 1 tablespoon of the butter with the oil in a small pan and cook the onion over low heat, covered, until softened but not browned. Uncover, then continue to cook gently until it begins to brown.

**2** Add the crushed cumin seeds and increase the temperature slightly. Cook, stirring occasionally, until the onion browns and begins to caramelize around the edges. Cool. Preheat the oven to 400°F.

**3** Sift the flour and baking powder into a large bowl and add the oats, 1/2 teaspoon salt, a generous grinding of black pepper and the brown sugar. Rub in the remaining butter, then add the onion, walnuts and thyme. Stir in enough of the buttermilk to make a soft dough.

**4** Roll or pat out the mixture to just over 1/2 inch thick and stamp out 2–2 1/2-inch round scones. Place on a floured baking sheet, brush with milk and sprinkle on a little coarse sea salt and a few extra cumin seeds. Bake for 12–15 minutes, until well-risen and golden brown. Cool the scones briefly on a wire rack and serve warm.

# Cheese & Mustard Scones

Depending on their size, these cheese scones can be served as little canapé bases, tea-time snacks or even as a quick pie topping.

**Makes 12**
2¼ cups self-rising flour, plus extra for dusting
1 teaspoon baking powder
½ teaspoon salt
3 tablespoons butter or sunflower margarine

1½ cups grated aged Cheddar cheese, plus extra for sprinkling
2 teaspoons whole-grain mustard
about ⅔ cup milk
ground black pepper

**To serve (optional)**
garlic-flavored cream cheese
chopped fresh chives
sliced radishes

**1** Preheat the oven to 425°F. Sift the flour, baking powder and salt into a large bowl, then rub in the butter or sunflower margarine. Season to taste with pepper and stir in the grated cheese.

**2** Mix the mustard with the milk until thoroughly combined. Add the mixture to the dry ingredients and mix quickly until the mixture just comes together.

**3** Knead the dough lightly on a lightly floured surface, then pat it out to a depth of ¾ inch. Use a 2-inch cutter to stamp out rounds. Place on a nonstick baking sheet and sprinkle on extra grated cheese.

**4** Bake for about 10 minutes until risen and golden. You can test scones by pressing the sides, which should spring back. Cool on a wire rack. Serve spread with garlic-flavored cream cheese, topped with chopped chives and sliced radishes, if desired.

> **Cook's Tip**
> Do not over-mix the dough, or the scones will be heavy, tough and chewy.

# Sunflower & Almond Sesame Crackers

Full of flavor, these slim savory crackers taste great with cheese and celery, or could be served with hummus or a similar dip.

**Makes about 24**
1 cup ground sunflower seeds
scant 1 cup ground almonds
1 teaspoon baking powder
2 tablespoons milk
1 egg yolk
2 tablespoons butter, melted
¼ cup sesame seeds

**1** Preheat the oven to 375°F. Reserve ¼ cup of the ground sunflower seeds for rolling out and mix the remaining ground seeds with the ground almonds and baking powder in a bowl.

**2** Mix the milk and egg yolk in a cup, then stir the mixture into the dry ingredients, with the melted butter, mixing well. Gently work the mixture with your hands to form a moist dough.

**3** On a cool surface that has been lightly dusted with some of the reserved ground sunflower seeds, roll out the dough to a thickness of about ¼ inch, sprinkling more ground seeds on top to prevent sticking.

**4** Sprinkle the dough with sesame seeds and cut into rounds, with a 2-inch cookie cutter. Lift onto a nonstick baking sheet.

**5** Bake the crackers for about 10 minutes, until lightly browned. Cool on a wire rack.

> **Variation**
> Sprinkle some poppy seeds on top of a few of the crackers before baking.

# Oatcakes

Old-fashioned they may be, but oatcakes are delicious, especially with cheese.

**Makes 8**

1½ cups medium oats, plus extra
    for sprinkling
½ teaspoon salt
pinch of baking soda
1 tablespoon butter, plus extra
    for greasing
5 tablespoons water

**1** Preheat the oven to 300°F. Mix the oats with the salt and baking soda in a mixing bowl.

**2** Melt the butter with the water in a small saucepan. Bring to a boil, then add to the oat mixture and mix thoroughly to form a moist dough.

**3** Turn the dough onto a surface sprinkled with oats and knead into a smooth ball. Turn a large baking sheet upside-down, grease it, sprinkle it lightly with oats and place the ball of dough on top. Sprinkle the dough with oats, then roll out to a 10-inch round.

**4** Cut the round into eight sections, ease them apart slightly and bake for 50–60 minutes, until crisp. Let cool on the baking sheet, then remove the oatcakes with a spatula.

> **Cook's Tips**
> • To achieve a neat round, place a 10-inch cake board or plate on top of the oatcake. Trim any excess dough with a knife, then lift off the board or plate.
> • Oatmeal is ground from the whole kernel of the cereal and is graded according to how finely it is ground. Health-food stores carry of variety of types, but standard oats are ideal for this recipe.

# Rosemary Crackers

Rosemary is said to grow best for a strong-willed woman. If you have some in your garden, make these excellent crackers, and top them with cream cheese and rosemary flowers.

**Makes about 25**

2 cups all-purpose flour
½ teaspoon baking powder
a good pinch of salt
½ teaspoon curry powder
6 tablespoons butter, diced
2 tablespoons finely chopped
    young rosemary leaves
1 egg yolk
2–3 tablespoons water
milk, to glaze

**To decorate**

2 tablespoons cream cheese
rosemary flowers

**1** Put the flour, baking powder, salt and curry powder in a food processor. Add the butter and process until the mixture resembles fine bread crumbs. Add the rosemary, egg yolk and 2 tablespoons of the water. Process again, adding the remaining water, if needed, to make a firm dough. Wrap in plastic wrap and chill in the refrigerator for 30 minutes.

**2** Preheat the oven to 350°F. Roll out the dough thinly on a lightly floured surface and cut out the crackers using a 2-inch fluted cutter.

**3** Transfer them to a large baking sheet and prick with a fork. Brush with milk to glaze and bake for about 10 minutes, until pale golden. Cool on a wire rack.

**4** Spread a little cream cheese on each cracker and place a few rosemary flowers on top, using tweezers to position the flowers, if this makes it easier.

> **Cook's Tip**
> If you do not have a food processor, simply rub the butter into the flour mixture in a bowl, then add the remaining ingredients and combine.

# Index